D0840378

ANNALS OF COMMUNISM

Each volume in the series Annals of Communism publishes selected and previously inaccessible documents from former Soviet state and party archives in the framework of a narrative text that focuses on a particular topic in the history of Soviet and international communism. Separate English and Russian editions are prepared. Russian and American scholars select and annotate the documents for each volume; together they explain the selection criteria and discuss the state of relevant research and scholarly interpretation. Documents are chosen not for their support of any single interpretation but for their particular historical importance or their general value in deepening understanding and facilitating discussion. The volumes are designed to be useful to students, scholars, and interested general readers.

EXECUTIVE EDITOR, ANNALS OF COMMUNISM

Jonathan Brent, Yale University Press

AMERICAN EDITORIAL ADVISORY COMMITTEE

Ivo Banac, Yale University
Jeffrey Burds, University of Rochester
William Chase, University of Pittsburgh
Victor Erlich, Yale University
Sheila Fitzpatrick, University of Chicago
Gregory Freeze, Brandeis University
J. Arch Getty, University of California at
  Riverside
Robert L. Jackson, Yale University
Leon Lipson, Yale University

Czeslaw Milosz, University of
  California at Berkeley
Norman Naimark, Stanford University
General William Odom, Hudson
  Institute and Yale University
Daniel Orlovsky, Southern Methodist
  University
Mark Steinberg, Yale University
Mark von Hagen, Columbia University
Piotr Wandycz, Yale University

RUSSIAN EDITORIAL ADVISORY COMMITTEE

K. M. Anderson, Russian Center for the
  Preservation and Study of Documents
  of Recent History (RTsKhIDNI)
N. N. Bolkhovitinov, Russian Academy
  of Sciences
A. O. Chubarian, Russian Academy of
  Sciences
V. P. Danilov, Russian Academy of
  Sciences
F. I. Firsov, formerly of Moscow State
  University and the Comintern
  Archive in the Russian Center for the
  Preservation and Study of Documents
  of Recent History (RTsKhIDNI)
V. P. Kozlov, State Archival Service of
  the Russian Federation
V. S. Lelchuk, Russian Academy of
  Sciences

S. V. Mironenko, State Archive of the
  Russian Federation
O. V. Naumov, Russian Center for the
  Preservation and Study of Documents
  of Recent History (RTsKhIDNI)
R. G. Pikhoia, State Archival Service of
  the Russian Federation
A. N. Sakharov, Russian Academy of
  Sciences
T. T. Timofeev, Russian Academy of
  Sciences
Ye. A. Tiurina, Russian State Archive of
  the Economy (RGAE)
General D. A. Volkogonov, advisor to
  the president of the Russian
  Federation

SERIES COORDINATOR, MOSCOW

N. P. Yakovlev

Stalin's Letters to Molotov 1925–1936

Edited by
Lars T. Lih, Oleg V. Naumov, and
Oleg V. Khlevniuk

Russian Consulting Scholars
L. Kosheleva and L. Rogovaia
V. Lelchuk and V. Naumov

Translated from the Russian by Catherine A. Fitzpatrick

Foreword by Robert C. Tucker

Yale University Press

New Haven and London

Published with assistance from the National Endowment for the Humanities and the Open Society Fund.

Copyright © 1995 by Yale University.
All rights reserved.
This book may not be reproduced, in whole or in part, including illustrations, in any form (beyond that copying permitted by Sections 107 and 108 of the U.S. Copyright Law and except by reviewers for the public press), without written permission from the publishers.

Designed by James J. Johnson and set in Sabon Roman type by The Composing Room of Michigan, Inc. Printed in the United States of America by Vail-Ballou Press, Binghamton, New York.

Library of Congress Cataloging-in-Publication Data

Stalin's letters to Molotov, 1925–1936 / edited by Lars T. Lih, Oleg V. Naumov, and Oleg V. Khlevniuk ; Russian consulting scholars L. Kosheleva . . . [et al.] ; translated from the Russian by Catherine A. Fitzpatrick, ; foreword by Robert C. Tucker.
     p.   cm. — (Annals of communism)
    Includes bibliographical references and index.
    ISBN 0-300-06211-7

    1. Stalin, Joseph, 1879–1953—Correspondence. 2. Molotov, Vyacheslav Mikhaylovich, 1890-   —Correspondence. 3. Heads of state—Soviet Union—Correspondence. 4. Soviet Union—Politics and government—1917–1936. I. Lih, Lars T. II. Naumov, Oleg V. III. Khlevniuk, Oleg V. IV. Kosheleva, L. IV. Series.
DK268.S8A4   1995
947.084'2'092—dc20   94-44050
                                              CIP

A catalogue record for this book is available from the British Library.

The paper in this book meets the guidelines for permanence and durability of the Committee on Production Guidelines for Book Longevity of the Council on Library Resources.

10 9 8 7 6 5 4 3 2

Contents

Foreword, *Robert C. Tucker*   vii

Preface, *Russian Editors and Scholars*   xiii

Acknowledgments   xv

Note on the Documents and the Narrative   xvii

Introduction, *Lars T. Lih*   1

CHAPTER ONE   1925   67

CHAPTER TWO   1926   97

CHAPTER THREE   1927   133

CHAPTER FOUR   1929   145

CHAPTER FIVE   1930   187

CHAPTER SIX   1931–1936   224

Appendix: The Eastman Affair   241

Glossary of Names   251

Index   269

Foreword

On his accession to power in Moscow in 1985, Mikhail Gorbachev set out to reform the crisis-ridden Soviet system and sponsored openness (*glasnost'*) as a means to that end. Events of the Soviet past, and especially of Stalin's autocratic rule, became subjects of discussion in the press, and researchers began to receive access to long-closed official archives containing documents bearing on those events. After the collapse of the Soviet state in 1991, access to the archives further improved.

One of the significant consequences is the appearance of this volume. It contains letters and notes written by Stalin to his trusty follower Viacheslav Molotov during the years from 1925 to 1936. In 1969, then in retirement at the age of seventy-nine, Molotov turned these materials over to the Central Party Archive. Now, at long last, they see the light of publication.

The reader of this volume has been well served by its editors. Oleg V. Naumov, assistant director of the Russian Center for the Preservation and Study of Documents of Recent History, Oleg V. Khlevniuk, and their associates have provided a general preface, highly informative introductions to the letters for each year or group of years covered, notes to the letters themselves, and a glossary of names. The introductions include, in some instances, the texts of other formerly top secret letters by one or another high-placed person in Stalin's entourage. The American editor, Lars T. Lih, a foremost Western specialist on the 1920s in the Soviet Union, has contributed an interpretive general introduction that provides ample background information and develops the view that the letters cast much light on how Stalin went about running the Soviet state during those years. That they certainly do.

It was Stalin's custom to spend lengthy periods from the later summer into the fall at his villa on the Black Sea coast, where he would devote himself to thinking out state affairs while at rest. He corresponded with Molotov (in some instances letters are addressed to other Politburo members as well). Molotov, for his part, kept him informed of developments in Moscow and carried out directions contained in Stalin's letters. No copies of Molotov's letters to Stalin in the course of this correspondence have come to light.

The question of selectivity on Molotov's part arises. The Russian editors point out that most of the letters are from 1925, 1926, 1927, 1929, and 1930, and that only a relative few are from 1931 through 1936 (there is only one from 1936). There are no letters for 1928 and 1934, two key years in Soviet history and in Stalin's rule. Commenting on the small number of letters from 1931 through 1936, the Russian editors state that these letters represent just a small portion of the correspondence between Stalin and Molotov during this period and add: "The contents of these letters suggest that only the most 'harmless' documents, those that in no way touched upon Stalin's and Molotov's darkest and most criminal activities, were selected for the archive." This point is presumably well taken.

Molotov's own life was in grave danger from Stalin in 1952 and early 1953, when the now increasingly crazed dictator was preparing to do away with him and possibly other members of his entourage in a new bloody purge that only his sudden death from a stroke forestalled. Speaking of that time in one of his conversations with Feliks Chuev, Molotov observed: "I think that if he [that is, Stalin—R.T.] had lived another year or so, I might not have survived, but in spite of that, I have believed and believe that he carried out tasks so colossal and difficult that no one of us then in the party could have fulfilled them."[1] Naturally, since Molotov remained true to Stalin to the very end of his own life (he died in 1986 at the age of ninety-six), he would hardly have turned over to posterity any letters from Stalin that would reveal him—and by implication Molotov himself as his henchman—in an evil light.

Even after all this is taken into account, we must agree with the Russian and American editors of this volume that the letters Molotov allowed to survive throw valuable light on various events of those years and help resolve some matters on which historians have differed. Take, for example, the subject of Stalin and foreign affairs. He was not only concerned with economic policy and the internal power struggle in the 1920s (as some have thought) but also engrossed in foreign affairs. This we see in letters bearing on China and Great

---

1. F. Chuev, *Sto sorok besed s Molotovym: Iz dnevnika F. Chueva* (Moscow, 1991), 279.

Britain, where revolutionary tendencies seemed afoot in 1926–1927. Stalin went beyond being interested and took it upon himself to be his own foreign commissar acting through Molotov. He was critical, not to say contemptuous, of his official foreign commissar, Maksim Litvinov, a basically Western-oriented old Bolshevik and a Jew, whom he would replace with Molotov in 1939 to signal his readiness to do business with Hitler. Western leaders who negotiated with Stalin during World War II would have been interested in his comment in a letter to Molotov (9 September 1929), apropos negotiations with the British government: "Remember we are waging a struggle (negotiation with enemies is also struggle), not with England alone, but with the whole capitalist world."

Lih raises the question: Did Stalin dismiss world revolution in favor of building up the Soviet state (as Trotsky, for one, alleged at the time), or did he remain dedicated to world revolution? Lih's answer, based on the letters, is that in Stalin's mind the Soviet state and international revolution coalesced, and the letters provide support for this view. They likewise bear out the proposition, which has been developed in the scholarly literature, that Stalin was a Russian imperial Bolshevik for whom the further progress of the international Communist revolution and the territorial expansion of Soviet Russia around its periphery were one and the same process.[2] Thus Stalin's letter of 7 October 1929 bruits the idea of organizing "an uprising by a *revolutionary* movement" in adjacent Manchuria. Armed intervention (with mainly Chinese-manned brigades) would "establish a revolutionary government (massacre the landowners, bring in the peasants, create soviets in the cities and towns, and so on)." Here is a preview of the efforts that Stalin made beginning in 1945 to encourage separatist movements in Manchuria and Sinkiang provinces in China, and, more broadly, of the sovietization imposed after World War II on Soviet-occupied neighboring countries in the process of imperial aggrandizement under Communist banners. Also revelatory of Stalin's Russian imperial bolshevism is a passage inspired by a public speech of Molotov's in January 1933: "Today I read the section on international affairs. It came out well. The confident, contemptuous tone with respect to the 'great' powers, the belief in our own strength, the delicate but plain spitting in the pot of the swaggering 'great powers'—very good. Let them eat it."

What can Stalin's letters to Molotov tell us about his personality? Insofar as

2. Robert C. Tucker, *Stalin in Power: The Revolution from Above, 1928–1941* (New York, 1990), 45–50.

the letters that Molotov was willing to share with posterity cast light on the matter, they tell us, first of all, that Stalin was totally consumed by politics. The lengthy sojourns in the south were less vacations in the ordinary sense than opportunities to concentrate his boundless energy on politics, to read Soviet newspapers and other official documents, to think out his political positions on men and events, and to communicate his political will to the oligarchy via the ever-obedient Molotov. Although he sometimes added regards to Molotov's wife at the end of a letter, one would not know from them that he too had a wife (until late 1932, when she committed suicide) and children of his own. Unlike most Russians, who have their easygoing interludes, this Georgian-born leader was a thinking, reacting, plotting politician during every waking hour. As Lih puts it, he was Stalin "at work." Indeed, until the day of his fatal stroke, 1 March 1953, at which time he was actively plotting and preparing his own "final solution" for the Jews of Soviet Russia and the elimination of, among highly placed others, Molotov (and his Jewish wife), Stalin remained actively "at work."

The Stalin of the letters, as Lih again argues, was an astute and effective leader who came to the fore in the post-Lenin Bolshevik hierarchy largely by virtue of his uncommon leadership capability: his capacity to assess person-alities and situations and prescribe measures for dealing with them that served his interests. He was neither the mediocrity that an old stereotype made him out to be, nor just a political boss and machine politician who rose to supreme power by exploiting the authority to make appointments that he possessed as the party Central Committee's general secretary. Not that placement—and re-placement—of cadres was a matter of small concern to him. But he was inde-fatigable in his striving to function as a leader. What that meant to him is reflected in a 1929 letter in which he dismissed the old Bolshevik Ye. Yaro-slavskii because "he is weak in the *political leadership* department (he loves to *swim along* 'with the tide' of the sentiment of the 'masses')." Stalin's strength in that "department" secured the removal of three opponents from the Politburo in 1929–1930: Bukharin, Rykov, and Tomskii, whom he called "rightists" (in fact they were Bolsheviks on the moderate left). It likewise propelled him to official public recognition as Lenin's successor—as the Soviet regime's new supreme leader or *vozhd'*, in other words—and thereby paved the way for his transformation of the regime and system during the 1930s. In this process, he made himself into an absolute autocrat on the model of sixteenth-century Ivan the Terrible, a hero in his eyes.

But in speaking of Stalin as a highly effective leader, a qualification is called for. His formidable leadership skills were effective in the quest for personal power and subsequently for the aggrandizement of the reconstituted Russian empire that was the USSR. But these very skills proved absolutely disastrous for the country and its people, and for the ruling Communist Party itself: in the course of the terroristic mass collectivization of the peasantry and the Great Terror in the 1930s, in Stalin's relations with Hitler in 1939–1941, in his direction of the Red Army during the ensuing Soviet-German war, and in the Cold War against the West afterwards. How and why this was so is a topic beyond the scope of this Foreword, but the fact must be stated. The fundamental explanation, I would maintain, is that Stalin's supreme aim, to which he was willing to sacrifice everything other than power, was glory. And his quest for glory had catastrophic consequences for Soviet Russia and the world.

Given the censorship that Molotov must have exercised in selecting the letters that survived, we would not expect them to reveal another key facet of Stalin's personality—the qualities that underlay his murderous rampage in the 1930s and beyond, whose still uncounted victims number in the tens of millions and stamp him as, if not the greatest single criminal in world history, then, along with Hitler, one of the two greatest. And yet, the letters have something to say to us even on this score.

First, they show that his mind worked conspiratorially and was at its most creative, so to speak, in so functioning. We see the Stalin of the letters devising conspiratorial explanations for the manifold shortages and breakdowns caused by his madcap industrialization under the five-year plan (1928–1932)— explanations that found the causation in "wrecking" activities by covert enemies. And we see him devising scripts for show trials of these alleged "wreckers" who would be forced under torture to confess to conspiring against the Soviet state. Now, a mind so strongly given to thinking in conspiratorial terms was one that would also carry on a conspiratorial war against political adversaries or those considered to be such. In this sense, the letters of the early 1930s cast light on Stalin's own great conspiracy of the middle to later 1930s against the regime and the Communist Party as then constituted.

Second, the letters show that Stalin was totally devoid of the most elementary human feeling for those who fell victim to one or another of his political designs. Their suffering and deaths, and the suffering of their loved ones, were matters of complete indifference to this man who so feared for his own life, was in fact such a coward, that the security arrangements concerning his own personal safety were unprecedentedly elaborate. Thus, writing in early August 1930 about the shortage of coins in the financial system, Stalin finds "wrecker elements from the Gosbank bureaucracy" responsible and prescribes a purge of the Finance and Gosbank apparatus that would involve "definitely shoot[ing] two or three dozen wreckers from these apparaty, including several dozen common cashiers." Still more to the point, he was completely indifferent to the massive famine and starvation that resulted from his relentless pressure—reflected in the letters—to export very large quantities of grain in order to buy foreign machinery and help with industrialization.

Given Stalin's indifference to the suffering and death directly resulting from his policy decisions and his habitually calm and collected manner in public appearances as well as in meetings with high-level foreign visitors, he acquired the reputation of being an unemotional person who was cold-bloodedly calculating in all his statecraft. He could be that on occasion. But behind the scenes—and the letters are very revealing in this respect—he was an extremely emotional man. But this emotionality was one-dimensional. His basic emotion was anger, vindictive and vengeful anger. When Soviet officials or others acted in ways that contravened his dictates or, in general, displeased him, he would explode in rage. His letters to Molotov occasionally reveal these outbursts of anger. When, for example, shortages appeared that showed his regime in a negative light, an infuriated Stalin would insist that supposedly guilty officials be put to death as "wreckers" and "saboteurs." They had to be treated as conspiring class enemies. As Lih observes, "The vivid invective of the letters belies the image of the cold-blooded Stalin."

By the mid-1930s, once Stalin held absolute power, his vindictive anger inflicted suffering and death, not only on individuals and small groups, but on entire sections of the population, including a very large proportion of the ruling Communist Party. Indeed, this man's anger became genocidal in sweep.

All the more pressing for the historian becomes the question of what typically aroused it. The letters themselves cannot give us the answer to this question. As a biographer of Stalin, I will conclude with the proposition that what frequently aroused Stalin's death-dealing anger and vindictiveness was speech or action that, directly or indirectly, negated his lifelong search for glory, that contradicted his image of himself as the leader of genius that he needed to be and not the catastrophic one that he was.

ROBERT C. TUCKER

Preface

In December 1969 at the age of seventy-nine, Viacheslav M. Molotov turned over to the Central Party Archive at the Institute of Marxism-Leninism seventy-nine original letters and notes he had received from Josef Vissarionovich Stalin. For many decades Molotov occupied top positions in the Soviet Union's party-state hierarchy as a Politburo member, chairman of the Council of Commissars, and minister of foreign affairs. The son of a bailiff from Viatsk province, Molotov began his dizzying career by becoming one of Stalin's most loyal comrades-in-arms during the 1920s; he did not hesitate to support Stalin in the struggle against all opposing factions, and he was prepared to obey any order the leader would give him. In a certain sense, the 1920s and 1930s could be considered the summit of Molotov's political career. Like other members of the Politburo, Molotov played a relatively independent political role until Stalin's total rule was fully established. Molotov's support was important to Stalin's effort to ensure a majority in the Politburo. For this reason, Stalin corresponded regularly with his supporters, guiding their actions, carefully following their moves, and giving them advice and directions. Stalin was a particularly active correspondent when he was vacationing outside Moscow.

During the many years that Soviet political history has been studied, scholars (primarily Western) have provided many interesting assessments of the struggle within the upper echelons of the Kremlin leadership; of the nature and mechanisms of party-state rule in the 1920s and 1930s; and finally, of the personality of Stalin himself. But researchers' opportunities were limited. Their conclusions were drawn from indirect testimonies and secondhand documents. The publication of primary sources thus acquires particularly great significance, especially letters written by a Soviet leader. In these letters Stalin reveals, in the most candid and direct way, the development of the basic ideas that were later implemented as official policy. Relatively few such primary documents have previously been available. And this collection of letters from Stalin to Molotov is uniquely valuable.

Stalin's letters to Molotov from 1925, 1926, 1927, 1929, and 1930 and a number of notes the two leaders exchanged during meetings of the Politburo constitute the main body of the documents. The selection for the year 1926 also includes six coded telegrams that Stalin and Molotov exchanged during their discussions of international affairs and one coded telegram from Tovstukha to Stalin. The period from 1931 through 1936 is represented by only a few documents. Letters from other years (notably 1928) are missing altogether. It is not known whether Molotov turned over all the documents in his possession or only a portion of them. Nevertheless, despite their fragmentary nature, the letters preserved contain unparalleled information, and they enable us to substantially broaden and refine our understanding of the nature and mechanism of the Soviet Union's party-state leadership in the 1920s and 1930s. They also offer an invaluable source for studying Stalin as an individual.

The introductory sections for each year and the notes help to elucidate the meaning of Stalin's letters. We do not claim to provide an exhaustive analysis of these letters. Our task is modest: to enable researchers and interested readers to familiarize themselves with the texts, to provide insight into their meaning and content, and to present the historical background of the correspondence.

Many of the political events about which Stalin wrote are unfamiliar to historians. Documents concerning the activities of top government officials have only recently become available. They have as yet been poorly studied, and for the most part they have not become generally familiar to the academic audience. For this reason, as much new material as possible is presented in the introductory sections and in the notes; the majority of these new documents are published in full, not extracted. Unfortunately, a certain number of important sources are still inaccessible. The final decisions on a number of issues mentioned in the letters, for example, were made under the rubric of the "Special File," the highest form of secrecy in the Soviet Union. Documents given this classification, including documents that concern many of the issues relating to foreign policy that are discussed in the 1927 letters, are still in the Russian Presidential Archive and are inaccessible to researchers. All decisions that were sent to the Special File are flagged in the notes.

RUSSIAN EDITORS AND SCHOLARS

Acknowledgments

I would like to thank the following people: Jonathan Brent, for inviting me to participate in the Annals of Communism series, a project of the highest scholarly value; Robert C. Tucker, for taking time away from his biography of Stalin to write a foreword to this volume; Jane Hedges, for her expert assistance and high standards. A grant from the National Council of Soviet and East European Affairs partly supported the research on which my introduction was based; the council, however, is not responsible for its content or my findings.

LARS T. LIH

Note on the Documents and the Narrative

All the letters from Stalin to Molotov presented in this volume are located in the Russian Center for the Preservation and Study of Documents of Recent History (Rossiiskii tsentr khraneniia i izucheniia dokumentov noveishei istorii, hereafter RTsKhIDNI). Stalin's letters are located in *fond 558, opis 1, delo 5388.* The archival and reference numbers of other documents are provided.

Stalin's letters to Molotov are all handwritten in pen or pencil, except for number 83, which is typed. Not all the letters carry original dates. When Molotov presented his collection to the archive, he penciled an estimated date on each letter, but in a number of cases he was mistaken. Stalin himself wrote the year 1926 on several letters dealing with events that definitely occurred in 1927. All corrections to the dates are discussed in the notes. The date appearing in brackets at the top of the letter is the corrected date. The letters are presented in chronological order and are numbered consecutively.

In the letters, words that were underlined once appear here in *italic,* words that were underlined twice in **bold.** It is not possible to ascertain whether the underlining was done by Stalin, by Molotov, or by a later reader, since all of the underlining was added by hand. All ellipses (. . .) in the letters are in the originals. (When the letters are quoted elsewhere in the text, underlining is not always retained, and ellipses used elsewhere indicate omissions made by the editors unless otherwise noted.) Some of the letters include comments written by other members of the Politburo: brief comments are presented in the notes, longer remarks appear after Stalin's text.

The Russian editors and scholars wrote the text that introduces the letters for each year. They also prepared the biographical material in the Glossary of Names (the information provided is generally restricted to the period covered by the letters). The U.S. edition was prepared directly from the transcript provided by the Russian editors, without reference to the original letters. The U.S. editor edited the translation, wrote the Introduction, and added all material in brackets, unless otherwise noted. Notes by the Russian editors appear without attribution. Notes by the U.S. editor and the translator are so labeled. A number of notes are repeated in full so that each letter can be read without reference to earlier ones.

Some of these letters have already appeared in Russian in Soviet periodicals. The letters from 1925 (letters 1 through 10) can be found in *Izvestiia TsK*, no. 9 (1990): 184–92. Letters 50, 56, 57, 59, 62, 65, 66, 68, 78, and 79 were published in *Kommunist*, no. 11 (1990): 94–106.

Stalin's Letters to Molotov

Molotov and Stalin

Introduction

—Do you dream about Stalin?
—Not often, but sometimes. The circumstances are very unusual—I'm in some sort of destroyed city, and I can't find any way out. Afterwards I meet with him. In a word, very strange dreams, very confused.

V. M. MOLOTOV

IN 1969, THE MAN whose long association with Stalin resulted in such eerie dreams, Viacheslav M. Molotov, turned over a packet of letters to party authorities. For the most part, Stalin wrote these letters to Molotov during the years 1925 to 1936 while away from Moscow on what appear to be rather frequent vacations. Although generally addressed to Molotov, the letters were often intended for Stalin's allies in the Politburo. In his memoirs, Molotov describes these letters as both personal and official; they contain musings on political events, arguments meant to persuade fellow Politburo members, and specific instructions.[1] Detailed, handwritten letters were evidently necessary given the lack of a reliable telephone link between Moscow and Sochi (where Stalin's Black Sea resort was located). We therefore have primitive communications technology to thank for a unique set of documents that throw a searching light on how Stalin approached his job of running the Soviet state.

The letters put us in the middle of many crucial episodes during a dramatic period of transformation. We see Stalin fighting against party rivals like Trotsky and Bukharin, trying to maneuver in the

1. F. Chuev, *Sto sorok besed s Molotovym: Iz dnevnika F. Chueva* (Moscow, 1991), 277. Molotov's conversations with Chuev are available in English: *Molotov Remembers: Inside Kremlin Politics,* ed. Albert Resis (Chicago, 1993). A biographical sketch of Molotov can be found in Roy Medvedev, *All Stalin's Men* (New York, 1985).

rapids of the Chinese revolution, insisting on the completion of all-out collectivization, and ordering the execution of scapegoats for economic failures. The value of the correspondence is greatly enhanced by the comprehensive annotation provided by the Russian side. They have elucidated much that would otherwise have remained mysterious and have also given us supplementary archival documents of the highest interest.

Stalin at Work

In 1925, when the Stalin-Molotov correspondence begins, Stalin had been general secretary of the Communist Party for several years. The official duties of the Secretariat concerned internal party matters that were supposed to be below the level of high policy, and the post of general secretary was not yet the unchallenged leadership position it later became as a result of Stalin's ascendancy. The letters sometimes reflect an almost conscious apprenticeship on Stalin's part: he extends his policy-making role into economic and diplomatic affairs with greater and greater assurance.

Molotov had actually held the post of party secretary prior to Stalin. A decade younger than Stalin, Molotov was renowned for his bureaucratic efficiency, but he did not have any independent political authority. In 1922 the party leaders decided it would be better to have a senior party figure head up the Secretariat, and Stalin was given the job. Molotov remained in the Secretariat and soon became a full member of the Politburo.

Molotov always seemed rather cold and unemotional, occasionally revealing a streak of aggressive pedantry that was extremely irritating to other party leaders. They called him Stone Bottom, a nickname that was dismissive and yet respectful of his huge capacity for work. His hero-worship of Stalin seems genuine enough, and his role as Stalin's right-hand man is evident from the letters. He would argue with his boss on occasion, but always in an effort to point out what would be in Stalin's best interest. Molotov was later rewarded for his loyalty with a number of important posts, including head of the government and minister of foreign affairs.

Toward the end of Stalin's life, Molotov fell into disfavor. He was forced to participate in the Politburo meeting that approved the arrest of his wife (Molotov abstained). Nevertheless, after Stalin's death, Molotov remained loyal to Stalin's memory, and his unreconstructed views led eventually to a falling out with Nikita Khrushchev and to his expulsion from the party. Molotov doggedly applied for reinstatement and was rewarded with a party card shortly before his death in 1986.

The present collection of letters begins at a time when the Bolshevik party was approaching a turning point. The decade from the beginning of World War I to 1925 was a period of social and economic breakdown and reconstitution for Russia. The low point occurred in the winter of 1920–1921. The economic upswing made possible by the end of hostilities associated with the civil war was further strengthened by the New Economic Policy (NEP) that was introduced in the spring of 1921. The essence of the new policy was a short-term toleration of private capitalists and middlemen, combined with a longer-term acceptance of a regulated market as the key economic link between socialized industry and peasant farms. The Bolsheviks assumed that, at some future date, industry would be advanced enough to allow Russian agriculture to be reorganized into large productive units. In the meantime, industrial growth had to rely on the surplus produced by small peasant farms.

By 1925 the economy was on the verge of reaching prewar levels. This recovery was shaky and infirm, however, since the orgy of destruction and demoralization that had occurred from 1914 to 1921 could not be made up in a few years' time. Furthermore, the rest of the world had not stood still. Thus the Bolsheviks were left in an even weaker international position than previous Russian governments had occupied. Still, by late 1925 the Bolsheviks were preparing to make an advance beyond simple recovery under the guidance of a general strategy that had a number of optimistic assumptions built into it: the superior productivity of nationalized industry, the availability of marketed surpluses of agricultural goods, and a relatively benign international environment.

Perhaps because of this optimism, Stalin devotes little attention to economic questions in the letters from 1925, 1926, and 1927. He comments in 1926: "I am not alarmed by economic matters. Rykov will be able to take care of them. The opposition wins absolutely zero points on economic matters" (letter 20). Although Aleksei

Rykov was official head of the government in the mid-1920s, he was a relatively colorless figure whom historians have left in the background. Stalin's remark hints that his role may have been greater than we suspected.

In the letters from the mid-1920s Stalin's principal economic concern is to ensure that the Politburo maintains control over economic questions, despite the resistance of planning specialists, "monopolistic" state syndicates, and lower-level trading cooperatives. One item of particular interest is Stalin's skeptical attitude in 1925 toward the Dneprostroi project—a proposed hydroelectric station that later became a symbol of Stalin's industrial achievements (letters 2 and 3). We know that Stalin voted against the project in April 1926, but here we see that his misgivings date back to a much earlier stage. Stalin felt that a commission that had been established under Trotsky's leadership would be too hasty in beginning the project. (He need not have worried, for in fact Trotsky used his influence to slow it down.)[2] Stalin learned about the Dneprostroi commission from a newspaper article, and indeed this seems to have been his main source of economic information, at least while he was on vacation.

The mid-1920s were a turning point for bolshevism politically as well as economically. The Bolsheviks had always felt that one of the reasons they were able to survive in an extremely hostile world was the unity of what they called the top leadership nucleus. Unlike almost all other Russian parties, the Bolsheviks had not allowed the inevitable dissensions and the clash of ambitions to drive the party apart during the civil war and the first years of NEP. Everyone realized that this remarkable political feat stemmed from Lenin's unique position in the party and that things would be very different after his death. Since no one could duplicate Lenin's status, the remaining leaders had to develop new methods for ensuring unity. This process is reflected in the letters from 1925 through 1927, which are strongly preoccupied with the political battle within the Politburo against Trotsky and Zinoviev. Stalin's attitudes toward his rivals are reflected in many other letters throughout the collec-

2. Anne D. Rassweiler, *The Generation of Power: The History of Dneprostroi* (Oxford, 1988).

tion. Taken together, the letters suggest the need to reconsider the way we look at the leadership struggles after Lenin's death.

In 1925, most observers felt that the country was run by a triumvirate consisting of Zinoviev, Kamenev, and Stalin, with Trotsky already relegated to the sidelines. Trotsky had been openly at odds with his Politburo colleagues for several years before 1925. By the end of 1923, he had managed to enrage the rest of his Politburo colleagues so thoroughly that they formed a shadow Politburo: the *semerka* (the seven), an institution that plays a large role in Stalin's letters from the mid-1920s. The seven's sole purpose was to conduct Politburo business without Trotsky's participation. Trotsky did not even know the seven existed until Zinoviev told him when they joined forces in 1926.

Stalin's letters to Molotov give us a close-up view of some dramatic episodes in this battle among the top leaders. In 1925 the Politburo took Stalin's suggestion and compelled Trotsky to issue a public refutation of a book written by his American admirer Max Eastman. The "Eastman affair" has previously been described as a cynical cover-up in which the triumvirate forced Trotsky to tell conscious lies. The letters and other documents allow a much different interpretation.

Another split within the Politburo was dramatically revealed at the XIV Party Congress in late 1925. For reasons of both policy and ambition, Zinoviev and Kamenev rebelled and called for Stalin's removal from the post of general secretary. Their effort failed utterly; during the winter of 1925–1926 Zinoviev even lost control of his political base in Leningrad. Even though Zinoviev had formerly been one of the most prominent Trotsky-baiters in the leadership, he now felt it expedient to join forces with his erstwhile foe. Thus was formed the united left opposition, which openly challenged the Politburo majority from a leftist standpoint until late 1927, when its leaders were thrown out of the party. Trotsky ended up in exile; Zinoviev and Kamenev recanted and were soon reinstated.

A large number of Stalin's letters in 1926 and 1927 deal with foreign policy, particularly with revolutionary stirrings in England and China. Stalin's intense involvement belies the image of an isolationist leader interested only in "socialism in one country." The letters show us that Stalin did not make a rigid distinction between the interests of world revolution and the interests of the Soviet state: both concerns are continually present in his outlook.

Although the British government had recognized the Soviet Union in 1924, the Conservative Party that was returned to power at the end of the year was uncomfortable with any dealings with bomb-throwing Bolsheviks. Relations were further strained by the enthusiasm with which the Bolsheviks greeted the brief general strike of 1926 and the moral and material support they gave to the striking miners. Back at home, the left opposition attacked the Politburo for not being revolutionary enough. The optimism of 1926 did not last long: working-class militancy in England petered out and the Conservative government broke off diplomatic relations in 1927. When a Labour government was formed in 1929, it promptly extended recognition to the Soviet Union; still, revolutionary feeling among the British working class did not resurface.[3]

Relations with China were even more complex, since China was experiencing its own revolutionary upheaval in the mid-1920s. The movement against the imperialist powers was spearheaded by the government at Canton controlled by the Kuomintang, the nationalist party founded by Sun Yat-sen. Allied to the Kuomintang was the newly formed Chinese Communist Party. Thanks in large part to Russian political and military advisors, the Kuomintang was prepared in 1926 to undertake the Northern Expedition in an effort to unite a country rendered powerless by internal divisions. The Northern Expedition was a phenomenal military success, but it quickly led to divisions within the camp of the Chinese revolutionaries. By the middle of 1927, the Chinese Communists found themselves isolated and driven underground, first by Chiang Kai-shek and then by the so-called left Kuomintang government located in Wuhan.

The Bolshevik leaders viewed events in China with the hope that a nationalist and anti-imperialist government would unite the country and strike a blow at the world power of Western capitalism. To this end, they counseled the Chinese Communist Party to work as closely as possible with the Kuomintang and later with the

3. Daniel F. Calhoun, *The United Front: The TUC and the Russians, 1923–1928* (Cambridge, 1976).

Wuhan government. The left opposition roundly criticized this "rightist" policy of cooperation with the bourgeoisie that led eventually to disaster for the Chinese Communists.[4]

Policy toward both China and Great Britain was thus a matter of intense dispute among the Bolshevik leaders. The dramatic Politburo showdown with Zinoviev in June 1926 involved policy toward the British trade unions. In spite of this partisan dimension, the letters reveal Stalin's genuine enthusiasm about revolutionary prospects in 1926 as well as his reaction to defeat in 1927. Particularly revealing are the letters from 1927 written at the moment when Stalin had to face up to the ruin of his China policy.

After 1927 the prospect of revolution elsewhere diminished, and Stalin's foreign policy concerns were confined to such issues as diplomatic recognition from Great Britain and the United States. His interest in China now focused on the Chinese Eastern Railway, which ran through Manchuria. This railroad, built during tsarist times, was of strategic importance to the Soviet government as the most efficient route to Vladivostok. The de facto ruler of Manchuria, a warlord named Chang Tso-lin, wanted complete control over the railroad. The dispute over the railroad culminated in a brief armed clash in 1929 between the Soviet government and Chang's son (Chang Hsueh-liang).[5] Even though the dispute over the Chinese Eastern Railway was entirely a matter of state, Stalin viewed it through the prism of revolutionary interests. He even outlined a scenario for retaining control over the railroad by instigating an instant revolution in Manchuria.

From 1925 to 1927, Stalin worked closely with both Nikolai Bukharin, editor of *Pravda* (the party newspaper) and principal party theorist, and Aleksei Rykov, head of the Soviet government and top economic administrator. There are no letters to Molotov from 1928, which is a pity but which adds to the dramatic effect when the curtain rises in 1929 and we find Stalin and Molotov plotting against their erstwhile allies, Bukharin and Rykov. The reason for the conflict was Stalin's radical "offensive along the

4. C. Martin Wilbur and Julie Lien-ying How, *Missionaries of Revolution: Soviet Advisers and Nationalist China, 1920–1927* (Cambridge, Mass., 1989).

5. For background on the conflict over the Chinese Eastern Railway in 1929, see E. H. Carr, *Foundations of a Planned Economy*, vol. 3 (New York, 1976–78), 895–910.

whole front," which attempted to combine a frantic pace of industrialization with all-out collectivization in agriculture. Stalin's general offensive meant the end of NEP and its use of the market to link the peasants with state industry. Bukharin and Rykov, who found this policy ill conceived and dangerous, were condemned as leaders of the "right deviation."[6]

The letters from 1929 and 1930 touch on all aspects of this great transformation. Stalin's high-pressure industrial policies led to an upheaval in the economy that left the government struggling to maintain a semblance of control. The letters show Stalin's response to this emergency as he ceaselessly shuffles personnel in order to put the right person in the right position. A more destructive response to the unending stream of foul-ups and breakdowns was to assign all blame to enemies within the Soviet government itself. An ideology centered on "wrecking" finds expression in the letters. For many observers, upward mobility via promotion off the shop floor (*vydvizhenie*) was a key source of support for the Stalinist system. It is thus ironic to find Stalin inveighing against vydvizhenie as disruptive (letter 69).

Only scattered passages in the letters show Stalin's attitude toward grain procurement and collectivization, but taken together they illuminate the mind-set that gave rise to the momentous decision in late 1929 to combine all-out collectivization with massive repression of the kulaks (better-off peasants). The letters also show Stalin's intensely personal anger against the leaders of the right deviation. More surprisingly, we find the same anger, justified with the same rhetoric, directed against people who are usually regarded as far removed from the right deviation: the former Trotskyist Georgii Piatakov and the loyal Stalinist Sergo Ordzhonikidze. The letters thus force us to reexamine the political logic by which Stalin defined his enemies within the party.

The nature of the correspondence changes drastically after 1930, and we have only thirteen rather fragmentary letters from the years 1931–1936. The reasons for this change are unclear. Molotov re-

---

6. Invaluable background for many of the issues discussed in Stalin's letters can be found in R. W. Davies, *The Soviet Economy in Turmoil, 1929–1930* (Cambridge, Mass., 1989).

placed Rykov as head of the government in late 1930, and it could be that other means were found to transmit Stalin's instructions. It is also possible that Molotov found it expedient to suppress incriminating material. Nevertheless, the letters from this period are not without interest. In September 1935, for example, Stalin gives a provisional outline of the new Constitution adopted the following year, thus documenting a strong directive role early in the drafting process (letter 83).[7] Stalin wanted the Constitution to reflect only "what has *already* been achieved"; he and Molotov evidently had somewhat macabre theoretical disputes over exactly what stage of socialism had been reached by the mid-1930s.

The list of topics covered in the letters is a long and varied one. Just as revealing are the patterns that emerge from the collection as a whole, which give us an unparalleled look at Stalin as leader. A complete analysis of Stalin's leadership would cover at least three dimensions. We need to consider Stalin as an *official* and examine the constraints faced by anybody in the position of top leader in a country undergoing revolutionary transformation. We need to look at Stalin as a *Bolshevik*, since the basic mental tools Stalin applied to his job were derived from the Bolshevik political culture in which he had spent his adult life. Nor can we neglect Stalin as an *individual* with his own particular psychological makeup and mental habits.

Stalin's letters fill in the gap between public speeches about the general direction of policy, on the one hand, and specific decisions about day-to-day matters, on the other; they are documents of leadership and persuasion aimed specifically at the top echelons of the Bolshevik party. As such, they throw valuable and much-needed light on all three dimensions of Stalin as a leader. Because Stalin is explaining his views on urgent policy questions, we observe him as an official, dealing with the whole range of problems that would confront any ruler of Russia. Because he is trying to obtain support in the Politburo, we can examine the arguments that Stalin thought would work with fellow Bolsheviks. Although we will never learn what Stalin said privately to himself, the letters provide us with the

7. J. Arch Getty, "State and Society under Stalin: Constitutions and Elections in the 1930s," *Slavic Review* 50 (1991):18–35.

next best resource for learning about Stalin as an individual: how Stalin defined the world in confidential correspondence with his closest political friend.

Along with my commentary on specific topics, I shall advance a general interpretation of Stalin as a leader that is based on my reading of the letters. My argument, in brief, is as follows: Stalin had a conscious and coherent approach to governing that I shall call the antibureaucrat scenario. The constructive side of this scenario allowed Stalin to use his undeniable leadership skills to get things done and to maintain Politburo support. These skills were the original basis of Stalin's power. On the other hand, the antibureaucrat scenario also defined governing as a continual struggle with class enemies of various types and hues. The scenario thus gave expression to the angry and vindictive sides of Stalin's personality.

The suspicious and punitive features of Stalin's scenario were always present, but they became more pronounced in 1929 and 1930 when the country was plunged into the whirlwind of the general offensive. We observe Stalin's anger at those he perceived as enemies become increasingly intense. Indeed, the ring of enemies seems to close in on him: first the international "capitalist encirclement," then domestic class enemies like the kulaks, next the "bourgeois specialists" working for the Soviet government itself, and finally some of his closest comrades. Although the correspondence fades out in the early 1930s, we are well on our way to the murderous purge campaigns of 1937–1938. The same outlook that allowed Stalin to run the government for so many years also pushed him close to destroying it.

The Antibureaucrat Scenario

To understand Stalin at work, we need to understand his views on running a government. It is not difficult to discover these views, for this was a subject that mattered deeply to Stalin; he gave it considerable thought and set forth his conclusions on a number of occasions. His own summary of his views seems no more than a couple of banal platitudes: the need for proper "selection of officials" and "checking up on fulfillment" of policy directives. These bland slogans only reveal their full meaning, however, when set into the context of a dramatic and politicized scenario of class conflict and revolutionary transformation. The details of this scenario can be found in Stalin's published speeches; the letters to Molotov reveal how the scenario guided him in his day-to-day work.

Stalin's scenario can be summarized as follows: There is no objective obstacle to the successful construction of socialism in Russia. The soviet system of government, the state control of the commanding heights of the economy, and the natural resources of Russia itself—all of these provide the potential for successfully completing the revolution. Correct leadership thus becomes the crucial factor. The first task of leadership is to define the correct line. The core leadership of the party—its "leading nucleus"—must accurately size up the situation and deduce the necessary tasks facing the party at any one time. The main threat to defining the correct line comes from wavering on the part of leaders who in their hearts lack faith in the revolution.

Defining the correct line is only the first step. Next it must be spelled out so that all other party members understand both the overall picture and their own role in it. This requires clarity in presentation and a careful selection of slogans and directives. But it would be criminal laxness to believe that the party line will be carried out automatically. Proper leadership requires unremitting attention to "selection of officials" and "checking up on fulfillment." The main threat here is Russia's low level of culture, which forces the worker-peasant state to rely on many "class-alien elements" in its government bureaucracy. As a result, vigilance is one of the basic duties of each party member.

These are the bare bones of Stalin's outlook, stated in somewhat dry propositional form. In order to understand the emotional power of this view, we have to recast it in the form of the dramatic antibureaucrat scenario that portrays well-intentioned but naive Communists doing battle with sophisticated bureaucrats who try to fool and corrupt them. Stalin's attitudes emerge in vivid language taken from three speeches given at different stages of his career.

In 1920, Stalin was head of Worker-Peasant Inspection (Rabkrin). This agency was the descendent of the tsarist Ministry of State Control, which was devoted mainly to auditing accounts of other government agencies. Lenin had ambitious plans for the Worker-Peasant Inspection and saw it as an instrument of mass participation in government. Although Stalin was nominally the head of Worker-Peasant Inspection, his other duties during the civil war prevented him from giving much of his time to it. Stalin left the Worker-Peasant Inspection in 1922 when he took over the post of general secretary.

In October 1920, Stalin addressed a group of officials from the Worker-Peasant Inspection. He stressed the vital importance of progressing from the seizure of political power to the genuine control over the state *apparat*: "Comrades, the people who really run the country are not those who elect delegates, whether to parliament in the bourgeois system or to soviet congresses under the Soviet system. No, those who factually run the country are those who really master the executive *apparaty* [or, the apparaty of fulfillment], those who lead these apparaty." This task was difficult because the workers and peasants did not have any prerevolutionary experience in administration. One consequence of this situation was that "although bureaucratism has been smashed, the bureaucrats have remained. Painting themselves as soviet officials, they have entered our state apparaty. Here they use the insufficient experience of workers and peasants who have just come into power; they spin out their old machinations in order to plunder state property; they introduce their old bourgeois morals." As Worker-Peasant Inspection officials tried to do their job, they would undoubtedly run into opposition from "overzealous bureaucrats, as well as some Communists who give in to the voices of these bureaucrats." When encountering this, their motto should be: "Don't spare individuals, no matter what position they occupy; spare only the cause, the interests of the cause."[8]

For our second speech we turn to the XII Party Congress in 1923. This was the last party congress in Lenin's lifetime; he was already incapacitated by strokes and did not attend. In his speech, Stalin depicted himself as developing Lenin's outlook. In addition to political considerations, Stalin felt that there was a "moral aspect" to Lenin's demand for an improved apparat: Lenin "wanted to get to

8. J. V. Stalin, *Sochineniia,* 13 vols. to date (Moscow, 1946–), 4:366–68.

the point where the country contained not a single bigwig, no matter how highly placed, about which the man in the street could say, 'that one is above control.'" Years later, in the mid-1930s, a murderous version of this populist rhetoric dominated the mass media.

Another of Lenin's slogans was "selection of officials." Stalin explained this slogan by arguing that it was insufficient merely to give directives—you had to find officials who could understand these directives and regard them as their own. For this reason the Central Committee needed to know each high official through and through.[9]

Our final example comes from the speech Stalin gave at a meeting of the Central Committee in January 1933. Stalin argued that the period of revolutionary transformation was drawing to a close: it was time to make the new structures work in a productive and efficient manner. The main obstacle was still the "enemy within" (to borrow a phrase from J. Edgar Hoover), portrayed in vivid and melodramatic fashion as crushed and resentful class enemies: "Thrown out of their groove, and scattered over the whole face of the USSR, these 'former people' [the elite disinherited by the revolution] have wormed their way into our plants and factories, into our government offices and trading organizations, into our railway and water transport enterprises, and, principally, into our collective and state farms. They have crept into these places and taken cover there, donning the mask of 'workers' and 'peasants,' and some of them have even managed to worm their way into the party." What did these class enemies carry with them into these places?—a feeling of hatred toward Soviet power, a feeling of burning enmity toward the new forms of economy, life, and culture. Inspired by this hatred, the alien elements set out to organize sabotage; certain professors, for example, went so far as to inject plague and anthrax germs into cattle. Stalin insisted that "the task is to eject these 'former people' from our own enterprises and institutions and render them permanently harmless." Unfortunately some people within the party thought that the class struggle was dying down, since the enemy classes had been defeated in open battle. Such people have either degenerated or are two-faced; they must be driven out of the party

9. Stalin, *Sochineniia*, 5:197–222.

and their smug philistine attitude replaced by revolutionary vigilance.[10]

These three speeches give an idea of the emotions Stalin invested
in the antibureaucrat scenario. In spite of an increase in the violence
and obsessiveness of the rhetoric, the fundamental outlook remains
the same: the system is basically good; problems arise from hostile
individuals within the system and their ability to fool otherwise
dedicated revolutionaries; only a united leadership devoid of wavering can combat the bureaucrats.

Turning now to Stalin's correspondence with Molotov, we observe that the slogans "checking up on fulfillment" and "selection
of officials" are ubiquitous. Some examples will show how Stalin
applied these in practice. His efforts to improve the oil industry in
the Urals demonstrate his attitude toward selecting officials (letters
42, 44, 46, 57). Given the decision to develop this industry, Stalin's
contribution was to get a competent person for the top party post—
someone who was a "Communist/oilman." Once this person was
found, he was to be given the "combat assignment" to develop oil,
drive out incompetent "wreckers," and protect the Urals from having personnel be "looted" by other localities and institutions.

The shortage of "big people"—energetic and talented administrators—is a constant complaint. In letter 60, Stalin wants to help
the Commissariat of Trade by sending over Rozengolts from the
Worker-Peasant Inspection, even though he realizes that Sergo
Ordzhonikidze, the head of Worker-Peasant Inspection, will be upset. He ends with the typical Stalin sentiment: "Do people pity
Khinchuk [a trade official]? But the cause should be pitied even
more. Do they not want to offend Sergo? But what about the
cause—can such an important and serious matter be offended?"

Once having selected the man for the job and given him vast
powers, Stalin had to worry about whether he would do what he
was supposed to do. Hence the importance of the slogan "checking
up on fulfillment." His obsessive concern is revealed in an exhorta-
tion about grain procurement in 1929 (letter 42):

10. Stalin, *Sochineniia*, 13:159–233. A fuller study of Stalin's theory of leadership and its relation to bolshevism will be presented in my "What Was Bolshevism:
Narratives of Identity in the 1920s" (work in progress).

The Politburo has adopted my proposals concerning grain procurement. This is good, but in my opinion, it is inadequate. Now the problem is *fulfilling* the Politburo's decision. There is no need to insist that all procurement organizations (especially in Ukraine) will *evade* this decision. . . . Therefore, it is necessary to demand the following from procurement organizations, the OGPU, the Collective Farm Center, and so forth:

a) copies of their instructions to subordinate organs concerning the *fulfillment* of the Politburo's decision; b) regular reports every two weeks (even better, once a week) about the *results of the fulfillment* of the decisions. The Worker-Peasant Inspection and the Central Control Commission should be involved in this as well. I don't know how you regard this matter and the outlook for grain procurement (Mikoian probably thinks that since the decision has been reached, he now has 130 million poods of an untouchable reserve sitting in the grain elevators). . . . And grain procurement this year will provide the basis for everything we're doing—if we foul up here, everything will be wiped out. And the danger of a foul-up will grow if we don't insist that the Central Committee's decision *be fulfilled* with unrelenting *firmness* and *ruthlessness.*

In 1930, Stalin dreamed of a Fulfillment Commission that would solve all his problems: "Without such an authoritative and rapidly acting commission, we will not be able to break through the wall of bureaucratism and [improve] the slipshod performance in our bureaucracies. Without such reforms, the center's directives will remain completely on paper" (letter 68). (This commission was actually set up in late 1930, but nothing came of it.) When Stalin wanted to give Molotov a pat on the back, it is no wonder that he paid him the ultimate compliment and praised his "Leninist checking up on fulfillment" (letter 70).

When set into the context of the antibureaucrat scenario, the two slogans have both a constructive and a destructive side. "Checking up on fulfillment" is the task of any responsible administrator who wants to ensure that central policies are actually carried out. According to Stalin's antibureaucrat scenario, however, class-motivated hostility is the main reason bureaucrats do not follow directives. If conscious or unconscious sabotage is the problem, repression is bound to be at least part of the solution. "Selection of officials" did not mean simply choosing and promoting the most competent people. There was a moral dimension: Officials needed to be chosen who would look on party directives as their own and who would not be seduced by "bourgeois specialists." But if the selected officials proved less reliable than anticipated, this moral dimension could easily give rise to disappointment and vindictive anger.

Let us now consider how the antibureaucrat scenario fits into the three dimensions of Stalin as leader. First, Stalin as an official: any politician trying to run an unwieldy bureaucracy is likely to develop some sort of antibureaucrat scenario. Richard Neustadt's classic *Presidential Power* shows this process at work in the case of the American presidency.[11] In Stalin's case, we have to add his position as top leader in a country undergoing a state-guided revolutionary transformation. Stalin had to run the country with the help of officials whose trustworthiness was dubious and whose competence was perhaps even more dubious. He was forced to grant enormous power to these people and to give them next-to-impossible tasks. Obsession with shuffling personnel and intense suspicion of appointees was built into the situation, and the antibureaucrat scenario reflected these structural realities.

Stalin did not create his particular version of the antibureaucrat scenario in a vacuum, and so we have to consider Stalin as a Bolshevik. His scenario had roots in what might be called the popular bolshevism that arose during the civil war. Both before and after the October revolution of 1917, the Bolsheviks blamed the breakdown of the economy on the sabotage of capitalists and bureaucrats and presented themselves as the only force capable of crushing this sabotage. When the economic breakdown continued during the civil war, the population transferred this explanation to the Bolshevik state itself. The population invented a new category—the "soviet bourgeoisie"—that Stalin took over and used for his own purposes.[12]

Stalin could plausibly claim Lenin's authority for his scenario, since Lenin also viewed public administration as a dramatic struggle against a class enemy. When Lenin insisted on the slogans "checking up on fulfillment" and "selection of officials" in 1922, he

11. Richard Neustadt, *Presidential Power: The Politics of Leadership* (New York, 1960).
12. Mary McAuley, *Bread and Justice* (Oxford, 1991), 400.

emphasized that they were part of "the struggle between two irreconcilably hostile classes [that] appears to be going on in all government offices." Lenin blamed his frustration with bureaucratic red tape on clever saboteurs: "The vile bureaucratic bog *draws us* into the writing of papers, endless talkfests about decrees, the writing of decrees, and real live work drowns in that sea of paper. Clever saboteurs deliberately draw us into this paper swamp. The majority of people's commissars and other government dignitaries unwittingly 'walk into the trap.' "[13]

The antibureaucrat scenario was thus derived from experiences that all the Bolshevik leaders had lived through. Shared experience gave Stalin's perceptions a basic legitimacy with the party elite: what he said made sense to them, even when they disagreed with it. The letters show the use that Stalin made of the scenario when exhorting his Politburo colleagues.

In spite of its links with Bolshevik political culture, the antibureaucrat scenario must also be considered from the point of view of Stalin as an individual. Stalin stood out among Bolshevik leaders in the attention he devoted to the problems of controlling the state. This point is usually made by emphasizing that Stalin was preoccupied with machine politics and with manipulating the state and party apparat. This is one way of putting it, and no doubt a valid one, but if we limit ourselves to this presentation, we risk underestimating Stalin in the same way his opponents did. An equally valid way of putting it is that no other Bolshevik leader took so seriously the basic problem confronting the Bolsheviks: how to run the country. Stalin's antibureaucrat scenario arose out of his reflections on that problem.

According to the scenario, good government was an eternal battle in which noble intentions were continually thwarted by the ill will of saboteurs. Without going deeply into psychological speculations, we may conclude that this scenario would recommend itself to a person predisposed to see the world in angry, punitive terms. Furthermore, as Stalin's goals became more ambitious and as the chaos of the general offensive led to greater and greater frustration, the intensity of the emotions he invested in the scenario rose to a murderous pitch.

13. Robert C. Tucker, ed., *The Lenin Anthology* (New York, 1975), 526–28, 717.

Political Opposition during NEP

In the letters from 1925 through 1927 Stalin is strongly preoccupied with the political battle within the Politburo against Trotsky and Zinoviev. These letters amply confirm some well-known images of Stalin. One is Stalin the Crafty Maneuverer. In 1925 Stalin seizes on a book published in the West as an opportunity to further discredit Trotsky, and in 1926 he directs a Politburo campaign to isolate Zinoviev and Kamenev. Another familiar image is Stalin the Catechist: the Stalin who learned in his days at the Tbilisi Theological Seminary to sum up any question with cut-and-dried formulae.

Yet even these familiar images require modification when we observe them in the context of relations within the Politburo. The Politburo majority (which included Zinoviev and Kamenev in 1925) relied on Stalin not just to do secretarial chores but to act as a leader: his influence within the Politburo was based on what his colleagues considered the cogency of his analysis and the soundness of his recommendations.

The Eastman Affair

The Eastman affair of 1925 provides an excellent case study of Stalin's leadership within the Politburo. This affair has usually been interpreted as a brazen cover-up of the existence of the document known as Lenin's Testament. In late 1922, a few months before his final stroke, Lenin dictated a short document that he termed a "letter to the [party] congress." In it, he characterized the top leaders; in a postscript added a few days later, he suggested that Stalin be removed from the post of general secretary of the party. Only Nadezhda Krupskaia, Lenin's wife, knew the full contents of this document until after Lenin's death in early 1924, at which time she turned it and related documents over to the Central Committee. The party leadership decided not to read Lenin's letter into the official record of the upcoming XIII Party Congress but rather to read it to each delegation off the record. Stalin offered his resignation as general secretary, but it was not accepted. The letter itself was not published.

Although this letter became widely known as "Lenin's Testament," it should be noted that Lenin himself did not give it this label; it was in fact one of a series of dictations on various matters. By 1925, Bukharin and others had given the title "Lenin's Testament" to the five articles Lenin published in early 1923, on the grounds that these final articles discuss matters of grand political strategy. For convenience, I will refer to Lenin's letter as the Testament, with the proviso that the appropriateness of this label is a matter of dispute.

The Western scholars who have discussed the Eastman affair (Leonard Schapiro, Isaac Deutscher, and Boris Souvarine, among others) all tell a similar story: after Lenin's death, his Testament was suppressed. In 1925 Max Eastman, an American journalist, wrote *Since Lenin Died,* in which he revealed the existence of the Testament and gave an accurate description of its contents.[14] The ruling triumvirate—Stalin, Zinoviev, and Kamenev—were horrified at the whistle being blown on their cover-up and forced both Trotsky and Krupskaia to write letters denying the existence of the Testament. Thus constrained to deny what he and other informed people knew to be true, Trotsky utterly discredited himself.[15] (Trotsky's and Krupskaia's letters are included in the appendix.)

This account needs to be reconsidered in the light of Stalin's letters to Molotov and the other remarkable documents presented by the Russian side.[16] Chief among the new documents is Stalin's long memorandum detailing the misstatements made in Eastman's book and demanding that Trotsky publicly repudiate these misstatements. From letter 6 it appears that Stalin wanted to publish his memorandum. This fact in itself forces us to reopen the case and ask whether the Eastman affair was a cynical cover-up or whether the

14. Max Eastman, *Since Lenin Died* (1925; Westport, Conn.: Hyperion, 1973). For page references, see text.

15. Leonard Schapiro, *The Communist Party of the Soviet Union,* rev. ed. (New York, 1971), 300–301; Isaac Deutscher, *The Prophet Unarmed: Trotsky, 1921–1929* (New York, 1959), 201–2; Boris Souvarine, *Stalin: A Critical Survey of Bolshevism* (New York, 1939), 414, 348.

16. For further background on the relationship between Trotsky and Eastman, see V. V. Shevstov, "Lev Trotskii i Maks Istmen [Max Eastman]: Istoriia odnoi politicheskoi druzhby," *Novaia i noveishaia istoriia,* no. 6 (1990): 141–63. Many important new documents that shed light on the Eastman affair can be found in Yuri Buranov, *Lenin's Will: Falsified and Forbidden* (Amherst, Mass., 1994). Buranov's book is unfortunately marred by serious inaccuracies, many of which are attributable to the very inadequate English translation.

Politburo was making what it considered legitimate demands. Our general picture of Politburo politics in the 1920s will be strongly influenced by the answer to this question.

Previous Western interpretations have all accepted that Eastman's book "correctly reproduced long extracts" of the Testament.[17] On reading *Since Lenin Died*, I was surprised to find this was far from true. Not only does Eastman give a highly distorted rendition of the Testament, but the distortions all clearly serve an explicit political purpose, unambiguously stated in the final sentence of the book: revolutionaries in other countries ought to remember that "they did not pledge themselves to accept, in the name of 'Leninism,' the international authority of a group against whom Lenin's dying words were a warning, and who have preserved that authority by suppressing the essential texts of Lenin" (130).

Eastman interprets the Testament as a "direct endorsement of Trotsky's authority" (31). In order to reach this conclusion, he had to remove the complimentary references to other leaders as well as the uncomplimentary references to Trotsky.[18] The blame for these errors should not fall primarily on Eastman, who relied on "three responsible Communists in Russia" who had read the Testament and "committed its vital phrases to memory" (30–31). In memoirs published in 1964, Eastman recalled that during the XIII Party Congress in 1924, Trotsky "told me, drawing me into a hidden corner of the palace, the principal phrases of Lenin's 'testament.' "[19] (In a memorandum to Stalin reproduced here, Trotsky implies that he did not meet with Eastman during this period.) Before publication, Eastman showed his manuscript to Christian Rakovskii, one of Trotsky's comrades who was working in France at the time, and Rakovskii approved publication. The responsibility for the distortions therefore seems to lie with the Trotsky group itself.

To understand the following course of events, then, we must start with the realization that *Since Lenin Died* is an inaccurate, highly

17. Schapiro, *Communist Party*, 300. A fuller study of Lenin's Testament and the issues raised in Stalin's memorandum on the Eastman book will be found in my "Road to Lenin's Testament" (work in progress).

18. A detailed discussion of Eastman's errors can be found in the appendix.

19. Max Eastman, *Love and Revolution: My Journey through an Epoch* (New York, 1964), 425.

politicized account that contrasts Trotsky, with his "saintly" devotion to the revolution (13), to all the other leaders of the party, who are nothing more than unscrupulous usurpers. After Stalin was alerted to the existence of *Since Lenin Died,* he must have been elated: all he had to do was send around a translation of Eastman's book to the Politburo (and later to local party officials) and Trotsky would be further discredited. What must Trotsky's colleagues have felt, for example, when they read a passage like the following: "If you danced on the corpse of Vladimir Ilich, you would insult his spirit less than by clapping censorship on his own last words to his Party and juggling under the table, with the cheapest tricks of the demagogue, the conscientious thoughts of that man whom he designated as the best of you" (92).

Stalin's lengthy memorandum on the Eastman book is a good example of his catechistic style, with its numbered points and its repetitive use of the phrase "Trotsky must be aware." On the whole, though, it must have struck his Politburo comrades as rather moderate and restrained. He passed over all genuine political differences and stuck to issues where he felt there could be no argument about Eastman's errors. He did not ask Trotsky to deny the existence of the Testament or to affirm any particular interpretation of it. Stalin did not accuse Trotsky of breaking discipline and revealing party secrets; rather, he chose to take at face value Trotsky's assertion that he had nothing to do with the Testament's transmission to Eastman. Stalin's main point was that by keeping silent, Trotsky was giving de facto legitimacy to slanderous accusations.

The demand that Trotsky disavow this open attack on the Russian Communist Party must have seemed perfectly legitimate to the Politburo. Trotsky complied with the request and wrote an open letter. A comparison of Trotsky's letter and Stalin's memorandum shows that Trotsky stuck fairly close to the points Stalin suggested. Trotsky also added some rhetorical flourishes that have caused confusion ever since:

> In several places in his book, Eastman says that the Central Committee "hid" from the party a number of highly important documents that Lenin wrote in the last period of his life (letters on the national question, the so-called testament, and so forth); this cannot be termed

anything other than a slander of the Central Committee of our party. . . . Vladimir Ilich did not leave any "testament" and the character of his relation to the party, not to mention the character of the party itself, excludes the possibility of such a "testament." When the emigré, foreign bourgeois, and menshevist press uses the term *testament,* it usually has in mind a letter—in a form distorted beyond recognition—in which Vladimir Ilich gave advice of an internal party character. The XIII Congress gave this letter, like all the others, its close attention and drew the conclusions appropriate to the circumstances of the moment. Any talk of a hidden or violated "testament" is a spiteful invention aimed against the real will of Vladimir Ilich and the interests of the party he created.[20]

This is the passage that has led scholars to assert that Trotsky consciously lied about the existence of the Testament. It is clear from the text of his letter and the accompanying open letter by Krupskaia that this was not his intention. Trotsky's point is that it is inappropriate to call Lenin's letter a "testament," in other words, a literal statement of last wishes that the party was beholden to carry out. It is worth noting that although Trotsky states that Eastman's text is defective, he is careful not to deny the conclusions that Eastman drew from the Testament. Trotsky's silence on this central point stands out clearly when his letter is contrasted with Krupskaia's letter, since Krupskaia does deal directly with this issue.

If Stalin was engineering a cover-up, he would not have insisted on publishing his own memorandum, for he discusses the Testament (under that name) at length. If we may judge from his comments to Molotov, Stalin even felt that instead of discrediting himself, Trotsky would actually gain in prestige by denouncing Eastman. In order to prevent this outcome, Stalin argues that his own memorandum should be published to show that Trotsky acted under Politburo pressure (letter 6). Later, Stalin opines that Trotsky "saved himself" by his compliance (letter 9).

On this revised understanding of the Eastman affair, the Politburo did not ask Trotsky to tell obvious untruths, nor did he do so. If Trotsky was discredited, it was because he or his friends allowed the publication of an inflammatory broadside.

20. Trotsky's letter, *Bolshevik,* 1925, no. 16:67–70. The full text of this letter appears in the appendix.

Even though the Western scholars who have written on the Eastman affair did not have access to Stalin's memorandum and his correspondence with Molotov, it is still puzzling why they chose to endorse the accuracy of Eastman's rendition of the Testament. One reason is that they were misled by Trotsky's rhetorical flourishes into the erroneous assumption that the Politburo wanted him to deny the very existence of the Testament. I suspect that another reason was their exclusive focus on Lenin's suggestion that Stalin be removed from the post of general secretary. This focus led them to overlook the political aims of Eastman's book and the distortions Eastman unwittingly perpetrated in order to serve those aims. These scholars were also comfortable with the level of cynicism they assigned to the Bolshevik leaders: according to their account, *all* the Politburo members, Trotsky included, were conscious liars blandly betraying their dead leader and denying the obvious. Painful as it may be to our preconceptions, it seems that, in this instance at least, the Politburo did not "laugh at all honesty as a limited prejudice" (as Boris Souvarine writes in his account of the affair).[21]

The new light thrown on the Eastman affair, when combined with evidence in other recently published documents, makes it difficult to put Politburo politics in the framework of a Trotsky-Stalin duel or even a duel between Trotsky and the triumvirate (Stalin, Zinoviev, Kamenev). Trotsky was not defeated because of Stalin's growing power. As the Russian historians Valerii Nadtocheev and Dmitrii Volkogonov have pointed out, the reverse is true: Stalin gained power because he was able to provide leadership in the Politburo's effort to neutralize Trotsky.[22] The Eastman affair shows how this worked. Stalin took the initiative, but he was able to convince his colleagues primarily because he had a good case. The rest of the Politburo agreed that Trotsky should make a public statement denouncing Eastman and used Stalin's memorandum as a basis for drafting the statement. Beyond that point, the Politburo majority broke up amid disputes on appropriate further action (with Zinoviev taking a harder line against Trotsky than Stalin did). In spite of the success of his memorandum, Stalin does not yet seem

21. Souvarine, *Stalin*, 414.
22. Valerii Nadtocheev, "'Triumvirat' ili 'semerka'?" in *Trudnye voprosy istorii* (Moscow, 1991); Dmitrii Volkogonov, *Triumph and Tragedy* (London, 1991).

the dominant figure. A different impression is given in the following
year, after Zinoviev and Kamenev went into opposition.

The Campaign against Zinoviev

By all accounts, Zinoviev was not a particularly attractive human
being. Neither in power nor in opposition was his conduct inspiring. Unlike Trotsky and Bukharin, Zinoviev has never been cele-
brated in a major biography as a symbol of resistance to Stalin, and
Western political parties never transformed him into an icon. From
the evidence of the letters, however, the leaders of the party majority
treated his opposition with greater seriousness than they did the
attacks by Trotsky, who was more renowned but also more margin-
alized.

Zinoviev and Kamenev openly challenged Stalin at the XIV Party
Congress a few months after the Eastman affair in 1925. Stalin's
forces moved quickly to dismantle Zinoviev's political base in
Leningrad. In spite of his former hostility to Trotsky, Zinoviev now
found it expedient to join forces with him. Their alliance was
formed soon after the defeat of the general strike in England, and
since Zinoviev was still head of the Comintern (the international
organization that united the Communist parties of the world), it
was natural that the Politburo showdown took the form of a challenge to the previous policy of cooperating with the British unions.

One of the first joint actions of the newly formed coalition was a
stormy Politburo meeting in early June 1926. Because of the political tension that surrounded this meeting, there was a flurry of letters
between the absent Stalin and his political friends in Moscow, and
we can follow the event in detail. In a biography of Trotsky, Isaac
Deutscher pictures Trotsky forcing a hesitant and vacillating
Zinoviev to reject the united front policies in England. With his
usual flair for journalistic detail, Deutscher sets the scene: "The
battle was joined, partly on Stalin's initiative, in the first days of
June. Immediately after Trotsky's return, Stalin met him at the Politburo" with a number of accusations.[23]

This picture is difficult to square with the train of events portrayed in the letters: Zinoviev prepares the theses condemning the

23. Deutscher, *Prophet Unarmed,* 269.

united front and leads the fight at the Politburo session. If Trotsky was the leader of the coalition on this issue, the fact was kept carefully hidden from the rest of the Politburo. Stalin was vacationing at the time, so Bukharin and Molotov provided the leadership of the offensive against Zinoviev and Trotsky.

Thus the letters force us to make a considerable adjustment in our picture of the early days of the united opposition. The point is not Deutscher's pardonable error about Stalin's physical whereabouts, but rather the misleading image of the leadership dispute as essentially a duel between Trotsky and Stalin. As the letters show, the duel was in fact between Zinoviev and the Politburo majority.

The next important clash between the newly united opposition and the Politburo majority occurred at a meeting of the full Central Committee in July. In preparation for this meeting, Stalin penned one of the more remarkable letters in the collection (letter 21). In it Stalin gives his reasons for considering the Zinoviev group as the leader of all schismatic tendencies in the party. He notes that previous opposition groups had stayed within definite bounds; furthermore, because Zinoviev occupied a much more central place in Bolshevik affairs than any previous opposition leader, he was better acquainted with the leadership's way of doing things. Another reason for worry was Zinoviev's potential power base as Comintern chief (Stalin does not mention Leningrad, which had been effectively taken away from Zinoviev earlier in the year).

Stalin recommends that Zinoviev and Trotsky be treated differently, with the brunt of the attack aimed at Zinoviev. This recommendation is partly justified by purely tactical considerations of divide and conquer, although it is possible that Stalin means what he says: Trotsky and his followers should be given a chance to return to the fold and work as team members. Stalin's recommendation was faithfully followed by his political friends, as shown by a statement Rykov made after the July Central Committee meeting, to the effect that Trotsky's actions do not require direct reprisal in the same way that Zinoviev's do, because "Comrade Trotsky made no such attempt at a split."[24]

Stalin's leadership amounted to more than the control over

24. Robert Vincent Daniels, *The Conscience of the Revolution: Communist Opposition in Soviet Russia* (Cambridge, Mass., 1960), 279.

appointments that is usually considered the main basis for his power. In his memoirs, Molotov repeatedly stresses his admiration for Stalin's ability to size up a situation and extract directives for action.[25] The two episodes portrayed in the letters—the 1925 Eastman affair and the 1926 campaign against Zinoviev—show that the Politburo came increasingly to rely on these skills.

What we view as crafty maneuvering may not have appeared that way to Stalin's Politburo colleagues. From their point of view, Stalin's proposal about Eastman's book was not an invitation to skullduggery but a legitimate demand that Trotsky disassociate himself from a scurrilous attack on the Russian Communist Party. Stalin's letter outlining the anti-Zinoviev strategy shows that he was no amateur at political infighting. But Stalin was not making any secret of his tactics: the letter is addressed to "Molotov, Rykov, Bukharin, and other friends." Stalin was eliminating a political rival, but he was also working toward a goal to which he and his fellow Bolsheviks accorded high legitimacy: preserving a united leadership team.

Stalin's catechistic style of exposition in his public speeches has struck many observers as the manifestation of a dogmatic mind. The letters show us that he employed the same dogged approach in his private correspondence. Yet his colleagues may have appreciated his conscious commitment to clarity in setting out his definition of the situation. In spite of (or perhaps because of) the numbered paragraphs and the litany-style repetitions, some of the letters are compelling expositions of complicated arguments. In the opening paragraph of his letter outlining the campaign against Zinoviev (letter 21), Stalin mentions that he reflected on the question a good deal but has now worked it all out—and thereupon follow the familiar numbered paragraphs. It would seem that the other Politburo members had come to rely on his ability to analyze a situation and devise a course of action.

According to Stalin's antibureaucrat scenario, the unity of the top leadership regarding the correct line was an essential precondition for the fight against the real enemies: the bureaucrats running the government. He therefore had no compunction about quashing

25. See, for example, Molotov's unfavorable comparison of Sergei Kirov to Stalin in Chuev, *Sto sorok besed,* 307–13.

Politburo colleagues who got out of line. Yet despite the vigor of the political infighting in 1925 and 1926, and despite Stalin's contempt for his rivals ("Really, Grisha's [Zinoviev's] brazenness knows no bounds" [letter 20]), it is evident that he did not yet regard them as enemies of the party and the revolution. It would take several years of conflict and frustration before Stalin arrived at the level of titanic anger and rejection we find in the letters from 1929 and 1930.

The Outside World

Bukharin opened the XV Party Conference in 1926 with a speech that contained these stirring words: "The international revolution is now on the move in three columns. It is moving in the East with the march of the Chinese people, with its many hundreds of millions. It is moving in the far West with the measured tread of the British coal miners; it is moving in the Soviet Union, with our growing offensive against the capitalist elements of our economy. These three forces will become more and more decisive, and to them will be given the final victory."[26]

What was Stalin's reaction to this enthusiastic picture of imminent world revolution? Did he think it was mere verbiage, or was he genuinely caught up in a moment of enthusiasm? Did Stalin dismiss world revolution in favor of building up the Soviet state, or did he remain at heart a Bolshevik dedicated to overthrowing capitalist society everywhere?

Observers have long puzzled over these questions. One point of view derives from Trotsky's critique of "socialism in one country" as a betrayal of the revolution. According to this view, Stalin decided early on that the chances of revolution elsewhere were nil. By inclination as well as conviction, Stalin was ready to turn his back on the rest of the world and devote his energies to building up a powerful Soviet state. Only when pressed by the critique made by the united left opposition did he feel it necessary to make even verbal obeisance to the icon of Bolshevik internationalism. He had only contempt for the Comintern, except perhaps as a minor tool of Soviet foreign policy. Some scholars have even speculated that he did not

26. *15 Konferentsiia VKP(b)* (Moscow, 1927), 45.

want to see a successful revolution elsewhere: Who needs powerful socialist rivals?

Another view is that the question should not be put in either-or terms: either the interests of world revolution or the interests of the Soviet state. We should rather seek to understand how the two coalesced in Stalin's mind. Stalin was indeed deeply committed to the interests of the Soviet state, but we still need to examine how he understood those interests. Stalin was not hypocritical in his support for world revolution, since from his point of view no sacrifice of state interests was involved. His caution about revolutionary prospects in particular cases did not mean he dismissed all revolutionary prospects for the foreseeable future.[27]

The publication of Stalin's letters to Molotov gives us a chance to move toward resolving these issues, for several important episodes of both Comintern policy and Soviet diplomacy are treated in detail. In 1926 and 1927, Stalin is concerned with what appear to be revolutionary situations in England and China. After 1927, as the revolutionary tide ebbs, Stalin's attention in the letters turns toward problems arising from state-to-state relations. Since Stalin was talking in private with like-minded colleagues, there was little partisan pressure to sound more revolutionary than he felt. Let us review the clues provided by the letters before assessing the new evidence. We will first examine Stalin's feelings about the prospects for revolution in 1926 and 1927.

Policy toward the British trade unions was a priority issue in 1926. The Politburo majority's official line was that the situation in England was moving in the direction of revolution but that it would be unwise to break with the reformist trade unions in the ostentatious fashion demanded by Zinoviev and Trotsky. The united left opposition interpreted the policy of the united front as de facto collaboration with the reformist union leaders, and thus a betrayal of Leninist principles. Their particular target was the Anglo-Russian Committee that had been established as a link between the Soviet trade unions and the General Council of the British Trade Unions Congress. In response,

27. For different points of view on Stalin's attitude toward revolution outside the USSR, see Isaac Deutscher, *Stalin: A Political Biography* (Oxford, 1949), chap. 10; Robert C. Tucker, *Stalin in Power: The Revolution from Above, 1928–1941* (New York, 1990).

the Politburo insisted that their only motive was to unmask the trade union leaders as the vacillating reformists that they were. Letters 13–19 contain Stalin's exposition of the majority point of view in preparation for the Politburo clash with Zinoviev in June. Stalin emphasizes his complete agreement with Bukharin and the others in Moscow. Given the highly partisan context, however, it is difficult to say whether Stalin's protestations are sincere.

Much more revealing are various remarks in letter 23, written in August 1926. Stalin first notes that a delegation from the British coal miners will soon arrive; they should be given an enthusiastic reception. More Soviet money needs to be collected for the striking miners. "The situation in England is serious, and it obliges us to make serious 'sacrifices.'" The Americans had promised to give the miners a million dollars, and it would be shameful if the Soviet Union gave any less. (Stalin need not have worried, since in the end the Americans gave very little.)[28] Even sending money is an insufficient gesture: Stalin suggests following the wishes of the British Communists and imposing an embargo on coal imports.

Stalin then latches on to what he considers a missed opportunity for unmasking the British labor leaders as cowards: Didn't they go on vacation rather than account for their actions? He mentions that he is keeping up with the British Communist newspapers, so he knows they have not "trumpeted" these facts as they should. Stalin's suggestion got a restrained response from Mikhail Tomskii, the leader of the Soviet trade unions. Tomskii had visited England and had acquired a greater sense of political reality; he doubted whether unmasking the reformist leaders' vacation trips would produce a serious political effect.

Stalin goes on to ask how the Comintern Executive Committee is reacting to new, more radical slogans advocating new elections in England. The mention of the Comintern reminds him of a project to publish the Comintern's journal more frequently: Why isn't Bukharin pushing this matter more energetically? A weekly journal would greatly improve the work of the Comintern and its member parties. (On Stalin's attitude toward the Comintern, see also letter 82, from 1935.)

28. Charles Loch Mowat, *Britain between the Wars, 1918–1940* (London, 1955), chap. 6.

Let us consider a few other comments from 1926 before assessing the evidence. In letter 12, written before the outbreak of controversy within the Politburo, Stalin insists that a pamphlet documenting Soviet support for the striking coal miners be translated into all the major Western languages. In letter 26, we learn that Stalin preferred to loan rather than give the General Council the money they requested. His motivation: to show Europe that the Soviets were sober people who knew how to count kopecks. Finally, in letter 28 Stalin argues against unduly irritating the British reformists over their failure to protest their government's intervention in China.

Taken together, Stalin's remarks indicate that he was very involved in the British situation and genuinely hoped for a more radical outcome. The letters also seem to acquit him of any real interest in collaborating with reformists: unmasking always gets top priority. One would not deduce from these letters that he was contemptuous of the Comintern. On the other hand, he is certainly not above using a gesture of revolutionary solidarity as a way of burnishing the Soviet government's financial reputation. Stalin saw no anomaly in advancing both sets of interests simultaneously.

The other burning issue of the mid-1920s was the Soviet and Comintern role in the Chinese revolution. The course of events in China is inconceivable without the crucial influence of Russian political and military advisors like Mikhail Borodin and Vasilii Bliucher. Many books have been devoted to the rights and wrongs, the insights and mistakes, of Comintern policy and its disastrous outcome for the Chinese Communist Party, yet the letters shed new light on the attitudes of both Stalin and his Politburo colleagues. Let us restrict ourselves here to passages that help us understand Stalin's general attitude toward revolution outside the Soviet Union.

At the beginning of 1926, Stalin thought the Kuomintang government in Canton would be best advised not to attempt to unify the country with a risky enterprise like the Northern Expedition. In spite of his caution on the military front, he felt the Kuomintang would strengthen its political base and achieve a stronger anti-imperialist thrust if it carried out a thorough agrarian reform.[29]

29. Stalin's views can be found in his addition to a memorandum written by Trotsky; the text can be found in *Kommunisticheskaia oppozitsiia v SSSR, 1923–27*, 4 vols. (Benson, Vt.: Chalidze Publications, 1988), 1:179.

When Chiang Kai-shek went ahead and launched the highly successful Northern Expedition, Stalin was elated and assumed that a new stage of the revolution had commenced. He explains his feelings to Molotov when criticizing Lev Karakhan, the top Soviet diplomat in China at the time: "He has outlived his usefulness: he was and *has remained* the ambassador of the *first* stage of the Chinese revolution and is entirely useless as a leader in the *current* new situation, both the Chinese and the international situation. . . . Karakhan will never understand that Hankow will soon become the Chinese Moscow" (letter 28). (Hankow was one of the cities in the Wuhan complex where the Kuomintang set up its capital during the Northern Expedition. His remark about a "Chinese Moscow" reflects his view that the whole country would be united under one anti-imperialist government, not that there would be a socialist revolution in China.)

The crux of what Stalin called the new stage of the revolution was the opportunity for widespread agrarian reform. Stalin seems to have believed that giving the peasants land would strengthen the Kuomintang and that an implicit deal could therefore be struck on the following basis: the Kuomintang armies would provide military cover, and the Chinese Communist Party would stir up the peasant masses. A letter written in June 1927 shows that Stalin was willing to make considerable sacrifices to obtain political space for the Chinese Communists. By this time, the Moscow leaders had begun to realize that the "left Kuomintang" government in Wuhan was on the verge of turning against the Communists. Stalin here gives his reasons for staving off the evil day by means of direct subsidies (letter 33):

> Losing Wuhan as a separate center means losing at least some center for the revolutionary movement, losing the possibility of free assembly and rallies for the workers, losing the possibility of the open existence of the Communist Party, losing the possibility of an open revolutionary press—in a word, losing the possibility of openly organizing the proletariat and the revolution. In order to obtain all this, I assure you, it is worth giving Wuhan an extra 3–5 million—only with some assurance that Wuhan will not surrender to the tender mercies of Nanking [headquarters of the right Kuomintang] with our money wasted for nothing.

The break came only two weeks later, and Stalin had to face the ruin of all his hopes for revolutionary collaboration with the Kuomintang. After taking a day to read through all the documents sent down from Moscow, Stalin penned letter 36, a long series of glum reflections on the future of the Chinese Communists.

The letter contains political advice for the immediate future: the Chinese Communists should leave the government but not the Kuomintang itself. The Politburo quickly adopted this advice, and instructions to that effect were sent off to China even before Stalin returned from vacation.[30] Stalin insisted that the blame for the failure of Comintern strategy lay with the leaders of the Chinese Communist Party; this too became official policy. Stalin's charge against the Chinese leaders was that they failed to take advantage of the political space Stalin thought they had: they did not mobilize the peasants or infiltrate the army. He dismissed them in the same way he dismissed Karakhan: they had been recruited in the first phase of the revolution and were unsuitable for its second, more radical phase.

Stalin's letter is considerably more pessimistic than are his later public statements. He describes in vivid terms what the Chinese Communist Party will have to undergo as the tide of revolution ebbs away: "[going] underground, arrests, beatings, executions, betrayals and provocations among their own ranks, etc." Stalin's scenario for the Chinese Communists is derived from Bolshevik experience between the revolution of 1905 and the outbreak of revolution in 1917; Stalin thinks it likely that the Chinese Communists will have to wait a similar length of time before a new revolutionary outburst occurs in China.

In an article published only a fortnight later, Stalin mentions the pessimistic 1905–1917 scenario as *less* likely than the possibility of a swift return to the storms of revolution. From letter 38 it appears that Stalin's change of heart was the result of objections by Molotov and perhaps Bukharin. The more optimistic reading of the Chinese situation led to a number of abortive revolts by Chinese Communists that compounded the damage done during the Kuomintang alliance. Stalin no doubt reflected that his first instincts had been correct.

Another aspect of Stalin's letter not reflected in later public state-

30. Helmut Gruber, *Soviet Russia Masters the Comintern: International Communism in the Era of Stalin's Ascendancy* (New York, 1974), 494–500; C. Martin Wilbur, *The Nationalist Revolution in China, 1923–1928* (Cambridge, 1983), 144.

ments is his conception of future Soviet aid to the Chinese Communists. The proposed aid seems to consist of better Marxist literature and better advisors. "We should regularly send to China, not people we don't need, but competent people instead." These political advisors will play the role of "nannies" for the present amorphous and weak Central Committee. "As the revolution and the party grow, the need for these 'nannies' will disappear."

In the following letter, Stalin notes some misgivings on the part of some of his political friends about past policy but defiantly affirms: "Never have I been so deeply and firmly convinced of the correctness of our policy, both in China and regarding the Anglo-Russian Committee, as I am now" (letter 37). As he did throughout his political career, Stalin blamed any unfortunate results on the failure of local leaders to understand the Politburo's correct policy.

To sum up: Stalin sees the success of the Chinese Communist Party as a matter of both state and revolutionary interest. Although by instinct he is cautious about revolutionary prospects, he can also be carried away by apparent success. He assumes that the Soviet model should guide the Chinese Communists, but he also assumes that Soviet "nannies" are only a temporary necessity.

After 1927 the letters touch more on state diplomacy than on revolutionary strategy. This gives us the opportunity to observe Stalin's amalgamation of state and revolutionary interests from another angle: his insistence on imposing revolutionary considerations on normal diplomacy. Letter 44 (August 1929) provides several examples. By acting tough in state negotiations with England and China, the Soviet Union is also striking a blow for revolution:

> The point is not only or not even mainly how to resolve this or that "conflict." The point is really to use our tough position to *unmask* completely and to undermine the authority of Chiang Kai-shek's government, a government of lackeys of imperialism, for attempting to become the model of "national governments" for the colonial and dependent countries . . . [thus] mak[ing] it easier to carry out the revolutionary education of the workers in colonial countries (and the Chinese workers above all).

Conversely, revolutionary success redounds to the Soviet state: "This [unmasking] is a very important and necessary revolutionary task, which will, at the same time, raise the prestige of the Soviet government in the eyes of the workers of all countries (and above all in the eyes of the working class of the USSR)."

A version of the antibureaucrat scenario is at play here. Back in 1925, Stalin had warned that capitalist encirclement might corrupt the Soviet foreign service, leading the policy specialists to forget the cause of world revolution.[31] This seems to be the thought behind the repeated sneers directed at Maksim Litvinov, acting head of the foreign service. "Litvinov does not see and is not interested in [the revolutionary aspect of policy]. But the Politburo [a party institution] should take all this into account" (letter 44). Litvinov is therefore associated with Bukharin and Rykov: "These people don't see the growth of the power and might of the USSR, nor those changes in international relations that have occurred recently (and will go on taking place)" (letter 51; see also letter 45). This corruption by the outside environment is a typical symptom of the right deviation (discussed in the section "Right Deviation").

The most dramatic diplomatic event of 1929 was the armed intervention arising out of the clash over the Chinese Eastern Railway. This was a surgical military operation against weak resistance with little fear of intervention by other powers—in other words, something on the order of Panama or Grenada. The war was not given wide publicity at home; one American journalist called it "the war nobody knew."[32] Still, Stalin was elated by its success: "Let them know what the Bolsheviks are like! I think the Chinese landowners won't forget the object lesson taught them by the Far East Army" (letter 53). He also allowed that Litvinov's speech on the subject wasn't so bad; in this speech Litvinov mocked the Americans for their attempt at diplomatic intervention.

The strangest amalgamation of state and revolutionary interests occurs during the preparation for this intervention (letter 51). At one point, Stalin wanted to expand the operation from a limited incursion to a more grandiose revolutionary uprising. His projected scenario makes it seem so simple: Organize and equip two Chinese brigades and give them the task of fomenting a rebellion among the Manchurian troops; then have them occupy Harbin and declare a revolutionary state authority. After that, attract the peasants by

31. Stalin, *Sochineniia*, 7:167–90.
32. Eugene Lyons, *Assignment in Utopia* (New York, 1937).

smashing the landowners, organize soviets in town and country, and go on from there. This revolutionary daydream seems atypical of the cautious Stalin, and there is no indication anything was done with it. But perhaps we can see it as a first sketch of what has been called "revolution from abroad," a term later applied to the countries on the USSR's western border.[33]

As the general offensive of the five-year plan came into full swing, the imperatives of Stalin's domestic revolution sometimes interfered with normal diplomatic relations. Several of the letters written after 1929 touch on this problem. In letter 72, for example, Stalin comments on a 1931 speech by Molotov defending the Soviet Union against charges of using forced labor. Stalin wants Molotov to argue that dekulakized peasants work only on a voluntary basis with the same rights as free labor. In letter 65, on the other hand, Stalin hoped to use the domestic campaign against "wreckers" for diplomatic purposes: Since the government had confessions of sabotage by British nationals, why not publish them prior to upcoming talks with the British government about debts and concessions? It is not clear exactly what Stalin hoped to gain from this maneuver; it is probably just as well that someone appears to have talked him out of it.

Other scattered comments suggest Stalin's attitude toward relations with the capitalist world: he thought they were dangerous (because the capitalists are enemies ill disposed toward the Soviet Union), unpleasant (because so many bourgeois politicians are just petty crooks), but necessary. American readers will be interested in his comments in 1932 on possible diplomatic recognition by the United States: "United States—this is a complicated matter. Insofar as they want to use flattery to drag us into a war with Japan, we can tell them to go to hell. Insofar as the oil industrialists of the United States have agreed to give us a loan of 100 million rubles without requiring from us any political compensation, we would be foolish not to take their money" (letter 74).

Stalin's chip-on-the-shoulder defensiveness is readily apparent in a comment on yet another Molotov speech: "Viacheslav! Today I read the section on international affairs. It came out well. The confi-

33. Jan T. Gross, *Revolution from Abroad: The Soviet Conquest of Poland's Western Ukraine and Western Belorussia* (Princeton, 1988).

dent, contemptuous tone with respect to the 'great' powers, the belief in our own strength, the delicate but plain spitting in the pot of the swaggering 'great powers'—very good. Let them eat it" (letter 76).

Having reviewed the evidence supplied by the letters, we can return to the dispute over Stalin's attitude toward the outside world. The letters refute the Trotsky-derived interpretation of "socialism in one country" as an isolationist rejection of revolution elsewhere. To be sure, Stalin never ignored the interests of the Soviet state and he was often cautious to the point of pessimism about the prospects for immediate revolution. But the letters show that he was also capable of hope and enthusiasm when revolution seemed to be on the move and ready to put his money where his mouth was. The letters also document his unremitting hostility toward and suspicion of the capitalist world even when he was forced to deal with it. He was vigilant lest the foreign policy professionals succumb to the disease of rightist degeneration and lose the ability to see the revolutionary aspect of diplomacy. All in all, Stalin comes out of the letters with his revolutionary credentials in good order.

Thus Stalin did not see state interests and revolutionary interests in "either-or" terms. But this leaves open the question of exactly how he amalgamated the two in his mind. One key factor was the prestige of the Soviet state at home and abroad. The capitalist world would never accord even basic legitimacy to the Soviet Union, much less accept it as an equal or admire it. The Soviet Union could appeal only to the disinherited; only as an embodiment of the revolutionary idea could the Soviet Union acquire a leadership role worthy of a great power. Yet I do not mean to suggest that Stalin was interested in world revolution only as a propaganda tool for the Russian empire. Because he identified himself with the prestige of the Soviet state, he also identified himself with its leading idea. As first servant of the state, he was also first servant of world revolution.

Grain Tribute and Collectivization

Starting in 1929, Stalin led the Bolshevik party and the Soviet state in a war against the peasantry—or, as Stalin's loyalists would say, against the better-off peasants (kulaks) who sabotaged necessary policies. The campaign had two theaters of conflict. One was a struggle over grain: Stalin insisted that the peasants had to pay what he openly called a tribute in order to help finance industrialization. The other area of conflict was a struggle over how the peasants ran their farms: Stalin wanted to transform the basic production units of the countryside from small individual farms to large-scale collective ones (*kolkhozy*).

The amount of material in the letters that bears on these events is not large, but what exists is highly suggestive and illuminates key aspects of the thought processes that gave rise to some of the most important decisions in Soviet history. What connection did Stalin see between collecting the tribute and transforming peasant production relations? What lay behind the fateful decision in late 1929 to unleash all-out collectivization coupled with dekulakization? In what ways did Stalin prod state and party to embark on this campaign?

Obtaining the grain tribute and imposing collectivized production are separate goals. It is quite possible to pursue each of them independently; in fact, they might even be seen as contradictory. During the civil war, the Bolsheviks felt compelled to exact a heavy tax from the peasantry, and for just this reason they found it expedient to move slowly in attempting to transform production relations.

In the late 1920s and early 1930s, in contrast, the two goals were pursued in tandem. The usual interpretation is that mass collectivization was adopted in order to obtain the tribute, on the assumption that it is easier to apply state coercion to large-scale collective farms than to scattered individual farms. Yet as Stephan Merl has cogently argued, this assumption is by no means self-evident.[34] The collectivization drive greatly disrupted production and alienated the peasantry, thus making it even more difficult to collect the tribute. By 1934 Stalin had taken so much grain from the peasants that he inflicted mass starvation (letters 74 and 77 give some indication of the pressure the Politburo was putting on the country in order to extract grain). Yet what was decisive was not the existence of collective farms but the massive investment in repressive resources Stalin made in the early 1930s in order to make the system work at all.

34. Stephan Merl, *Die Anfänge der Kollektivierung in der Sowjetunion* (Wiesbaden, 1985).

Given that the state prepared to stop at nothing, the same amount of grain could have been extracted from individual farms, perhaps even with less coercion.

It thus remains an open question exactly why Stalin linked the two goals. If we turn to his speeches of 1928, when he was seeking to rally the party leadership behind his strategy, we find the following argument: This year we have had to apply coercive "emergency measures" to get the grain we need to keep industrialization on track. We are all agreed that using such methods is costly and unsatisfactory in the long run. We cannot live forever with this continual war with the peasants, with no reserves, and with hunger threatening the city and the towns. (Stalin's obsession with a reserve fund can be observed in many of his 1929 letters, particularly letters 44 and 53.) Collective farms are the only route of escape from this chronic crisis. Since the collective farms will be supported by state economic assistance, the state will have a greater opportunity to ensure deliveries by economic means. An expanding collective farm movement will also undercut the authority of the kulaks, whose sabotage is a principal reason for the difficulties we have encountered in grain collection.

Thus Stalin did not publicly advocate collectivization as a necessary tool for coercing the peasants. Ironically, given the way things turned out, Stalin originally defended collectivization as a way of making up for the political and economic damage caused by collection of the tribute and of avoiding the permanent confrontation with the peasants implied by repeated use of emergency measures.

The question is whether this public advocacy accurately reflects Stalin's private thinking. The clues provided by the letters are at least consistent with the thesis that Stalin did not see collectivization as a method for collecting the tribute. Stalin's single-minded insistence on getting grain to export comes through loud and clear. Grain procurements are the key to everything; without exports there will be no new factories. The need is so urgent that it is impossible even to wait for better grain prices (letter 60). Yet in letter 41 from August 1929, collective farms themselves show up as one of the main barriers to successful procurement. Later in the year he pronounces himself reasonably satisfied with the procurement campaign (letters 51 and 53), but his satisfaction did not stop him from giving the green light to the all-out collectivization campaign. His attitude in 1930 is similar: his anger at impediments to the collectivization drive in letters 61 and 63 is separate from his exhortations for better procurement in letters 57, 59, 60 (see also 67).

Turning now to the collectivization drive itself, we can ask whether the letters provide any clue to the decision in late 1929 to proceed with all-out collectivization, coupled with "liquidation of the kulaks as a class." The basic argument in favor of collective farms had always been their ability to make efficient use of up-to-date equipment. It was clear that industry was in no position to provide this equipment, and prior to December 1929 Stalin had never argued that collective farms could increase production without new equipment.

All during 1929, regional officials tried to attract central attention and resources by accelerating the rate of collectivization in their areas. The most extreme case was Khoper county in the lower Volga region: local party officials announced in late August that they would complete all-out collectivization by the end of the five-year plan. A phenomenal rate of collectivization then followed. In June, only 2.2 percent of Khoper farms had been collectivized; by October, the total had reached at least 30 percent for the whole county, with much higher percentages reached in some areas.[35]

It is unclear to what extent local officials acted on their own initiative, but there is no doubt that central party officials gave much attention and encouragement to the frantic pace of collectivization in Khoper. Less sanguine were state officials responsible for administering the collective farm movement; they looked into the situation and sent back critical reports to Moscow. As a result, a commission under T. R. Ryskulov was sent out to Khoper in late October. By the end of November, this commission reported back to Moscow and dismissed the skeptics who argued that administrative pressure was behind the rush to form collective farms in Khoper. Ryskulov retorted that these skeptics were completely confused: the rate of collectivization should be accelerated, not reduced.

The goings-on in Khoper form the background for an excited passage from Stalin's letter dated 5 December 1929 (letter 53):

35. For background on Khoper, see R. W. Davies, *The Socialist Offensive: The Collectivisation of Soviet Agriculture, 1929–1930* (Cambridge, Mass., 1980).

The collective farm movement is growing by leaps and bounds. Of course there are not enough machines and tractors—how could it be otherwise?—but simply pooling the peasant tools results in a colossal increase in sown acreage (in some regions by as much as 50 percent!). In the lower Volga [where Khoper was located], 60 percent of peasant farms have been transferred (already transferred!) to collective farms. The eyes of our rightists are popping out of their heads in amazement. . . . [ellipsis in original]

In an important speech at the end of December, Stalin again used Khoper to show why collective farms brought tremendous advantages even without expensive new equipment. By simply banding together, the peasants were in a position to plow under virgin and abandoned land on a scale that lay beyond the powers of individual peasant farmers. In this same speech, Stalin announced the new slogan "liquidation of the kulaks as a class." He argued that it would have been irresponsible to liquidate the kulaks any sooner because they could not have been replaced.

With the clue provided by the letter of 5 December, we can surmise the following: Stalin regarded Khoper as a testing ground for all-out collectivization. In November 1929, high officials were still arguing about the results of this experiment, so Stalin waited for the report of the Ryskulov commission. The news he received excited him because it gave him the green light, not only for all-out collectivization, but also for dekulakization. Even without tractors, it was possible for collective farms to replace the kulak farms without damaging agricultural output.

The decision made in late December and in early January 1930 led to a wave of forced collectivization and other excesses that threatened to destroy the country, so the leadership was forced to call a temporary halt in March 1930, when Stalin published his article "Dizziness from Success." A mass exodus of peasants from existing collective farms followed immediately. Stalin's determination to press on with collectivization is revealed in a 1930 letter written at the end of the summer (letter 61). The immediate occasion for his outburst was a campaign in favor of settlement associations, a new form of rural organization:

You seem very unconcerned about the statute for settlement associations and the accompanying agitation in the press. Keep in mind that this ill-omened statute was offered to us as the *new* word, which claims to be *setting itself up against* the "old" word, i.e., the statute for the agricultural *artel* [basic form of a collective farm]. And the whole point of the settlement (*new*) statute is the desire to give the individual the possibility of *"improving his (individual) farm."* What kind of nonsense is this? Here we have the *collective farm* movement advancing in a growing wave, and then the clever ones from the Commissariat of Agriculture and from the agricultural cooperative societies want to *evade* the question of collective farms and busy themselves with *"improving"* the individual peasant farm! It seems to me that the rightists have achieved some sort of revenge here, sneaking in this statute on settlement associations, because people in the Central Committee, since they're overburdened with work, haven't noticed the little trick.

Stalin's practical conclusions show the emphasis he put on devising correct slogans and conducting educational propaganda in the press (letter 63):

> An illusion has arisen of a *retreat* from the slogan "For the collective farms!" to the slogan "For the settlement associations!" It doesn't matter what they want in Moscow—in practice there's been a *switch* from the vital and triumphant slogan "For or against the collective farms" to the mongrel, artificial slogan "For or against the settlement associations." And all of this at a time when we have a growing surge of peasants into the collective farms! . . .
>
> In my opinion, we should, *first,* give an *internal* directive to local party committees not to get carried away with settlement associations. . . . *In the second place,* it would be well to overhaul *Pravda* and all of our press in the spirit of the slogan, "Into the collective farms." . . . In a word, [we should] launch a systematic and persistent campaign in the press for the collective farm movement as the major and decisive factor in our current agricultural policy.

These remarks suggest that collectivization would never have been completed without unremitting pressure from the very top. The state bureaucracy was not a machine bent on achieving a single aim but a complex organism reflecting various currents and pressures. In this case, specialists in the Commissariat of Agriculture were trying to do their job—improve agricultural productivity—by giving support to individual farmers. Stalin realized that this provided an alternative to the collective farms, and he moved to cut off the route of escape.

By 1929–1930, Stalin had immense power. It is striking, for example, how quickly press campaigns followed upon pronouncements in these letters. In August 1929 he complains about the lack of cooperation in grain procurement shown by collective farms; a press campaign follows in September. Immediately after his letter of 5 December on the breakthrough in Khoper, the press announces that tractors are not an inevitable prerequisite of collectivization. Finally, historians have observed a shift toward a harder line on collectivization in September 1930—that is, immediately after the letter just cited on the danger of a slowdown.[36]

Yet Stalin's power to get his way on specific issues did not guarantee the success of his leadership in carrying out a revolutionary policy like collectivization. Guided by his antibureaucrat scenario, Stalin realized that he had to struggle continually against the bureaucracy and its tendency to follow the path of least resistance. This required energetic checking up on fulfillment: top party leaders should not allow incorrect policies to slip past them because of inattention. The antibureaucrat scenario also helped Stalin interpret the source of this bureaucratic resistance. In the case of the statute on settlement, it was a de facto alliance between the specialists working in the Commissariat of Agriculture and the rightists within the party. In the next two sections, we shall look more closely at Stalin's dealings with these two sets of enemies within the state apparat and the party.

Wreckerism Rampant

The general offensive of 1929–1930 was accompanied by steadily mounting repression against any expert or bureaucrat who seemed to question the practicality of the industrialization and collectivization campaigns. Starting in late 1929, the Worker-Peasant Inspection, the agency that both Lenin and Stalin had seen as a weapon against bureaucratism, conducted a wide-ranging purge of economic bureaucracies. In this period, its task was to find any unused production reserves and to remove the bureaucrats who allegedly hid them. More and more engineers and other specialists were arrested for counterrevolutionary activity. As the superhuman pressure on

36. For background, see Davies, *Socialist Offensive*, 372–81.

the country created more frequent foul-ups and breakdowns, more scapegoats were accused of wreckerism. A particularly grisly execution came in September 1930: forty-eight specialists in the meat industry were executed after a secret trial in which they were found guilty of "sabotaging the meat supply." A public trial of engineers accused of forming an industrial party devoted to wreckerism began in November; this was followed in the spring of 1931 by another trial devoted to a mythical "Union Bureau" of Mensheviks.

These hysterical but deadly accusations of improbable conspiracies have often been called a witch-hunt. One challenge for observers in such cases is to probe the mixture of belief and cynicism that motivated the witch-hunters. Stalin's letters from 1930 provide rich material on this score. His cynicism is prominently on display. A striking instance is the execution of the forty-eight "saboteurs" in the meat industry. Journalistic accounts from the period all stress how much this particular act of barbarity shocked Soviet society even amid the growing repression.[37] It appears from letter 65 that the decision to murder these unfortunate specialists resulted from a burst of vindictive anger by Stalin, impatient with Politburo foot-dragging: "We must immediately *publish all* the testimonies of all the wreckers of the supplies of *meat, fish, tinned goods,* and *vegetables.* For what purpose are we preserving them, why the 'secrets'? We should publish them along with an announcement that the Central Executive Committee or the Council of Commissars has turned over the matter to the OGPU . . . and after a week have the OGPU announce that *all* these scoundrels will be executed by firing squad. They should all be shot" (letter 65; see also letter 57). Less than two weeks later the executions were carried out.

For Stalin, judicial forms had meaning only as agitational theater. In letter 63, he muses whether or not it would be expedient to bring Kondratiev and his "co-conspirators" to trial: "By the way, how about Messrs. Defendants admitting their mistakes and disgracing themselves politically, while simultaneously acknowledging the strength of the Soviet government and the correctness of the method

37. William Henry Chamberlin, *Russia's Iron Age* (Boston, 1935), 154; Eugene Lyons, *Assignment in Utopia* (New York, 1937), 349–61; H. R. Knickerbocker, *The Red Trade Menace: Progress of the Soviet Five-Year Plan* (New York, 1931), 268; William Reswick, *I Dreamt Revolution* (Chicago, 1952), 294–98.

of collectivization? It wouldn't be a bad thing if they did." In letter 65, he insists that accusatory documents be published with an appropriate "interpretation" from the press underscoring the political moral to be drawn.

Stalin was thus cold-bloodedly set on maximizing the political exploitation of his victims. But another question is still unanswered: Was Stalin consciously framing innocent victims, or did he really believe in the guilt of the accused? Judging from the evidence of the letters, it would appear that he was a believer. Given the farfetched nature of the alleged crimes, this conclusion is very hard to credit—yet just for that reason, we should make the strongest possible hypothetical case in its favor before dismissing it. Even if we decide that Stalin must have been aware of what he was doing, it is still striking that he felt compelled to play the role of a believer in confidential correspondence with his closest political friends.

The basic mode of proof used by the secret police was the forced confession. Stalin expressed no doubts about the reliability of this method; on the contrary, he seems to have thought that prisoner testimonies were "indisputable documents" (letter 65) that would convince anyone who read them. He continually urges that relevant testimonies be presented to elite and mass audiences (see letters 56, 57, 59, and 65). The introductory section for the year 1930 contains Stalin's remarkable letter about the forced testimonies to the head of the secret police, V. R. Menzhinskii, in which Stalin hopes that even Western workers will be impressed by the confessions.

There are other indications that Stalin took these testimonies quite seriously. If we compare letter 62 with the letter to Menzhinskii just mentioned, it appears that Stalin was genuinely concerned about the threat of intervention allegedly discovered by the secret police. Although Stalin gave strong hints to the police, he evidently did not simply dictate a desired scenario, and the testimonies did not show everything he wanted them to show. Even though he is convinced that there is a "direct line" between the arrested "saboteurs" and Bukharin, he is forced to admit that the police have not yet found any indication of it (letters 57, 67).

What the letters tell us about the so-called Syrtsov-Lominadze affair is also revealing. S. I. Syrtsov was a fast-rising party official who had strongly supported Stalin's line ever since the extraordinary measures were introduced in 1928. In 1930 he was head of government for the Russian republic, and many observers felt he was being groomed to replace Rykov as head of government for the Soviet Union as a whole. Yet in the fall of 1930, Syrtsov (along with V. V. Lominadze, a party official from the North Caucasus) was expelled from the Central Committee and accused of forming an "underground factional center." Most analysts assume that the trouble stemmed from Syrtsov's publicly stated views, particularly a speech he gave in August in which he obliquely criticized the ferocious pace of the general offensive. The Syrtsov-Lominadze affair rounded off the repressions of 1930 with evidence of a split within the Stalinist leadership group itself.

The letters raise the possibility that the affair was triggered by an informer's report that Stalin received in late October. In the weeks prior to this report, Syrtsov is mentioned a couple of times, not with great approval but not as someone who was about to be removed (letters 64, 69). In letter 64 Syrtsov is associated with the right deviationist Rykov, but only in the context of a bureaucratic dispute over the use of forced labor. Stalin explodes in anger only in letter 71, which was written after he received the informer's denunciation. Thus it seems that Stalin did not first choose Syrtsov as a victim and trump up a case against him, but rather that Syrtsov's views were declared beyond the pale after Stalin became convinced of his guilt.

Many observers, both at the time and later, have pointed out the numerous absurdities and self-contradictions in the charges made in the newspapers and at the circus-like show trials. Is it possible that anyone with minimum intelligence could have been taken in by this nonsense for half a minute? But perhaps this is not the right question to ask. Given a secure cognitive framework, all sorts of anomalies can be ignored or explained away. In our society, we are aware that our court system produces many absurdities and miscarriages of justice, yet because we believe in its basic principles, we do not lose faith in the system as a whole.

So it was with Stalin and his friends. They could explain away any anomalies in their system as a product of the same bureaucratism and wreckerism in the secret police that existed in all other state agencies. They considered it prudent to institute procedural safeguards in the more important cases. Prominent among these is the confrontation (*ochnaia stavka*), in which the accused met his accuser face-to-face in front of interested officials. The complete inadequacy of this safeguard may be apparent to us, but that does not mean it was apparent to the leaders of the Bolshevik party. (This hypothetical description of the Stalinist mentality is vividly illustrated by Molotov's memoirs.)

We should not be too hasty in dismissing the system of forced confessions as obviously unacceptable to any intelligent person. The use of torture has a long and distinguished history in Western jurisprudence. Historians have shown that torture was instituted for cases in which evidence was inherently hard to come by: witchcraft, for example, or adultery. It replaced trial by ordeal when rationalist criticism undermined the legitimacy of the earlier method of pronouncing judgment in otherwise undecidable cases.[38] This history gives us a clue about the compelling power that the method of forced confessions had over the Stalinist leadership. The alternative to believing in forced confessions was simply *not knowing*—and this was intolerable in an atmosphere permeated by insecurity and struggle.

A dispute over foreign policy in 1929 illustrates Stalin's reaction to cognitive insecurity. When the Labour Party took over the British government after an election in spring 1929, the Soviet government expected a quick resumption of the diplomatic relations broken off by the Conservatives in 1927. The Bolsheviks were determined not to make recognition conditional on the resolution of such highly contentious issues as tsarist debts or Comintern propaganda. Prior to recognition, therefore, they would discuss only the *procedure* for resolving the controversial issues, not their *substance*. This rather subtle distinction led to misunderstandings at a meeting in July between British Foreign Secretary Arthur Henderson and the Soviet ambassador to France, V. S. Dovgalevskii; according to a source close to Litvinov, the problem was also attributable to "lack of a common language well-understood by both."[39] The Russians received the impression that Henderson had insisted on substantive talks; Henderson later denied that he had done so.

38. Robert Bartlett, *Trial by Fire and Water: The Medieval Judicial Ordeal* (Oxford, 1988).

39. Louis Fischer, *The Soviets in World Affairs* (1930; reprint New York, 1960), 604.

The dispute within the Soviet government involved the best way to deal with the uncertainty surrounding Henderson's real intentions. Litvinov seems to have argued that it was a misunderstanding and that any move on the British side to clear it up should be met by a forthright Soviet response. Stalin was convinced it was a trap; even after Henderson made conciliatory statements in September, Stalin argued for a suspicious, go-slow attitude (letters 40, 42, 44, 47, 51).

This background makes letter 47 a revealing instance of how Stalin dealt with inherent uncertainty. Stalin was convinced that Litvinov's informants were unreliable; the only way to arrive at a correct interpretation was through the "logic of things." Stalin arrived at his own insight into Henderson's intentions by viewing the situation in the light of general considerations: the Bolsheviks were dealing with enemies, diplomatic politeness was only a "masked" attempt to take advantage of the Soviets, left-wing bourgeois governments often tried to gain legitimacy by acting tough with the Soviets. In the welter of ambiguous signals, Stalin used maxims like these to give him the confidence to dismiss Litvinov's views in an aggressive fashion. Yet it seems clear that this aggressiveness arose from an underlying cognitive insecurity. As the top leader in revolutionary times, Stalin had no access to unbiased information and was condemned to permanent radical uncertainty. He had to fall back on his own sense of the "logic of things." If forced confessions seemed to confirm his logic, they undoubtedly acquired a compelling power in his mind.

Another circumstance that protected Stalin's belief in the guilt of his victims was the vagueness of the categories used to define it: "sabotage," "wrecking," "faction," "center," and a host of others. "Center," for example, could refer to anything from a shadow government to a casual get-together of malcontents. Stalin's habit of running together names ("In addition, the disciples of Bogolepov-Groman-Sokolnikov-Kondratiev should be turned out" [letter 67]) is more than a rhetorical device: it manifests an outlook that seizes on almost any contact between individuals as a token of a purposeful organization. Because Mikhail Kalinin spoke to some of the arrested "scoundrels," he is on his way to joining a counterrevolutionary organization: the Central Committee should be notified (letters 59 and 63). The reasoning recalls Stalin's earlier interest in discovering that Yevgenii Preobrazhenskii had visited Trotsky in Berlin (letter 11 from 1926).

The people of the Soviet Union would probably have been better off if Stalin had been more cynical than he was. Robert Tucker has pointed out how much pain and suffering went into the mass production of confessions during 1937.[40] These confessions served no earthly purpose; they were promptly filed away and forgotten. Tucker speculates that Stalin insisted on these confessions as proof to posterity that his vision of a world filled with enemies was basically correct. It was a repetition on a grandiose scale of his insistence in 1930 that people read and heed the testimonies of arrested wreckers.

In this section we have seen the antibureaucrat scenario turn murderous. Bureaucrats are no longer merely a focus for exasperation; they are cast as evil wreckers. This outlook was not inconsistent with the cynical scapegoating that accompanied the antiwrecker campaign throughout the 1930s. The Russian historian O. V. Khlevniuk has described the situation in 1937:

> If food was delivered in irregular fashion, this was because of enemies who had infiltrated the collective farms, and appropriate trials were already being organized. If the accident rate at work was high, a simple explanation was already at hand in the form of exposed wreckers. The housing problem was not solved for years, and even finished houses could not be lived in because of incomplete and unsound work— wreckerism again. Wreckers were active in trade, which worked incredibly badly. Wreckers in transport—that's the reason trains jumped the rails. In general, the Stalinist leadership used a means of manipulating public opinion that was simple but effective enough under the circumstances: everything good came from the party, from Soviet power, and from the leader; everything bad came from enemies and wreckers.[41]

This excellent description falls short of a complete explanation because it makes Stalin and his friends too cynical and knowing. The letters indicate that, at least in 1930, Stalin genuinely believed that the wreckers were guilty as charged. Not only did he believe, but he thought that others believed. His capacity for rational ma-

40. Tucker, *Stalin in Power.*
41. O. V. Khlevniuk, *1937: Stalin, NKVD i sovetskoe obshchestvo* (Moscow, 1992), 81–82.

nipulation must have been severely limited by his own angry credulity.

Right Deviation

Up to now we have seen Stalin lashing out at various groups defined as enemies: capitalist governments, kulaks, and "class-alien elements" employed by the Soviet state. In all these cases, Stalin's anger, however irrational, was directed against people toward whom Bolsheviks had long been hostile. In this section we shall examine a phenomenon that is much harder to understand: Stalin's lashing out at fellow Bolsheviks, not just avowed rivals for the leadership like Trotsky or Zinoviev, but party comrades who protested their loyalty to Stalin's general line. Was this an aberration explainable only in terms of Stalin's individual psychology? Or was it based on a political logic that Stalin shared with his victims?

To answer these questions we must examine the phenomenon of the right deviation.[42] There is an air of paradox about the right deviation. On the one hand, it was an ephemeral political opposition, quickly called into being by Stalin's change of course in 1928 and as quickly defeated. On the other hand, it seemed to the Stalinist leadership to be a permanent enemy that could never be entirely rooted out, one that threatened to undo all of Stalin's work even after his death. In his memoirs, Molotov maintains that the right deviation was a permanent temptation that was much more dangerous than the left opposition.[43]

Clearly the Stalinist leadership had an expanded definition of the right deviation that encompassed more than the opposition to the extraordinary measures of 1928 and the breakneck industrialization of the first five-year plan. The right deviation in this expanded sense was not just a right-wing counterpart to the left opposition. The left opposition can be defined by specific beliefs or policy commitments; the same cannot be said of the right deviation, since it was defined less by any specific set of beliefs than by the logic of Stalin's attitude. To understand this logic, we must return to the

42. The standard study of the right deviation in the strict sense is Stephen F. Cohen, *Bukharin and the Bolshevik Revolution* (New York, 1971).
43. For an example, see Chuev, *Sto sorok besed,* 171.

antibureaucrat scenario and look more closely at the relationship between the wily specialist and the naive Communist.

In expounding this feature of the antibureaucrat scenario, Stalin often used the imagery of infection. A vivid example of this imagery can be found in letter 66, when Stalin calls M. N. Riutin a "counterrevolutionary scum [*nechist'*]" who should be sent far away from Moscow. *Nechist* is a term taken from Russian folk belief; it means literally "the unclean one" and refers to the devil or indeed to anyone with whom one should not share the same food and drink. Stalin's combination of foreign Marxist jargon and earthy peasant abuse is eloquent not only stylistically but also politically, revealing a concept of pollution that could only be removed by a "cleansing" (*chistka,* usually translated as "purge").

Stalin's political epidemiology traced the infection of the right deviation through the following chain: surrounding classes, lower-level bureaucrats, bourgeois specialists, Communist administrators, party leaders. Once the party leaders were infected, they were a menace to the cause and could not be tolerated.

If the idea of infection is taken seriously, it presents two problems: how to deal with the lower-level bureaucrats who are the source of the infection, and how to deal with the infected leaders. The letters show Stalin acting to resolve both problems before and after the official discovery of the right deviation in 1928. They reveal that the logic that defined the right deviation was already in evidence during NEP, although there was an increase in emotional intensity after 1928.

If specialists and other lower-level bureaucrats are seen as wreckers, the response is straightforward: round them up and wring confessions out of them. If they are seen as a source of infection, the problem is more insidious: How can anyone work with them without losing one's Bolshevik immunity? In the long run, the bourgeois specialists would be replaced by "our people." The letters show Stalin's responses to this dilemma in the short run: pressure, reliable Communist administrators, and a united leadership front.

The need to exert pressure on state economic organs was part of official NEP doctrine. Bukharin argued that without the spur of competition, state industry was threatened by monopolistic degradation. The solution to this problem was not to reintroduce competition within state industry but rather to exert firm political leadership. Stalin agreed; in letter 4 (28 July 1925), he writes: "The syndicate's inertia is understandable: it doesn't feel like expanding production since expansion means more headaches—why bring on unnecessary headaches if the syndicate is doing fine without them? This ruinous inertia that arises from its monopoly position has to be overcome no matter what."

Thus, nothing special is occurring when Stalin informs Molotov in 1926 that "we are drafting immediate and *concrete* measures to reduce *retail* prices (we will put brutal pressure on the trade and cooperative network)" (letter 30). More uniquely characteristic of Stalin is his angry outburst in 1926 against lower-level cooperative and state procurement agents who "violated" policy directives by offering prices higher than officially permitted (letter 27):

> An extremely bad impression is produced by the constant communiqués in the press (especially in the economic press) about the complete violation of directives from the Commissariat of Trade and the party by the cooperatives and by the local and central procurement agencies. The virtual impunity of these obvious criminals is grist for the mill of the Nepmen [private middlemen] and other enemies of the working class—it demoralizes the entire economic and soviet apparat, it turns our directives and our party into a meaningless toy. This can't be tolerated any further if we don't want to be captured by these bastards who claim to "accept" our directives but in reality mock us.

Stalin insists that these violators must be arrested and a circular sent out to local party committees: "These violators are enemies of the working class and . . . the struggle with them should be merciless" (letter 27). (Stalin was still fuming about these violators in an impromptu speech given several months later in January 1927.)[44]

If this sort of pressure was considered appropriate even during NEP, it is less surprising that during the five-year plan Stalin would rely more and more on the security police (OGPU) to carry out economic tasks. An illustrative example from 1929 is letter 41 on improving grain procurements. The sources of difficulties include petty speculators, "Nepman elements" in the cooperative and state economic organs, and uncooperative collective farms. The answer

---

44. Stalin, *Sochineniia*, 9:158–59.

in each case is to send in the OGPU—otherwise the government is limiting itself to mere propaganda. In the next letter, Stalin is still worried, even though the Politburo has adopted his suggestion: it is unlikely that either the procurement agency or the security police will carry out the directives without vigorous checking up on fulfillment by the top leadership.

In 1930 the "OGPU-ization" of economic administration seems to take a step forward when Stalin feels that bank policy would be much improved if the hierarchy were cleansed of unreliable Communists and replaced with people from the OGPU and the Worker-Peasant Inspection (letter 63). Stalin uses the expressive and untranslatable phrase *proverochno-mordoboinaia rabota*. The closest American idiom I can think of is "kick butt"; the general idea is "checking up by punching people in the face."

An alternative to crude pressure of this sort is to send in reliable Communists who will keep tabs on top-level specialists. Unfortunately, Stalin's fear that the specialists would subvert the party's control made the relationship between specialists and Communists inherently unstable in his eyes. His attitude can be documented by his references to one of the most important "nonparty specialists," Vladimir Groman, a former Menshevik whose contribution during the 1920s to the methodology of planning was so great that he probably deserves the title "father of Soviet planning." In July 1925, Stalin complains that the Politburo is losing control of important economic decisions to Gosplan (the state planning agency)— in fact, not even to Gosplan but to middle-level experts. The real leadership of Gosplan comes from "Smilga and Strumilin . . . plus Groman" (letter 5). As party members, Smilga and Strumilin were supposed to keep an eye on things, but were they really reliable? In letter 10, Stalin calls Smilga a "fake" economic leader.

In 1929, while the general offensive is in full swing, Stalin demands reliability of a more violent and radical sort. He wants Mikoian to "*smash* the nest of Gromans, Vinogradskiis, and other such bourgeois politicians ensconced in Gosplan, the Central Statistical Administration, and so on. Hound them out of Moscow and put in their place young fellows, our people, Communists" (letter 44).

By 1930 Groman is a wrecker who should be shot. But apart from his out-and-out wrecking, Groman is a source of infection.

His example inspired the smaller fry, the cashiers, and various other specialists (who should also be shot). No doubt if all were known, a "direct link" (that is, a chain of acquaintances) could be found between Groman and the leaders of the right deviation. Groman also seemed to infect any Communist administrator who supervised him. In 1925, Piatakov was preferable to the "sham" Smilga, but now he too is a "dubious Communist" who lets "financial wreckers" get away with murder (letter 57).

As these remarks show, Stalin felt that lower-level elements were encouraged by infected leaders at the top—and therefore no wavering or dissension among the top leadership could be tolerated. A united front is needed in both economic and political spheres. If procurement agencies compete among themselves, grain holders will see their chance and hold out for a better price (letter 41). In the same way, if the party leadership is openly divided, the bureaucrats will rejoice. As Stalin warns Molotov in September 1929, even the appearance of reconsidering the self-criticism campaign will discourage the best elements of the party and gladden the hearts of bureaucrats everywhere (letter 49).

By these means—pressure, reliable watchdogs, united leadership front—Stalin sought to quarantine the source of infection, but with only partial success. What if a senior Bolshevik—a Politburo member—became infected? By what symptoms would you recognize the disease? What political consequences arise from the presence of the infected leader? Answers to these questions can be found in a speech Molotov gave at the Party Conference in 1926. We learn from letter 29 that Molotov asked Stalin to look over this speech before it was printed. We may thus infer that Molotov regarded the speech as an expression of their joint outlook.

Molotov's speech is a political sermon on the necessity of faith. "Faith in victory, assurance about one's own forces, a genuine conviction about the correctness of one's line and the unwavering decisiveness in struggle that flows from it—this is what will decide the outcome [of our struggle]." If faith can move mountains, lack of faith is deadly. Lack of faith is not an unimportant matter, not just a psychological quirk—no, it stems from a whole "ideology of unbelief." Those party members who lack faith "will waver, will wobble, will get confused, will not have a line, and will confuse everybody they can. This is the logic of things." It is absolutely intolerable to permit waverers to remain in the leadership: "In this period of undoubtedly tense and long-drawn-out struggle for victory, it is necessary that our hands not shake, that our will not waver, that our thinking not be paralyzed."[45]

In other words, the symptom of the disease is lack of faith, and if top leaders are infected, the result will be widespread wavering and confusion. In 1926 this analysis was directed against the left opposition, with the support of Bukharin and Rykov. In 1929, during the fury of the general offensive, it was turned against the right deviation. In their notes for 1929, the Russian editors have given us a Politburo statement from August of that year condemning Bukharin; it is instructive to compare this text to Molotov's earlier attack on the left. Bukharin is making "masked attacks" against the party. A case in point: in a recent speech he cited Marx's dictum "Doubt everything." Doesn't this show that "Com. Bukharin is engaged in spreading unbelief [nedoverie] in the general line of the party"? His struggle with the leadership arises out of the inevitable wavering of the petit bourgeois stratum during a time of intense class struggle. And since Bukharin's sallies against the Central Committee destroy the appearance of a united leadership front, they "nourish the illusions" of capitalist elements who hope that resistance might pay off. In other words, Bukharin has been infected by petit bourgeois wavering, and the resulting lack of faith demoralizes the party and encourages the class enemy.

The letters supplement this political analysis by revealing Stalin's intensely personal anger with Bukharin. When describing his feelings, Stalin resorts to a revealing social imagery that associates Bukharin with the milieu of the specialists. In one of his outbursts of hard-to-translate invective, Stalin casts him in the role of a prerevolutionary *intelligent*: he is a "typical representative of the spineless, effete *intelligent* in politics, leaning in the direction of a Kadet lawyer" (letter 42). (The Kadets, or Constitutional Democrats, were members of the leading liberal party in the decade before the revolution.) Stalin's conflation of Bukharin with the educated specialist helps explain why he was so sure that Bukharin was somehow inspiring the bureaucrats to frustrate the party's aims: he would feel more at home in the left wing of a

45. *15 Konferentsiia,* 654–75.

party of petit bourgeois socialists than in the Communist Party, where he is a decrepit, rotten defeatist (letter 67).

We then observe the strange debate between Bukharin and Stalin in 1929, in which Bukharin protests that he has no differences with the general line and Stalin insists that he does. In a private conversation that someone reported to Stalin, Bukharin evidently claimed that his difficulties with the Central Committee stemmed from his personal difficulties with Stalin. Stalin would have none of it: "If his disagreements with the present Central Committee are explainable by Stalin's 'personality,' then how does one explain his disagreements with the Central Committee *when Lenin lived*? Lenin's 'personality'? But why does he praise Lenin so much *now*, after his death? Isn't it for the same reason that all renegades like Trotsky praise Lenin (after his death!)? Our lawyer has completely tied himself in knots" (letter 43).

Thus Stalin claimed that Bukharin's dislike of him arose from profound political causes and Bukharin claimed that it did not. It is ironic that Bukharin's present-day reputation rests on the assumption that Bukharin was wrong and Stalin was right.

Bukharin is the paradigmatic right deviationist. But according to Stalin's version of the antibureaucrat scenario, any party leader who worked closely with specialists risked infection. According to the usual categories of party history, Georgii Piatakov, Aleksei Rykov, and Sergo Ordzhonikidze belong in completely different slots: Rykov was a right deviationist, Piatakov a Trotskyist, and Ordzhonikidze a loyal Stalinist. Yet the letters reveal how Stalin lashed out at each of them in strikingly similar terms.

As longtime head of the Soviet government and top economic administrator, Rykov was the coleader of the right deviationist group. In his memoirs, Molotov dwells on the disgrace of being called a Rykovite by Stalin as late as 1950.[46] Like almost anyone in his position, Rykov wanted to have efficient, businesslike relations with the specialists working under him and was irritated by the systematic distrust that interfered with productive work. At the same Party Conference in 1926 where Molotov delivered his sermon on faith, Rykov read aloud a long letter from a specialist of his acquaintance who was on the verge of quitting. The specialist gave a

---

46. Chuev, *Sto sorok besed*, 469.

long list of all the reports he had to make to inquisitive government agencies and ended with a description of some petty harassment by the local OGPU officer. Rykov furiously scolded the security police for throwing its weight around just to show who was boss. He then drew the moral: "Of course, together with good specialists, there are also bad ones. But the working class should be able to separate out the good from the bad, and to help the good in every way while punishing the bad."[47]

This outburst by Rykov shows that Stalin's version of the anti-bureaucrat scenario was not the only one compatible with Bolshevik political culture. But Rykov's defense of specialists made him a prime target for Stalin's suspicion. Sometimes Stalin sounded as if Rykov's body had been snatched and he was no longer a Bolshevik but a specialist. In September 1929, Stalin was highly irritated by a recent speech in which Rykov evidently failed to denounce the right deviation. "In my opinion, it's the speech of a *nonparty soviet bureaucrat* pretending to take the tone of a 'loyal' person 'sympathizing' with the soviets" (letter 50).

After mentally expelling Rykov from the party in this way, Stalin insisted on removing him from key governmental posts in the name of ensuring effective party leadership of the government. He reasoned that only in this way could the rot in the top government agencies be effectively eliminated. Rykov and his infected associates could no longer be tolerated. "If Rykov and Co. try to stick their noses in again, beat them over the head. We have spared them enough. It would be a crime to spare them now" (letter 67).

But if Rykov and company were removed, who would take their place while remaining immune from infection? A plausible candidate was Piatakov, who had always been known as a vigorous, perhaps too vigorous, party administrator. In 1925, Stalin preferred him over the "sham" Smilga. Piatakov had joined the left opposition because of his desire for more energetic industrialization, but he was one of the first to recant and re-enlist when Stalin started his industrial push in the late 1920s. In 1930, Piatakov was head of the Gosbank.

47. *15 Konferentsiia*, 118–20.

It is not quite clear from the letters exactly why Stalin was angry at Piatakov in 1930. Many observers at the time felt that Piatakov was resisting the inflationary policies demanded by the party leadership. According to R. W. Davies, this is an unlikely explanation. Piatakov had recently presided over a complicated credit reform designed to ensure better central planning of credit. Owing to haste and lack of preparation, the reforms led to severe, unplanned inflation; as a result, a harsh deflationary policy was instituted soon after Piatakov's dismissal in the autumn of 1930.[48] Another possible explanation for Stalin's discontent is suggested by Piatakov's memorandum reproduced in the introductory section for the year 1930: some of his recommendations amounted to a de facto criticism of the overall thrust of economic policy.

Inflationary pressures were an inevitable result of massive industrialization; the small-change crisis discussed in the letters was a passing episode confined to the summer of 1930. Stalin's anger at the "wreckers" involved is amply documented here, and visiting journalists were struck by the ferocity of the campaign against "hoarders."[49] Stalin may have held Piatakov responsible for this mini-crisis. Most likely, Stalin was not for or against inflation, for or against the credit reforms, but simply irritated at Piatakov when things went wrong.

More important for our purposes is Stalin's interpretation of Piatakov's sins: Piatakov is a "genuine rightist Trotskyist" (letter 65; see also letter 66). If the right deviation was a set of policy positions like the left opposition, this description would be merely nonsensical. But holding Trotskyist opinions on industrial tempo is perfectly compatible with being a link in the chain of infection. Piatakov is under the thumb of his specialists; he is "a poor commissar alongside specialists" (letter 60). (The allusion is to the practice during the civil war of attaching Bolshevik commissars to the army in order to keep an eye on former tsarist officers.) Piatakov becomes "the most harmful element in the Rykov-Piatakov bloc plus the Kondratiev-defeatist sentiments of the bureaucrats from the soviet apparat" (letter 65). The knotted prose of the Russian original conveys an even stronger impression of an unbreakable conglomerate.

48. Davies, *Soviet Economy in Turmoil*, 431.
49. Knickerbocker, *The Red Trade Menace*, 256–57.

Both Rykov and Piatakov had blots on their escutcheons: their participation at one time or another in oppositional currents within the party. Perhaps someone who had never wavered in supporting Stalin would better withstand infection. In 1930, when plotting to remove Rykov from his governmental posts, Stalin felt it was essential to get someone like Sergo Ordzhonikidze to do the job. Alas!—in 1933, the conflict arose again, and this time with Ordzhonikidze himself (letters 78 and 79).

Ordzhonikidze (known to everybody simply as Sergo) was a fellow Georgian who had been a Stalin loyalist from the very beginning and yet had managed to retain his independence in a way that people like Molotov had failed to do. The letters show Stalin's great reliance on Sergo as well as his occasional impatience with his fiery temperament (see letters 25, 27, 31). The clash with Ordzhonikidze in 1933 is all the more revealing. By now, the scenario is familiar. An economic difficulty exists (this time it involves missing parts). Its cause is violation of party decisions by impudent enemies of the party. A punitive campaign against them is announced. Anyone who raises a warning hand about this campaign—no matter who—is acting in an "anti-party" manner. The evil motives of the lower-level violators are clear enough, but Stalin is also aggrieved by Ordzhonikidze: "For what reason [is he doing this]? Of course, not in order to rein in the reactionary violators of party decisions—rather to support them morally, to justify them in the eyes of party opinion, and, in this way, to discredit the party's unfolding campaign—which in practice means to discredit the policy of the Central Committee" (letter 79).

In early 1937 Ordzhonikidze committed suicide under circumstances that point to a growing conflict with Stalin over exactly this sort of issue. Ordzhonikidze's death removed one of the few remaining barriers to the purge campaign of 1937 that decimated the Soviet elite.

We began this section by noting the paradoxical quality of the right deviation: elusive yet fearsome. The imagery of infection helps account for its insidious power in the eyes of Stalin and Molotov. One is almost tempted to define the right deviation (in the expanded sense under consideration here) as the attempt to be a self-respecting Stalinist—more exactly, the attempt to combine loyalty with self-respect. A party leader assigned a difficult job would try to do it in the most professional way he could, and this meant establishing a working relationship with specialists and sometimes suggesting a local revision of the general line. But as soon as anything went wrong or otherwise irritated Stalin, the antibureaucrat scenario would come into play and Stalin would see his former comrade as infected by the class enemy, as a source of rot, and as an unclean spirit that had to be exorcised.

All three dimensions of leadership are needed to explain this result. As an official, Stalin was placed in a relationship that was bound to produce tension: the top party leader was exerting pressure on the economic bureaucracy. One's feelings about the specialists depended to a large extent on where one stood in this relationship. Ordzhonikidze changed his own attitude toward specialists in 1930 when he moved from the Worker-Peasant Inspection (used in this period as a party tool for prodding the specialists) over to the top post in the government economic bureaucracy.[50]

But an explanation based solely on the dynamics of bureaucratic politics is insufficient. Leonid Brezhnev confronted the same structural tensions Stalin faced but reacted quite differently. In part this was because the Soviet Union was no longer undergoing revolutionary transformation in Brezhnev's time. Brezhnev also had the advantage of many long years of experience with a system that was new and dangerously unpredictable in the early 1930s. For these reasons, Stalin's level of frustration and suspicion was bound to be much higher.

The main reason, however, that different people react differently to the same structural realities is that they interpret them differently in their own minds. For the source of Stalin's interpretation, we must turn to the other two dimensions of leadership: political culture and individual psychology. Stalin defined the problems he faced with the aid of the antibureaucrat scenario. He did not make up this scenario all by himself: some version of the scenario, and even much of the imagery of infection, was canonical within Bolshevik political culture. Even when Rykov was defending specialists, he had to admit that there were bad ones requiring police attention. The letters show that the essential logic that defined the

50. Sheila Fitzpatrick, "Ordzhonikidze's Takeover of Vesenkha: A Case Study in Soviet Bureaucratic Politics," *Soviet Studies* 37 (1985):153–72.

right deviation was present and active already in the mid-1920s—before Stalin's radical change of course. It was common party property, and when Stalin invoked it he could expect his words to resonate even with his victims.

Still, not every Bolshevik would invest the scenario with the same emotional intensity, and so we must look at Stalin's own psychological makeup. The vivid invective of the letters belies the image of the cold-blooded Stalin. The antibureaucrat scenario in itself does not account for Stalin's certainty about Bukharin's guilt or his ability to suspect close friends like Ordzhonikidze of deliberately encouraging policy violation. The person who wrote these letters was a general secretary, a Bolshevik, and an exceptional individual.

Conclusion

When a large new body of material such as Stalin's letters to Molotov becomes available, it is always difficult to assess its significance. This is doubly difficult at the present time, because of the ongoing archival revolution in Soviet history. My own conclusions are offered here as hypotheses intended to promote discussion.

These letters show Stalin at work; they reveal how he saw his job and how he approached the problems on his desk each morning. I have argued that the antibureaucrat scenario provides an essential key to understanding Stalin's outlook. This scenario served as a bridge between his day-to-day work (deciding on policy and getting it implemented) and his descent into criminality (campaigns against wreckers and right deviationists). The mundane slogans "checking up on fulfillment" and "selection of officials" were embedded in a politicized drama of class conflict that pitted the revolutionary party against the specialists and bureaucrats. The bureaucracy represented the petite bourgeoisie and, as such, provided a source of infection for party officials. Stalin interpreted the frustrations of his job as the result of sabotage, and he therefore lashed out with murderous anger.

The antibureaucrat scenario also formed a bridge between the Stalin of NEP and the Stalin of the general offensive. As early as 1925 and 1926, Stalin was angry at "violators" of policy directives and worried about loss of Politburo control. The intolerability of any wavering within the party leadership was already explicit doctrine. But Stalin's application of the antibureaucrat scenario became steadily more violent during the general offensive when society threatened to spin out of control. The cognitive framework stayed pretty much the same; the emotional intensity became much fiercer.

Finally, the antibureaucrat scenario unites the three dimensions of Stalin's leadership. This scenario represents the resources of Bolshevik political culture applied to a particular job by a particular individual. Most top executives will come up with some form of the antibureaucrat scenario, but Stalin's version arose from the revolutionary experiences of the Bolshevik party and its collective reflection on them. Although Stalin's scenario thus made sense to his colleagues, it also acquired a characteristically angry and vindictive tone when he applied it. The letters reveal this vividly because they were written as immediate reactions to various problems confronting Stalin.

The picture of Stalin that emerges from the letters will have a profound effect on a number of scholarly debates.[51] There have been two general approaches to deciphering the enigma of Stalin; each has been given classic expression by someone who worked with him and presumably knew him well. In 1928, after Bukharin broke with Stalin, he summed up his new view of Stalin to Kamenev: "Stalin is an unprincipled intriguer, who subordinates everything to the preservation of his own power."[52] Bukharin went on to complain that Stalin changed his views like a weathercock whenever it suited his interests.

This description has remained the basis of one popular interpretation of Stalin. It is not without foundation, for there is no doubt that Stalin was an adept intriguer; the Molotov letters provide some excellent examples. The question remains: Was Stalin an unprincipled or a principled intriguer? In contrast to Bukharin's view in 1928 is a comment Nikita Khrushchev made during the "secret speech" of 1956 in which he exposed many of the crimes of the dead tyrant: "We cannot say that these were the deeds of a giddy

51. For three recent book-length studies of the various debates concerning Stalin and Stalinism, see Giuseppa Boffa, *The Stalin Phenomenon* (Ithaca, 1992); Chris Ward, *Stalin's Russia* (London, 1993); Graeme Gill, *The Origins of the Stalinist Political System* (Cambridge, 1990).
52. Robert V. Daniels, ed., *A Documentary History of Communism*, 2 vols. (New York, 1960), 1:308.

despot. He considered that this should be done in the interest of the party, of the working masses, in the name of the defense of the revolution's gains. In this lies the whole tragedy!"[53]

In spite of its air of paradox, Khrushchev's portrait of a sincere Stalin has always had adherents. In my view, the letters weigh in heavily on Khrushchev's side of the debate: Stalin was a believer.

This conclusion bears on another debate over Stalin: How much control did he have over events? To put the debate in oversimplified terms: Was Stalin powerful and committed enough to achieve what he wanted, so that we can deduce his intentions from the results? Or was he the creature of processes beyond his ken, avoiding decisions until his hand was forced? The letters suggest the need to pose the question in other terms. They reveal a very powerful Stalin who was aggressively confident about his own opinions. When he was committed to a policy, he selected officials and checked up on fulfillment until that policy was carried out. His insistence on the collectivization drive is the most eloquent example in the letters.

On the other hand, control over events implies cognitive control. To assume that we can deduce Stalin's intentions from the actual results is to assume that he knew what he was doing—in other words, that he had insight into the workings of state and society and that he understood the effects of his actions. Few readers of the letters will want to defend these statements. I have argued that much of Stalin's opinionated intolerance arose from cognitive insecurity; as top leader in revolutionary times, he had no access to unbiased information and was condemned to permanent radical uncertainty. The overriding mood of the letters is not the confidence of power but the anger of frustration.

Another long-standing debate over Stalin concerns his commitment to world revolution and the meaning of "socialism in one country." The letters show that Stalin did not see revolutionary interests and state interests in either-or terms: his genuine involvement in the revolutionary upswing in England and China did not contradict his fundamental loyalty to the power and prestige of the Soviet state. Finally, the letters show that by the mid-1920s Stalin's ascendancy within the Politburo rested to a large extent on his

53. *Khrushchev Remembers*, trans. Strobe Talbott (Boston, 1970), 616.

leadership skills and his ability to make a good case for his recommendations.

Each reader of the Stalin letters will come away with a conception
of the person who wrote them. Here I offer my own impressions.
Much of the correspondence is devoted to the rough-and-tumble of
political infighting. Assuming that this was an inevitable part of the
Kremlin environment, I find that Stalin's image of himself as a
devoted, conscientious leader is not entirely without foundation.
He plainly worked very hard trying to resolve genuinely intractable
problems. His leadership skills are impressive. Although it is usual
to scorn his catechistic style and numbered paragraphs, I have a
feeling that if I were on a committee with Stalin and those prodi-
gious memos came my way, I would find them difficult to ignore.

On the other hand, the emotional range found in the letters is
frighteningly narrow; it almost seems confined to anger, irritation,
and vindictiveness. Praise, generosity, enthusiasm, humor—these,
while not entirely absent, are in short supply. Robert Daniels's char-
acterization based on Stalin's public writing is amply confirmed by
the letters: "an anxious, rigid, compulsive, combative mind."[54]
Stalin was caught up in events beyond his comprehension (we are
still struggling to understand them today), and his conceptual
equipment was plainly inadequate for grasping the real causes of his
problems or the effects of his actions. His ignorance and anger,
amplified by his sincerity and his leadership skills, led to crimes of
horrifying dimensions. It would take the powers of a Dostoyevsky
to fully describe the combination of cynicism and belief, of manipu-
lation and sincerity, that resulted in the tragedy of Stalin and his
times.

54. Robert V. Daniels, *The Nature of Communism* (New York, 1962), 115.

Institutional Background to the Letters

The Soviet political system was divided into party and state institutions. This division was more meaningful in Stalin's time than it became later, because, in the early years of the Soviet Union, the party felt that state institutions were filled with "class-alien elements" whose loyalty was dubious. In Stalin's letters, "soviet" often means "state institutions as opposed to party." Ironically, this usage meant that the term *soviet* acquired pejorative overtones when used by party members.

The soviets themselves were elective councils. These councils formed a pyramidal system topped by the Central Executive Committee, which was therefore the supreme authority in constitutional terms. A body with more real power was the Council of People's Commissars, whose members included the heads of the powerful ministries. (Henceforth, *People's* will not be included in the name of this council and of other commissariats.)

The Soviet government also managed industry directly, and important state institutions developed economic policy. The top decision-making body for the economy as a whole was the Labor Defense Council. The responsibility for the day-to-day coordination of industrial administration was given to the Supreme Economic Council, while Gosplan (State Planning Agency) developed planning techniques and prepared long-term economic strategy.

Let us turn now to the party. Its top leadership bodies were set up along the lines of a parliamentary system. The Central Committee was the parliament that theoretically had sovereign authority between elections (the electorate consisted of large party congresses held every other year or so during the 1920s). The Politburo was the equivalent of a cabinet, and the general secretary took the role of prime minister. The Secretariat thus became the party's civil service. Although Stalin as general secretary was clearly first among colleagues who were less and less his equal, he could not take Politburo support completely for granted.

One or two institutions straddled the always fluid border between state and party. One was the Soviet security police, called, among a long series of names, the OGPU or the GPU. Although

65

theoretically a state body, it was even more thoroughly politicized than most. Another crossover institution was the Worker-Peasant Inspection (Rabkrin). Following some suggestions in Lenin's last articles, this state inspection agency was amalgamated with the Central Control Commission, a party body that occupied a somewhat similar position within the party. The job of all these institutions—security police, Worker-Peasant Inspection, and Central Control Commission—was to help the party leadership "check up on fulfillment."

In 1925 full members of the Politburo were Joseph Stalin, Lev Kamenev, Lev Trotsky, Grigorii Zinoviev, Aleksei Rykov, Mikhail Tomskii, and Nikolai Bukharin; in January 1926 Viacheslav Molotov was promoted to full member and Kamenev demoted to candidate member (Klim Voroshilov also became a member at this time).

In 1930 the Politburo consisted of Stalin, Voroshilov, Lazar Kaganovich, Mikhail Kalinin, Sergei Kirov, Stanislav Kosior, Valerian Kuibyshev, Molotov, Jan Rudzutak, and Rykov. Rykov was removed at the end of 1930.

The Communist International (Comintern) was an organization uniting the world's communist parties; officially speaking, the Communist Party of the Soviet Union was just one "section" like all the rest. In practice, however, since the Soviet party was the only one in power, it easily dominated the institution. The Comintern was also headed by a Central Executive Committee.

In the years before the revolution, the Bolsheviks were the beneficiaries of Lenin's inexhaustible supply of terms of polemical abuse. These terms retained their importance in Comintern affairs particularly because they often arose from the problems of preparing for the revolution. *Opportunism* was the most inclusive term, embracing all the ways in which a party could evade the demands of the revolution and settle for mere reform. One road to opportunism was "boycottism" or "recallism" (*otzovizm*), a label given to a Bolshevik faction that refused to work within bourgeois institutions like a parliament or the trade unions. A very different road to the same destination was "liquidationism": the desire to liquidate the party underground and to be content with legal institutions only. A final failing was "tailism" (*khvostizm*), which meant following behind the masses and their momentary moods rather than providing firm leadership.

CHAPTER ONE

1925

THE LETTERS preserved from the correspondence between Stalin and Molotov begin in 1925, a crucial turning point in the Soviet government's political program. This year is generally viewed as the peak of Lenin's New Economic Policy (NEP). In the spring of 1925, a comprehensive program of economic liberalization for the countryside was passed. Agricultural taxes and the cost of machinery were substantially reduced, loans were expanded, land rental rights and the right to use hired labor were expanded, and control over small-scale peasant trade was loosened. In industry, craftsmen were given significant latitude, and the pressure on private traders—the "Nepmen"—was lessened.

The economic reforms were reinforced by a shift in political strategy toward weakening class contradictions and the class struggle and toward overcoming capitalist elements in an evolutionary manner. The renewal of the activity of the soviets allowed elections to be held that were freer than those in the past. The central government tried to curb harassment of the prosperous peasants and the "bourgeois specialists."

All of these events are fairly well known and have been repeatedly and carefully studied by scholars. In Stalin's letters, however, these problems, so central to the life of the nation at that time, are virtually unmentioned. Stalin was entirely consumed by the political struggle within the upper echelons of power. Indeed, this is a characteristic feature of all the letters published here. Stalin was interested in decisions on foreign or domestic policies primarily as they related to his struggle for power. This is revealed with particular candor in the second half of the 1920s, during the war with the party opposition.

The clash between the so-called troika—Stalin, Kamenev, and Zinoviev—on the one hand and Trotsky on the other hand began during Lenin's illness and grew particularly aggravated after his death. In August 1924, a large group of Central Committee members opposed to Trotsky convened a conference where they declared themselves the collective leaders and elected an executive organ, the "seven," consisting of all the members of the Politburo except for Trotsky (Bukharin, Zinoviev, Kamenev, Rykov, Stalin, Tomskii) plus Kuibyshev, the chairman of the Central Control Commission (CCC) of the All-Union Communist Party (Bolshevik).[1] The seven regularly met on the eve of Politburo sessions and decided all the fundamental issues. At the Politburo meeting itself, with Trotsky present, resolutions that had already been agreed on were formally approved. Stalin's letters to Molotov from 1925 provide a unique source for studying the activities of the seven and the role that Stalin played in this "underground Politburo."

As the letters reveal, two issues were the focus of Stalin's attention: approval of a program for the construction of the Dnepr Hydroelectric Power Station (Dneprostroi) and the Eastman affair. Each of these issues figured prominently in the campaign against Trotsky.

Trotsky not only headed the commission for the construction of the Dnepr Station but was a fervent advocate and promoter of the project. Stalin was against the plan—from all indications, primarily because Trotsky was involved. Stalin was unable to obtain support for his position among the seven. In April 1926 at a Central Committee plenum, he once again accused Trotsky of trying to upset the balance between the government's financial capabilities and the pace of industrial development. "How, for example, can the fact be explained," Stalin asked, "that Com.[2] Trotsky, who has forced the issue of the Dnepr construction, is forgetting about the resources required for this enormous undertaking? . . . How will we keep from falling into the predicament of that peasant fellow who, when he had saved up an extra kopeck, instead of repairing his plow and

1. Hereafter referred to as "the party"—Trans.
2. The Russian abbreviation for *tovarishch'* (comrade) is *t.* or *tov.* and has been rendered "Com." throughout the book—Trans.

fixing up his farm, bought a gramophone and . . . went bankrupt. Can we really not reckon with this danger? Can we really not reckon with the decision of the [XIV Party] Congress requiring our industrial plans to conform to our resources? Meanwhile, Com. Trotsky is obviously not reckoning with this decision of the Congress."[3]

Soon, however, virtually confirming the political motivation behind his protests, Stalin changed his mind. By October 1926 at the XV Party Conference, the construction of the Dnepr Station was presented as a priority task, with an emphasis on its profit and importance for the country's economy. For example, V. Ya. Chubar, chairman of the Ukrainian Soviet of Commissars, stated that "to postpone these works would mean to artificially slow the pace of the industrialization of an important part of the Union."[4] All fears of financial hardship were forgotten. On 25 November 1926, the Politburo decided that both Dneprostroi and the Semerechensk Railroad were top-priority projects of all-union importance.[5] On 31 January 1927, the Politburo decided "to organize the construction of Dneprostroi with our own resources" only if "the most competent foreign expertise could be involved."[6] By that time, Trotsky had been virtually removed from his job, and his name was in no way associated with Dneprostroi.

The battle over the construction of the Dnepr Station played a far less important role in Trotsky's political destiny, however, than did the Eastman affair. The Eastman affair grew out of a book published in the West by Max Eastman, an American Communist and journalist. Eastman had traveled to Russia numerous times, knew Russian, was married to a Russian woman (Ye. V. Krylenko, the sister of N. V. Krylenko, RSFSR[7] commissar of justice), and was thus able to gather a great deal of material about the struggle within the Soviet political leadership during the last months of Lenin's life and fol-

3. RTsKhIDNI f. 17, op. 2, d. 220, l. 110. [Archival references use Russian designations as follows: "f." for *fond* (fund); "op." for *opis'* (register); "d." for *delo* (file); "l." for *list* (page)—Trans.]

4. XV All-Union Party Conference. Transcript (Moscow and Leningrad, 1927), 150.

5. RTsKhIDNI f. 17, op. 3, d. 604, l. 3.

6. Ibid., d. 615, ll. 1–2.

7. RFSFR is the Russian acronym for the Russian Soviet Federal Socialist Republic, one republic of the USSR—Trans.

lowing his death. Eastman met several times with Trotsky and was his ardent supporter. In Eastman's portrayal, Trotsky was one of the few true leaders of the Russian revolution, who, after its culmination, fell victim to the scheming of unprincipled Kremlin intriguers. The book reveals many Kremlin secrets, including the circumstances of the publication of Lenin's last articles, his "testament," and so on.

After the appearance of Eastman's book, Trotsky found himself in a difficult situation. Almost immediately the heads of several Western Communist parties addressed inquiries to him, asking whether the facts reported by Eastman about Trotsky's persecution corresponded with reality. Submitting to party discipline (because the facts cited by Eastman were considered secret), Trotsky was forced to answer that Eastman was lying. But this meant that Trotsky himself was now lying, because much of what Eastman wrote was the truth. Initially, wishing to extract himself from an unpleasant situation with the least damage, Trotsky tried to simply offer several general rebuttals. Stalin, who had a vested interest in this incident, however, decided to publicize it as widely as possible and to exploit it vigorously to discredit Trotsky. On 17 June 1925, Stalin sent the following lengthy memorandum:

TO ALL MEMBERS AND CANDIDATES OF THE POLITBURO AND PRE-SIDIUM OF THE CENTRAL CONTROL COMMISSION

On 8 May of this year, the Politburo received a statement from Com. Trotsky addressed to "Com. Eric Verney" at the periodical *Sunday Worker* in reply to Eric Verney's inquiry about a book by Eastman, *Since Lenin Died*. Published and widely quoted in the bourgeois press, *Since Lenin Died* depicts Com. Trotsky as a "victim of intrigue," and the readers of the book are given to understand that Trotsky regards [bourgeois] democracy and free trade in a favorable light. In view of this presentation, Eric Verney asked Com. Trotsky to provide an explanation that would be published in the *Sunday Worker*.

Com. Trotsky's statement, as is known, was printed in *Pravda,* no. 104 (9 May 1925).

I personally paid no attention to Com. Trotsky's statement at the time because I had no notion of the nature of Eastman's book.

On 9 May 1925, Com. Trotsky received an inquiry from the Central Committee of the British Communist Party signed by Com. Inkpin in connection with Eastman's book. Com. Inkpin asks Com. Trotsky to make a statement concerning Eastman's book, because "the enemies of the Communist International in our country exploit your position in relation to the Russian Communist Party."

Here is the full text of the letter from Inkpin:

9 May 1925. To Com. L. Trotsky. Dear Com. Trotsky! The Central Committee of the British party has assigned me to send you the attached copy of the book by Max Eastman, *Since Lenin Died,* and the issues of the *New Leader, Lansbury's Weekly,* and *Labour Magazine* containing reviews of the book. These reviews will show you how enemies of the Communist International in our country exploit your position in relation to the Russian Communist Party.

Our Central Committee considers that it would be very useful if you would write and send an answer to these reviewers. Such an article would be of good service to the Communist movement in our country, and we for our part would do everything possible to give it the widest publicity. With Communist greetings, General Secretary Inkpin.

Com. Trotsky wrote the following letter in reply to Inkpin's letter:

Dear Com. Inkpin: Your letter of 9 May was evidently written before my answer to the inquiry from the *Sunday Worker* was received in London.

My brochure "Where Is England Headed?" will be, I hope, a sufficient reply to all the attempts of the Fabian pacifists, the parliamentary careerists, the Philistines, and the MacDonalds to use various events in our party as proof of the advantage of reformism over communism and of democracy over the dictatorship of the proletariat.

As soon as my brochure is reviewed by the Central Committee of our party, I will not delay in sending you the manuscript.

With Communist greetings, L. Trotsky

21 May 1925.

At the same time, Com. Trotsky sent to the Politburo in care of Com. Stalin a letter dated 19 May 1925, wherein Com. Trotsky, without providing a direct reply to the questions raised by Com. Inkpin, attempts to get by with a reference to his brochure "Where Is England Headed?" which has no relationship to Com. Inkpin's inquiry.

Here is the text of Com. Trotsky's letter:

To Comrade Stalin. Dear Comrade! In order to avoid any misunderstandings whatsoever, I consider it necessary to provide you with the following information regarding the English book by Max Eastman,

Since Lenin Died (I have just received this book and have managed to leaf through it quickly).

I became acquainted with M. Eastman as an American Communist at one of the first international congresses of the Comintern.

Three or four years ago, Eastman asked for my assistance in writing my biography. I refused, suggesting that he do some other work of more general interest. Eastman replied in a letter in which he argued that the American worker would become interested in communism not in response to the expounding of theory or history but in response to a biographical story; he and other American writers wanted to fashion a weapon of Communist propaganda out of the biographies of several Russian revolutionaries. Eastman asked me to give him the necessary facts and subsequently to review the manuscript. I replied that in view of his explanation I did not feel I could refuse to tell him the necessary facts, but I definitely refused to read the manuscript and thus accept direct or indirect responsibility for the biography.

Subsequently I gave Eastman information relating to the **first twenty-two years of my life,** before I arrived in London in 1902. I know that he visited my relatives and schoolmates and collected information about that same era. These materials are what gave him, apparently, the opportunity to write the book *Lev Trotsky: Portrait of a Youth,* the announcement of which is printed on the cover of the book *Since Lenin Died.*

The last time I saw Eastman must have been more than a year and a half ago; I lost track of him altogether after that. *I had no notion of his intention to write a book devoted to the discussion in our party.* And even he, of course, did not have this intention during that period when he met with me to collect facts about my youth.

It goes without saying that he could not have received any party documents from me or through me. Eastman, however, did speak and write Russian well, had many friends in our party, was married to a Russian Communist, as I was recently told, and consequently had free access to all our party literature, including, evidently, those documents that were sent to local organizations, distributed to members of the XIII Party Congress, etc. I have not verified whether he has cited these documents accurately or from rumor.

The press of the British mensheviks is trying to use Eastman's book against communism (the secretary of the British Communist Party sent me, along with Eastman's book, three issues of menshevik-type publications that included articles about that book). Meanwhile, my telegram was supposed to appear in the *Sunday Worker* (there is mention of this in the *Daily Herald*). I think that my pamphlet "Where Is England Headed?" will be quite timely under these circumstances and will dispel many illusions and much gossip spread by the menshevik and bourgeois press. I intend to do an appropriate supplement for the English edition.

In a private conversation, I told you that for half a year I have not received any Comintern documents. In particular, I have no idea whatsoever what the "inquiry" Treint raised about me involves. To this day I do not know why Rosmer and Monatte were expelled from the party, I do not know what their disagreements are with the party, and I do not know what they are publishing or even whether they are publishing anything at all.[8]

With Communist greetings, L. Trotsky

Moscow, 19 May 1925.

Only after this letter from Com. Trotsky and only because Com. Trotsky stubbornly refused to reply directly to Com. Inkpin's questions about the Eastman book did it become clear to me that I had to familiarize myself immediately with the contents of that book.

Acquaintance with Eastman's book convinced me that this book was not written naively, that its purpose is to discredit the government of the USSR and the Central Committee of the Russian Communist Party, and that for these purposes Eastman indulges in a whole range of slanders and distortions, referring to Trotsky's authority and to his "friendship" with Trotsky and to some secret documents that have not yet been published. I was particularly surprised by Eastman's statements concerning his "chats" with Com. Trotsky about Lenin's so-called testament and about the "main figures in the Central Committee," and also by his statement that the authenticity of [his text of] Lenin's so-called testament was confirmed by "three responsible Communists in Russia," whom "I (that is, Eastman) interviewed separately and who had all recently read the letter and committed its most vital phrases to memory."

For me it became clear that, given everything I have just related, it would be not only intolerable but outright criminal to hush up the question of Com. Trotsky's relationship with Eastman and his book *Since Lenin Died*.

8. Alfred Rosmer and Pierre Monatte were expelled from the French Communist Party in December 1924 because of their support for Trotsky. Albert Treint was one of the top leaders of the French Communist Party, and he supported the anti-Trotsky majority in the Soviet Politburo. For details, see Helmut Gruber, *Soviet Russia Masters the Comintern: International Communism in the Era of Stalin's Ascendancy* (New York, 1974)—U.S. Ed.

In view of that, after discussing the matter with the secretaries of the Central Committee, I ordered Eastman's book translated into Russian and sent the translation to Politburo members and candidates for their review.

I was also moved to act because, meanwhile, all and sundry bourgeois and social democratic parties have already begun to use the Eastman book in the foreign press against the Russian Communist Party and Soviet rule: they take advantage of the fact that in their campaign against the leaders of the Soviet government they can now rely on the "testimonies" of the "Communist" Eastman, a "friend" of Com. Trotsky who has "chats" with him, to the effect that Russia is ruled by an irresponsible bunch of usurpers and deceivers.

I have no doubt whatsoever that Eastman's book is libelous, that it will prove enormously profitable to the world counterrevolution (and has already done so!), and that it will cause serious damage to the entire world revolutionary movement.

That is why I think that Com. Trotsky, on whom Eastman occasionally claims to rely in his book when speaking against the leaders of the Russian Communist Party and the Soviet revolutionary authority, cannot pass over Eastman's book in silence.

I am not thinking at present of proposing to Com. Trotsky that he substantively respond in the press to the fundamental issues covered in Eastman's book, which are the fundamental questions of our disputes as well. Let the party and the International judge who is right and whose political position is correct, the position of the Central Committee or the position of Com. Trotsky.

But certain minimum obligations rest on party members; a member of the Central Committee and Politburo, such as Com. Trotsky is at this moment, has a certain minimum moral duty that Com. Trotsky cannot and should not refuse. This minimum requires that Com. Trotsky speak out in the press unequivocally against the crude distortions of facts that are known to everyone, distortions permitted in Eastman's book for the purpose of discrediting the Russian Communist Party. Obviously the silence of Com. Trotsky in this case may be construed only as a confirmation or an excuse for these distortions.

I think that Com. Trotsky should rebut at least the following distortions:

1) In the section, "Attacking the Old Guard," Eastman's little book says that "Trotsky's letter [the reference is to an appeal to the local committees in 1923 in connection with the Politburo's resolution on internal party democracy—J. Stalin] and some supplementary articles

in pamphlet form were practically suppressed by the Politburo" [53].[9]

Further, in chapter 9 of Eastman's book, it says that "Trotsky's book [the reference is to volume 3 of Trotsky's works and *Lessons of October*—J. Stalin] was practically suppressed by the Politburo until they [that is, the Central Committee of the Russian Communist Party— J. Stalin] were sure of the success of their manoeuvre" [80–81].

Finally, chapter 14 of Eastman's book says that "Trotsky's true texts do not appear in public to refute their [that is, the Central Committee's—J. Stalin] statements. These texts are read privately, con- scientiously, by those minds who have the courage and penetration to resist the universal official hysteria stimulated and supported by the State" [125]. I think that Com. Trotsky should refute these statements by Eastman as malicious slander against the party and the Soviet gov- ernment. Com. Trotsky cannot help but know that neither during the party discussions of 1923 or 1924, nor at any time whatsoever, did the Central Committee obstruct the printing of Com. Trotsky's articles and books in any way.

In particular, Com. Trotsky must recall that during the 1923 discus- sion he himself refused in his well-known statement in the press to reply to the arguments of representatives of the party majority. He must also remember the following statement "From the Editors" of *Pravda,* the central party organ:

"From the Editors. In reply to the question posed by a number of comrades concerning why Com. Trotsky is not responding to the criticism of Trotskyism, the editors of *Pravda* report that so far neither Com. Trotsky nor his close supporters have submitted any articles in response to the criticism of Trotskyism" (see *Pravda,* no. 284 [13 December 1924]).

2) The second chapter of Eastman's book speaks of the Russian Communist Party leaders as "suppressing the writings of Lenin him- self," [20] and in chapter 9 it says that they, that is, the party leaders, "clap[ped] the censorship on his [that is, Lenin's—J. Stalin] own last words to his Party" [92].

I think that Com. Trotsky should also refute these statements by Eastman as a lie and as libel against the leaders of the party, the Central Committee, and its Politburo. Trotsky knows quite as well as do all other members of the Central Committee that Eastman's reports do not correspond with reality to the slightest degree.

3) In the second chapter of his book, Eastman states that "all those

9. The text of the passages from Max Eastman's book (*Since Lenin Died* [1925]) are taken from the English original.

present at the meeting, including the secretaries, were not only against the policies proposed by Lenin, but they were against the publication of the article" [25] [the reference is to Lenin's article "How We Should Reorganize Rabkrin"—J. Stalin].[10]

I think that Com. Trotsky should also refute this statement by Eastman as an obvious slander. He cannot help but recall, first, that Lenin's plan as set forth in his article was not discussed substantively at this time; second, that the Politburo was convened in connection with the statements in Lenin's article about the possible schism in the Central Committee—statements that could have provoked misunderstanding in the party organizations. Com. Trotsky could not help but know that the Politburo then decided to send to party organizations, in addition to Lenin's printed article, a special letter from the Orgburo and the Politburo of the Central Committee stating that the article should not provide grounds for any perception of a schism in the Central Committee. Com. Trotsky must know that the decision to publish Lenin's article immediately, and to send a letter from the members of the Orgburo and Politburo about the absence of a schism within the Central Committee, was passed unanimously; any notion that the Politburo's decision on the publication of Lenin's article was passed under pressure from Com. Trotsky is a ridiculous absurdity.

Here is the text of the letter:

Letter to the Provincial and Regional Committees. Dear Comrades, *Pravda* no. 16 of 25 January carries Lenin's article "How We Should Reorganize Rabkrin." One part of this article speaks about the role of the Central Committee of our party and the need to take organizational measures that will eliminate the prospect of, or make as difficult as possible, a schism in the Central Committee if mutual relations between the proletariat and the peasantry become complicated in connection with the changes ensuing from NEP. Some comrades have directed the Politburo's attention to the fact that the comrades in the provinces may view this article by Com. Lenin as an indication of a recent internal schism within the Central Committee that has prompted Com. Lenin to advance the organizational proposals outlined in his article. In order to eliminate the possibility of such conclusions—which do not at all correspond to the real state of affairs—the Politburo and the Orgburo consider it necessary to notify the provincial committees of the circumstances surrounding the writing of Com. Lenin's article.

The return of Com. Lenin to highly pressured work after his illness

10. Actually, Eastman incorrectly thought the dispute was over another article by Lenin, "Better Fewer but Better"—U.S. Ed.

led to exhaustion. The doctors pronounced it necessary to prescribe for Com. Lenin a certain period of absolute rest without even reading newspapers (since for Com. Lenin reading newspapers is, of course, not entertainment or a means of relaxation but an occasion for intense contemplation of all the current political issues). It goes without saying that Com. Lenin does not take part in the Politburo sessions, and he is not even sent—again, in strict accordance with his doctors' advice—the transcripts of the sessions of the Politburo and the Orgburo. The doctors believe, however, that because complete mental inactivity is intolerable for him, Com. Lenin should be allowed to keep something like a journal, in which he notes his thoughts on various issues; when authorized by Com. Lenin himself, moreover, a portion of this journal may appear in the press. These external conditions underlying the writing of "How We Should Reorganize Rabkrin" demonstrate that the proposals contained in this article are suggested not by any complications inside the Central Committee but by Com. Lenin's general views on the difficulties that will face the party in the coming historical epoch.

In this strictly informational letter we will not consider the possible long-range dangers that Comrade Lenin appropriately raised in his article. The members of the Politburo and Orgburo, however, wish to state with complete unanimity, in order to avoid any possible misunderstandings, that in the work of the Central Committee *there are absolutely no circumstances that would provide any basis whatsoever for fears of a "schism."*

This explanation is provided in the form of a strictly secret letter, rather than being published in the press, to avoid giving enemies the opportunity to cause confusion and agitation through false reports about the state of Com. Lenin's health. The Central Committee has no doubt that if anyone in the provinces has drawn the alarming conclusions noted in the beginning of this letter from the article by Com. Lenin, the provincial committees will not delay in correctly orienting the party organizations.

Available Members of the Politburo and Orgburo of the Central Committee of the Russian Communist Party:

Andreev	Molotov
Bukharin	Rykov
Dzerzhinsky	Stalin
Kalinin	Tomskii
Kamenev	Trotsky
Kuibyshev	

Moscow, 27 January 1923

4) Chapter 3 of Eastman's book talks about Lenin's "testament."

"One of the most solemn and carefully weighed utterances that ever came from Lenin's pen was suppressed—in the interests of 'Leninism'—by that triumvirate of 'old Bolsheviks,' Stalin, Zinoviev and Kamenev. . . . They decided that it might be read and explained privately to the delegates—kept within the bureaucracy, that is to say,—but not put before the party for discussion, as Lenin directed" [28–29].[11]

I think that Com. Trotsky should also refute this statement by Eastman as a malicious slander. First of all, he cannot help but know that Lenin's "testament" was sent to the Central Committee for the exclusive use of the Party Congress; second, that neither Lenin nor Com. Krupskaia "demanded" or in any way proposed to make the "testament" a subject of "discussion before the entire Party"; third, that the "testament" was read to all the delegations to the Congress without exception, that is, to all the members of the Congress without exception; fourth, that when the Congress presidium asked the Congress as a whole whether the "testament" was known to all the members of the Congress and whether any discussion of it was required, the presidium received the reply that the "testament" was known to all and that there was no need to discuss it; fifth, that neither Trotsky nor any other member of the Congress made any protest about possible irregularities at the Congress; sixth, that by virtue of this, to speak of suppressing the "testament" means to slander maliciously the Central Committee and the XIII Party Congress.

5) The second chapter of Eastman's book says that the "article [the reference is to Lenin's article on the nationalities question—J. Stalin] which Lenin considered of 'leading importance,' and which he designed to have read at a party convention, but which constituted a direct attack upon the authority of Stalin, and a corresponding endorsement of the authority of Trotsky, was not read at the party convention, the triumvirate deciding that it was for the welfare of the party to suppress it" [23].

I think that Com. Trotsky should also refute this statement by Eastman as clearly libelous. He must know, first, that Lenin's article *was read* by all members of the Congress without exception, as stated at a full meeting of the Congress; second, that none other than Com. Stalin himself proposed the publication of Lenin's article, having stated on 16 April 1923, in a document known to all members of the Central Committee, that "Com. Lenin's article ought to be published in the press"; third, that Lenin's article on the nationalities issue was not

11. In this instance, Stalin's Russian version rearranges the order of the passages as presented by Eastman; in addition, Eastman's word *privately* is rendered as *v sekretom poriadke*, that is "secret"—U.S. Ed.

published in the press only because the Central Committee could not fail to take into consideration that Lenin's sister, Mariia Ilinichna, who had Lenin's article in her possession, did not consider it possible to publish it in the press. Com. Fotieva, Lenin's personal secretary, states this in a special document dated 19 April 1923, in reply to Stalin's proposal to print the article: "Mariia Ilinichna [Lenin's sister—J. Stalin] has made a statement," writes Com. Fotieva, "to the effect that since there was no direct order from Lenin to publish this article, it cannot be printed, and she considers it possible only to have the members of the Congress familiarize themselves with it . . ." and, in fact, Com. Fotieva adds that "Vladimir Ilich did not consider this article to be finished and prepared for the press"; fourth, that Eastman's statement that the Congress was not informed of Lenin's article therefore slanders the party.

6) In the second chapter of his book, Eastman, among other things, writes the following about Lenin's "testament": "There is no mystery about my possession of this and the foregoing information; it is all contained in official documents stolen by the counterrevolutionists and published in Russian, at Berlin, in the *Sotzialistichesky Viestnik* [Socialist herald]" [26].

Here Eastman once again distorts the truth. Not Lenin's "testament" but a malicious distortion of it was published in *Sotsialisticheskiy vestnik*.

I think that Com. Trotsky should make a declaration about this distortion.

7) In the second chapter of Eastman's book, Com. Kuibyshev is incorrectly portrayed as an opponent of Lenin's plan set out in the article about the Worker-Peasant Inspection: "The degree to which the policies outlined by Lenin have been followed may be inferred from the fact that Kuibishev . . . is now the People's Commissioner of Workers' and Peasants' Inspection, and the head of the Central Control Committee of the party" [25].

In other words, it seems that when the Central Committee and the Party Congress appointed Kuibyshev commissar of Worker-Peasant Inspection and chairman of the Central Control Commission, they intended not to implement Lenin's plan but to sabotage it and cause it to fail.

I think that Com. Trotsky should also make a declaration against this libelous statement about the party, for he must know that, first, Lenin's plan, developed in the article about the Worker-Peasant Inspection, was passed by the XII Party Congress; second, Com. Kuibyshev was and remains a supporter and promoter of this plan; third, Com. Kuibyshev was elected chairman of the Central Control Commission at the XII Congress (reelected at the XIII Congress) in the presence of Com. Trotsky and without any objections on the part of Com. Trotsky or other members of the Congress; fourth, Com. Kuibyshev was appointed head of Worker-Peasant Inspection at the Central Committee plenum of 26 April 1923 in the presence of Com. Trotsky and without any objections on his part.

8) Eastman states in the first chapter of his book: "When Lenin fell sick and was compelled to withdraw from the Government, he turned again to Trotsky and asked him to take his place as President of the Soviet of People's Commissars and of the Council of Labour and Defence" [16].

Eastman repeats the same thing in the second chapter of his book: "He [that is, Com. Trotsky—J. Stalin] declined Lenin's proposal that he should become the head of the Soviet Government, and thus of the revolutionary movement of the world" [18].

I do not think that this statement by Eastman, which, by the way, does not correspond at all to reality, could harm the Soviet government in any way. Nevertheless, because of Eastman's crude distortion of the facts on a matter concerning Com. Trotsky, Com. Trotsky ought to speak out against this undeniable distortion as well. Com. Trotsky must know that Lenin proposed to him, not the post of chairman of the Council of Commissars and the Labor Defense Council, but the post of one of the four deputies of the chairman of the Council of Commissars and Labor Defense Council, having in mind already two deputies of his own who had been previously appointed, Comrades Rykov and Tsiurupa, and intending to nominate a third deputy of his own, Com. Kamenev. Here is the corresponding document signed by Lenin:

To the Secretary of the Central Committee, Com. Stalin. Since Com. Rykov was given a vacation before the return of Tsiurupa (he is expected to arrive on 20 September), and the doctors are promising me (of course, only in the event that nothing bad happens) a return to work (at first very limited) by 1 October, I think that it is impossible to burden Com. Tsiurupa with all the ongoing work, and I propose appointing two more deputies (deputy to the chairman of the Council of Commissars and deputy to the chairman of the Labor Defense Council), that is, Comrades Trotsky and Kamenev. Distribute the work between them with my clearance and, of course, with the Politburo as the highest authority. 11 September 1922. V. Ulianov (Lenin).

Com. Trotsky must be aware that there were no other offers then or now from Com. Lenin regarding his appointment to the leadership of the Council of Commissars or the Labor Defense Council. Com. Trotsky thus turned down, not the post of chairman of the Council of Commissars or the Labor Defense Council, but the post of one of the four deputies of the chairman. Com. Trotsky must be aware that the Politburo voted on Lenin's proposal as follows: those in favor of Lenin's proposal were Stalin, Rykov, Kalinin; those who abstained were Tomskii, Kamenev; and Com. Trotsky "categorically refused"; (Zinoviev was absent). Com. Trotsky must be aware that the Politburo passed the following resolution on this matter: "The Central Committee Politburo with regret notes the categorical refusal of Com. Trotsky and proposes to Com. Kamenev that he assume the fulfillment of the duties of deputy until the return of Com. Tsiurupa."

The distortions condoned by Eastman, as you can see, are glaring.

These are, in my opinion, the eight indisputable points, Eastman's crudest distortions, that Com. Trotsky is obliged to refute if he does not wish to justify through his silence Eastman's slanderous and objectively counterrevolutionary attacks against the party and the Soviet government.

In connection with this, I submit the following proposal to the Politburo:

PROPOSE TO COM. TROTSKY THAT HE DISASSOCIATE HIMSELF DECISIVELY FROM EASTMAN AND MAKE A STATEMENT FOR THE PRESS WITH A CATEGORICAL REBUTTAL OF AT LEAST THOSE DISTORTIONS THAT WERE OUTLINED IN THE ABOVE-MENTIONED EIGHT POINTS.

As for the general political profile of Mr. Eastman, who still calls himself a Communist, it hardly differs in any way from the profile of other enemies of the RCP [Russian Communist Party] and the Soviet government. In his book he characterizes the RCP Congress as nothing but a "ruthless" and "callous bureaucracy," the Central Committee of the party as a "band of deceivers" and "usurpers," the Lenin levy (in which 200,000 proletarians joined the party) as a bureaucratic maneuver by the Central Committee against the opposition, and the Red Army as a conglomerate "broken into separate pieces" and "lacking defense capability," and these facts clearly tell us that in his attacks against the Russian proletariat and its government, against the party of this proletariat and its Central Committee, Eastman has outdone run-of-the-mill counterrevolutionaries and the well-known charlatans of White Guardism. No one, except the charlatans of the counterrevolution, has ever spoken of the RCP and the Soviet government in such language as the "friend" of Com. Trotsky, the "Communist" Eastman, permits himself. There is no question that the American Communist

Party and the Third International will properly evaluate these outstanding exploits of Mr. Eastman.

17 June 1925   J. Stalin.[12]

The following day, 18 June, the Politburo affirmed Stalin's proposal about Trotsky's statement of rebuttal in the press. Trotsky himself promised that within three days he would submit the text of his statement.[13] On 22 June, Trotsky in fact sent Stalin material entitled "On Eastman's Book *Since Lenin Died.*" Without citing any accusations, Stalin replied with a brief note:

> If you are interested in my opinion, I personally consider the draft completely unsatisfactory. I do not understand how you could submit such a draft regarding the counterrevolutionary book by Eastman, filled with lies and slander against the party, after you accepted a moral obligation at the Politburo session of 18 June to disassociate yourself resolutely from Eastman and to rebut categorically the factual distortions.

In an appeal to the Politburo, Trotsky tried to defend himself, attempting to prove that Stalin's accusations were nonsense. After meeting the usual rebuff, however, he began to revise the text of his statement for the press. Oversight of his revision was assumed by Bukharin, Zinoviev, Rykov, and Stalin. They demanded from Trotsky harsher accusations against Eastman and a categorical denial of the facts cited in Eastman's book. Trotsky conceded to all demands. The final text of his statement, which had satisfied the censors from the "seven," was ready by 1 July 1925.

Now Stalin and his supporters decided to take the affair outside the framework of the Politburo by first briefing a broad circle of party functionaries about it and then publicizing it generally. In early July, Central Committee members L. M. Kaganovich, V. Ya. Chubar, and G. I. Petrovskii submitted a statement that contained a request that "all the members of the Central Committee be sent all materials on the publication of Eastman's book" and that members of the Central Committee of the Ukrainian Communist Party be briefed. On 7 July 1925, after a poll of Politburo members, this request was fulfilled.[14] The materials on the Eastman affair were

12. RTsKhIDNI f. 17, op. 3, d. 507, ll. 8–23.
13. Ibid., ll. 1, 2.
14. Ibid., d. 510, l. 7.

typeset, published in the form of a small book (containing Stalin's letter, the Politburo's resolutions, Trotsky's correspondence with Stalin and with other members of the Politburo, and drafts of Trotsky's statement), and sent to Central Committee members. But Stalin had further plans to publish, both in the West and later in the USSR, the following documents: Trotsky's statement, a letter specially prepared by N. K. Krupskaia, in which she, as Lenin's widow, refutes Eastman, and the letter from Stalin himself that demonstrates his role in the struggle for party interests. But these plans, to which Stalin repeatedly referred in his letters to Molotov, were never fully realized.

Soon after the materials on the affair were sent to Central Committee members, Trotsky had occasion to take the offensive. On 16 July 1925, the French Communist newspaper, *L'Humanité,* published the original version of Trotsky's statement. On 27 July, Trotsky addressed a letter to Bukharin, who at that time was acting as chairman of the Comintern's Executive Committee. Trotsky expressed his puzzlement and protest over the French publication and demanded that the circumstances of the leak be investigated, hinting that publication had deliberately been arranged even after he, Trotsky, had made all the necessary concessions and had demonstrated his readiness to cooperate with the Politburo majority in defending the party's interests.[15] That day, after a poll of Politburo members, the following resolution was passed:

> a) To request *L'Humanité* to publish [a notice] that the text of Com. Trotsky's letter regarding Eastman's book that appeared in *L'Humanité* is incomplete and distorted.
>
> b) To request *L'Humanité* to publish the full (final) text of Com. Trotsky's letter about Eastman's book.[16]

Bukharin, in turn, ordered an investigation into the circumstances of the incident and informed Trotsky of this decision.[17]

Soon it became clear that the original version of Trotsky's article had been given to *L'Humanité* by D. Z. Manuilskii, a member of the Comintern's Executive Committee presidium, during his trip to France. The documents that remain do not enable us to determine the real circumstances behind Manuilskii's initiative. Nevertheless,

15. Ibid., f. 325, op. 1, d. 418, ll. 43–44.
16. Ibid., f. 17, op. 3, d. 513, l. 6.
17. Ibid., f. 325, op. 1, d. 418, l. 45.

as can be seen from the published letters, Stalin was involved in this conflict, and he was even forced to deny categorically that Manuilskii had acted in concert with him.

As the letters testify, Stalin was also unable to get the "seven" to agree to publish his own letter. The affair ended in a compromise. Only Trotsky's and Krupskaia's statements were published, first abroad, then in the USSR (in the journal *Bolshevik*, 1925, no. 16). As for the documents on the Eastman affair, it was decided that only a relatively small group of party officials should see them. After obtaining the approval of the "seven," on 27 August 1925, the Politburo decided to turn over all materials on the Eastman book to the Comintern's Executive Committee so it could "brief the central committees of the most important Communist parties." The Politburo also sent the documents, along with Eastman's book itself, to all the party's provincial committees and to members and candidate members of the Central Committee and the Central Control Commission; these items were given the status of a restricted distribution letter. At Trotsky's insistence, the correspondence concerning the *L'Humanité* incident was included in the package of documents sent to the Comintern's Executive Committee.

The publication and dissemination of documents on the Eastman affair had highly unfortunate consequences for Trotsky. Once again, to the mass of party bureaucrats at various levels, he appeared humbled and defeated, hanging his head before Stalin. The rank-and-file party members, especially his supporters, were shocked at Trotsky's recantation in *Bolshevik*. By declaring Eastman a slanderer, Trotsky seemed to be withdrawing from further struggle, disavowing his former accusations against the party leadership. Furthermore, by denying many well-known facts, Trotsky looked like a liar. "It's terrible, simply terrible! It's incomprehensible why Lev Davidovich [Trotsky] would do that. Surely he has put his head on the block with such a letter. He has made himself despicable . . ."[18] Trotsky himself was loath to recall this episode of his political biography.

18. N. Valentinov, *Novaia ekonomicheskaia politika i krizis partii posle smerti Lenina* (The New Economic Policy and the party crisis after Lenin's death) (Moscow, 1991), 295. N. Valentinov's real name was N. V. Volskii (1879–1964). After the October revolution, he was deputy editor of *Torgovo-Promyshlennaia gazeta* (Commercial and industrial newspaper). Later, he worked for the USSR trade delegation. He emigrated in 1930.

Stalin and Molotov

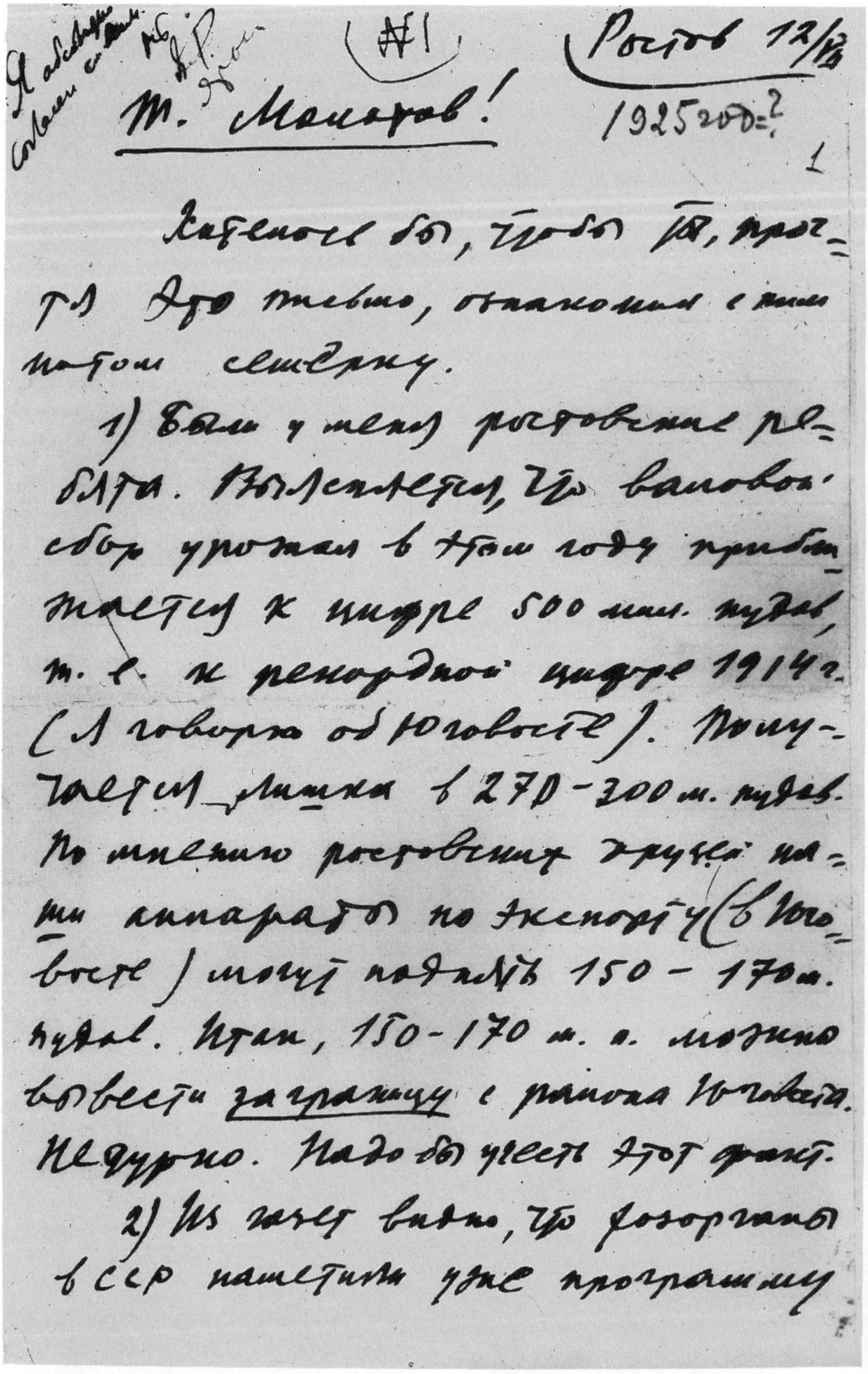
№1
Ростов 12/VII
1925
Т. Молотов!
Хотелось бы, чтобы ты, прочтя это письмо, ознакомил с ним нашу семерку.
1) Были у меня ростовские работн. Выясняется, что валовой сбор урожая в этом году приближается к цифре 500 милл. пудов, т. е. к рекордной цифре 1914 г. (я говорю об Юговостоке). Получается лишек в 270–300 м. пудов. По мнению ростовских друзей наши аппараты по экспорту (в Юговостоке) могут подать 150–170 м. пудов. Итак, 150–170 м. п. можно вывезти заграницу с района Юговостока. Недурно. Надо бы учесть этот факт.
2) Из газет видно, что хозорганы в ССР наметили уже программу

First page of letter from Stalin to Molotov, 12 July 1925 (RTsKhIDNI f. 558, op. 1, d. 5388, l. 1).

Letter 1   [12 July 1925]

Rostov 7/12

Com. Molotov,[1]
I would like you to show this letter to the seven after you have read it.
1) The fellows from Rostov were here to see me. It turns out that the gross yield of the harvest this year is approximately 500 million poods[2] [1.8 tons], that is, close to the record number in 1914 (I'm speaking about Yugovost). There is a surplus of about 270–300 million poods. In the view of our Rostov friends, our export offices (in Yugovost) could raise 150–170 million poods. Thus 150–170 million poods could be shipped *abroad* from the Yugovost region. Not bad. We should take this fact into account.
2) It is apparent from the newspapers that the USSR economic agencies have already designated a program to construct *new* factories. I'm afraid that they'll start building in the border regions without taking into account a number of unfavorable factors involved, and then if we miss the moment, it will be impossible to correct mistakes. For example, they want to build *new* factories in Peter[3] and Rostov; this is not expedient. In designing the construction program, I think that two considerations should be taken into account in addition to the principle of the factories' proximity to raw materials and fuel: the link with the countryside and the geographic-strategic position of the new factories' location. Our basic interior is: the Urals, the Volga region, the Black Earth south (Tambov, Voronezh, Kursk, Orel, etc.). These are exactly the areas (if you don't count the Urals) that are suffering from a lack of industry. Meanwhile, these are the areas that represent the most convenient rearguard for us in the event of military complications. Therefore, these are precisely the areas where industrial construction should be developed. In that respect, Peter is completely unsuitable. There will be pressure from the locals, of course, but that has to be overcome. This issue is so important for us that it ought to be placed on the agenda of the Central Committee plenum, if that is what is required to overcome local pressure. It would be good to know the opinion of the seven on this.

Regards,[4]
J. Stalin

P.S. I'm leaving for Sochi today.

---

1. In the upper right-hand corner there is a notation by Molotov: "1925=?" In the upper left-hand corner there is a comment by Bukharin, "I agree absolutely with everything. N.B.," under which are the signed initials "J.R." [Ya. E. Rudzutak] and "Yaros" [Ye. M. Yaroslavskii].
2. A pood is 36 pounds avoirdupois—Trans.
3. Leningrad, now known as St. Petersburg—Trans.

4. At the close of nearly every letter, Stalin wrote *Zhmu ruku* or *Krepko zhmu ruku* (I shake your hand, or I shake your hand firmly). These words have been rendered as "Regards" and "Warm regards" throughout the text—Trans.

Letter 2   [20 July 1925]

7/20/25

Com. Molotov,

In issue no. 159 (15 July) of *Ekonomicheskaia zhizn'* [Economic life], I read a notice, *"Examination of the Dnepr Construction Project"* [Dneprostroi],[1] from which it is evident that the party (and the Supreme Economic Council) may be dragged *bit by bit* into the Dneprostroi matter, requiring up to *200 million rubles,* if we do not take preventive measures in time. Com. Dzerzhinsky has published, it turns out, an "order" according to which Com. Trotsky has been requested to submit a technical and financial plan for the construction "by mid-October," so that *"the necessary loans for the preparatory operations can still be included in the budget for 1925–26."* The amount of 30,000 rubles has been released to Com. Trotsky for the preparation of the plan. The notice contains a few small reservations on the need for caution and so on. But since 30,000 rubles have already been released and a deadline for submission of the plan has been set, the project is beginning to take on a practical—and therefore serious—nature.

I do not think that we can afford to take on Dneprostroi either this year or next year given our financial situation. Only the other day we rejected the plan for the petroleum factory in the Transcaucasus,[2] although it is more realistic at present and a fourth of the cost. On what grounds must we accept the Dneprostroi plan, which is less realistic for the present and four times as expensive? Do we really have so much money? Is the Donbass (the region where Dneprostroi is to be located) really suffering such a fuel shortage—or is not the opposite the case? Why is there such haste with Dneprostroi?

We need, in the first place, new equipment for our worn-out factories and plants. Has that need really been satisfied?

We need, furthermore, to expand our agricultural machinery factories, because we are still forced to purchase abroad the most elementary agricultural tools for tens of millions of rubles.

We need, then, to build at least one tractor manufacturing plant, a new and large factory, because without one or more such factories, we cannot develop further.

We need, finally, to organize copper foundries, to develop lead production, to improve our military industry, because without that they will beat us with their bare hands.

Are those needs really all satisfied yet?

How can we, who suffer from a shortage of capital, forget all that?

I think that aside from all sorts of other dangers, we face another serious danger—the danger of squandering some of the kopecks we have managed to accumulate, of spending them for nothing, thoughtlessly, and thus of making our construction work more difficult. A month ago Com. Dzerzhinsky understood all this. And now apparently he's gotten carried away . . .

I very much urge you, Com. Molotov, to read this letter to Com. Dzerzhinsky. In view of the importance of the matter, read it to the seven and drop me a note to inform me of their opinion.

Regards,

J. Stalin

1. The reference is to the following short article from *Ekonomicheskaia zhizn'* (Economic life), no. 159 (15 July 1925):

The chairman of the USSR Supreme Economic Council, Com. F. Ye. Dzerzhinsky, has issued a special decree in connection with the completion of the blueprint for the construction of a hydroelectric power station on the Dnepr River (Dneprostroi) and the need for a technical and economic appraisal of the project and for the resolution of the basic issues involving its implementation.

The decree indicates that owing to the very close connection between the proposed hydroelectric construction project on the Dnepr and the proposals for restructuring the whole economy of the southern region, it is necessary to have an overall plan for technical and economic measures in this region and a financial plan for their implementation both during construction and after the station is opened for use.

The drafting of these plans is assigned to Com. L. D. Trotsky, member of the Supreme Economic Council presidium.

Com. Trotsky is assigned to organize an appropriate interdepartmental conference to allow the plan to be coordinated with the requests and needs of the Commissariat of Transport, the Commissariat of Agriculture and other offices, and to draft this overall economic, technical, and financial plan.

A report with a preliminary overall appraisal of the project and an exhaustive economic, technical, and financial plan is to be presented to the presidium of the Supreme Economic Council in mid-October; the necessary loans for the preparatory operations can still be included in the budget for 1925–1926.

A credit of 30,000 rubles is allocated for the project conferences. In addition, in light of the particular importance of the Dnepr Station for our entire economy, Com. Dzerzhinsky considers it necessary to include prominent specialists from North America in the appraisal of the project.

The Supreme Economic Council considers that it can ask the government for the exceptionally large sums required for the Dnepr construction project only if the mistakes of past construction projects are taken into account and only if, after a comprehensive review of world experience, it can be guaranteed that the proposed gigantic works will be expedient, timely, and economical.

2. The Finance Commissariat's protest against the Council of Commissars' resolution on the petroleum pipelines was reviewed at the Politburo session of 8 July 1925. It was decided to suspend the construction of the Baku-Batum gas pipeline and to review the matter once again the following year (RTsKhIDNI f. 17, op. 3, d. 510, l. 5).

Letter 3

[27 July 1925]

Com. Molotov,[1]

A week ago I sent to you a letter protesting against the plan for the immediate launching of electrification at the Dnepr rapids. I still don't have an answer. Did my letter get lost en route, or did you receive it? Drop me a line about what happened to the letter if you don't mind.

Best regards,
J. Stalin

1. In the upper right-hand corner is Molotov's notation: "July 1925"

Letter 4

[28 July 1925]

Sochi 7/28/25

Com. Molotov,

We have to think about [who will run] the party's Organizational and Assignment Department.[1] It seems Gei isn't right for the job. He's young, little known, without much of a record, and he won't be authoritative. Ask anyone—they'll tell you. Krinitskii isn't right either—or actually he is even less appropriate than Gei (for the same reasons). Is it perhaps time to take on [S. V.] Kosior and send Gei to Siberia? Perhaps we could take on Shvernik or Yanson? Just by himself, Bauman wouldn't be big enough, would he? I think he won't be adequate. Really, appointing someone for this department is a nut we've got to crack *before* the Congress.

The[2] other day I read in the newspapers that the textile syndicate evidently decided not to expand production very much in the coming year because of the shortage of raw materials, mainly cotton from Turkestan. **If** that is true and **if** the reason really has to do with the raw materials, then the syndicate's decision, in my view, is profoundly mistaken. It would be much more profitable for us to purchase more raw materials in America (by the way, American cotton is cheap **right now**) and process it here in our country than to purchase textiles from abroad. It is more profitable in all respects. This is a serious matter, worthy of attention. The syndicate's inertia is understandable: it doesn't feel like expanding production since expansion means more headaches—why bring on unnecessary headaches if the syndicate is doing fine without them? This ruinous inertia that arises from its monopoly position has to be overcome no matter what. Speak to Dzerzhinsky about it; show him my letter[3] and ask him to put pressure on the syndicate. I repeat, this is a serious question that merits attention. Either we resolve it properly in the interests of the state, the workers, and the unemployed, who could be placed in jobs if manufacturing were expanded, or, if we don't resolve it correctly, aside from everything else, we will lose tens of millions on this to foreign textile mill owners.

Warm regards,
J. Stalin

1. The Organizational and Assignment Department of the Central Committee (Orgraspred) was formed in 1924. It was a component of the Central Committee Secretariat with the following tasks: establishing and strengthening ties with local party bodies; instructing, registering, selecting, and assigning party cadres [trained staff] both to central as well as to local bodies; mobilizing, transferring, and nominating party officials; and performing specific assignments from the party's Orgburo and Central Committee Secretariat.

2. The text from here to the end is marked in red pencil.

3. Molotov sent the following letter to Dzerzhinsky on 7 August 1925 (RTsKhIDNI f. 82, op. 1, d. 141):

Com. Dzerzhinsky, I'm sending you two letters from Com. Stalin (in the second one from 28 July, I ask you to note the part marked in red pencil). Since I have learned that you are still running the affairs of the Supreme Economic Council, even from your sickbed (of course this is not good, and in the near future I will have a serious conversation with you about a vacation), I ask you to conduct an inquiry regarding Stalin's questions. I myself am completely in agreement with him. I do not doubt that you are also. I will expect from you reports on both Dneprostroi and the Textile Syndicate. Stalin has peppered me with questions about the status of these matters. I wish you a genuine recovery and a vacation soon! Regards! V. Molotov. August 7. P.S. I ask you to return the attached letters from Com. Stalin. V.M.

Letter 5

[July 1925]

Com. Molotov,[1]

The Labor Defense Council matter, of course, is not going well. Dzerzhinsky is upset,[2] he's overtired, but there's no smoke without fire, of course. In fact the Politburo itself is in an awkward position because it has been torn away from economic affairs. Take a look at *Ekonomicheskaia zhizn'* [Economic life] and you'll see that our funds are being allocated by Smilga and by Strumilin plus Groman, while the Politburo . . . the Politburo is changing from a directing body into a court of appeals, into something like a "council of elders." It's sometimes even worse than that: not Gosplan but Gosplan "sections" and their specialists are in charge. It's clear why Dzerzhinsky is unhappy. And work cannot help but suffer from that. I don't see any other alternative but to restructure the Labor Defense Council's membership and bring in Politburo members.[3]

Greetings,
Yours, Stalin

1. In the upper right-hand corner is Molotov's notation: "1926=?" In fact the letter was written in July 1925.

2. On 25 July 1925, Stalin sent Dzerzhinsky the following letter (RTsKhIDNI f. 558, op. 1, d. 5272):

> Sochi. 25 July. Dear Feliks, I learned about your letter of resignation from Molotov. I urge you not to do this. There is no basis for it: 1) the work is going well; 2) there is support within the Central Committee; 3) we'll reorganize the Labor Defense Council so that individual commissars cannot form blocs to the detriment of state interests; 4) we'll put Gosplan and its sections in their place. Hang on for a month or two more, and we'll fix things up right. Best regards, Yours, Stalin.
> P.S. How is your health?

3. On 15 October 1925, at a Politburo session, Stalin raised the issue "On the work of the Politburo and mutual relations among the central institutions." It was decided that in order to improve the work of the central institutions of the USSR (Council of Commissars, Labor Defense Council, Central Executive Committee presidium, Gosplan, etc.) and to establish complete coordination among them, as well as to ensure the Politburo's leadership of their work, two days a month would be set aside for special sessions of the Politburo on issues of state and, particularly, of economic organization. A Politburo commission for improving and coordinating the work of the central institutions of the Union was established at the meeting (ibid., f. 17, op. 3, d. 523, l. 4).

Letter 6   [1 August 1925]

Sochi 8/1/25

Com. Molotov,

1) I was told that Manuilskii sent *L'Humanité* the *first* draft of Trotsky's article for publication, not accidently, but *on purpose*. If that's true, it's an outrage. If it's true, then we are dealing, not with a "mistake," as you wrote me, but with the *policy* of a few people who for some reason are not interested in publishing Trotsky's article in its *final* edited version. This is unquestionably the case. This matter cannot be left as it is. *I propose raising the issue with the seven and condemning Manuilskii's intolerable action, since he has placed the Russian Communist Party and L'Humanité in a ridiculous position; in doing so, we must definitely find out who it was that instigated Manuilskii to take this malicious step.* As background, let me tell you several necessary facts: a) the documents were given to Manuilskii at Manuilskii's written request (it should be in the Central Committee's files) and *with the knowledge* of the seven (Zinoviev raised the issue of giving Manuilskii the documents at [a meeting of] the seven); b) the documents were given before the final version of Trotsky's article was available; c) they were handed over to brief the top people of the Comintern *and were not for publication* (see, by the way, Manuilskii's request); d) the question of publishing the documents, specifically, of publishing my memo on Eastman's book, was discussed by the seven, and in fact we all had in mind publishing my memo *after* the final version of Trotsky's article

was published; Manuilskii knew this; e) before Manuilskii's departure to Germany (in early July or late June) I asked Manuilskii *to return* to the Secretariat of the Central Committee *all* documents. He agreed, but yet he *did not return* the documents and took them with him. Those are the facts. *I urgently ask the seven to follow up on this matter* and thus put an end to such dirty tricks in our party.

2) I do not agree with the seven regarding the publication of *only* Trotsky's article in its final version. First, Krupskaia's article[1] must be published as well. Second, it is quite possible to publish some documents (including my memo on Eastman's book) *after* Trotsky's article is published, in order to prove that Trotsky wrote the article only under pressure from the Russian Communist Party (otherwise Trotsky might appear as the savior of the party's prestige).

3) Report to me on the fate of Trotsky's and Krupskaia's articles on Eastman: Were they published in England or not? I have asked for this three times and still do not have an answer.

4) I still don't have an answer from you to my letter about Dneprostroi. Give your answer verbally to Tovstukha—he'll write me.

5) I don't believe that Trotsky "didn't read" Eastman's article that you sent out to Politburo members. Trotsky is putting you on.

6) I read Trotsky's "answers" to the German delegation.[2] I do not agree with everything in them. Does *Pravda* agree with them? This is a platform for Trotsky's group.

7) I am getting better. The Matsestinskii waters (near Sochi) are good for curing sclerosis, reviving the nerves, dilating the heart, and curing sciatica, gout, and rheumatism. I should send my wife here.

Regards,
J. Stalin

1. Krupskaia's article, "Pis'mo v redaktsiiu *Sunday Worker*" (Letter to the editor of the *Sunday Worker*) was published in the journal *Bolshevik*, 1925, no. 16: 71–73. [For an excerpt, see the appendix.]

2. In July and August 1925 a German workers' delegation visited the USSR. On 25 July, they met with Trotsky. Trotsky's answers to the delegation were published in *Pravda* on 29 July 1925.

Letter 7   [Later than 1 August 1925]

To the Seven:[1]

At one time, the seven decided to publish Trotsky's article and Krupskaia's letter about Eastman in the Russian press after they were printed in the foreign press. They should have already appeared abroad by now, but for some reason they have not been printed in our country, so I do not consider it superfluous to remind you of this. Their publication would be of great significance—especially now when Manuilskii has contrived to shuffle the deck and thus has unwittingly raised the question of the authenticity of Trotsky's article. If it [Trotsky's article] were to be printed here, the question of its authenticity would be removed by itself. And that would be a plus for the party, and not only our party, but the foreign Communist parties, especially the Communist parties of England and America.

J. Stalin

1. In the upper right-hand corner is Molotov's notation: "1925 = ?"

Letter 8
[9 August 1925]

Sochi 8/9/25

Com. Molotov,
  Read this letter to Bukharin.
  I received your letter of 5 August.
  1) Apparently, the appointment of Gei[1] occurred before you received my letter about the appointment of Shvernik or someone else as head of the Organizational and Assignment Department. We really did have an agreement about Gei, but later I changed my opinion, about which I informed you, but, unfortunately, too late. Well, let's see how Gei will behave. A decision that has been made twice is no longer worth changing.
  2) Regarding Dneprostroi. I am a little worried because the project sounds like hundreds of millions and people want to decide it at full tilt. Preventive measures should be taken before *it is too late*; moreover, you should try to prevent the interests of the cause from suffering and [you should] not hesitate even if Dzerzhinsky and Trotsky will be somewhat offended. *The matter has to be decided by the seven.*
  3) As for Manuilskii, there is some kind of misunderstanding here, if not blackmail. Once again I state that 1) I gave the documents to Manuilskii, with the knowledge of the seven, to enable him *to brief* the top officials of the Comintern, *and not for publication;* 2) I told Manuilskii about the publication abroad, *along with* the publication of the *final text* of Trotsky's article, of several other documents—exactly which documents would be (and could only be) decided by the seven; 3) *I did not give and could not have given* **any directives** *to Manuilskii on the publication of Trotsky's* **unfinished** *draft article,* since I stood for and continue to stand for the publication of Trotsky's article in its *best* and not its worst form; 4) I could not have given such a directive to Manuilskii at all, since I demanded from him before his departure abroad **the return** to the Central Committee *of all* documents (he agreed to

this, but, for some reason, he did not do this). Ask Manuilskii why he didn't return the documents before his departure.[2]

4) The printing of Krupskaia's letter was decided by the seven; the review was assigned to me, Bukharin, Rykov, and Zinoviev. Bukharin, Rykov, and I reviewed it and approved it. Zinoviev was absent. People have a surprisingly short memory, especially Bukharin.

5) The seven decided to publish Trotsky's article and Krupskaia's letter in the Russian press *after* their publication abroad, *without opening, however, in any way a [public] discussion on this issue.* It's possible that this decision has now been abrogated by the seven. That, of course, is their affair. But if it hasn't been abrogated, they should be published in our press. Can you report anything to me in this regard?

6) As for the publication of my memo on Eastman, we can talk about that when I get back from vacation. There's no hurry.

7) Tell Bukharin that *Pravda* must *comment* on Trotsky's replies if it doesn't agree with them.

8) How's Frunze's health?[3]

9) Kotovskii was killed under what circumstances! It's a pity, he was an outstanding person.[4]

Regards,
J. Stalin

Don't berate me for such a long letter.

1. The Politburo considered the decision to appoint Gei as head of the Organizational and Assignment Department of the Central Committee of the party on 27 July and 3 August 1925 (RTsKhIDNI f. 17, op. 3, d. 513, l. 6, and d. 514, l. 2).

2. A draft of Zinoviev's letter to Manuilskii dated 12 August 1925 has been preserved (ibid., f. 324, op. 1, d. 551, ll. 131–33):

> Com. Manuilskii. Because the mistake with the printing in *L'Humanité* of the first draft of Trotsky's statement in the form of a final draft is obviously becoming significant, I urge you to recollect in more detail:
> 1) Didn't I tell you that you had to start with the publication of Stalin's letter (the first) and then provide excerpts with commentaries for all the rest after some time?
> How do you explain that Stalin's letter did not appear in *L'Humanité* and that the first draft was called final?
> 2) Didn't I tell you that there was no final draft of Trotsky's statement yet, since talks and correspondence with him were still continuing?
> 3) Didn't I send you to the Secretariat of the Central Committee to obtain all the documents?
> 4) Didn't I tell you that the decision of the comrades working on the matter was to reveal how Trotsky had arrived at the final draft, that is, that he was forced to renounce Eastman? Didn't I tell you to print the draft itself (the final one) of Trotsky's statement with commentaries from *L'Humanité* and others only after the final draft appeared in the British press? Didn't I tell you at the same time of the decision to publish a pamphlet opposing Eastman in English by the British Communists Gallacher and Pollitt?

3. Frunze died on the operating table on 27 October 1925; some people at the time blamed Stalin for his death (cf. Roy Medvedev, *Let History Judge* [New York, 1971], 48)—U.S. Ed.

4. A draft of a short article by Stalin dedicated to the memory of Kotovskii has been preserved (RTsKhIDNI f. 558, op. 1, d. 2809):

I knew Com. Kotovskii as an exemplary party comrade, an experienced military organizer, and a seasoned commander. I especially remember him at the Polish front in 1920, when Com. Budenny broke through to Zhitomir at the rear of the Polish army, while Kotovskii led his cavalry brigade in desperately heroic raids on the Poles' Kiev army. He was a threat to the Poles, because he knew how to "pulverize" them like nobody else could, as the Red Army soldiers used to say back then. The bravest among our most modest commanders and the most modest among the brave—thus I remember Com. Kotovskii. Long live his memory and glory. J. Stalin.

Letter 9   [18 August 1925]

8/18

Com. Molotov,[1]

The letter from Manuilskii is cowardly and conniving.

I stand *entirely* by my **declaration** on the swindling and dirty tricks, despite the dissatisfaction of some comrades.

Kamenev's declaration that Stalin's main aim in this affair was to get his own memo about Eastman published—this I consider dishonest. He is measuring others using his own yardstick . . .

You and Bukharin did the wrong thing by voting against the proposal on the documents concerning Eastman.[2] You should not be barring the Central Committees of the foreign parties from receiving the documents about Eastman. Kamenev and Zinoviev want to establish the preconditions for making Trotsky's removal from the Central Committee necessary, but they will not succeed in this because they don't have supporting facts. In his answer to Eastman's book, Trotsky determined his fate, that is, he saved himself.

Regards,
J. Stalin

1. In the upper right-hand corner is Molotov's notation: "1925 = ?"
2. On 11 August 1925, Molotov sent Stalin a coded telegram (RTsKhIDNI f. 17, op. 1, d. 5389, l. 11):

> By a poll of the absent members of the seven, a vote was taken on the following proposal passed by the available members, with Bukharin and Molotov voting against it: "In reply to the Comintern's request, the Bolshevik delegation is permitted to transmit, as confidential material, material from the Politburo on the question of Eastman's book to the members of the central committees of foreign Communist parties."

Letter 10 [August 1925]

Com. Molotov,[1]

I received your letter of 20 August. I spoke with Bukharin today.

1) You are proposing an agenda of five questions for the plenum:[2] 1) Foreign Trade, 2) the trade unions; 3) the Comintern; 4) wages; 5) land reform in Central Asia. I *do not object* to such an agenda. It is important to prepare the question of wages (the planned increase of wages and so on). This item was raised by the seven, and Shmidt was assigned to prepare it apart from the Politburo. Put pressure on him. While the issue is being prepared, it should be run past the Politburo ahead of time. It would be good to add the issue of industrial construction, with a report by Feliks [Dzerzhinsky] or Piatakov. (Smilga should not stick his nose in this; he's a fake as an economic leader, and besides, this is not a question of the economy as a whole, but of industry.) If Feliks cannot give a report now, it can be tabled until the next plenum, but with the proviso that a firm guarantee must be given that *not one* factory *of national significance* will be built for this period without the Politburo's sanction.

2) Nothing should be formalized on the issue of the Ukrainian Poor Peasants' Committees. The decision of the Ukrainian Central Committee on this issue coincides entirely with the decisions of the XIV Party Conference. It would be better to place a *report* of the rural conference on the agenda of the Central Committee plenum in the form of a separate issue and to describe in this report the Poor Peasants' Committees, other peasant committees, and so on. In fact, this will confirm the decision of the Ukrainian Central Committee. You should do the report. Without fail.[3]

3) The economic plan can be placed on the agenda of the *next* plenum, *if it turns out to be necessary*, giving the report not to Gosplan but to Rykov (Council of Commissars) or Kamenev (Labor Defense Council) with the involvement of the Central Control Commission.

4) We'll speak later about the agenda for the Congress.

5) If you have time, write more—I will answer in detail (I have lots of time).

6) Bukharin says that you are now heavily overworked. I will try to be in Moscow on the 10th, or even earlier, in order to take off some of the load.

I'm healthy. I've made a fairly good recovery.

Regards,

Yours, J. Stalin

P.S. The theses on the trade unions are in general acceptable, but the individual formulations need reworking because they are weak and the individual formulations are insufficiently precise. They definitely have to be revised in the spirit of Andreev's well-known speech.

J. Stalin

---

1. In the upper right-hand corner is Molotov's notation: "8/1925=?"

2. The following questions were reviewed at the party plenum of 3–10 October 1925: 1) On Foreign Trade (Kuibyshev and Krasin reporting). 2) On the work of the trade unions (Tomskii reporting). 3) On wages (Shmidt reporting). 4) On the Central Committee's meeting on the work in the countryside (Molotov reporting). 5) On the current issues in agricultural policy (Kamenev reporting). 6) On the situation in the foreign Communist parties (Zinoviev reporting). 7) On the agenda, venue, and deadline for convening the XIV Party Congress (Molotov reporting). 8) On the dissolution of the wages commission of the Central Committee and Central Control Commission.

3. The Conference on the Work in the Countryside, at which Molotov spoke, approved the decision of the Ukrainian Central Committee to reorganize the committees of poor villagers [komnezamy] into voluntary organizations to help improve the farms of the poor peasants and middle peasants. The task of "unifying the peasantry to promote mutual aid and aid to those in need" was given to the "peasant committees" [krestkomy] (RTsKhIDNI f. 17, op. 2, d. 197, l. 57).

CHAPTER TWO

1926

THE LETTERS SHOW THAT Stalin was chiefly occupied with the struggle against his political opponents in 1926, just as he had been in 1925. After the final break with Zinoviev and Kamenev at the XIV Party Congress in late 1925, Stalin and his supporters were soon faced with a united opposition headed by Trotsky, Zinoviev, and Kamenev that coalesced by the middle of 1926. In late 1925 and early 1926, relative calm could be observed in the high echelons of power. The two sides were waiting each other out, watching one another, analyzing the new situation, and, for a time, avoiding open polemics. A reflection of this situation was the August Guralski and Vojskov Vujovich affair. V. V. Kuibyshev spoke about it in some detail at the July plenum of the Central Committee and Central Control Commission:

> I believe that I must read aloud the appropriate documents . . . so that all the plenum members can see how attempts to factionalize were made soon after the Party Congress, . . . they . . . finally culminated in a real factional fight. In light of recent events, this Guralski and Vujovich affair is of particular interest.
>
> The Politburo has in its possession a letter . . . from Gertrud Gessler, member of the Communist Party of France:
>
> Moscow.
> 10/1/1926
> On 3 January Comrade Guralski approached me and asked me to come to his room to discuss a certain matter.
> Comrade Vujovich was also there. I was offered a trip to carry out the following assignment for the opposition of the Russian [Com-

munist] Party. I was to travel to Berlin, Paris, and perhaps Rome to meet with certain leading party comrades in order to persuade them not to take a definite position with regard to the party discussion in Russia. I was to report to them that the situation in Russia was not at all clear, that within a short time the mood in the party would change completely and turn to the left, and that, for two months at least, the large foreign parties should not take a stand in favor of the Central Committee of the Russian Party . . . I was supposed to inform everyone that the opposition was held hostage in Russia and was denied the opportunity to communicate with those abroad.

From the first moment it was clear that this was a question of a dangerous factional fight on an international scale, and I agreed to accept the assignment for the time being in order to follow developments.

. . . Several times I specifically asked who I was supposed to represent when I arrived in Europe, and I always received the same answer, that I was traveling on behalf of the opposition of the Russian Communist Party and that three people had direct responsibility: Guralski, Vujovich, and Zinoviev. On Friday the 8th, I saw Guralski—and was alone with him again—and he informed me that the whole affair was off, since a truce had been declared the previous evening between both factions of the party on the Comintern question for a period of six months. Guralski informed me that the Politburo had made substantial concessions to his group on the previous evening and that it had been decided that the Comintern work should be allowed to proceed calmly without major changes. He himself had spent almost the entire evening with Zinoviev and Piatnitskii in order to discuss various lines of work, and, on this basis, it was decided within the opposition at Com. Kamenev's suggestion that the entire plan for my trip was to remain in effect for the present. Guralski himself supposed that this whole compromise would fall apart within two months and [suggested that] I should be prepared to arrange things so that I could leave afterward. Of course, he said, Piatnitskii wasn't there when this was decided; only Guralski, Zinoviev, and Kamenev were present. Gertrud Gessler, member of the Communist Party of France.

This statement from Com. Gessler was discussed in a special commission made up of Coms. Piatnitskii, Lozovskii, and Manuilskii. This commission received the assignment from the Russian delegation, interrogated Guralski, Vujovich, Roy, and Gessler, and established that

1) Com. Guralski, together with Com. Vujovich, attempted in early January of this year to send a special agent to make the rounds of the

most important Comintern sections (France, Germany, and Italy) for the purpose of conducting factional work; 2) while sharing the views of the Leningrad opposition, they acted on their own personal behalf and used the name of Com. Zinoviev for factional aims . . .; 5) when confronted with Com. Gessler's letter, Guralski tried to disparage the testimonies of comrades who had fulfilled their party duty, claiming that people had been sent to him to provoke him into a factional act. [The commission concluded:]

. . . On the basis of this information, the commission resolves to limit itself to a strict reprimand of Coms. Guralski and Vujovich and, in light of Guralski's particularly active role in this attempt to create a faction, to remove him from work in the Comintern and to reassign him at the discretion of the Central Committee.

The laxity of this resolution in comparison to the deed committed by Guralski and Vujovich, in addition to the mitigating circumstances cited, is motivated by the necessity to avoid complications in the work of the Comintern and to quickly eliminate by internal party means the aftermath of the disputes at the XIV Party Congress.

19 January 1926. Signed: Piatnitskii. D. Manuilskii. A. Lozovskii.

This resolution was later confirmed by the Politburo on 11 February. Thus both the commission and the Politburo saw this attempt by Vujovich and Guralski (Guralski is a member of the Russian [Communist] Party) to create factions in the foreign Communist parties as a sequel to the disputes at the XIV Party Congress. . . . Despite the fact that the Politburo's work [had been hampered by] many indications of factional intolerance and frequent continuation of former mistakes, both the Central Control Commission and the Politburo considered it possible to believe that the opposition would work in harmony with the party's decisions.[1]

The period of relative calm in the internal party struggle did not last long. One cause of renewed clashes between the united opposition and the Stalinist majority was events in Great Britain. On 1 May 1926, a miners' strike began. On 4 May, the General Council of the British Trades Union Congress declared a general strike in support of the miners. But on 12 May, by a ruling of the same General Council, the general strike was halted. At the same time, the General Council refused to accept money from the Soviet trade unions sent to aid the striking British workers. The united opposi-

1. RTsKhIDNI f. 17, op. 2, d. 246, vyp. 4, ll. 1–5.

tion claimed that the events in Great Britain proved that Stalin and Bukharin had been mistaken in their policy on the international trade union movement. Zinoviev, then chairman of the Comintern Executive Committee, prepared theses on the lessons of the British strike. The majority of the Politburo rejected them, and Bukharin prepared countertheses that defended cooperation with the social democratic trade unions. Bukharin's theses were accepted by the Politburo.

Having prevailed on the issue of the British strike, the Politburo majority adopted an active offensive against the opposition. Stalin formulated the program and conception of this overall offensive frankly in his letter to Molotov of 15 June 1926 (letter 20). The chief pretext for the new attack against the opposition was the so-called Lashevich affair.

On Sunday, 6 June 1926, about seventy Communists from the Krasnopresnenskii District in Moscow gathered at a dacha along the Savelovskaia rail line. The meeting had been initiated by a group of former district committee party workers who had joined the opposition. They invited M. M. Lashevich—an old Bolshevik, then first deputy of the USSR Revolutionary Military Council, and a supporter of Zinoviev—to speak at the meeting. A participant at the gathering then informed M. N. Riutin, secretary of the Krasnopresnenskii District Party Committee, about the meeting. Riutin, in turn, sent a dossier to the Central Committee. On 8 or 9 June, a specially created investigative body of the Central Control Commission interrogated the known participants at the meeting.[2] On the basis of these materials, the meeting was characterized as underground and factional. On 12 June, based on the report of the investigative commission, the Central Control Commission issued penalties against seven of the participants. Lashevich was given a strict reprimand with a warning. The Central Control Commission also decided to propose that the next plenum of the Central Committee expel Lashevich from the Central Committee, remove him immediately from his position at the Revolutionary Military Council, and deny him the right to occupy any responsible posts for a period of two years.[3]

2. Ibid., d. 695, ll. 10–35.
3. Ibid., f. 613, op. 1, d. 46, ll. 21–22.

The initial inspection by the investigative commission did not establish that any other people had been involved in the case except those who had actually attended the meeting. But Stalin was still dissatisfied. As can be seen from his letter to Molotov of 25 June (letter 21), Stalin decided to link the case of Lashevich with Zinoviev and thereby strike a blow against the opposition. He was able to realize his plan at the July 1926 plenum of the Central Committee and Central Control Commission. Just as Stalin had suggested, the Lashevich affair virtually became the Zinoviev affair at the plenum. Furthermore, the evidence concerning dissent and factional activities gathered by the Central Control Commission and OGPU (for example, the "affairs" of Medvedev, Guralski, and Vujovich) were presented at the plenum, once again in complete accord with Stalin's proposals, as links of a single chain and a manifestation of the vigorous activity of a powerful, conspiratorial oppositional organization. The plenum thus asserted that "the opposition has decided to cross the boundary between legitimately promoting its views and creating an illegal all-union organization, opposing itself to the party and thus paving the way for a split in the party's ranks."[4] The plenum laid the political responsibility at Zinoviev's door and expelled him from the Politburo.

After the July plenum, the removal of opposition members from the ruling party and state bodies was accelerated. In October 1926, a joint Central Committee and Central Control Commission plenum resolved to remove Zinoviev from the post of chairman of the Comintern, to dismiss Trotsky from the Politburo, and to dismiss Kamenev as a candidate member of the Politburo.

One of the last episodes in the trouncing of the opposition in 1926 was the conflict with Kamenev described by Stalin in a letter dated 23 December (letter 30). In a speech at a session of the VII expanded plenum of the Comintern on 15 December 1926, Stalin noted that in March 1917, Kamenev had sent a telegram of greetings from his Achinsk exile to the Provisional Government and to Great Prince Mikhail Romanov (who was briefly tsar after Nicholas abdicated). Stalin also claimed that in April 1917 at the VII Confer-

4. *KPSS v rezoliutsiiakh* (Resolutions of the CPSU), vol. 4 (Moscow, 1984), 49–50.

ence of the Bolshevik party this fact almost cost Kamenev his membership in the Central Committee; only Lenin's intervention saved him from losing the election.

Kamenev, supported by Zinoviev and Trotsky, made a speech of rebuttal. According to his statement, the Siberian newspaper *Yeniseiskii kray* [Yenisey region] of 8 March 1917, had been the first to print the false information about the telegram of greetings. Several weeks later, this article had been reprinted in Petrograd by opponents of the Bolsheviks. On 8 April 1917, *Pravda* carried a rebuttal. The incident was closed and the question of the greeting was never raised again, even at the VII Party Conference. Kamenev's version was confirmed by numerous testimonies submitted by the opposition to the Central Committee from eyewitnesses who had been political exiles in Achinsk in 1917 and delegates at the VII Party Conference. On 16 December 1926, Zinoviev, Smilga, and G. F. Fedorov, members of the Central Committee elected in 1917 to the VII Party Conference and supporters of Kamenev, made an official statement to the Politburo about the telegram. They also affirmed that the Kamenev telegram had never existed and that the issue had never come up during the elections at the Party Conference. The opposition demanded that their statement be published in *Pravda*.

On 18 December 1926, the Politburo majority approved the official text of a reply to the statement from Zinoviev, Smilga, and Fedorov, which stated in part:

> The Politburo considers the incident at the VII expanded plenum of the Comintern Executive Committee an incident that does not have any direct relationship to fundamental disagreements. For this reason, the Politburo, not wishing to overshadow fundamental issues with the issue of one of Com. Kamenev's mistakes (although a severe one), does not consider it expedient to publish the statement made by Com. Zinoviev and the other comrades in the daily newspapers.[5]

As a result, the opposition members' statement was placed in *Bolshevik* (1926, nos. 23–24), along with documents that refuted the version of the story given by Kamenev and his supporters. The selection of documents included an official statement, "From the

5. RTsKhIDNI f. 17, op. 3, d. 607, l. 7.

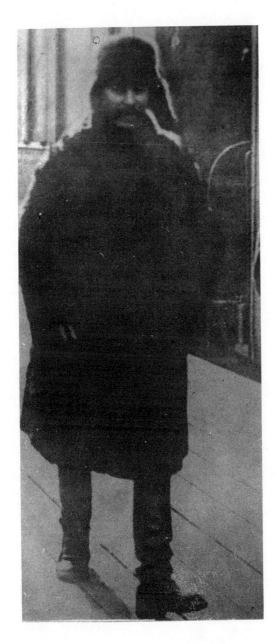

Stalin

Здравствуй!

Приехал на место в воскре-
сенье вечером. Погода пока
не важная. Виды на урожай
по Сев. Кав-зу хорошие. Хорошо.

Бухарин рассказывал,
что: 1) Троцкий был в Москве еще
в среду утром; 2) к нему ез-
дил в Берлин Преображенский
(на свидание?). Интересно.

Ну, всего хорошего.

И. Сталин

Понедельник. Сочи.

Letter from Stalin to Molotov, [24 May 1926] (RTsKhIDNI f. 558, op. 1, d. 5388, l. 18).

Central Committee of the All-Union Communist Party (Bolshevik)," which outlined the position of the Politburo majority, and a reprint of the article from the newspaper *Yeniseiskii kray* of 8 March 1917, without any commentary or mention that this article had been refuted by *Pravda* in April 1917. The published documents included several selected statements from witnesses among the exiles who confirmed the facts outlined in *Yeniseiskii kray* and from several delegates to the April Party Conference who supported Stalin's version of the events.

Thus the selection of materials placed in *Bolshevik* was openly tendentious. Not a single one of the numerous documents collected by the opposition members to counter the charges was even mentioned; all of them have remained in the archives to this day. Meanwhile, Stalin gleefully told Molotov of the latest victory over the opposition, gloating over its weakness and powerlessness.

Letter 11   [24 May 1926]

Hello,[1]

I got here Sunday evening. The weather was lousy. The harvest outlook in the North Caucasus is good. That's good.

Belenkii told me that 1) Trotsky was back in Moscow as early as Wednesday morning; 2) Preobrazhenskii went to visit him in Berlin (for a rendevous?).[2] Interesting.

> Well, all the best,
> J. Stalin
> *Monday. Sochi.*

1. Molotov's notation in the upper right-hand corner: "1926=?"
2. In the spring of 1926, Trotsky and his wife were in Berlin for medical treatment (see L. Trotsky, *Moia zhizn'* [My life] [Moscow, 1991], 496).

Letter 12   [26 May 1926]

Hello again,[1]

Since you are all busy with large matters, some trivial matters may slip by you. I think it won't be out of order to remind you of several necessary details:

1) You must remind Bukharin of the article against the "workers' opposition." It shouldn't be put off any longer. It must be written immediately. It's more advantageous for us if Bukharin writes it, and not Grisha [Zinoviev], who has criminally missed all deadlines.[2] It would be strategically advantageous if Bukharin would write it. Bukharin is fully within his rights to do so, since Grisha has sabotaged the assignment from the Politburo.[3]

2) We must publish the **complete** text of the resolution of our workers (from all regions) in support of the British strikers in general and the coal miners in particular in **all** the most important languages of the West as quickly as possible. I think it should be published in the form of a brochure with a foreword by Bukharin or Tomskii. Neither Grisha nor Lozovskii are needed here. The preface should be written by either Bukharin or Tomskii. This is a fighting matter and should not be allowed to fall by the wayside. It can be published by the Trade Union Council or the State Publishing House. It shouldn't be published by Comintern itself—this can do harm. Better have it come from the trade unions.[4]

3) Tell me something about that alarming matter that Uglanov and Yagoda reported to us.[5] If everything's all right, telegraph the message "Feeling fine"; if things are bad, telegraph in code the message "Feeling sick."

That's it for now. The weather has gotten better.

26/5/26
J. Stalin

1. Molotov's notation on this letter is: "5/26/1926."

2. In 1924, S. P. Medvedev, a leader of the former "workers' opposition," drafted a letter criticizing the party's policy (published in *Kommunisticheskaia oppozitsiia v SSSR, 1923–27* [Communist opposition in the USSR, 1923–27], 4 vols. [Benson, Vt.: Chalidze Publications, 1988], 1:90–101). The letter was distributed among some members of the Baku Party Organization. At that time, several Communists expelled from the Communist Party in Baku were charged with attempting to create an "underground opposition group," whose ideological mentor was Medvedev and another leader of the former "workers' opposition," A. G. Shliapnikov. Zinoviev was assigned to write an article criticizing Medvedev's "platform." He did not carry out this assignment, however. On 10 July 1926, *Pravda* carried an editorial, "Rightist Danger in Our Party," with a detailed analysis and severe criticism of Medvedev's letter. From all indications this editorial was written by Bukharin.

3. From Stalin's speech on 15 July 1926, at the party plenum (RTsKhIDNI f. 17, op. 2, d. 246, vyp. 1, ll. 75, 76):

> Com. Zinoviev agreed to write an article criticizing Medvedev. Why didn't he write it? Why has he dragged this out a year and not spoken against Medvedev? . . . Why has Com. Zinoviev sabotaged the decision for a whole year, although he himself agreed to criticize Medvedev's Menshevist letter? Why? Yesterday he tried to explain this as follows: since there was a marked tendency to the right in the party, I, Zinoviev, decided to spare Medvedev [as a representative of the left—U.S. Ed.]. . . .
>
> Com. Trotsky feigns surprise that we are raising the issue of the Medvedev letter precisely now, when it was written a year ago. And in fact why was there such a delay? Because we waited a year for Com. Zinoviev, who sabotaged the Politburo's decision. Because about three months ago the Central Committee received a statement from Comrades Shliapnikov and Medvedev in which not only do they fail to renounce the letter from Com. Medvedev, but, on the contrary, they demand that it be printed in *Pravda*. Because back in April of this year, after receiving the statement from Comrades Shliapnikov and Medvedev, I sent the members of the Central

Committee a letter with my signature in which I once again reminded Com. Zinoviev of his duty to criticize the Medvedev letter. I received no reply to this letter whatsoever. . . .

Allow me to read some extracts from my letter: "Some time ago the so-called workers' opposition provided a platform of its views in the form of the well-known letter by Com. Medvedev to members of the 'workers' opposition' in Baku. This platform of the 'workers' opposition' states that the policy of the Comintern is leading 'to the disorganization of the workers' movement in that country [the reference is to Norway—J. Stalin] and to the establishment of "Communist" parties with few material resources. They are maintained at the expense of the Russian workers, using resources that cost them blood and sacrifices but which they themselves cannot enjoy under current conditions,' that 'in reality hordes of petit bourgeois timeservers are created; maintained on Russian gold, they depict themselves as the proletariat and represent themselves in the Comintern as the most revolutionary workers.' The platform goes on to say that 'our [that is, the "workers' opposition"—J. Stalin] evaluation of the Western European social democratic parties differs profoundly from those evaluations that are given by our leaders [that is, the Central Committee—J. Stalin].' Finally the platform states that 'we [that is, the "workers' opposition"—J. Stalin] consider that associations like the "Trade Union International" [Profintern] are in practice, deliberately or not, an instrument for creating a gulf between, on the one hand, the worker masses of Russia and the Communist masses of Western Europe and, on the other hand, the decisive mass of the entire proletariat. It is a direct hindrance, unjustified by the real situation, to an authentic united front of the working class within each country and at the international level.' . . .

The Central Committee assigned Com. Zinoviev to publish a statement in the press against the letter . . . , but Com. Zinoviev for more than a year now has not seen fit to fulfill this assignment. . . . Is it not clear that Com. Zinoviev needs to remain silent about the 'workers' opposition' in order to secure himself the bloc he is establishing with that very 'workers' opposition'? Are Com. Zinoviev and Com. Medvedev in agreement that the Communist parties in the West are not authentic workers' parties but 'hordes of petit bourgeois timeservers'? Yes or no? Are Com. Zinoviev and Com. Medvedev in agreement that Amsterdam is more valuable than the Profintern, that the Profintern should be liquidated? Yes or no? If Com. Zinoviev is not in agreement with these fundamental points of the 'workers' opposition,' then [why] is he forming a bloc with it at the present moment, and why is he not fulfilling the Central Committee's decision about publishing a statement against the platform of the 'workers' opposition'? What does all this tell us? That Com. Trotsky and Com. Zinoviev have formed a bloc with the 'workers' opposition.'

In his statement to the Central Committee on 18 July 1926, Zinoviev wrote (ibid., d. 696, ll. 46, 47):

More than a year ago, with . . . the seven, the question was raised whether or not to make a statement in the press against Medvedev's letter. I held the opinion that we should have an article in *Bolshevik* and publish Com. Medvedev's letter itself in full. I have not changed my opinion. Even now I consider that it would be correct to publish the letter itself in the party's theoretical organ and to provide a serious and sharp analysis of it. Among the seven, Comrade Stalin at first considered that this wasn't necessary, and then was inclined to say that perhaps we should try to write such an article. The factional seven expressed the opinion that I should write this article. [After Zinoviev joined with Trotsky, he condemned the seven as a factional organization—U.S. Ed.] I did not write it partly because I was overloaded with other work but partly because the mood in the seven was hesitant: there wasn't a firm decision to definitely publish an article. Over the course of the next year and later, no one from the seven ever reminded me even once that this article had to be written. . . . The claim that the Central Committee of our party gave me an assignment to publish an article against Com. Medvedev is a lie. It never happened.

No Politburo decision to assign Zinoviev the task of writing this article has been found.

4. In 1926, the Trade Union Council published a collection in Russian, *Angliiskaia stachka i rabochie SSSR* (The British strike and Soviet workers), simultaneously issuing it in German in Moscow and Berlin.

5. The editors were unable to determine the reference here.

Letter 13

[1 June 1926]

CODED TELEGRAM FROM MOLOTOV AND BUKHARIN TO STALIN[1]

On 28 May, Molotov sent you a detailed letter about Zinoviev's theses on the lessons of the British strikes. We believe that it is extremely important for you to study these theses immediately and send us your opinion. Zinoviev is reevaluating our analysis of capitalist stabilization and the tactics of the Comintern, slinging mud at the Comintern's existing policy, and making references to the party and to individual Central Committee members as he did earlier in "Philosophy of the Era,"[2] and he is ready to take upon himself the initiative of breaking immediately with the General Council. Trotsky also advocates a demonstrative break with the General Council. I believe this is consummate stupidity of the "recallist"[3] variety and the Central Committee should ruthlessly oppose it. Opportunism disguised by "leftist" phrases should be exposed. Zinoviev's theses must be refuted and opposed with politically precise theses from the Central Committee, including our right and duty to criticize ruthlessly and expose the rightists and all the leftists of the General Council, but without initiating a break with the General Council. Among us there is full unanimity on the basic point. Bukharin prefers not to present our own countertheses but to make instead appropriate corrections to Zinoviev's theses. We are postponing a discussion of the British lessons for five days while we think over our theses. We're expecting your immediate reply. Zinoviev made a speech at Sverdlov University[4] in the spirit of his theses. Trotsky echoed him. Bukharin spoke out against them without naming names.

Molotov. Bukharin.

1. The telegram is printed on a form from the party's Transcaucasian Regional Committee. In the upper part of the form is written: "Tiflis. Transcaucasian Regional Committee. Decipher in the presence of Com. Ordzhonikidze. Hand deliver to Com. Stalin" (RTsKhIDNI f. 82, op. 1, d. 144, l. 1).

2. An article by G. Ye. Zinoviev (frequently reprinted, for example, G. Ye. Zinoviev, "Filosofiia epokhi," Leningrad, Priboy, 1925; Moscow, Moskovskiy rabochiy, 1925, etc.).

3. "Recallist" is a label given to a Bolshevik faction that refused to work within a bourgeois institution like a parliament or a trade union—U.S. Ed.

4. The Sverdlov Communist University, a party-run academy for training party and Soviet personnel.

Letter 14

[1 June 1926]

CODED TELEGRAM FROM MOLOTOV TO STALIN[1]

Bukharin is writing countertheses to Zinoviev's. Zinoviev and Trotsky are causing us to be in a terrible rush. In my view, our theses must provide a determined attack against Zinoviev and Trotsky's attempts to conduct a radical although cowardly review of the policy of the Comintern, the party, and the Trade Union Council; our theses should expose not only ultra-leftism but that which screens it, that is, leftism in the Comintern, as Lenin taught. The opportunistic "recallism" on the matter of the break with the General Council must be exposed. Simultaneously we must: 1) emphasize the conditional nature of the stabilization and the growth of complications that may lead to revolution in the capitalist countries, although the outcome may go either way; 2) [emphasize] the betrayal of the rightists and the capitulation of the leftists in the General Council; in fact the leftists bear the main objective responsibility for this, because they have a majority in the General Council; 3) demonstrate that we have joined and can remain in the Anglo-Soviet [sic] Committee,[2] for the sake of contact with the masses of British workers, without restricting in any way our right to criticize any action by the General Council or our support of the revolutionary elements of the British workers' movement. The Communist Party of England should be decisively defended against Trotsky's charge in *Pravda* of 26 May that it is an element of "unrevolutionary inhibition." Your opinion is needed immediately. It would be better if you came in person to Moscow; then (we) would postpone the decision on the British issue until 7 June. Awaiting your reply.

Molotov

1. In the upper part of the telegram is written: "Decipher in the presence of Com. Ordzhonikidze. Hand deliver to Com. Stalin" (RTsKhIDNI f. 82, op. 1, d. 144, l. 2).

2. The Anglo-Russian Committee, a joint committee of the trade unions of Great Britain and the USSR, was created in London on 6–8 April 1925 at a conference of representatives of the Soviet Trade Union Council and the General Council of the British Trades Union Congress (TUC). It was dissolved in September 1927 after diplomatic relations between Great Britain and the USSR were broken off.

Letter 15 [2 June 1926]

CODED TELEGRAM FROM STALIN TO MOLOTOV[1]

2 June 1926

Moscow

Central Committee

To Molotov:

I received the coded telegram today. I haven't received Molotov's letter yet. I will read the theses immediately and report back to you. I don't understand how they can rush you when you have the majority. Postpone the matter for another week and tell them to go to hell. The matter of the theses is an important one, and we have to think it through without haste. Apparently they want to take advantage of the British issue in order to get back everything they had lost before. They must be put in their place.

Stalin

1. RTsKhIDNI f. 558, op. 1, d. 3263, l. 1.

Letter 16

[3 June 1926]

CODED TELEGRAM FROM STALIN TO MOLOTOV[1]

Central Committee

All-Union Communist Party

Com. Molotov,

Decipher Immediately

Basically Grisha's [Zinoviev's] theses proceed from the premise that 1) stabilization is ending or has already ended; 2) we are entering into or have already entered into a phase of revolutionary explosions; 3) the tactic of gathering forces and working in the reactionary trade unions is losing its viability and is receding into the background; 4) the tactic of a united front has outlived itself; 5) we must build our own trade unions by relying on the "minorities" movement. Hence Grisha's proposal to take upon himself the initiative for an outright break with the General Council.

In the given historical circumstances, this entire premise, in my view, is fundamentally incorrect because it plays into the hands of Amsterdam[2] and the Second International[3] and dooms our Communist parties to sectarianism.

I think that:

1) Stabilization has not ended, although it [circumstances] has been and continues to be shaky;

2) The provocation of the [general] strike by the British Conservatives was capital's attempt to solidify stabilization—that is, in this case, capital, not the revolution, was on the attack.

3) This attempt did not lead to a strengthening of stabilization, nor could it. But it also did not lead to a triumphant development of the workers' revolutionary struggle or to the destruction of stabilization; moreover, as a result of the strike, some categories of workers were not able to preserve even their former conditions of work and struggle.

4) As a result, we do not have a new phase of stormy onslaught by the revolution but a continuing stabilization, temporary, not enduring, but stabilization nonetheless, fraught with new attempts by capital to make new attacks on the workers, who continue to be forced to defend themselves.

5) Our task is to continue to gather forces and [form] a real united front; to prepare the working class to resist new attacks by capital; to turn this defense

into a broad-based revolutionary attack by the proletariat against capital, into a transition to a struggle for power.

6) Hence the need for more intense work by the Communists in the reactionary trade unions for the purpose of internally transforming them and of taking control of them.

7) Hence the need for a determined struggle against Zinoviev and Trotsky, who have been advocating splitting the trade union movement and have opposed a united front, to the advantage of Oudegeest and Sassenbach.

8) Hence a determined struggle against Zinoviev and Trotsky, who are pushing the British trade union movement into the arms of Amsterdam and the American Federation of Labor (AFL).

9) Hence a decisive rebuttal of Zinoviev and Trotsky's line, which leads to the Communist parties' isolation from the masses and to the abandonment of the masses to a monopoly of leadership by reformers.

10) Hence a decisive rebuttal of any attempt to take upon ourselves the initiative of splitting the [Soviet] Trade Union Council from the British trade union movement, since a break with the General Council under these conditions must lead to a break with the trade unions of England in favor of Amsterdam.

11) The break with the General Council will surely lead to a disruption in the policy of a unified trade union movement in France and Germany as well, since the reformers in France and Germany are no better than the British reformers.

12) Work with the Profintern[4] and the "minorities" must be stepped up and their authority increased.

13) The British Communist Party must be unconditionally defended against Zinoviev and Trotsky's efforts to discredit it.

14) A number of the practical proposals made by Com. Lozovskii should be approved, and complete agreement should be established between Tomskii and Lozovskii.

15) Ruthless criticism of centrists and leftists in the General Council is absolutely necessary.

16) This criticism does not and cannot exclude the possibility [and] the necessity of preserving the Anglo-Soviet [sic] Committee.[5]

17) Separately from the Comintern theses, we should make a decision to have the Trade Union Council pass a resolution (after hearing a report by [its] presidium concerning the results of the May strike) criticizing the treachery of the rightists and the lack of character of the leftists. The resolution should be broadcast over the radio and also sent to the British Communist Party and the [trade union] minority as well as to the General Council for their information.

18) The trade union minority and the British Communist Party should launch a vigorous campaign for new elections to the executive committees of the unions and the General Council aiming at the expulsion of the Thomas traitors[6] and their hangers-on among the leftists; the British party should support their replacement with new revolutionary leaders.

19) Bukharin's theses should take account of the decisions of the Politburo

and its British Commission[7] about the British strike, keeping in mind that Zinoviev has broken with these decisions in his theses.

20) Zinoviev's theses must be completely refuted as liquidationist[8] and replaced by our theses.

21) The rejection of Grisha's theses could lead to threats of resignation which should not frighten you in any way.

22) I don't think my trip is necessary.

23) If talks are still needed on a direct line, then send a note over the wire and I will answer.

Sent June 3

J. Stalin

1. RTsKhIDNI f. 558, op. 1, d. 3266, ll. 1, 2.

2. The Amsterdam International of Trade Unions was an international association of trade unions formed in July 1919 at a congress in Amsterdam. Soviet trade unions did not join. The Amsterdam International of Trade Unions was condemned as reformist in the USSR.

3. The International Association of Socialist Parties, founded in Paris in 1889. The Bolsheviks countered it with the III Communist International, founded in Moscow in 1919. The II International was condemned in the USSR as opportunist and social-reformist.

4. The Profintern (Red International of Trade Unions) was an international organization of leftist trade unions that existed from 1921 to 1931 under the influence of the USSR.

5. The Anglo-Russian Committee, a joint committee of the trade unions of Great Britain and the USSR, was created in London on 6–8 April 1925 at a conference of representatives of the Soviet Trade Union Council and the General Council of the British Trades Union Congress (TUC). It was dissolved in September 1927 after diplomatic relations between Great Britain and the USSR were broken off.

6. James Henry Thomas is used here as a symbol of the moderate trade union leaders that Communists felt had betrayed the working class by calling off the general strike—U.S. Ed.

7. No information was found in Politburo minutes concerning the creation and activity of the British Commission of the Politburo.

8. The Liquidators were a movement within Russian Marxism that allegedly favored liquidating the underground party and preserving only the legal institutions—U.S. Ed.

Letter 17

[3 June 1926]

CODED TELEGRAM FROM STALIN TO MOLOTOV[1]

Moscow

Central Committee

All-Union Communist Party

Com. Molotov,

Decipher Immediately

Ending of Coded Telegram No.[2]

In Bukharin's theses, you must definitely note Zinoviev's very important mistakes on the matter of the British strike, on Pilsudski,[3] and on the Chinese revolution[4] and criticize them thoroughly in whatever way you choose, because these mistakes are in the air and find support among those in the Comintern with rightist tendencies.

1) At the very first session of the Politburo during the start of the British strike, Zinoviev came with a draft of directives for the British Communists that he had developed with the help of certain Comintern members who are among those sympathizing with the opposition. In the draft, as Politburo members well know, there turned out not to be a single word on the need to shift the general strike toward greater political struggle; nor was there any hint of the slogan "Down with the Conservative government, long live the workers' government." The majority of the Politburo introduced this new directive and new slogan into Zinoviev's draft as amendments that Zinoviev was obliged to accept. This omission of the most important slogan about the strike movement in England is not trivial; it plays into Thomas's hands.[5] There is no guarantee that such mistakes will not be repeated in the work of Zinoviev and his supporters. In order to protect the party from such blatant mistakes, Zinoviev's mistakes must be discussed in our theses.

2) At the notorious Politburo session about a month ago, Zinoviev came with a purely liquidationist proposal about the desirability of the Communist Party quitting the Kuomintang,[6] thus [leaving it] in the hands of its right wing. When the Politburo majority remarked that Zinoviev's proposal would lead to the liquidation of the revolutionary movement in China, Zinoviev and Radek, after unsuccessful attempts to defend their proposal, were forced to withdraw it and accept the Politburo's proposal to intensify the work of the Communist Party within the Kuomintang and to concentrate our efforts against the right wing within the Kuomintang. Since there is no guarantee that Zinoviev won't make such a mistake again, it's essential to discuss this in our theses.

3) At a meeting of the Politburo's Polish Commission,[7] on the day the first reports were received about Pilsudski's taking Warsaw, Zinoviev presented, in the presence of Unshlikht, Dzerzhinsky, Domski, Wenecki, and many others, a draft of directives to the Polish Communists, saying that the Communists' neutrality in Pilsudski's struggle with the fascists was impermissible. Thus according to Zinoviev's theses, Pilsudski is viewed as an antifascist and the Pilsudski movement is viewed as a revolutionary movement, but there is not a single word about the fact that Communist support of Pilsudski is even more impermissible.

The majority of the commission introduced a basic amendment on the impermissibility of supporting Pilsudski, and Zinoviev was obliged to accept this amendment, revising the entire draft of the directive. I am certain that the mistakes of the Polish Communists about which Zinoviev so gleefully writes now are entirely a reflection of Zinoviev's deeply opportunistic view of the alleged revolutionary nature of the Pilsudski adventure. Because there is no guarantee that these mistakes will not be repeated, it is essential to take account of them in Bukharin's theses. In informing you about all this, I ask you to circulate this document among our closest friends.

3 June, 9:00 P.M.

Stalin

1. RTsKhIDNI f. 558, op. 1, d. 5297.

2. No telegram number was provided in the original.

3. In May 1926, as a result of Pilsudski's military coup, the so-called Sanats regime was established in Poland.

4. On the debates between the Politburo majority and the opposition concerning the issue of the Chinese revolution and the policy regarding the Kuomintang, see the letters for 1927.

5. James Henry Thomas is used here as a symbol of the moderate trade union leaders that Communists felt had betrayed the working class by calling off the general strike—U.S. Ed.

6. The Kuomintang (National People's Party) was founded in 1912 and was the ruling party in China from the mid-1920s through the 1940s.

7. No information about the creation or activity of the Politburo's Polish Commission has been discovered in the Politburo minutes.

Letter 18

[3 June 1926]

CODED TELEGRAM FROM TOVSTUKHA TO STALIN[1]

Sent from Moscow, 3 June 1926

Received and deciphered June 3

Tiflis, Transcaucasian Regional Committee

To: Ordzhonikidze

Decipher immediately for Com. Stalin

Yesterday countertheses about England, signed by Bukharin, Tomskii, and Molotov, were sent out to all the members of the Politburo. The remainder have given their consent in full. Today the British issues were discussed at the Politburo, with a transcript made at Zinoviev's insistence. We received your telegram during the meeting. We state our absolute agreement with you, including the details. The battle at the Politburo was tremendous—six hours. Trotsky voted in favor of Zinoviev. Zinoviev's theses were rejected. The theses of the three were accepted in principle and sent to the commission. Zinoviev demanded that he be allowed to defend his point of view in the Comintern. The Politburo declined his request. Trotsky also voted against this. Details to follow in a letter. We're sending the theses of the three today to Sergo [Ordzhonikidze]. We are also sending them to Sochi.

Tovstukha

1. RTsKhIDNI f. 558, op. 1, d. 3266, l. 3.

Letter 19 [4 June 1926]

CODED TELEGRAM FROM STALIN TO MOLOTOV[1]

Moscow

Central Committee

All-Union Communist Party

Decipher Immediately
    The coded telegram was received. I knew that there would be complete agreement. Continue on in the same spirit. Greetings.

Stalin

Deciphered and sent on 4 June, 11:00 A.M.

1. RTsKhIDNI f. 558, op. 1, d. 3340.

Letter 20 [15 June 1926]

6/16/26

Greetings, Molotov,

Greetings, Bukharin,

I returned to Sochi today, 15 June. In Tiflis I came down with a stomachache (I got food poisoning from some fish) and am now having a hard time recovering. Today I read your letters (undated) and Bukharin's letter (also undated). My opinion:

1) Your theses turned out nicely. Grisha [Zinoviev] should be exposed on the Polish issue as well, since he himself *dragged* Warski into it and now tries to foist him on you. Really, Grisha's brazenness knows no bounds.

2) There was no need to tell the Comintern that the theses passed *unanimously*. The unanimity was *formal*, but in reality there was no unanimity whatsoever. To cover up the disagreement with Grisha **now** would mean to abet him in his anti-party work and put ourselves in a stupid position.

3) If Lashevich is organizing illegal meetings, if Grisha Zinoviev is organizing R. Fischer's flight to Germany,[1] and if Sokolnikov is being sent to France to the Congress[2]—it means that they have decided, along with Trotsky, to break up the party through the Comintern. I don't really believe that's possible, but a lot of conflict is quite possible. From this it follows that we are coming—we must come, if we want to protect the party from any surprises—to the need for a new regrouping of people from the opposition. As to the measures against Lashevich, you are correct. It would also be good to prepare the issue regarding Zinoviev one way or the other. The best way, I think, would be to give the

plenum the Politburo's report on the Special File[3] issues and, when discussing it in the plenum, mention all the squabbles in the Politburo, so that the plenum can have its say.[4]

4) If Trotsky tells Bukharin that he soon hopes to have a majority in the party, that means he hopes to intimidate and blackmail Bukharin. How little he knows and how much he underestimates Bukharin! But I think pretty soon the party will punch the mugs of Trotsky and Grisha along with Kamenev and turn them into isolated splitters, like Shliapnikov.

5) Sokolnikov should be recalled from France immediately, and the French Central Committee should be told that Sokolnikov has no assignments on French matters from either the party's Central Committee or from the Comintern.

6) I am not alarmed by economic matters. Rykov will be able to take care of them. The opposition wins absolutely zero points on economic matters.

7) It's very good that Bukharin has made up his mind to report in Moscow and Peter [Petrograd].[5]

> Well, goodbye for now.
> Best regards,
> J. Stalin
> 15 June 1926

P.S. Rudzutak together with Mikoian proposes postponing the plenum to 20 July.[6] I have no objections. J. Stalin

---

1. The reference is to Ruth Fischer's travel from Moscow to Germany for medical treatment without the sanction of the Comintern's Executive Committee.

2. The reference is to the V Congress of the French Communist Party, which took place in Lille on 21–26 June 1926.

3. The Special File contained the final decisions on a number of issues that were treated with the highest degree of secrecy in the Soviet Union. Documents given this classification are still in the Russian Presidential Archive and are inaccessible to researchers.

4. On 17 June 1926, at a Politburo meeting, the agenda for the Central Committee plenum for 10 July 1926 was approved: 1) new elections for the soviets; 2) the housing issue; 3) grain procurement; 4) a resolution of the Central Control Commission presidium on Lashevich, Belenkii et al. (RTsKhIDNI f. 17, op. 3, d. 568, l. 3).

On 8 July 1926, the Politburo decided to add an additional item, the British miners' strikes, to the agenda (ibid., d. 573, l. 2).

5. Bukharin gave a report to Moscow party activists on 8 June 1926, and to Leningrad party activists on 11 June 1926.

6. A joint plenum of the Central Committee and the Central Control Commission of the party opened on 14 July 1926.

Letter 21

Sochi, 6/25/26

To Molotov, Rykov, Bukharin, and other friends,

I have long pondered the matter of the Lashevich affair, going back and forth, linking it with the question of the opposition groups in general; several times I came to various opinions and have finally settled on the following:

1) Before the appearance of the Zinoviev group, those with oppositional tendencies (Trotsky, the workers' opposition, and others) behaved more or less loyally and were more or less tolerable;

2) With the appearance of the Zinoviev group, those with oppositional tendencies began to grow arrogant and break the bounds of loyalty;

3) The Zinoviev group became the mentor of everyone in the opposition who was for splitting the party; in effect it has become the leader of the splitting tendencies in the party;

4) This role fell to Zinoviev's group because a) it is better acquainted with our methods than any other group, b) it is stronger in general than the other groups and has control of the Comintern Executive Committee ([Zinoviev is] chairman of the Comintern Executive Committee), which represents a serious force; c) because of this it behaves more arrogantly than any other group, providing examples of "boldness" and "determination" to those with other tendencies;

5) Therefore the Zinoviev group is now the most harmful, and the blow must be struck precisely against this group at the plenum;[1]

6) Not only should Lashevich be removed *from the Central Committee,* Zinoviev should be removed from the *Politburo*[2] with a warning that he will be removed from the Central Committee if he does not cease his work in preparing a schism;

7) Either we strike this blow now with the calculation that Trotsky and the others will once again become loyal, or we risk turning the Central Committee and its bodies into nonviable institutions incapable of work, and we will very soon have to deal with a tremendous fuss in the party that will harm the cause and our unity;

8) It's possible that after this, Zinoviev will submit his resignation from the Comintern. We should accept it. At any rate, after being removed from the Politburo, Zinoviev can no longer be chairman; all the member parties will understand that and will draw the necessary conclusion **themselves.** In the Comintern, we will then shift from a system with a chairman to a system with a secretariat.[3] This will disarm the Zinoviev group and liquidate Zinoviev's arrogance in preparing the schism (remember what was said about Stockholm at the Congress!);[4]

9) I assure you that in the party and the country this affair will get by without

the slightest complications—no one will feel sorry for Zinoviev, because they know him well;

10) Previously I had thought that a *broad* resolution on unity was needed *at the plenum*. Now I think that it would be better to leave such a resolution for the [XV] *Conference* ([where we could provide] a theoretical foundation and so on) or for the *Congress*. At the plenum, we can and should limit ourselves to a *brief* resolution on unity in the narrow sense of the word *in connection with the Lashevich affair*, citing Lenin's resolution on unity at the Tenth Congress.[5] This resolution should say that Zinoviev is being removed from the Politburo not because of differences of opinion with the Central Committee—there are no less profound disagreements with Trotsky, after all, although the issue of removing Trotsky from the Politburo is not on the agenda—but because of his (Zinoviev's) policy of *schism*. I think this will be better: the workers will understand it, since they value party unity, and this will be a serious warning for the other opposition groups. Dzerzhinsky can be brought into the Politburo to replace Zinoviev. The party will take this well. Or the number of Politburo members can be raised to ten by bringing in both Dzerzhinsky and Rudzutak. Obviously, with a *broad* plenum resolution (the previous plan), we would be forced to *unite* Zinoviev and Trotsky *officially* in one camp, which is perhaps premature and strategically irrational now. Better to break them individually. Let Trotsky and Piatakov defend Zinoviev, and we will listen. At any rate that will be better at this stage. Then we'll see.

We'll speak in more detail when I come to Moscow. I think I'll be in Moscow three or four days before the plenum. What do you say to that?

P.S. I don't know about you, but I think that with the Lashevich affair, the Zinovievites have cut their own throats, especially if this affair is linked with the Guralski affair. *And indeed it must be linked.*

Best regards,
J. Stalin.

1. A statement from thirteen members of the plenum (I. Avdeev, I. Bakaev, L. Kamenev, N. Krupskaia, M. Lashevich, G. Lizdin, N. Muralov, A. Peterson, G. Piatakov, K. Solovev, L. Trotsky, G. Yevdokimov, G. Zinoviev) was addressed to the plenum but not incorporated into the record (RTsKhIDNI f. 17, op. 2, d. 696, l. 68):

> The question of the "affair" of Com. Lashevich, placed on the 24 June agenda of this plenum by decision of the Politburo, was turned into the "affair" of Com. Zinoviev at the very last moment by a 20 July resolution of the Central Control Commission. We consider it necessary to state that in the draft resolution of the Central Control Commission there is not a single fact, not a single report, not a single suspicion that was not known six weeks ago when the Central Control Commission passed a resolution on the "affair" of Com. Lashevich and others. The name of Com. Zinoviev does not appear in that resolution. Yet, in the final draft of the resolution it is stated completely categorically that "all threads" lead to Com. Zinoviev, as chairman of the Comintern Executive Committee. This matter, as is abundantly clear to everyone, was decided not by the Central Control Commission but by a group whose leader is Com. Stalin. We are dealing here with a new stage in the implementation of a plan that was conceived long ago and is being systematically carried out. . . .

2. By a decision of the July 1926 joint plenum of the Central Committee and Central Control Commission, Zinoviev was removed from the Politburo, and Lashevich was expelled as candidate

member of the Central Committee (*KPSS v rezoliutsiiakh* [Resolutions of the CPSU], vol. 4 [Moscow, 1984], 36).

3. The VII expanded plenum of the Comintern's Executive Committee of 22 November 1926 voted to "relieve Com. Zinoviev of his deputies as chairman of the Comintern's Executive Committee and of his work in the Comintern." The plenum eliminated the position of chairman of the Comintern's Executive Committee. A new executive body of the Comintern was formed: the Political Secretariat.

4. The reference is to Krupskaia's speech at the XIV Party Congress on 20 December 1925. At that time, in defense of Zinoviev, she said (XIV Congress of the Russian Communist Party [Bolshevik], *Transcript* [Moscow, 1926], 165, 166):

> Our Congress must be concerned to search and find the correct line. That is its task. We cannot reassure ourselves with the idea that the majority is always right. The history of our party includes congresses when the majority was wrong. Let us recall, for example, the Stockholm Congress [IV Joint Congress of the Russian Social Democratic Workers' Party in 1906, at which the Bolsheviks had fewer representatives than the Mensheviks]. The majority should not be content with being the majority but should dispassionately search for the correct decision.

5. In 1921, the X Party Congress passed a resolution banning factions within the party—U.S. Ed.

Letter 22   [3 August 1926]

8/3 (Tuesday)

Molotov,[1]

1) Kamenev has turned in his resignation **before** the review in the Politburo of the question of the export-import plan, and he proposes that Mikoian replace him.[2]

2) The Politburo has reviewed the question of the export-import plan and pronounced it "unfavorable," having created the Rudzutak commission to improve matters in the Commissariat of Trade.[3]

3) We will accept Kamenev's resignation on Thursday (5 August) and appoint Mikoian, after polling the Central Committee members on this matter.[4]

4) We're thinking of sending Kamenev to Japan and Aralov to China (the Chinese government demands Karakhan's removal, and we'll have to do it); Kopp could perhaps go to Italy, by recalling Kerzhentsev to Moscow, since he hasn't worked out in Italy.[5]

5) Things are generally not going so badly. **All** the big Western parties have come out in support of our Central Committee (including both France and Czechoslovakia) against the opposition.

6) Bukharin has still not returned.[6] There are six people now in the Politburo: Rykov, Rudzutak, Kalinin, Stalin, Trotsky, and Kamenev (Kamenev votes since there are no other candidates in Moscow).

7) You already know about Kuibyshev's appointment to the Supreme Economic Council.[7] The opposition is keeping a low profile in the Politburo.

Greetings to all friends in Sochi.

Best regards,
Stalin

Send me a transcript of your speeches as soon as possible. We decided to publish the Lashevich affair in the next issue, that is, the debates on this affair.[8]

1. In the upper right-hand corner is Molotov's notation: "From Moscow (?). 1926=?"

2. Kamenev notes in his letter to the Central Committee of 25 July 1926 (RTsKhIDNI f. 17, op. 3, d. 579, ll. 13, 14):

> The work of the Commissariat of Trade involves a large amount of economic maneuvering and requires 100 percent support and complete trust on the part of the Politburo and Labor Defense Council. . . . This support and trust in my work at the Commissariat of Trade was missing from the Politburo and Labor Defense Council from the very beginning. . . . It is entirely clear that as long as I am at the head of it, the Commissariat of Trade cannot count on any trust or any real support. . . . There exists an intention to use the entirely unavoidable mistakes of the Commissariat of Trade, not for helpful criticism, but for political purposes. Such an important government body cannot work in such an atmosphere, and I cannot take responsibility for fulfilling its responsibilities. . . . I assume that Com. Mikoian, who has repeatedly been named in recent days in the capacity of [head of] the Commissariat of Trade, will be able to cope with this task.

3. The agenda item "On progress in the fulfillment of the foreign currency plan of 1925–1926 (in trade and nontrade areas)" was reviewed at the Politburo on 29 July 1926 (ibid., d. 577, ll. 4, 5).

4. On 5 August 1926, the Politburo dismissed Kamenev from his work at the Commissariat of Trade and appointed Mikoian commissar for domestic and foreign trade (ibid., d. 579, l. 3).

5. In Bukharin's speech to the July plenum of the Central Committee on the Politburo's decisions regarding the British miners' strikes and the events in Poland and China, he states (ibid., op. 2, d. 246, vyp. 1, l. 15):

> We had the issue of the Chinese Eastern Railway, the main strategic artery, which is our revolutionary forefinger pointed into China. The comrades in the opposition have proposed that we get rid of the Chinese Eastern Railway as quickly as possible, to give it up, since it is a "blister" on our foot. . . . But when have we ever turned down revolutionary opportunities merely because they were fraught with difficulties? Such suggestions were made, but they were rejected. After we had suffered a number of defeats in China, a certain diplomatic reshuffling was proposed: to send Kopp to China and Karakhan to Japan. The point was that a furious campaign was being waged against Karakhan, who embodied our support of the national revolutionary movement, whereas Com. Kopp was known for his skeptical attitude to the whole national-revolutionary movement.

On 12 August 1926, the Politburo decided to appoint Kopp Soviet representative in Italy, freeing him from his responsibilities in Japan, and to appoint [L. B.] Kamenev representative to Japan (ibid., op. 3, d. 580, l. 5). On 30 December 1926, Aralov was appointed Soviet representative to the national government in China.

6. Bukharin was in Leningrad at the time. On 28 July 1926, he gave a speech to the Leningrad Party Organization's activists.

7. On 29 July 1926, the Politburo appointed Kuibyshev chairman of the Supreme Economic Council (ibid., op. 3, d. 577, l. 4).

8. A transcript of the discussion of the Lashevich affair at the July 1926 plenum of the Central Committee was included in the fourth issue of the transcript of the July plenum of the Central Committee for 1926 (ibid., op. 2, d. 246, vyp. 4).

Letter 23

To Molotov (for our friends),[1]

1) The delegation of British coal miners should be arriving any day, if it has not already arrived. They should be met "by all the rules of the game" and *as much money as possible* should be collected for them. I've heard that the Americans have promised 1 million dollars. We have to collect and send possibly 1 million or 2 million rubles (**less** than the Americans is impossible) or perhaps a whole 3 million. The situation in England is serious, and it obliges us to make serious "sacrifices."[2]

2) I think we must tell Andreev that he should insist on an embargo.[3] The embargo is *now* the most urgent issue. The *British Communists are waging an intensified campaign* for the embargo. The General Council should not be allowed to get away with mere calls to collect money. That is not enough *now*. *Now* [we] should push the embargo as hard as possible. By the way, how is Andreev's work coming along?[4]

3) I think that neither our own press nor the British Communist press has exploited Thomas's and Henderson's **fleeing** from an accounting of the congresses of the "Labour Party" and the "General Council's trade unions" (they "went on vacation," one to Canada and the other to Australia).[5] We should *trumpet* in both our own and the British press that these traitors *fled* from responsibility, so that when the strike was discussed, their absence would keep them from being insulted. We should broadcast the fact that the General Council and the Executive Committee of the Labour Party **helped** them flee from an accounting, and thus took upon themselves the responsibility for their betrayals and so on. It's strange that the British (and our) press is silent about it (I read the British Communist newspapers, and I know that these facts are not exposed there.)

4) How did the Comintern react to your letter about the campaign to dissolve Parliament and have new elections? What do the British Communists think about it?

5) You should not indefinitely postpone the matter of publishing the Comintern's *Kommunisticheskiy internatsional* [Communist International] as a weekly. You and Bukharin should get that going.[6] It will be enormously important for improving and reorganizing all the work of the Comintern and its member parties. What does Bukharin think of this?

6) How is the economic situation doing? How are things with [agricultural] procurements? How about exports? Give me a brief report if there is time.

Well, all the best,

J. Stalin

27 August 1926

Re: Stalin's letter (of 27 August)[7]

On Point 1, a) Tomskii has promised to organize *today* an appeal from the

Central Committee of Miners to the British coal miners regarding the **four-month strike**. The appeal should say that our support will continue and will be *the same as before*. It will **say directly** that [our] Central Committee of Miners is certain that the wish of the Trade Union Council for 1 percent [contribution] *will be passed*. This is important for *today* because on 2 September there will be a conference of striking coal miners.[8]

b) We should make a decision to send the 2 million rubles at a ceremonial meeting between the trade unions and a delegation of miners right before the Trades Union Congress (before 6 September). We'll discuss this last item b) at the Politburo.

I am entirely for points 2 and 3. Plus, a campaign should be launched, especially and above all in England, with political slogans (dissolution of the Parliament, "Down with the Conservative government, for a genuine workers' government").

Molotov
1 September

1. Shvarts checked with me today about sending the greetings and should clear it with Molotov at two o'clock, 1 September.

2. I'm for aid, as Molotov and I agreed.

3. I don't object to exposing Thomas and Henderson, but I don't think it will produce a serious political effect for us.

Tomskii
1 September

1. In the upper left-hand corner is the note: "We have read this. Agreed. Bukharin, J. Rudzutak, V. Kuibyshev, N. Yanson, Yem. Yaroslavskii."

2. As a sign of solidarity with the striking miners, the Trade Union Council decided to allocate a portion of one day's pay to the strikers. The British General Council was sent 2.25 million rubles, which it refused to accept. Subsequently, at the request of the Miners' Federation of Great Britain, the Trade Union Council sent these funds directly to the federation.

3. The reference is to an embargo on coal shipments to Great Britain.

4. A. Andreev took part in the work of the Anglo-Russian Committee (see note 2 in letter 26).

5. James Henry Thomas is used here as a symbol of the moderate trade union leaders that Communists felt had betrayed the working class by calling off the general strike—U.S. Ed.; Arthur Henderson was secretary of the British Labour Party from 1911 until 1934.

6. The journal *Kommunisticheskiy internatsional*, the organ of the Comintern's Executive Committee, was published from 1919 to 1943. By decision of the Comintern presidium on 15 September 1926, the journal became a weekly.

7. The following notes from Molotov and Tomskii are appended to Stalin's letter.

8. On 4 September 1926, the Politburo accepted by voice vote Tomskii's draft of the statement from the Trade Union Council to the British Federation of Miners (RTsKhIDNI f. 17, op. 3, d. 585, l. 3).

Letter 24   [30 August 1926]

Hello, Molotov,

1) Matters are coming to a head and we cannot avoid raising the issue of removing Grigorii [Zinoviev] from the Comintern. This is indicated by the *resolution* of a number of the Western parties (England, Germany) on his removal. The first agenda item ("international questions") for our (forthcoming) conference also speaks to this. It would be incomprehensible and unnatural if we (the Russian Communists) were to "squirm out of" the question of removing him at the same time as circumstances make the question unavoidable and two Western parties have definitively *proposed* removing him. Therefore, we can and must make a decision about the expediency of removing him.[1]

2) The formal handling of the matter should be done at an expanded plenum of the Comintern Executive Committee. If *all* parties or a great majority of them speak in favor of removing Grigorii, such an expression of will can be safely considered the authentic will of all the parties, that is, of the entire Congress. A final decision can be made by the [next] Congress.

2)[2] We should *already* be thinking about the outline or the first (rough!) draft of the theses on the trade unions and the economic situation. Are there any such rough drafts in the Secretariat, that is, did the Secretariat receive these "drafts"? If not, we have to hurry.[3]

3) Don't you think it would be expedient to introduce to the trade unions a "system" or an "institution" of activists *by unions*, or perhaps *by various branches* of the manufacturing trade unions? If this "system" has not yet been introduced, it ought to be, because it would both *promote* new people and bring the trade unions *closer* to production and, in general, would *invigorate* the trade unions. It is only necessary to ensure that the *activist* group (in textiles, petroleum, coal, and so on) is *broad*, that it consist not only of trade union officials, not only of Communists, but of nonparty workers as well (say fifty-fifty), and so on. What do you think about this?

4) Don't you think that the matter of Kamenev must be raised at the Central Committee plenum? Is the Commissariat of Foreign Affairs working to get Kamenev set up in Japan?

Well, all the best,
J. Stalin
30 August 1926

P.S. I read *Stetskii's article on the new opposition*.[4] The article is good, but there are a few individual apples in it that *spoil the whole barrel*. According to Stetskii, it seems that *we are not supposed to* strive to achieve "complete predominance of the proletarians and the semi-proletarians in the soviets." That's not correct. The difference with the opposition is *not* in that, but, first, in that the proletariat cannot *physically* predominate in those districts where there are very few proletarians; second, in that the predomination must be understood as *political* and not just statistical; and third, in that we *radically disagree* with the *methods of achieving the predominance* that the opposition has recommended to us. It's very bad that no one helped Stetskii correct such blunders.

1. The October joint plenum of the Central Committee and Central Control Commission passed the following resolution (*KPSS v rezoliutsiiakh* [Resolutions of the CPSU], vol. 4 [Moscow, 1984], 67, 68):

> By virtue of the fact that Com. Zinoviev does not express the line of the All-Union Communist Party (Bolshevik) in the Communist International and, because of his factional activity, has lost the trust of a number of Communist parties (German, British, French, American, etc.), who have announced this in their resolutions, the Central Committee and Central Control Commission do not find it possible for Com. Zinoviev to continue working in the Communist International.

2. Stalin's repeat of "2" is present in the original.

3. Stalin's letter was written on the eve of the XV Party Conference, which took place from 26 October to 3 November 1926. A report was heard at the conference on the work and future tasks of the trade unions. At the end of 1926, the VII Congress of Trade Unions was convened, apparently in response to Stalin's wish to make the trade unions more active.

4. Stetskii's article, "Kak novaia oppozitsiia prishla k trotskizmu" (How the new opposition came to Trotskyism), was published in *Pravda* on 26 August 1926.

Letter 25   [4 September 1926]

9/4

Molotovich,[1, 2]

Sergo was here to see me the other day. He is furious with the Central Committee's *statement* concerning his *recall*.[3] He views the formulation of the **recall** as punishment, as an insult given by the Central Committee for some unknown reason. He feels that the phrase about Sergo being transferred to Rostov "*in Mikoian's place*" is a hint that Mikoian is *higher* than Sergo, that Sergo is only good enough to be Mikoian's deputy, and so on. He understands that the Central Committee never had and never could have a desire to offend him, to insult him, to place him underneath Mikoian, and so on, but he believes that those who receive a copy of the Central Committee's resolution could understand it as in fact an attack on Sergo, and it should be formulated better and more precisely. I think that we must satisfy him, since he is *objectively* put in the position of an offended person because of an accidental mistake in the formulation. The formulation could be *corrected* approximately as follows:[4]

1) To comply with Com. Ordzhonikidze's request to relieve him of his duties as first secretary of the Transcaucasian Regional Party Committee and reject the demand of the Transcaucasian organizations (the national central commit-

tees and the Transcaucasian Regional Committee) to keep Com. Ordzhonikidze in his old post.[5]

2) To postpone for several months, in view of Com. Ordzhonikidze's definite refusal to transfer immediately to Moscow,[6] the question of appointing Com. Ordzhonikidze commissar of Worker-Peasant Inspection and deputy chairman of the Council of Commissars.[7]

3) To accept the proposal of the North Caucasian Regional Party Committee to confirm Com. Ordzhonikidze as first secretary of the North Caucasian Committee (if Com. Ordzhonikidze consents).

The sooner you take care of this little thing, the better, and then a new copy of the Central Committee's resolution will have to be sent to everyone who received the old copy.

You might say that this is all nonsense. Perhaps. But I must tell you that this nonsense may seriously harm the cause, if we don't correct it.

Nazaretian is playing a very unsavory role in this affair, which only wounds Sergo's pride and eggs him on—I don't know what his specific purpose is.

Well, all the best,

J. Stalin

1. By turning Molotov's last name into a patronymic, Stalin is demonstrating informality and friendship—Trans.

2. In the upper left-hand corner is Molotov's notation: "1926–?"

3. On 30 August 1926, the Politburo approved by voice vote the proposal of the North Caucasian Regional Party Organization to recall Ordzhonikidze from the Transcaucasus and to confirm him as first secretary of the North Caucasian Regional Committee in place of Mikoian (RTsKhIDNI f. 17, op. 3, d. 584, l. 5).

4. Stalin crossed out the next phrase: "The approved proposal is adopted."

5. On 1 September 1926, the following letter was sent to Stalin (RTsKhIDNI f. 85, op. 26, d. 5):

TO THE GENERAL SECRETARY OF THE CENTRAL COMMITTEE OF THE PARTY COMRADE STALIN. DEAR KOBA:

In connection with the proposed transfer of Sergo from the Transcaucasus, we, a group of his comrades who have worked with him for a long time in the Transcaucasus, consider it our party duty to warn and caution you, as the leader of our entire party and country, of the difficulties that could arise in our work and also to provide an evaluation of the situation that may emerge in the Transcaucasus and the individual Transcaucasian republics without Sergo, as well as [raise] the question of his significant role in our very complicated situation.

First of all, two caveats:

1) In order not to be accused of defending narrow local interests, we state that we understand perfectly well and are aware of the urgent need to strengthen the leadership from the ranks of those who have spent many years as our most prominent comrades. But we cannot for a minute forget that in the tranquil and peaceful construction of socialism in our Union as a whole, tranquility in the Transcaucasus and the peaceful coexistence of its peoples play a very great role.

It seems unnecessary to mention the enormous significance of the Transcaucasus in the life of the Union to one who has taught us to carry out a cautious, flexible policy, imbued with an internationalist spirit.

2) We also do not want to be accused of intimidation with the goal of keeping Sergo in the Transcaucasus. We do not think that you suspected us of being led in this matter by a feeling of personal attachment to Sergo rather than an awareness of political necessity and expediency.

The alarm that naturally arises in each of us and in each rank-and-file member of the party has a very serious foundation. Everyone recalls how the ongoing work of the Transcaucasian party bodies and the Soviet, trade union, and organizational bodies was set up, what difficulties were overcome in the past, with what efforts the peaceful coexistence of the peoples of the Caucasus was established, and what role Com. Sergo played in that work. Just as clearly we see all the difficulties [that will arise] in future work without a person who is able to unite around himself all the people most active and decent in our republic and in the entire Transcaucasus without regard to nationality.

The first important difficulty that will arise after the departure of Com. Sergo from the Caucasus is the strengthening of elements sowing mistrust and ethnic enmity among the nationalities of the Transcaucasus. The mutual trust of peoples in the Caucasus found a real bulwark not only in the political line of the highest party bodies but also in the person of Com. Sergo himself; with his departure, this trust could be shaken. Sergo was able, with unshakable firmness, confidently and without fears and glances over his shoulder, to implement this line without leaning toward the nationalist extortions of the "Hurrah" patriots in the republics nor toward the ultra-internationalist phrase-mongers about which both Ilich [Lenin] and you in particular warned.

The second difficulty, no less important, is the strengthening inside the party of elements that were suppressed until now by the authority of Com. Sergo and who will, with his departure, undoubtedly open furious fire on the majority of the party and its leading bodies, making use of the platform of the "new opposition" and hiding behind the names of its leaders. There are already obvious signs of this. Sergo's departure will unleash these elements as well.

The third difficulty arises from the complicated relations among the three republics. Com. Sergo's authority in all three republics is extremely high. There isn't a corner of these republics where Sergo's name isn't known. Sergo's name is linked not only with liberation from the landowners and the nobility and with national cultural liberation from the chauvinist policy of tsarism but also with the political stability of the republics and the federation and to an even greater extent with the stable peace between the Transcaucasian nationalities.

The fourth difficulty arises from the impossibility of replacing Com. Sergo with someone of equal authority or someone capable of resolving the complex issues of our daily life and of our overall policy with the same energy, discernment, and objectivity. Although the nationalities problem has been resolved in principle, a correct, practical implementation in real life is still required; the slightest deviation or violation of this policy will cause the nationality issue to spring up again in full bloom. The distribution among the republics of any material wealth, funds, and so on will provoke the nationalities issue. All issues here are complicated by the ethnic aspect (land, pastures, water rights, etc.). Under these conditions, Com. Sergo's exclusive authority in all three republics has been of crucial significance in resolving these issues, and under his leadership, they have been settled smoothly, easily, and without offending anyone. Sergo's objectivity is above any suspicion, starting with Khulo and Lanchkhuta and ending with Zangezur and Shemakha. . . .

This list of difficulties is hardly complete. In sum, all sorts of difficulties could create a very dangerous situation in the Transcaucasus. . . .

We openly state that we cannot cope with the work that Com. Sergo was able to. All of our fears force us to ask you to note these concerns when you make the final decision in the matter of Sergo; in calculating the political interests of both the Union as a whole and the particular interests of the Transcaucasus and its republics, we ask you to refrain from the proposed transfer of Com. Sergo to Moscow.

This letter was already written when we received Com. Molotov's telegram informing the Transcaucasian Regional Party Committee of Com. Sergo's appointment as secretary of the North Caucasian Regional Committee (in place of Com. Mikoian). . . .

With all the sincerity and candor characteristic of Bolsheviks, we must inform you that we consider this decision a mistake. . . .

Proceeding from all of these concerns, the Transcaucasian Regional Committee, on behalf of all the party organizations of the Transcaucasus, urgently requests the Central Committee to review its decision of 8/30/26.

1. Makharadze 2. Lukashin. 3. Nazaretian. 4. Eliava. 5. Kartvelishvili. 6. Karaev. 7. Guseinov. 8. Kasimov. 9. R. Akhundov. 10. Mravian. 11. V. Sturua. 12. Asribekov. 13. P. Ivanov 14. A. Gegechkori. 15. D. Bagirov. 16. Mirzoian. 17. K. Rumiantsev. 18. M. Orakhelashvili. 9/1/26.

On 9 September 1926, the Politburo rejected the request from the Transcaucasian Regional Committee to review Ordzhonikidze's appointment as first secretary of the North Caucasian Regional Committee (ibid., f. 17, op. 3, d. 586, ll. 4, 5).

6. The original text of the second point was as follows: "The appointment of Com. Ordzhonikidze as commissar of Worker-Peasant Inspection and deputy chairman of the Council of Commissars should be postponed for several months in view of Com. Ordzhonikidze's refusal of immediate" and so on.

This text was crossed out by Stalin himself.

7. The question of Ordzhonikidze's appointment as commissar of Worker-Peasant Inspection was decided in July 1926, as shown by a coded telegram from Stalin to Ordzhonikidze of 27 July 1926 (ibid., f. 558, op. 1, d. 3259):

> For Sergo. In view of Kuibyshev's promotion to the Supreme Economic Council, we will raise the issue of your appointment as commissar of Worker-Peasant Inspection and deputy to Rykov. For formal reasons the matter of a new chairman for the Central Control Commission will remain open until the Party Conference, although Kuibyshev will leave the chairmanship at the next Central Control Commission plenum. In reporting this to you, we ask you not to kick up a fuss; nothing will come of it anyway. Stalin.

And on 29 July 1926 (ibid., d. 3341):

> The suggestion was not mine, but all our friends', including Rykov along with Molotov. The question has been put off for several weeks.

Letter 26   [8 September 1926]

9/8

I received your letter.[1]

1) Our delegation in Berlin handled itself rather well.[2] The report of the Trade Union Council is generally all right. The appeal from the Trade Union Council is good. Tomskii's interview is good. I do not insist on a *loan* [as opposed to an outright grant] to the General Council or the Federation of Coal Miners. I think that the question of the loan can be postponed for the time being. I raised the issue of the loan in order to show "Europe" that we are not a republic "made out of money," but people with calculation, able to save a kopeck, that we give loans in order to be repaid, and so forth. But this matter can be postponed or perhaps dropped altogether.

2) I already sent a coded telegram about China. I am certain that Kopp and Serebriakov will not carry out our policy; they will only give Chang [Tso-lin] the opportunity to exploit our *minor differences* and ruin our cause. Sending Kopp back to Japan will mean virtually negating the Politburo's decision on Kopp and Kamenev. It will not look good if decisions made by the Politburo *with one set of members* are nullified by the same Politburo *with another set of members* without sufficient grounds.[3] Of course, at present you can see things better [in Moscow], but we still ought not run from one extreme to another because Chang, encouraged by Kopp, has taken it into his head to blackmail us.

Well, all the best.

Regards,
J. Stalin

1. In the upper left-hand corner is Molotov's notation: "1926=?"

2. In August 1926 at a meeting of the Anglo-Russian Committee in Berlin, the Soviet trade union delegation proposed launching a broad campaign of support for the British miners' struggle that included declaring an embargo on the shipping of coal to Great Britain. A delegation of the British General Council rejected these proposals.

3. On 12 August 1926, when the decision was made to appoint Kopp Soviet ambassador to Italy and Kamenev Soviet ambassador to Japan, Politburo members Bukharin, Rudzutak, Rykov, Stalin, Trotsky, and candidate Politburo members Andreev, Kaganovich, and Kamenev were present at the Politburo session (RTsKhIDNI f. 17, op. 3, d. 580, l. 1). On 2 September 1926, the following Politburo members were in the session: Bukharin, Kalinin, Molotov, Rudzutak, Tomskii and candidate members Andreev, Mikoian, and Petrovskii.

Letter 27   [16 September 1926]

Hello, Molotov,[1]

I received your letter of 12 September.

1) It's good that the misunderstandings with Serebriakov and Kopp have finally been eliminated.[2] Otherwise we would have demolished our own policy, *those people* would have been hostage to Chang and the Japanese, and we in turn would have found ourselves hostage to *those people*. Chang's strength derives, incidentally, from the fact that he now knows (*Kopp and Serebriakov have let him know it*) that we will not embark on military intervention, that even back then, half a year ago, we were not thinking of advancing on Harbin, that he thus has nothing to fear and can allow himself to be brazen, selling **"such and such"** to the Japanese or (especially) the British in order to get some sort of help. That's the whole point. Kopp and Serebriakov told Chang (because of their indiscretion) a secret of our diplomacy, the secret that we are only scaring Chang, but we will not go to war over the Chinese Eastern Railway. They got the idea they could buy off Chang and the Japanese with softness and gabbiness! Obviously they also had a factional purpose here, carried out according to the line of the Commissariat of Foreign Affairs with the help of Litvinov.

2) Now I can say with complete confidence that Chang will restrict himself to *making jabs* and that it will not come to seizing the Chinese Eastern Railway at this stage. Chang, and Japan (and England) through him, are probing, testing the strength of our resistance. That is precisely why Karakhan should not have been recalled *now*.[3] But only for that reason. Because it seems to me that Karakhan, who has gotten himself utterly entangled in the underhanded schemes of the Fengites[4] and other Chinese "generals," now constitutes a negative factor *from the perspective of the substance of our policy in China*. We will have to consider the issue of the Chinese Eastern Railway and Chang in the near future.

3) I did not write to you last time about Sergo in detail. But now I must inform you that both Sergo and—especially—Nazaretian left me with an unpleasant impression in connection with the incident involving his "recall" from the Transcaucasus. I had it out with Sergo, called him petty, and stopped seeing him (he is now in New Mt. Athos). The matter of the composition of the secretariat of the Transcaucasian Regional Party Committee must now be discussed separately. Nazaretian will not do as a replacement for Sergo in the secretariat (he does not have the stature; he's not serious and not always truthful).

4) As far as the target figures go, I think that we have to put on the pressure now and definitely reduce the staffs of the commissariats and self-financing bodies *from above*.[5] Otherwise talk about economic austerity will remain empty. Industry's share must definitely be increased.

5) Negotiations with Krupskaia are not only ill timed *now*, they are politically harmful. Krupskaia is a splitter (see her speech about "Stockholm" at the XIV Congress).[6] She has to be beaten, as a splitter, if we want to preserve the unity of the party. We cannot have two *contradictory* lines, fighting splitters *and* making peace with them. That's not dialectics, that's nonsense and helplessness. It's possible that tomorrow Zinoviev will come out with a statement on Molotov's and Bukharin's "lack of principle," [saying] that Molotov and Bukharin "offered" Zinoviev (through Krupskaia) a "bloc" and that he, Zinoviev, "rejected this intolerable flirtation with disdain," and so forth and so on.

6) You are absolutely right about the "August bloc." Not just one but several of Ilich's [Lenin's] articles should be published, and along with them, we should tell the story of how this bloc emerged. We must definitely unleash Sorin on this matter. A speech by you and Bukharin is absolutely necessary. It is a serious matter.[7]

7) It's good to hear that trade and wages are going fairly well.[8]

8) It would not be a bad idea to destroy the Nechaev fledglings.[9]

9) Demian's [Bednyi's] poem won't do. It's pretty dry and lifeless. I wrote him about it.

10) I am getting a little better, but my arm still hurts.

11) Bukharin is a swine and perhaps worse than a swine[10] because he considers it beneath his dignity to write even two lines about his impressions of Germany. I'll get my revenge for that.

Well, that's it for now.

> Best regards,
> J. Stalin
> 16 September 1926

Addition to the letter

An extremely bad impression is produced by the constant communiqués in the press (especially in the economic press) about the complete violation of directives from the Commissariat of Trade and the party by the cooperatives and by the local and central procurement agencies. The virtual impunity of these obvious criminals is grist for the mill of the Nepmen [private middlemen] and other enemies of the working class—it demoralizes the entire economic and soviet *apparat,* it turns our directives and our party into meaningless toys. This can't be tolerated any further if we don't want to be captured by these bastards who claim to "accept" our directives but in reality mock us. *I propose requiring the Commissariat of Trade (and the Worker-Peasant Inspection [to do the following]:*

1) The violators of the pricing policy on state procurements must be *removed* and *turned over to the courts,* and the names of the criminals published.

2) Immediately *remove* and *turn over to the courts* the violators of the pricing policy concerning sales of industrial goods to the public (the reduction of retail prices), publish [their full names] and so on.

3) Put out a party circular about how these violators are enemies of the working class and how the struggle with them should be merciless.

I adamantly insist on my proposal and ask all of you to accept it. Understand that without such measures we will lose the campaign in favor of *Nepman elements who are sitting in our state procurement and cooperative bodies.* Without these measures, it will be a disaster.

Awaiting your reply,

J. Stalin

16 September 1926

1. In the upper left-hand corner of the letter there is a notation: "We have read it: Molotov, Bukharin, Uglanov, J. Rudzutak."

2. On 7 September 1926, the Politburo made the following decision regarding China (RTsKhIDNI f. 17, op. 3, d. 585, l. 3): "In light of the information from Com. Kopp on his need for continuing treatment, the resolution of the Politburo from 2 September of this year should be rescinded."

3. On 27 August 1926, at Chicherin's suggestion, Karakhan was recalled to Moscow to report (ibid., d. 584, l. 5). On 21 September Karakhan was requested to speed up his trip to Moscow by not stopping in either Canton or Japan (ibid., d. 589, l. 3).

4. Fengites were followers of Gen. Feng Yü-hsiang. In 1925 Soviet representatives established contacts with Feng, whose units at that time controlled a number of districts in northern China and, by the end of 1925, occupied Tientsin. Military advisors and materials were sent under the command of Gen. Feng, who had declared himself an advocate of national revolution. In 1926, Feng maneuvered back and forth between various forces inside and outside China.

5. On 20 September 1926, the Politburo made the following decision (ibid., d. 588, l. 3): "Continue work to reduce expenditures on the administrative and economic apparaty . . . by a minimum of 15 percent."

6. For Krupskaia's speech at the XIV Congress, see letter 21, note 4.

7. In Vienna in August 1912, a conference of representatives of a number of Russian social democratic groups and tendencies took place. In the course of the meetings, a bloc emerged that united the supporters of Trotsky, a number of representatives of the Latvian Regional Social Democratic Party, the Bund, the Transcaucasian Regional Committee, and other organizations. It opposed the decisions of the Russian Social Democratic Workers' Party VI Conference.

On 5 October 1926, *Pravda* published Molotov's speech at the opening of the courses for local party workers. In this speech, Molotov noted that an oppositional bloc had formed in the party uniting "tendencies [all the way] from those of Medvedev and Shliapnikov to those of Trotsky and Zinoviev"; he compared this bloc to the "August bloc" of 1912–1914. Molotov devoted an entire section of his speech to the story of the August bloc; he ended with the statement that the August bloc had shared the fate of the Menshevik party and that the struggle with the August bloc had allowed the Bolshevik party "to grow into the powerful leader of the proletarian revolution." The journal *Bolshevik* (1925, no. 16) reprinted Lenin's articles about the August bloc and published Sorin's article "The August Bloc."

8. On 8 September 1926, the Central Control Commission reviewed the Commissariat of Trade's violation of a Politburo's directive about the acquisition of foreign stocks. Measures were taken to prevent such violations in the future (ibid., f. 613, op. 1, d. 47, l. 14).

9. Probably a reference to the case of N. V. Nechaev. On 21 September 1926, the Kursk Province Control Commission expelled Nechaev for conducting "oppositional underground work" and distributing opposition materials. At the same time, some of Nechaev's coworkers who knew about his views received strict reprimands. In late 1926 and early 1927, the Nechaev matter was reviewed by the Secretariat of the Central Control Commission and the Orgburo. The decision to expel Nechaev from the party remained in effect (ibid., d. 48, l. 120b, and d. 63, l. 25).

10. The author's intent here appears to be jocular—Trans.

Letter 28   [23 September 1926]

Comrade Molotov,

I received your letter of 20 September.

1) Regarding wages, I think you have got it fairly well.[1] It's important that the lower strata receive something tangible. It would also be good to give something to the oil workers who do not get very much on the whole, but if there isn't an opportunity at this moment they will have to be turned down, despite the complaints of the Baku people.[2]

2) If *Trotsky* "is in a rage" and thinks of "openly going for broke," that's all the worse for him. It's quite possible that he'll be bounced out of the Politburo now—that depends on his behavior.[3] The issue is as follows: **either** they must submit to the party, **or** *the party* must submit to **them**. It's clear that the party will cease to exist as a party if it allows the latter (second) possibility.

3) As for *Smirnov*, after the warning that he has already had, only one thing remains—expel him, at least temporarily.[4]

4) I think that the plenum cannot "gloss over" the question of *Medvedev*.[5] Perhaps you have a means of "glossing over"—if so, tell me what it is.

5) Perhaps you are right that the question about the opposition bloc must be raised at the conference.[6] Still, we shouldn't get ahead of ourselves; better to observe how that bloc will behave now.

6) You and Bukharin must hurry up with your speech on the question of the August bloc—there's no reason to wait now, I think.

7) I wrote Demian [Bednyi] that his tale is "dry and lifeless" and "won't do" (or something to that effect) and that "*it should not be printed.*" I don't have a copy or I would send it to you immediately. As for this tale being a bad

"symptom" in the sense of Demian's position worsening—I doubt it. We'll talk more when I come.

8) Don't give Karakhan his way on China—he'll ruin the whole thing, that's for sure. He has outlived his usefulness: he was and *has remained* the ambassador of the *first* stage of the Chinese revolution and is entirely useless as a leader in the *current* new situation, both the Chinese and the international situation, given the **new** events which he doesn't understand and *can't understand on his own*, for he is a person who is terribly frivolous and limited (in the sense of revolutionary outlook). But as for audacity and impudence, arrogance and conceit—he's got plenty of those. That's what is especially dangerous. Karakhan will never understand that Hankow will soon become the Chinese Moscow . . .

Well, best regards,
J. Stalin
23 September 1926

Sochi. I am getting better, more or less.

P.S. I am not certain that an open appeal to the General Council from the Trade Union Council regarding a joint protest against the bombing of Wanhsien is correct.[7] It will look as if we are taunting both the General Council and the Conservatives needlessly. Is this necessary? It would be better to take other, more effective routes.

1. On 20 September 1926, the Politburo approved the proposal of its committee on wages. The committee proposed raising the wages only of workers employed in production. A list of branches of industry where wages were to be raised was also approved (coal, ore, metal, etc.) (RTsKhIDNI f. 17, op. 3, d. 588, ll. 1, 2).

2. On 30 September 1926, the Politburo recognized the need to raise the wages of individual groups of workers in the petroleum industry (ibid., d. 590, l. 2).

3. In October 1926, a joint plenum of the Central Committee and Central Control Commission decided to relieve Trotsky of his duties as a member of the Politburo because of his factional activity.

4. On 8 September 1926, V. M. Smirnov was expelled from the party for factional activity. On 26 November 1926, after acknowledging his mistakes, he was reinstated.

5. At a joint plenum of the Central Committee and Central Control Commission in October 1926, Shliapnikov and Medvedev, the former leaders of the "workers' opposition," were condemned for anti-party activity.

6. The Central Committee plenum of October 1926 added an item concerning the opposition and the internal party situation to the agenda of the XV Party Conference, which had already been published in the press.

7. The British navy's bombing of the Chinese city of Wanhsien took place on 5 September 1926.

Letter 29   [7 November 1926]

Com. Molotov,[1]

I don't see any reason why the speech in its current form shouldn't be printed without any corrections from me, if we all (including myself) give our speeches to be printed without any preliminary checking. I have only now realized the whole awkwardness of not having shown anyone my speech. Is your persistence regarding the corrections saying in fact that I was mistaken in not sending around my own speech to friends? I already feel awkward after the disputes of a couple of days ago. And now you want to kill me with your modesty, once again insisting on a review of the speech. No, I had better / refrain. Better print it in the form that you consider necessary.

J. Stalin

7 November

1. The text is written on the Central Committee's stationery. In the upper left-hand corner is Molotov's handwritten remark: "Re: my speech at the XV Party Conference. V.M." Stalin and Molotov were in Moscow at the time. The XV Party Conference took place from 26 October to 3 November 1926. Stalin gave a speech on the opposition and the internal party situation.

Letter 30   [23 December 1926]

Hello, Viacheslav,[1]

You don't have to hurry back—you could easily remain another week (or even more) past the deadline.

Things are going pretty well here for us.

1) state procurements and exports are going all right;

2) revenues to the state budget are not coming in very well;

3) the *Chervonets* is doing fine;[2]

4) industry is creeping ahead a little bit;

5) we decided to lower the wholesale price on a number of consumer goods;[3]

6) we are drafting immediate and *concrete* measures to reduce *retail* prices (we will put brutal pressure on the trade and cooperative network).[4]

The Congress of Trade Unions passed "normally" as Tomskii would say; that is, we preserved everything we had but added nothing new to our arsenal.[5]

The expanded plenum of the Comintern Executive Committee[6] went all right. The resolution of the XV Conference was passed unanimously (one Bordiga supporter from Italy abstained). Our oppositionists are really fools. Why the hell they jumped into the fray I don't know, but they got well and truly whipped. When Kamenev made an irresponsibly harmful speech, I had to remind him in the closing remarks of the telegram to M. Romanov. Kamenev came out with a "rebuttal," saying, "It's a lie."[7] Zinoviev, Kamenev, Smilga, and Fedorov brought a "statement" of "rebuttal" to the Politburo, demanding that it be published. We published the statement in *Bolshevik* with the Central Committee's answer and with documents that slaughtered Kamenev politically. We consider that Kamenev is knocked out of commission and won't be in the Central Committee any longer.

Well, that's it for now. More later in person.

Regards,

Koba

23 December 1926

1. The letter was sent from Moscow.

2. Ten-ruble bank note in circulation 1922–1947—Trans.

3. The Politburo considered reducing the wholesale prices of consumer goods on 23 December 1926 (RTsKhIDNI f. 17, op. 3, d. 607, ll. 4, 5.).

4. In February 1927, the Central Committee plenum approved the resolution "On the reduction of retail and wholesale prices" (*KPSS v rezoliutsiiakh* [Resolutions of the CPSU], vol. 4 [Moscow, 1984], 137–48).

5. The VII Congress of USSR Trade Unions took place on 6–18 December 1926.

6. The VII expanded plenum of the Comintern Executive Committee took place in Moscow from 22 November through 16 December 1926, with 191 representatives from the Communist parties of various countries in attendance. The plenum discussed the following issues: the international situation and the tasks of the Comintern; the disputes inside the Soviet party; lessons of the British strike; the Chinese question; the work of the Communists in the trade union movement; questions of individual parties.

7. On 15 December 1926, Kamenev stated that this reference to a telegram to M. Romanov was a repetition of the gossip that chauvinist socialists had spread against the Bolsheviks. At the evening session of the Comintern plenum, he made the following statement (RTsKhIDNI f. 85, op. 1c, d. 173, ll. 3, 4):

> Yesterday Com. Stalin reported from the Comintern podium that I had supposedly sent a telegram to Mikhail Romanov during the first days of the February revolution. . . .
> The editorial board of *Pravda*, of which I was a member at that time, along with Comrades Lenin and Zinoviev, learned of this slander from the newspaper *Yedinstvo* [Unity], which was under the direction of a well-known renegade and scoundrel and later monarchist, Aleksinskii, who in those days waged a furious campaign against the Bolsheviks in general and against each one of us in particular. . . . This provincial lie personally directed against me was judged by all of us to be petty and insignificant gossip, and we limited ourselves to several lines of rebuttal, stating that the telegram was sent on behalf of a rally in a provincial town in Siberia, where, as an exile, I had also spoken; it was sent against my wishes. . . .
> It goes without saying that no one—including Stalin—even thought of ascribing any significance whatsoever to this gossip when, two weeks after the appearance of this lie at the April (1917) conference, I—as Lenin had proposed—was elected along with him, Zinoviev, and Stalin to the first legal Central Committee of our party. Since then, for ten years, no one has dared to return to this slander.
> After ten years of collaboration, to repeat such a charge as a means of struggle is to condemn oneself in the most brutal fashion.

CHAPTER THREE

1927

HISTORIANS HAVE frequently regarded 1927 as a year of crisis for moderate policies and as the prologue to Stalin's "great breakthrough" of the early 1930s. There were many signs of the government's departure from NEP. Economic policy was becoming less reasoned and balanced. Attacks on "bourgeois elements" were increasing. The political regime grew harsher. The struggle with the opposition in the party was waged with increasing strength, chiefly with the help of the OGPU.

Particularly influential in Soviet society at the time was intensified propaganda about a drastic deterioration of the international situation and the proximity of a new war. The facts behind this high-powered campaign include the 23 February 1927 note from Austin Chamberlain, British foreign minister, accusing the USSR of conducting "anti-British propaganda"; the attack on the Soviet embassy in Peking on 6 April 1927, instigated by the Chinese government; the search by the British police on 12 May 1927 of the offices of Arcos, an Anglo-Soviet joint-stock company; Great Britain's severing of diplomatic relations with the USSR at the end of May; and the murder of P. L. Voikov, Soviet ambassador to Poland, on 7 June 1927.

Official Soviet propaganda ascribed great significance to each of these incidents. The government used international problems as an excuse to crack down internally. Newspapers reported the OGPU's discovery of new, hostile plots. In mid-May a group of former noblemen who worked in various Soviet government offices were detained as hostages. On the day following the murder of Voikov, by order of the OGPU collegium, the twenty hostages were executed without trial. That summer and fall, various militarized activities, for example, a "defense week" and mobilization drills, were organized.

Stalin's letters to Molotov preserved from 1927 are almost entirely devoted to foreign policy issues. He was greatly concerned with the state of the international Communist movement. In that regard, 1927 was a year of crisis. The united front policy suffered a number of failures in Great Britain and continual conflict undermined the viability of the Anglo-Russian Committee, the symbol of the united front policy of cooperation between the Communists and the social democrats. In September 1927, the British trade unions finally withdrew from the Anglo-Russian Committee.

Tragic, bloody events took place in China that same year. For several years, Moscow had encouraged the Chinese Communists to cooperate with the Kuomintang, restraining them from any independent actions for the sake of preserving and strengthening the "revolutionary-democratic bloc" with the Chinese bourgeoisie. Even after Chiang Kai-shek massacred the Communists in Shanghai in 1927, the Soviet Politburo majority continued to hew to a version of this policy. The regime of the "left Kuomintang" in Wuhan preserved for a time its alliance with the Soviet government, which endeavored to use Wuhan as a weapon against Chiang Kai-shek. As can be seen from the letters, Wuhan was given no small amount of aid, and Stalin insisted on increasing it.

There were many signs, however, that the Wuhan regime would not orient itself toward Moscow or cooperate for long with the Communists. Nevertheless, Stalin continued to insist on the correctness of the chosen course. Thus when fresh disaster broke out in Wuhan, the Soviet government was largely caught by surprise. In mid-July 1927, the Chinese Communist Party was banned and many Communists were persecuted.

When he realized the scope of the disaster in China, Stalin immediately laid the groundwork for an organized retreat: in his letters he persuaded his gloomy allies on the Politburo that their China policy had been correct and that the crackdown against the Communist Party was provoked by objective circumstances and was mainly the fault of the Chinese Communists themselves. The Stalin-

Stalin and the Politburo: A. A. Andreev, K. Ye. Voroshilov, A. A. Zhdanov, L. M. Kaganovich, M. I. Kalinin, A. I. Mikoian, V. M. Molotov, N. S. Khrushchev, L. P. Beriia, N. M. Shvernik

Дорогой Вячеслав!

1) Просмотрел (очень бегло) "стенограмму засе-
дания ЦКК" по делу Зиновьева и прочаго.
Получается впечатление сплошного конфуза
для ЦКК. Допрашивали и обвиняли не члены ЦКК,
а Зиновьев и Троцкий. Странно, что подпи-
сались некоторое число ЦКК. А где Серго?
Куда и почему он спрятался? Позор! Не
имел бы ничего против того, что комис-
сия по обвинению Тр. и Зин. превратилась в
трибуну по обвинению ЦК и КК с защити-
ем "дела" против Сталина, которого нет в Москве и на которого можно ввиду этого ве-
шать всех собак. Неужели эту "стенограмму"
отдадут на руки Троц-му и Зин. для распро-
странения? Этого еще не хватало.
2) Обрати внимание на документы о "Труде". Надо произвести чистку в "Труде". Оччень...

23/VII - 26.

Letter from Stalin to Molotov, 23 July 1927 (RTsKhIDNI f. 558, op. 1, d. 5388, l. 48).

Bukharin leadership required all of these arguments to repel the opposition's attack.

The events in Great Britain and, especially, China provided the members of the opposition with powerful arguments against the party's leadership. This was the opposition's last chance, and it made the utmost use of it. The internal party confrontation reached its apex in the fall of 1927. By the end of the year, supporters of Trotsky and Zinoviev, like the leaders of the opposition themselves, were expelled from the party, and many were persecuted.

Letter 31   [23 June 1927]

Dear Viacheslav,[1]

1) I had a look (very quickly) at the "transcript of the Central Control Commission session" on the Zinoviev and Trotsky affair. The impression given is one of utter confusion on the part of the Central Control Commission. Zinoviev and Trotsky, not the Commission members, did the interrogating and the accusing. It's odd that some of the Commission members didn't show. Where's Sergo? Where has he gone and why is he hiding? Shame on him! I resolutely protest against the fact that the commission to charge Trotsky and Zinoviev has turned into a forum for charges against the Central Committee and the Comintern, with an emphasis on the "case" against Stalin, who is not in Moscow and on whom therefore any accusation can be pinned. Will Trotsky and Zinoviev really be handed this "transcript" to *distribute!* That's all we need.

2) Note the documents on *Trud* [Labor]. A purge should be conducted in *Trud*.[2]

23 June 1926

1. Stalin has placed the date 23 June 1926 under the text of the letter, although the events about which Stalin was writing took place in 1927. Zinoviev and Trotsky's defense was heard by the Central Control Commission, whose members were Yanson, Shkiriatov, and Ilin, on 13 and 14 June 1927 (RTsKhIDNI f. 613, op. 1, d. 48, l. 57).

On 24 June 1927, the Central Control Commission reviewed the question "On the violation of party discipline by Comrades Zinoviev and Trotsky." The Central Control Commission recommended that the joint plenum consider removing Zinoviev and Trotsky from the Central Committee. This decision was published in *Pravda* on 26 June 1927. Trotsky protested to the Central Control Commission about the omissions and distortions in the published transcript of his speeches at the Central Control Commission.

2. No evidence of such a purge has been discovered.

Letter 32

[24 June 1927]

6/24/26

Dear Viacheslav,[1]

I just received your last letter by courier. Regarding China, I think that 3 or 4 million can now be sent out of the 10 million, and the question of the 15 million should be postponed. Another 15 million is being asked of us, apparently in order to avoid an immediate attack against Chiang Kai-shek if we don't give those 15 million.[2]

As for the holy trinity (R.+Or.+V.),[3] I am remaining silent about them for the time being since there will still be plenty of opportunities to discuss them later. Or. is a "good fellow," but a phony politician. He was always a "simple-minded" politician. V. is probably just "not the type." As for R., he is "scheming," supposing that this is what "real politics" is all about.

Greetings,
J. Stalin

1. The upper left-hand corner of the letter contains a date inserted by Stalin: "24 June 1926." The events discussed in the letter took place in 1927.

2. The reference is to subsidies given the Wuhan government for organizing an expedition against Chiang Kai-shek's group.

3. We can only guess who Stalin is referring to here. Judging from the next letter, "R., Or., and V." were in some way connected with Mikoian, who was commissar of trade at this time—U.S. Ed.

Letter 33

[27 June 1927]

Dear Viacheslav and Nikolai,[1]

1. I received your last letters (24 June) and the Politburo resolution about the Anglo-Russian Committee.[2] Hack "them" to pieces pretty well (I mean the General Council), not by making a lot of noise, but thoroughly. They may break off [with us] in order to "demonstrate" their "independence" from Moscow and earn Chamberlain's praise. But they will lose more in breaking off now than [if they had broken off] during the coal strike period, since the real threat of war affects all workers, and very profoundly. They will try to make much of the executions, but that won't work for very long, especially if you try to provide some well-argued declaration on that score. You should throw it right back in "their" faces that they are helping their masters launch and wage a war.

2. I already wrote about Feng [Yü-hsiang] in the coded telegram. Apparently the report about Feng corresponds to reality.[3] I'm afraid that Wuhan[4] will

lose its nerve and come under Nanking.[5] It's not worth arguing with Wuhan over Borodin (if Wuhan wants to remove him). But we must insist adamantly on Wuhan not submitting to Nanking while there is still an opportunity to insist. Losing Wuhan as a separate center means losing at least some center for the revolutionary movement, losing the possibility of free assembly and rallies for the workers, losing the possibility of the open existence of the Communist Party, losing the possibility of an open revolutionary press— in a word, losing the possibility of openly organizing the proletariat and the revolution. In order to obtain all this, I assure you, it is worth giving Wuhan an extra 3–5 million—but only with some assurance that Wuhan will not surrender to the tender mercies of Nanking, with our money wasted for nothing.

3. I received a telegram the other day from Wang Ching-wei and gave him a fairly lengthy reply of my own. Read it and tell me your opinion in brief.

4. I have no objections regarding Lozovskii.

5. Regarding the expediency of making our relations with Chiang "official," I have my doubts. The analogy with Chang Tso-lin doesn't hold up. We recognized Chang three years ago. If the matter were to come up today, we would not officially recognize him. To recognize Chiang *now* (this minute) would mean striking a blow against Wuhan (Wuhan still exists) and throwing down the gauntlet to Chang Tso-lin (remember the Chinese Eastern Railway). It would be better to wait on Chiang and keep the status quo.

6. It's not surprising that R. has gone into leftism in a big way. That means that he has lost for a minute the opportunity to "scheme," "maneuver," and so on. But Mikoian is a greenhorn in politics, a talented greenhorn, but a greenhorn all the same. When he grows up, he'll improve.

Well, regards,

J. Stalin

27 June 1926

1. Stalin dates the letter 27 June 1926. In fact the events discussed in the letter took place in 1927. On the back of the letter, in Bukharin's hand, is: "I've read it through, Bukh."

2. On 24 June 1927, the Politburo approved the idea of a trade union declaration criticizing the British General Council's position because its position had led to a break with the Anglo-Russian Committee and to support for the Conservative government. The declaration included a response to the General Council's criticism of the execution of twenty White Guards in the USSR on 9 June 1927 (RTsKhIDNI f. 17, op. 3, d. 641, l. 3).

3. On 10 June 1927, at a secret meeting with the Wuhan leaders, Feng Yü-hsiang, the commander in chief of the national government's forces, made his alliance with Wuhan conditional upon the latter's break with the Communists. On 21 June, after a meeting between Feng Yü-hsiang and Chiang Kai-shek, their intention to act in unison was announced. In a telegram to the Wuhan government, Feng demanded submission to Nanking and the dismissal of Borodin, political advisor to the Kuomintang Central Committee sent from Moscow in 1923. For information on Feng Yü-hsiang, see note 4 to letter 27.

4. Wuhan is where the national government headed by Wang Ching-wei was located. The majority of the top posts in this government were held by representatives of the left wing of the Kuomintang, and two ministries (labor and agriculture) were headed by Communists.

5. The reference is to Chiang Kai-shek's group, whose center was located in Nanking after the coup of 12 April 1927.

Letter 34

[Early July 1927]

Dear Viacheslav,[1]

I'm sick and lying in bed so I'll be brief.

1. The Trade Union Council's declaration is good,[2] Rykov's answer is bad.[3]
2. Tomskii's report is weak.[4]
3. I would be for giving Ishchenko and Valentinov a *warning*.[5]
4. Trotsky should go to Japan.
5. I could come for the plenum if it's necessary and if you postpone it.[6]
6. Bukharin's article about China turned out well.[7]

Greetings,
J. Stalin

1. The upper right-hand corner of the letter has a notation from Molotov: "1926=?" In fact the letter was written by Stalin in early July 1927. The upper left-hand corner has a notation from Bukharin: "I've read it. Bukh."

2. The reference is to the Trade Union Council's resolution concerning the results of Tomskii's negotiations with British representatives regarding the Anglo-Russian Committee, which was approved by the Politburo on 28 June 1927 (RTsKhIDNI f. 17, op. 3, d. 642, l. 5). This resolution criticized the General Council, because its policy was leading to the collapse of the Anglo-Russian Committee and to support of the Conservative government.

3. The reference is to Rykov's reply to the telegram from [George] Lansbury and [James] Maxton, activists of the British workers' movement, who had protested the execution of twenty people by order of the secret police. Rykov claimed that the campaign against the death penalty was deliberately launched by the bourgeoisie to cover up the organization of an anti-Soviet imperialist bloc and to prepare for intervention in the USSR.

4. The reference is to Tomskii's report at the Trade Union Council plenum on 28 June 1927.

5. Ishchenko's and Valentinov's factional activities were on the agenda of several Central Control Commission meetings in the fall of 1927.

Ishchenko was accused of violating party discipline "by distributing without consent of party bodies . . . among nonparty people his appeal to the Congress of Water Transport Workers, which contained slanderous attacks against the line of the Central Committee." It was determined that "his speech at the Trade Union Council plenum was slander against the party."

Valentinov was accused of making an anti-party speech at the Trade Union Council plenum "defending proposals from the Trotskyist opposition." The Central Control Commission resolution stated that his speech was "an attempt to discredit before nonparty members the party's leadership of the trade union movement through juggling and distortion of the facts."

By decision of the Central Control Commission, both men were expelled from the party (RTsKhIDNI f. 613, op. 1, d. 49, ll. 124, 127ob., 137, 137ob.).

6. The joint plenum of the Central Committee and Central Control Commission opened on 29 July 1927.

7. The reference is to Bukharin's article "Tekushchii moment kitaiskoi revoliutsii" (The current moment in the Chinese revolution), published in *Pravda,* 30 June 1927.

Letter 35

Dear Viacheslav,[1]

1. When I sent my big coded telegram about China, I didn't know about T'ang Shen-chih's machinations or about the behavior of the Wuhan government in connection with this. (I also didn't have the materials concerning the disarming of the workers' guard in Wuhan.)[2] Obviously, with all these new materials you were justified in approving new directives. We used the Wuhan leadership as much as possible. Now it's time to discard them. An attempt should be made to take over the periphery of the Kuomintang and help it oppose its current bosses. The fact that the periphery of the Kuomintang is being persecuted by military upstarts tells you that this task may be successful.[3] Therefore, if there is a chance, we ought not to link withdrawal from the national government (which is necessary now) with withdrawal from the Kuomintang (which may become necessary in the near future).

2. I am not afraid of the situation in the group. Why—I'll explain when I come.

3. When should I come exactly?

Greetings,
J. Stalin
8 July 1926

1. Stalin dated the letter 8 July 1926, although the events mentioned in the letter occurred in 1927.

2. The reference is to the disarming of workers' detachments in Wuhan, which took place in June 1927 by order of Wang Ching-wei, head of the national government in Wuhan.

3. By the word *periphery*, Stalin seems to mean local organizations of the Kuomintang—U.S. Ed.

Letter 36

7/9/26

To Molotov and Bukharin,[1]

Damn the both of you: you misled me a little bit by asking my opinion on the *new* directives (about China) and not providing me with *concrete* fresh material. The draft of the new directives talks about both T'ang Shen-chih and disarming the workers (the "*virtual* disarming," T'ang Shen-chih "*virtually* became the tool of the counterrevolutionaries," and so on). But first, no *concrete* facts are provided there, and second, neither the press nor the coded telegrams (which I had at the time) said anything about the existence of *such facts.* And not only did **you** mislead me a little bit, but **I** also misled you, perhaps, with my long and quite angry reply by coded telegram.

After I received the draft of your new directives, I decided: *so*, the opposition has finally worn Bukharin and Molotov down with a flood of new "theses," and they have succumbed, finally, *to blackmail*; *so*, Klim [Voroshilov] will be glad now that he is freed from the *payments* to Wuhan, which is why he was only too happy to vote for the new directives. And so forth and so on in the same spirit. Now I see that was all wrong. Yesterday I spent the whole day reading the new materials brought by the courier. Now I am not worried that new directives have been sent but rather that they have been sent too late. I don't think that leaving the national government and the Kuomintang can ease the plight of the Communist Party and "put it on its feet." On the contrary, leaving will only make it easier to beat up the Communists, create new discord, and perhaps even prepare something like a split. But there is no other way, and, in any event, in the end we had to come to this. This period has to be gotten through, absolutely.

But that is not the main thing now. The main thing is whether or not the *current* Chinese Communist Party can manage to *emerge with honor* from this new period (the underground, arrests, beatings, executions, betrayals and provocations among their own ranks, etc.), to come out hardened, tempered, without splitting up, breaking into pieces, disintegrating, and degenerating into a sect or a number of sects. We cannot exclude this danger at all, nor can we exclude the possibility of an interval between this bourgeois revolution and a *future* bourgeois revolution—analogous to the interval that we had between 1905 and 1917 (February). Moreover, I believe that *such* a danger is more real (I mean the danger of the disintegration of the Chinese Communist Party) than some of the seeming realities so abundant in China. Why? Because unfortunately, we don't have a real or, if you like, actual Communist Party in China. If you take away the middle-ranking Communists who make good fighting material but who are completely inexperienced in politics, then what is the current Central Committee of the Chinese Communist Party (CCP)? Nothing but an "amalgamation" of general phrases gathered here and there, not linked to one another with any line or guiding idea. I don't want to be very demanding toward the Central Committee of the CCP. I know that one can't be too demanding toward it. But here is a simple demand: fulfill the directives of the Comintern. Has it fulfilled these directives? No. No, because it did not understand them, because it did not want to fulfill them and has *hoodwinked* the Comintern, or because it wasn't able to fulfill them. That is a fact. Roy blames Borodin. That's stupid. It can't be that Borodin has more weight with the CCP or its Central Committee than the Comintern does. Roy himself wrote that Borodin did not attend the CCP Congress since he was forced to go into hiding. . . . Some (some!) explain this by the fact that the bloc with the Kuomintang is to blame, which ties the CCP down and does not allow it to be independent.[2] That is also not true, for although *any* bloc ties down the members of the bloc one way or another, that doesn't mean that we should be against blocs in general. Take Chiang's five coastal provinces from Canton to Shanghai, where there is no bloc with the Kuomintang. How can you explain that Chiang's agents are more successful at disintegrating the "army" of the Communists, than the Communists are at disintegrating Chiang's rear guard? Is it not a fact that a whole number of trade unions are breaking off from the CCP, and Chiang continues to hold strong? What sort of CCP "independence" is that? . . . I think the reason is not in these factors, although they have their significance, but in the fact that the current Central Committee (its leadership) was forged in the period of the nationwide revolution and received its baptism by fire during this period and it turned out to be *completely unadaptable* to the new, agrarian phase of the revolution. The CCP Central Committee *does not understand* the point of the new phase of the revolution. There is *not a single* Marxist mind in the Central Committee capable of understanding the underpinning (the social underpinning) of the events now occurring. The CCP Central Committee *was unable to use* the rich period of the bloc with Kuomintang in order to conduct energetic work in *openly* organizing the revolution, the proletariat, the peasantry, the revolutionary military units, the revolutionizing of the army, the work of *setting the soldiers against* the generals. The CCP Central Committee has lived off the Kuomintang for a whole year and has had the opportunity of freely working and organizing, yet it did nothing to turn the conglomerate of elements (true, quite militant), incorrectly called a party, into a real party. . . . Of course there was work at the grass roots. We are indebted to the middle-ranking Communists for that. But characteristically, it was not the Central Committee that went to the workers and peasants but the workers and peasants who went to the Central Committee, and the closer the workers and peasants approached the Central Committee, the farther away from them went the so-called Central Committee, preferring to kill time in behind-the-scenes talks with the leaders and generals from the Kuomintang. The CCP sometimes babbles about the hegemony of the proletariat. But the most intolerable thing about this babbling is that the CCP *does not have a clue* (literally, not a clue) about hegemony—it kills the initiative of the working masses, undermines the "unauthorized" actions of the peasant masses, and reduces class warfare in China to a lot of big talk about the "feudal bourgeoisie" (now it has finally been determined that, as it turns out, the author of this term is Roy).

That's the reason why the Comintern's directives are not fulfilled.

That is why I'm afraid of letting such a party float freely on the "wide open sea" before it has to (it will crash before it has managed to harden itself . . .).

That is why I now believe the question of the party is the main question of the Chinese revolution.

How can we fix the conglomerate that we incorrectly call the Chinese Communist Party? The recall of Ch'en Tu-hsiu or T'an Ping-shan will not help here, of course, although I don't object to recalling them and teaching them a thing or two. Other measures are needed. A good Marxist-Leninist literature must be created in the Chinese language—fundamental, not made up of "little leaflets"—and the necessary funds must now be allocated for this, without delay (you can say to Klim that this will cost much less than maintaining one hundred of his hemorrhoidal bureaucrat/counterrevolutionaries for half a year). Furthermore, we have expended too much effort on organizing a system of advisors for the armies in China (moreover, these advisors turned out not to be on the ball *politically*—that is, they were never able to warn us in time of the defection of their own "chiefs"). It's time to really busy ourselves with the organization of a system of *party advisors* attached to the CCP Central Committee, the Central Committee departments, regional organizations in *each province*, the departments of these regional organizations, the party youth organization, the peasant department of the Central Committee, the military department of the Central Committee, the central organ [party newspaper], the federation of trade unions of China. Both Borodin and Roy must be purged from China, along with all those opposition members that hinder the work there. We should regularly send to China, not people we don't need, but competent people instead. The structure has to be set up so that all these party advisors work together as a whole, directed by the chief advisor to the Central Committee (the Comintern representative). These "nannies" are necessary at this stage because of the weakness, shapelessness and political amorphousness, and lack of qualification of the current Central Committee. The Central Committee will learn from the party advisors. The party advisors will compensate for the enormous shortcomings of the CCP Central Committee and its top regional officials. They will serve (for the time being) as the nails holding the existing conglomerate together as a party.

And so on in the same spirit.

As the revolution and the party grow, the need for these "nannies" will disappear.

Well, that will do.

Regards to you,
J. Stalin

P.S. *Report back on receiving this letter. Report your opinion as well.* If you find it necessary, you can give it to the other Politburo members to read.

J. Stalin

1. In the upper right-hand corner, the date written by Stalin is 9 July 1926, although the events mentioned in the letter occurred in 1927. At the top of the letter there are the following notations: "I've read it. Bukharin. Read it. A. I. Rykov, A. Andreev, M. Tomskii, Voroshilov, A. Mikoian."

2. Stalin is referring to the views of the united opposition headed by Zinoviev and Trotsky—U.S. Ed.

Letter 37   [11 July 1927]

Dear Viacheslav,

1) I received Zinoviev's article "The Contours of the Coming War."[1] Are you really going to publish this ignorant piece of trash? I am decidedly against publication.

2) I read the Politburo directives on the withdrawal from the national government in China. I think that soon the issue of withdrawing from the Kuomintang will have to be raised.[2] I'll explain why when I come. I have been told that some people are in a repentant mood regarding our policy in China. If that is true, it's too bad. When I come, I will try to prove that our policy was and remains the only correct policy. Never have I been so deeply and firmly convinced of the correctness of our policy, both in China and regarding the Anglo-Russian Committee, as I am now.

3) When should I be in Moscow?

J. Stalin
11 July 1927

1. Zinoviev's article "Kontury griaduschchei voiny i nashi zadachi" (Contours of the coming war and our tasks) outlined the views of the united opposition on both foreign policy and domestic issues. The article was sharply criticized at a joint meeting of the Central Committee and Central Control Commission in August 1927.

2. The expulsion of the Communists from the Kuomintang occurred at the initiative of the Kuomintang's Central Executive Committee on 26 July 1927. The Chinese Communist Party was banned, and many Communists and their supporters were persecuted.

Letter 38   [16 July 1927]

7/16/26

To Molotov:[1]

1) We'll talk about China when I come. You didn't understand my letter. The letter says that we can't **rule out** an interval [between revolutions], but that doesn't mean that a new upsurge in the next period is ruled out. In short, let's talk when I get there. You have apparently decided to distribute the documents of the opposition to the members and candidates of the Central Committee and the Central Control Commission.[2] But what do you have to counter these documents with? Surely not just Bukharin's last article?[3] But really, it's just not good enough! To distribute documents **in that way** doesn't help us.

2) Your hastiness in setting up official diplomatic relations with Chiang

[Kai-shek] makes a bad impression. What is this—a bow to Chamberlain or something else of the kind? What's the big hurry?

3) I'll be in Moscow on Saturday morning the 23rd. I wanted to put it off another two days, but the weather here is starting to turn bad.

Greetings,
Stalin

1. Stalin dates the letter 16 July 1926. In fact, the events mentioned in the letter occurred in 1927.

2. The reference is to statements from the opposition on the Chinese question.

3. Bukharin's article "Na krutom perevale kitaiskoi revoliutsii" (On the steep pass of the Chinese revolution) was published in *Pravda* on 10 July 1927.

CHAPTER FOUR

1929

IN THE LETTERS WRITTEN IN 1929, as in those written in previous years, Stalin advocated an extremely harsh response to all issues that fell under the purview of the country's top leadership. Once again, he proposed resolving the growing problem of grain procurement through coercive emergency methods. From the letter of 10 August (letter 41), it is apparent that Stalin is responsible for insisting on grain procurement even if it required crude force.

No less vigilantly did Stalin cut off attempts to voice even the slightest dissent on the "ideological front." As the letters illustrate (letters 39, 42, 43, 44), a campaign was organized on Stalin's orders to expose the well-known party propagandists Ya. Sten and L. Shatskin. In their articles published in *Komsomolskaia pravda*, Sten and Shatskin criticized "conformism in the party" and some members' lack of principle; they called on members to think about the party line in an independent, critical way, using their own experience. On Stalin's instructions, these platitudes were characterized as attempts to undermine party discipline, and Sten and Shatskin were described as "slipping into the political and organizational positions of Trotskyism on individual issues."

Stalin's foreign policy positions were no less harsh. In 1929, the Soviet leadership's attention was chiefly focused on establishing diplomatic relations with Great Britain and overcoming the conflict with China regarding the Chinese Eastern Railway (CER). A significant portion of the letters to Molotov in 1929 are devoted to these matters in particular.

The Conservative government of Great Britain suspended diplomatic relations with the Soviet Union in June 1927. Over time, larger and larger circles of the British public favored restoring relations. Thus, when the Labour government won the election in the spring of 1929, it began almost immediately to prepare for negotiations with the USSR. British leaders tried to combine the restoration of diplomatic relations with a settlement of some outstanding disputes between the USSR and Great Britain—primarily the debts of the tsarist government, British citizens' claims on property nationalized in the Soviet Union, and the ban on distributing "Communist propaganda" in Great Britain, which Britain viewed as interference in its internal affairs.

On 17 July 1929, the Labour government notified the Soviet government of its readiness to resume relations and requested that a Soviet representative be sent to work out a procedure for discussing the disputed matters. In late July, V. S. Dovgalevskii was sent to Great Britain as the authorized representative of the government of the USSR. He had strict instructions to negotiate only on the procedure for resolving the disputed matters, not on their substance. The Kremlin demanded that diplomatic relations be restored before any mutual claims could be settled.

At the very first meeting in London, British Foreign Minister Arthur Henderson informed Dovgalevskii that the British government could establish diplomatic relations only through Parliament, whose next session started on 29 October. In order not to lose the intervening three months, he proposed that negotiations on the disputed matters should commence immediately. Moscow rejected the offer, and Dovgalevskii left Great Britain right away.

On 4 September 1929, Henderson reiterated the British government's readiness to conduct negotiations on the procedure for renewing diplomatic relations. On 6 September Maksim Litvinov, Soviet commissar of foreign affairs, announced that the USSR had agreed to talks between Henderson and Dovgalevskii to begin on 24 September in London. On 5 October 1929, the House of Commons approved the restoration of diplomatic relations with the USSR.

The letters show that Stalin was directing the negotiations with Great Britain. They also reveal that his insistence on a harsh, uncompromising position led him into conflict with Litvinov, although the precise nature of the conflict remains unclear.

The diplomatic interplay with Great Britain coincided with the sharp conflict over the CER, the railroad under the joint administration of the USSR and China. The chairman of the board of the CER (the *taipan* of the railway) was appointed by the Chinese, and the administrator of the railroad was a Soviet citizen. Other positions were held by both Soviet and Chinese citizens.

On 10 July 1929, the Chinese police occupied the CER central telegraph station and arrested a number of Soviet officials. The taipan demanded that the Soviet administrator, A. I. Yemshanov, turn over the administration of the railroad to Chinese appointees. When Yemshanov refused, his aide, Eismont, and other officials were expelled from China. The new director, his assistant, and other officials were appointed by the taipan. Many Soviet citizens were arrested. An armed conflict broke out on the Soviet-Chinese border.

On 16 August 1929, the USSR broke off diplomatic relations with China. That same month, by order of the Revolutionary Military Council, the Special Far East Army was formed. Military units were deployed along the Soviet-Chinese border. Together with this display of force, there were attempts to settle the conflict peacefully. With the intercession of the German ambassador to Moscow (Germany undertook to defend Chinese interests in the USSR and Soviet interests in China), the Soviet and Chinese governments tried to come up with a declaration resolving the conflict in late August. The attempt failed; the stumbling block was the Soviet government's refusal to appoint a new CER administrator and assistant. Moscow agreed to reconsider the matter of replacing Yemshanov and Eismont only if the Chinese government would appoint a "new chairman of the board [taipan] to replace the current one, who is directly responsible for violating the agreement and for aggressive actions on the CER."[1] The Chinese government rejected this stipulation.

Both sides had reason to be uncompromising and to drag out the talks. From Stalin's letters, it becomes evident that he was counting on provoking an uprising in Manchuria by dispatching special military detachments to the region. In early October, Soviet troops

1. *Dokumenty vneshnei politiki SSSR* (Documents of USSR foreign policy), vol. 12 (Moscow, 1967), 489.

commenced active military operations. In November, the Chinese suffered a defeat in Manchuria.

On 19 November 1929, A. Simanovskii, a Soviet official in Khabarovsk, received from a Chinese official in Harbin, Ts'ai Yun-shan, a statement that he was authorized to open talks immediately to settle the Soviet-Chinese conflict. On 22 November, Simanovskii reported to Ts'ai that the Soviet government advocated a peaceful settlement of the conflict but that the Chinese government had to fulfill some preliminary conditions: to officially consent to restoring the status of the CER that had existed prior to the conflict, to restore the rights of Yemshanov and Eismont, and to immediately release all arrested Soviet citizens.

The Chinese accepted all the Soviet demands. As a result of the negotiations, a preliminary protocol ending the Soviet-Chinese conflict was signed in Nikolsk-Ussuriysk on 3 December 1929.[2] On 22 December, the Khabarovsk protocol on the restoration of the CER's prior status was signed.

Among Stalin's concerns in 1929, the struggle with the Bukharin group figured prominently. In spite of the political defeat of the "rightists" in April 1929 at both the plenum of the Central Committee and the XVI Party Conference, Bukharin, Rykov, and Tomskii preserved some authority in the party-state apparat. All of them remained members of the Politburo. In addition, Rykov occupied the high government posts of chairman of the Council of Commissars and chairman of the Labor Defense Council. The "rightists" remained on good personal terms with many members of the Politburo. This state of affairs in the Politburo and the position of the Bukharin group provide the background for understanding Voroshilov's letter to Ordzhonikidze of 8 June 1929.

> Moscow, 8 June 1929
> Dear Friend,
>   I am extremely glad to hear about your general condition and that your wound is healing well. Everything is going well and the sun will make up for what the "old bod" finds difficult to handle. I know that you're mad at me for being silent. Please note, however, my great friend, that neither Unshlikht nor [S. S.] Kamenev (my deputies) are here, and I am taking the rap all alone. Of course this circumstance is no justification,

2. Ibid., 594–96, 601–2.

but still you must be more indulgent with me. What's going on with our affairs? I think you know everything that's interesting and important from Koba [Stalin], and the rest is being reported fairly accurately by the newspapers. It will hardly be news to you that Bug-arin[3] has been appointed to the Scientific-Technical Administration of the Supreme Economic Council. The information was published in the newspapers. The newspapers just don't know the details that accompanied this "act." The correspondents of the bourgeois European newspapers explain Bukharin's appointment as his removal from politics, as his dismissal from the leadership. There are quite a few people in our country who think the same thing. But in reality Bukharin begged everyone not to appoint him to the Commissariat of Education and proposed and then insisted on the job as administrator of science and technology. I supported him in that, as did several other people, and because we were a united majority we pushed it through (against Koba). Now I somewhat regret my vote. I think (I fear) that Bukharin will directly or indirectly support the idea that this was a removal from power. Mikhail [Tomskii] is still at loose ends. For the time being, he has been nominated to the Central Union of Consumer Organizations, but neither Tomskii nor Liubimov is especially sympathetic to that idea. There is now talk of nominating Liubimov commissar of finance, and if that goes through, then it is quite likely that Tomskii will have to go to the Central Union of Consumer Organizations.

At the last Politburo meeting, a rather nasty affair broke out between Bukharin and me. The Chinese affair was being discussed. Some favored a demonstration of military force on the Manchurian border. Bukharin spoke out sharply against this. In my speech I mentioned that at one time Bukharin had identified the Chinese revolution with ours to such an extent that the ruin of the Chinese revolution was equivalent to our ruin. Bug-arin said in reply that we have all said different things at different times, but only you, Voroshilov alone, had advocated support for Feng and Chiang Kai-shek, who are presently slaughtering workers. This unpardonable nonsense so infuriated me that I lost my self-control and blurted out in Nikolashka's [Bukharin's] face, "You liar, bastard, I'll punch you in the face," and other such nonsense and all in front of a large number of people. Bukharin is trash and is capable of telling the most vile fabrications straight to your face, putting an especially innocent and disgustingly holy expression on his ever-

3. Literally *Bukhashka,* a play on Bukharin's name with the Russian word *bukashka,* or insect—Trans.

lastingly Jesuitical countenance; this is now clear to me, but, still, I did not behave properly.

But the trouble is my nerves. The damned things get me into trouble. After this scene, Bukharin left the Politburo meeting and did not return. Tomskii did not react at all. Rudzutak, who was chairman, should have called me to order, I think, but got by with just mumbling something.[4]

It is hard to say to what extent Stalin feared that his too vigorous and harsh attacks on the "rightists" would provoke a counterattack in the Politburo and push his wavering supporters toward Bukharin. As usual, Stalin spent a long time preparing, step-by-step, for the final blow against the Bukharin group. Bukharin was removed from the Politburo in November 1929; Tomskii, in July 1930; and Rykov, in December 1930. In each case, their removal was preceded by a campaign of harassment and provocation. Bukharin was the main target of these attacks in 1929.

The excuse for the latest attacks against Bukharin was his speech at the All-Union Congress of Atheists (*Pravda*, 12 June 1929) and the publication of a long article, "The Theory of 'Organized Mismanagement'" ([Teoriia "organizovannoy bezkhoziaistvennosti"], *Pravda*, 30 June 1919).

On 8 July 1929, the Politburo passed the following resolution:

> a) To consider that Com. Bukharin's speech at the antireligious Congress and his article "Organized Mismanagement" is a continuation in masked form of the struggle against the party and its Central Committee.
>
> b) To propose to the editors of *Pravda* and other organs of the party press that the resolution of the recent Central Committee plenum be followed and that such articles and speeches not be published in the future.[5]

Bukharin tried to resist. On 22 July 1929, he sent the following letter to all the Politburo members and candidate members and also to Ye. M. Yaroslavskii.

Dear Comrades,

I received an excerpt from the Politburo's decisions of 8 July 1929 that partly deals with the agenda item "On the article and speech of

4. RTsKhIDNI f. 85, op. 1/s. d. 110, ll. 1–20b.
5. Ibid., f. 17, op. 3, d. 748, l. 5.

Com. Bukharin." According to this decision, the publishing of "such articles and speeches" is prohibited by virtue of "the resolution of the recent Central Committee plenum" because the speech at the antireligious congress and the article about [Hermann] Bente's book supposedly represent "in masked form" a "struggle against the party and its Central Committee."

This extraordinary decision, which is without precedent in the history of the party, appears to me to be profoundly unjust for reasons of both substance and form.

I gave the speech at the Congress of Atheists, in accordance with the Politburo's resolution, *on behalf of the Central Committee of the party.* In order to avoid the slightest misunderstanding, I asked Com. Yaroslavskii, who was, as is known, a speaker on the internal party question at the Central Committee plenum and therefore a fairly competent person regarding the decisions of the plenum on this matter, to give his *preliminary* consent to an outline of this speech; after I gave the speech, *the council* of the atheist congress, whose chairman is the very same Com. *Yaroslavskii,* decreed by special decision that the speech should be printed as a pamphlet; *the editors of Pravda,* headed by Com. Krumin, also found nothing in the speech that would contradict the party line; finally, after all, I personally participated in one of several sessions of the Politburo *after* the speech was published, and *no one* expressed any negative reaction toward it. Unfortunately, the Politburo does not indicate how the speech departs from the party line, a departure that was not noted by anyone for approximately six weeks.

The article "The Theory of 'Organized Mismanagement'" did not deal at all with issues that were a subject of dispute at the plenum, and I cannot understand what *could* be the disagreement with the party line. This article was printed after the second reform in *Pravda*'s editorial staff, that is, *after* the creation of an internal collegium of Com. Yaroslavskii, Krumin, and Popov. They apparently found nothing in the article that would contradict the party line and the decisions of the last plenum, which, of course, were also supported by Com. Yaroslavskii, a member of the internal collegium.

From all of this it follows that without any precise indication of what makes my speech and article incorrect, the editorial staff, which had not noted these inaccuracies, has been told, in effect, not to place a single other article under my byline. If this is what is intended, then I would ask the Politburo to pass a direct and precise resolution on this subject, which, of course, will be accepted by me for my information and guidance.

With comradely greetings,
N. Bukharin [6]

6. Ibid., d. 753, l. 12.

That same day Bukharin sent to the members of the Politburo and the Central Control Commission presidium a communication regarding some letters from the Komsomol member G. Platonov (a clear provocation organized against Bukharin).

Dear Comrades,

In connection with the letters from the Komsomol member G. Platonov that have been distributed by Com. Stalin,[7] I must express my profound regret that the Central Committee Secretariat did not first ask me about this case. Platonov's letters represent the product of the fantasy of a mentally ill person; his account of a conversation with me is extremely dissimilar to the actual conversation; I would express it far more sharply if it were not a question of a mentally ill person. . . .

G. Platonov twice tried to meet with me in Teberda, and twice I refused because he made an entirely strange impression. The third time he approached me and stated categorically that I *must* speak to him no matter what, that he was severely ill, that he suffered from severe nervous attacks, that he had just suffered such an attack before coming to see me, that he had escaped from the observation of a doctor, and so on. After such an introduction, I could not send him home, because he had to calm down. For an hour and a half he poured out to me the details of his family life (his father was a missionary, his wife is of bourgeois background, his surroundings are bourgeois), the constant conflicts, his (Platonov's) "fanaticism" (and immediately the lack of determination to break with his bourgeois surroundings, and so forth, and so on). In great agitation he then told me about the Baku affair (about which I did not have the slightest notion), about the execution of workers by the heads of the GPU, about the forgery of documents by the GPU, about the judicial protection of Communists guilty of raping some schoolgirl, about the concealing of all these affairs from the masses, about the cover-up of the execution of the conspirators; next followed stories about the uprising in Gandzhe, the rebellion in the Kononovo settlement, where troops supposedly refused to act, and so on. I told him that these affairs were not known to me at all. Then Platonov began to get outraged at the "ugly methods of struggle" against me personally, began to tell me facts about this area, stating that he did not agree with them, that he could not understand it, and so on. Displaying com-

7. The letters were sent out on 19 July for the information of the members and candidate members of the Central Committee, the members of the Komsomol Central Committee Bureau, and the members of the presidium of the Central Control Commission (annotation to the document).

plete familiarity with the "red notebooks" (the transcript of the joint meetings of the Politburo and the Central Control Commission presidium and the plenums) and, in particular, with my speeches, Platonov asked me if I had made various proposals (about individual taxation, grain imports, regional prices, and so on). In replying affirmatively to these questions, I literally told him the following: The decisions of the party and its Central Committee are binding for everyone. There can be no question of factional struggle. I am obliged to defend the party decisions and will always do so, not because I value "ranks and orders" and not because I "recant" but because that is the basis of party life, especially at such a difficult moment; as for the methods of struggle against me, politics is a hard thing, you have to reconcile yourself to that. He, Platonov, should calm down and not talk about any "ugly methods" and should not speak out about his "doubts" but should *get treatment*; he should break off from his bourgeois surroundings.

That was the *real* content of the "chat." The entire point of the conversation from *my* side was to calm the sick fellow down, to remind him constantly of his "fanaticism," to emphasize that he should say [to his bourgeois surroundings] "the hell with you," and so on. Virtually the next day Platonov suddenly disappeared.

I think the picture is completely clear. The bourgeois family, the "religious background," and so on prevent Platonov from "advancing." With the maniacal zeal of a "fanatic," he decided to look good during the purge and cover up any "religious background," sincerely believing, in all probability, that this would be done through a "sensational exposé." It is easy to see that [in his letters] all of *his* account is taken from the "red notebooks" [and not from our conversation] and that despite a certain ability to re-create arguments from the newspapers, there are obvious signs of illness even in the letters (the mention of fanaticism, the demand that Com. Stalin reply, the desire—after the letter!—to correspond with me, the repeated references to religious background, and so on). I think that his letter should most likely be sent to his personal physician. I write all this on the premise that Platonov *was not feigning* attacks and so on. If that is not the case, then the picture is different but no less clear. I cannot help but note that the letter of a sick person directed against a member of the Politburo was sent out to many addressees without that Politburo member ever being asked.

> With comradely greetings,
> 22 July 1929
> N. Bukharin

P.S. I ask you to distribute this report to the same addressees to which the letters from Platonov were sent.[8]

After Stalin's letter to Molotov of 9 August (letter 40), in which Bukharin's letters were described as "underhanded," the Politburo, on 13 August 1929, passed the following resolution by voice vote, "On the Letters of Com. Bukharin of 22 July 1929."

To approve the following resolution:

The two recent letters from Com. Bukharin of 22 July 1929, addressed to the Central Committee, testify that Com. Bukharin continues to use the method of struggle with the party and its Central Committee chosen by him of late, making indirect sorties against decisions of the Central Committee (in "private" conversations: the "chat" with Com. Kamenev and now the "chats" with the Komsomol member Com. Platonov and others) and permitting himself further masked attacks on the party line in speeches and articles ("Notes of an Economist," then the speech "The Political Testament of Lenin," and recently the speech at the All-Union Congress of Atheists and the article "The Theory of 'Organized Mismanagement'"). Furthermore, each time the party catches Com. Bukharin at this, he squirms out of a direct answer and an admission of his mistakes and in reality covers them up. Regarding the two recent letters from Com. Bukharin, the Politburo must state the following:

a) In vain does Com. Bukharin pretend not to understand the decisions of the Politburo condemning his article "The Theory of 'Organized Mismanagement.'" First, in this article, Com. Bukharin makes the same mistake in evaluating the development of capitalism that was pointed out at the last plenum of the Comintern: "The reconcilers' notion about the waning of internal contradictions within capitalist countries and the possibility of organizing the domestic market while preserving anarchy only in the world market is refuted by the entire development of capitalism during the past years and in reality means a capitulation to reformist ideology."

Second, under cover of the "analogy" between the proletarian dictatorship's method of economic management and the methods used by contemporary capitalist monopolies, Com. Bukharin essentially continues his defense of views condemned at the April plenum of the Central Committee, thus continuing his battle against the party's policy of an intensified offensive against the capitalist elements and their

8. RTsKhIDNI f. 17, op. 3, d. 753, ll. 13–14.

removal. His actions can only nourish the illusions of capitalist elements about a retreat from the proletariat's socialist offensive.

b) Com. Bukharin also pretends that his speech at the Congress of Atheists does not contradict the line of the party and its Central Committee. Meanwhile, in reality, under cover of the slogan "Doubt everything," deployed by Marx to destroy capitalism and overthrow the bourgeois government, Com. Bukharin is engaged in spreading unbelief [nedoverie] in the general line of the party, which promotes the triumphant construction of socialism. Thus, instead of helping to mobilize the broad masses of workers under the Communist banner of the working class, in this speech, Com. Bukharin completely violates the Marxist method of dialectics; furthermore, he continues his struggle against the party leadership. His views reflect the vacillations of petit bourgeois segments [of the population]. These vacillations are inevitable when class warfare is aggravated during the offensive against capitalist elements.

c) Although not believing it necessary to dwell on Bukharin's "justifications" regarding his "chat" with Komsomol member G. Platonov, the Central Committee cannot overlook the fact that even Com. Bukharin's letter—without dwelling here on the unworthy attacks on the Central Committee—confirms that he is using any excuse to continue the battle against the party's policy.[9]

Yet another conflict between the right opposition and Stalin broke out over the reorganization of Pravda's editorial staff. In June 1929, the Politburo disbanded the position of managing editor (otvetstvennyi redaktor) of Pravda (Bukharin had held the post until April 1929) and created a separate editorial collegium to direct the ongoing work at the newspaper. The collegium consisted of Krumin, Popov, and Yaroslavskii. Several days later, Rykov, Bukharin, Uglanov, Krupskaia, and others submitted a statement protesting the decision to the Central Committee.

To the secretary of the Central Committee of the party:
On the issue of the organization and composition of the editorial staff of Pravda: I voted against it for the following reasons.
1. The present editorial staff (Coms. Yaroslavskii, Krumin, Popov) includes not a single member of the Central Committee. For the entire history of our party (except for the time when the editorial staff of the central organ [party newspaper] was chosen by a congress along with

9. Ibid., ll. 7, 8.

the Central Committee), highly authoritative members of the Central Committee have headed the central organ. This is all the more necessary and possible now because the Central Committee has many more members than ever before.

2. Com. Yaroslavskii is the most popular figure among the three. Many in the party will place the major responsibility for running *Pravda* on him. But he (Com. Yaroslavskii) is also one of the top officials of the Central Control Commission and is a member of its presidium.

In his work at *Pravda* as chief member of the inner core of the editorial staff, he is completely subordinate to the Central Committee and is responsible to it for the central organ. As a member of the Central Control Commission presidium, he represents an organ elected by the Congress, responsible [directly] to the Congress, and possessing oversight functions [and thus independent of the Central Committee]. I think that such a position does not correspond to the spirit of the party rules and to the Leninist principles of organization of the Central Control Commission.

3. The Politburo resolution does not contain any directives about dividing functions between a full editorial staff and an inner circle within it, just as there are no directives to divide the duties among the three members of this inner editorial collegium. Such a situation could cause uncertainty about the work and responsibility of each member of both the full editorial collegium and the inner circle.

4. The one member of the three (the actual editorial staff) who can devote all his time to the everyday direction of the central organ is, at the Politburo's suggestion, a recent Menshevik, Com. Popov. I do not object to giving former Mensheviks a great deal of work, but I categorically oppose granting them the political role associated with guiding the work of the central organ. This factor is particularly important now that such old party members and central organ workers as Mariia Ilinichna Ulianova have been removed from the leadership of the newspaper.

5. The last Central Committee plenum decided to dismiss Com. Bukharin from the editorship of the central organ, but before I left Moscow, neither the plenum nor the Politburo had discussed the question of changing the actual organization of the central organ's editorial staff and of eliminating the institution of the managing editor.

I think the old system was more suitable: a managing editor chosen by the Central Committee plenum and a collegium under him (or even better, two assistants under him). Because of the exceptional significance of the central organ in the leadership of the party and the country, the managing editor must be one of the members or candidate members of the Politburo.

22 June 1919

With Communist greetings,

A. I. Rykov

I vote *against* this proposal.

Reasons:

1) There is no justification for eliminating the position of managing editor.

2) There is not a single member of the Central Committee on the editorial staff, which means a drastic narrowing of the role of the central organ and is without precedent.

3) There is also no Central Committee member in the internal "working" collegium, whereas Com. Yaroslavskii is a member of the Central Control Commission, an organ that is supposed to maintain oversight.

4) M. I. Ulianova has been virtually removed from the job, although she is a longtime employee of *Pravda* and initiated the workers' correspondents' movement.[10] No preliminary discussion was held with her.

5) Com. Maretskii has been dismissed.

6) N. N. Popov has been brought in, who was a Menshevik during the civil war.

N. Bukharin

I do not object to the editorial collegium, but, instead of Com. Popov, I vote for Com. M. I. Ulianova as a member of the editorial collegium.

6/12

Kotov

I vote for the institution of a managing editor and against dismantling this position; I abstain regarding the proposed staff of the editorial collegium of *Pravda*.

Kulikov

10. The workers' correspondents (*Rabkor*) were factory workers who provided newspapers with stories of achievements and abuses in their factories. The movement began in 1923—U.S. Ed.

1) I vote *against* eliminating the position of managing editor and creating an editorial collegium.

2) I abstain regarding the composition of the editorial staff.

6/12/29

N. Uglanov

1) In the past, there were editorial staffs without managing editors, but I hesitate to judge whether it is possible to get by without a managing editor now. Moreover, even when no one was called the managing editor, such a person always existed in practice. 2) The editorial staff (expanded) consists of many very busy officials who cannot really serve as more than consultants, and even so they are not the only consultants, of course. *Pravda* requires a very thorough coverage of all issues; everyone expects no less from it. 3) I abstain regarding the question of a smaller editorial staff.

6/12/29

N. Krupskaia[11]

On 6 September 1929, the Politburo passed a resolution by voice vote, "On *Pravda*'s editorial staff":

To the members and candidate members of the Central Committee of the party.

Copy to the presidium of the Central Control Commission of the party.

In connection with the distribution of a statement submitted to the Central Committee by Coms. Rykov, Bukharin, and others containing reasons for their votes on the question of *Pravda*'s editorial staff, the Politburo considers it necessary to address in particular the reasoning of Com. Rykov, who repeats in more detailed form the reasoning of Com. Bukharin on this question.

1. The Politburo states that Com. Rykov's protest against replacing of the individual editor of *Pravda* with an editorial collegium is thoroughly misleading. Com. Rykov states that previously the central organ was headed by authoritative Central Committee members; this cannot in any way conceal the reality of the completely intolerable *estrangement* of *Pravda* from the Central Committee since last year, even though it was formally headed by a Politburo member, Com. Bukharin. In fact, Com. Rykov's reference to "authoritative" Central Committee members is only a rotten attempt to conceal the fact that

11. RTsKhIDNI f. 17, op. 3, d. 756, ll. 18, 19.

beginning in the summer of 1928, a group of young comrades who were completely untested in the party and hardly authoritative began to run *Pravda:* Slepkov, Maretskii, and Ye. Tseitlin (Com. Bukharin's personal secretary). Central Committee members know very well that in the period 1928–1929, *Pravda's* Leninist party line was upheld, not because of Com. Bukharin's presence as managing editor, but rather because of the change in *Pravda's* editorial collegium last August, with the appointment of Coms. Krumin and Savelev, and also because of the direct, daily guidance from the Central Committee.

2. The Politburo states that Com. Rykov's statement (as well as that of Com. Bukharin) concerning the "removal" of Com. M. I. Ulianova from the direction of the newspaper is false. Com. Ulianova is still a member of the editorial collegium; just as before, she is the secretary of the editorial staff. It should be added that prior to 1928, Com. Ulianova was not a member of *Pravda's* editorial collegium.

3. The Politburo notes Com. Rykov's unworthy attack (and also that of Com. Bukharin) on Com. N. N. Popov. In addition, the Politburo notes that (in August 1928) Com. Popov was unanimously confirmed as a member of the editorial staff of another leading organ of the party, *Bolshevik;* in 1924, at the *suggestion* of Coms. *Bukharin* and Skvortsov-Stepanov, he was brought onto the *Pravda's* editorial staff.

4. The Politburo is compelled to make special mention of Com. Rykov's statement that the confirmation of the Central Control Commission presidium member Com. Yaroslavskii as a member of *Pravda's* editorial collegium supposedly "did not correspond to the spirit of the party rules and to the Leninist principles of organization of the Central Control Commission." It is easy to see that in an attempt to find at least some sort of principled reason for his erroneous position, Com. Rykov has, in the end, lost his way completely. This is apparent even from Com. Rykov's protest against, on the one hand, introducing into the editorial staff *one* member of the Central Control Commission (Com. Yaroslavskii) and, on the other hand, not bringing into this staff *another* member of the Central Control Commission (Com. Ulianova). Com. Rykov *now* objects to Com. Yaroslavskii because he is a member of the Central Control Commission presidium, although *previously* he [Rykov] himself repeatedly voted to transfer Com. Yaroslavskii to *Pravda's* editorial staff.

Turning to questions of principle, [we see that] not only do Com. Rykov's claims have nothing in common with bolshevism, but they are completely identical to the previous attempts by the Trotskyists to see the Central Control Commission and the Central Committee as in opposition. Thus it is apparent that in this case Com. Rykov's references to the party rules and the "Leninist principles of organization of the Central Control Commission" only prove his own lack of political principles.

Since the Politburo was occupied with a number of complicated and urgent matters (the economy, the CER, British-Russian relations, etc.), it did not have the opportunity to react immediately to the documents of Coms. Rykov, Bukharin, et al.

The Politburo can now state that the correctness of the Central Committee's decision about the composition of *Pravda*'s editorial staff has been completely and, in fact, obviously confirmed over the past months, during which time *Pravda*'s necessary link to the Central Committee and its correct political line have been fully ensured. As a result, the popularity of the central organ in the party and among the broad working masses has undeniably increased.

9/6/1929

Politburo of the Central
Committee of the All-Union
Communist Party (Bolshevik)[12]

Stalin's next move was also aimed at Rykov and Bukharin. The pretext was Rykov's speech at the Moscow region Congress of Soviets (*Pravda*, 28 September 1929). In tone and content it was the speech, not of a disgraced opposition figure, but of a confident chairman of the Council of Commissars. The audience greeted it, according to *Pravda*, with "stormy, prolonged applause." Stalin's reaction followed immediately. On 30 September, he wrote to Molotov, Voroshilov, and Ordzhonikidze (letter 50) and proposed condemning Rykov and stripping him of the right to chair Politburo meetings.

Simultaneously charges were readied against Bukharin in connection with the so-called Vorobiev affair. On 19 September 1929, at the party cell at the Industrial Academy of the Supreme Economic Council, a report from cell member Vorobiev was heard. In 1928–1929, Vorobiev was close to the group of Communists who supported Bukharin. This group met at the apartment of Uglanov, a supporter of Bukharin and the secretary of the Moscow City Party Committee, and included Bukharin's pupils, Maretskii, Astrov, Zaitsev, Slepkov, and others. In the second half of 1929, Vorobiev

12. Ibid., ll. 8, 16–17.

went over to Stalin's side and began to testify about the "factional activity" of the "rightists" in the Moscow Party Committee, reporting on the moods and comments of those around Bukharin during the period of his clash with Stalin. Vorobiev's detailed testimony was recorded in the transcript of the cell meeting at the Industrial Academy and then sent to the Central Committee.

On 5 October 1929, the Politburo reviewed the Vorobiev affair and Rykov's speech and passed a general resolution.

a) To send to the Central Control Commission for review the material received from the bureau of the Industrial Academy cell and the resolution of the Moscow Committee. (Approved unanimously.)

b) To state that in Com. Rykov's speech at the Moscow region Congress of Soviets, he overlooked the central question of the party's policy. Com. Rykov did not emphasize the decisive role of the party in guaranteeing—despite the rightists and the appeasers of the right deviation and as a result of the systematic struggle with them—the enormous successes in fulfilling the five-year economic plan. Com. Rykov also completely overlooked the question of the struggle with the right deviation and did not disassociate himself from the rightists despite the well-known resolutions of the party and the Comintern. Com. Rykov also completely overlooked the very important question of the party's policy concerning grain procurements, about which the party had and continues to have radical disagreements with the right deviationists.

All of this illustrates that Com. Rykov violated the decision of the April plenum of the Central Committee, which emphasized that the right deviation is the main danger in the party and obliged each party member, especially Central Committee members, to wage a determined struggle against the right deviation and against any appeasement of it. (Approved by all except one, Com. Rykov. Com. Bukharin was absent.)[13]

As the letter of 7 October 1929 (letter 51) reveals, Stalin decided to use Vorobiev's testimony at the Central Committee plenum. Vorobiev's charges, among other materials, figured in the review of the Bukharin question that took place at the Central Committee plenum in November 1929. As Stalin had intended, Bukharin was removed from the Politburo.

13. Ibid., d. 761, l. 6.

Letter 39

Com. Molotov,

For Monday's Politburo meeting

I strongly protest publishing Sten's article in *Komsomolskaia pravda* (see *Komsomolskaia pravda*, no. 169), which is *similar to Shatskin's article*, several days after the Politburo's condemnation of Shatskin's article.[1, 2] This is either stupidity on the part of the editors of *Komsomolskaia pravda*[3] or a *direct challenge* to the Central Committee of the party. To call the subordination of Komsomols (and that means party members as well) to the general party line "careerism," as Sten does, means to call *for a review* of the general party line, for the *undermining* of the iron discipline of the party, for the *turning* of the party into a *discussion club*. *That is precisely how* any opposition group has begun its anti-party work. Trotsky began his "work" with this. Zinoviev got his start that way. Bukharin has chosen this same path for himself. The Shatskin-Averbakh-Sten-Lominadze group is embarking on this path, demanding (essentially) the *freedom* to review the general party line, the *freedom* to weaken party discipline, the *freedom* to turn the party into a discussion club. *For this* the Shatskin-Sten group is trying to turn *Komsomolskaia pravda* (if it has not already turned it) into *its own* battle organ. *For this* it is trying to turn *Molodaia gvardiia* [Young guard] into *its own* theoretical journal. For this *Komsomolskaia pravda is counterposed to Pravda*, and *Molodaia gvardiia* [is] counterposed to *Bolshevik*. It is time to call for order and disband this group, which is straying, or has already strayed, from the path of Leninism to the path of *petit bourgeois (Trotskyist) radicalism*. It is time, because only in this way can these young comrades be corrected and retained for the party.

It is necessary to:

1) Immediately take a close look at the composition of the staffs of *Komsomolskaia pravda* and *Molodaia gvardiia* and put at their head comrades who are *experienced in the party;*[4]

2) Criticize the ideological vacillations of the Shatskin-Sten-Averbakh-Lominadze group;[5]

3) Show that the Slepkovites[6] and the Shatskinites are as similar as two peas in a pod.

I think that the sooner we finish with this affair, the better. To delay would mean hurting the cause and perhaps losing a number of young comrades who could be valuable party workers in the future. To delay would mean allowing a group that has strayed from the path to corrupt young comrades and to go on corrupting our glorious revolutionary youth in the future. That would be completely intolerable.

J. Stalin

29 July 1929

1. Ya. Sten, "Vyshe kommunisticheskoe znamia Marksizma—Leninizma" (Raise high the banner of Marxism-Leninism); L. Shatskin, "Doloi partiinuiu obyvatel'shchinu" (Down with party philistinism), *Komsomolskaia pravda* (18 June 1929). Shatskin's article was condemned in a resolution of the Politburo on 22 July 1929, and Shatskin himself was relieved of his duties as a member of the editorial collegium of *Pravda* (RTsKhIDNI f. 17, op. 3, d. 750, l. 5). The Politburo once again returned to this matter on 25 July 1929 and proposed that the editors of *Komsomolskaia pravda* provide an article clarifying Shatskin's error and that the Komsomol Bureau discuss measures to strengthen the newspaper's editorial staff (ibid., l. 2).

2. According to Stephen Cohen, Sten, Shatskin, and Lominadze were the best-known members of "a group of radical anti-Bukharinists sometimes called the 'Young Stalinist Left' [who had been] protégés of Stalin since the early twenties" (Stephen F. Cohen, *Bukharin and the Bolshevik Revolution* [New York, 1971], 459–60). This letter thus shows Stalin's impatience with signs of independence on the part of his own supporters—U.S. Ed.

3. *Komsomolskaia pravda* was the official newspaper of the Komsomol, the party's youth organization—U.S. Ed.

4. On 15 August 1929, the Politburo approved the new editorial collegium of *Komsomolskaia pravda* proposed by the Komsomol Bureau. The position of managing editor of the newspaper was eliminated. Those duties were handed to a collegium of three within the editorial staff (ibid., d. 753, l. 4).

5. On 8 August 1929, the Politburo approved a resolution from the Komsomol on *Komsomolskaia pravda*. The editors of *Pravda* and *Bolshevik* were asked to discuss the mistakes in the articles by Sten and Shatskin (ibid., d. 752, l. 3).

6. Stalin is referring to a group of young theoreticians and journalists who shared Bukharin's ideological and theoretical views. A. N. Slepkov was one of the better-known representatives of this group. [Stalin is therefore equating "left" and "right" deviation from his "general line"—U.S. Ed.]

Letter 40 [9 August 1929]

Hello, Com. Molotov,[1]

Voroshilov and I have discussed your letter (Sergo has long since left for Nalchik) and have come to the following conclusions.

On England. If Henderson does not provide a new reason, in terms of a concession (which is rather unlikely), it would be better to wait on the question of England until a decisive increase in the grain procurements [has been attained], that is, until the middle or end of October. In middle or late October it will be possible to convene a *regular* session of the Central Executive Committee, hear the report from the Commissariat of Foreign Affairs, and pass something like the following resolution:

"1) [The Central Executive Committee] approves the course of action adopted by the Commissariat of Foreign Affairs;

2) Considers that there are no grounds for violating the universal principle of preliminary establishment of normal diplomatic relations as the necessary legal basis for the ensuing settlement of all disputes, claims, and counterclaims;

3) Assigns the Council of Commissars the task of organizing a delegation to the Anglo-Soviet conference, as soon as ambassadors are exchanged."

I think this is the only decision we can make. To accept Henderson's suggestion would mean entangling ourselves and pushing ourselves into a trap. To accept Henderson's suggestion would mean:

a) discouraging Italy, Germany, France, and the others who recognized us *without preliminary conditions* and pushing them toward a break with us;

b) strengthening those elements in America that do not want to recognize us;

c) justifying the way the Conservatives broke with us;

d) helping all the Deterdings and Chamberlains to move the focus of attention from normal economic relations to the question of debts, claims of private persons, and propaganda;

e) tacitly agreeing to pay debts, not only to England, but to Germany, France, and so on because consenting to Henderson's proposal would create a *precedent* that **everyone** would definitely latch on to;

f) facilitating the creation of a united anti-Soviet front.

Worse than all this, even if we were to agree to Henderson's proposal, we *would not achieve the restoration of relations* because we would still not come to an agreement on the disputed matters, since [Prime Minister] MacDonald apparently wants to *diverge dramatically from the agreement of 1924*[2] and impose completely unacceptable terms on us.

Now Henderson and MacDonald *are exactly where we want them* because we can accuse them of being more bourgeois than the fascists in Italy, than the capitalists in France and Germany who recognized us without any preliminary conditions. But (if we accept Henderson's proposal) *we will be exactly where they want us,* because they will accuse us of not valuing the cause of peace and thus not making concessions on the disputed matters, and then they will say that they don't believe it is possible to recognize the USSR.

To accept Henderson's conditions means to get into a trap our enemies have set for us.

The proposed draft resolution of the Central Executive Committee is in my view the only acceptable answer to the fraud of the bourgeoisie and its lackeys from the "Labour government."

Regarding Bukharin (publication of the Comintern resolutions, etc.), we are in full agreement with you.[3]

Rakovskii should be sent to an even more remote place so that he can't lie anymore about the Bolsheviks in the press.[4]

I consider both of Bukharin's letters to be underhanded. This Kadet[5] professor apparently doesn't understand that you can't fool Bolsheviks with such fraudulent letters. He is a typical Kadet lawyer.

The business of *Komsomolskaia pravda* came out quite well.

That's it for now.

Regards,

J. Stalin

9 August 1929

Kalinin, Stalin, and Voroshilov

#37

Здравствуй, т. Молотов! 10/VIII/1929

Читал постановление ЦК РКП о хлебозаготовках. При всех его достоинствах оно, по-моему, совершенно недостаточно. Сейчас главное в деле хлебозаготовок: 1) наличие большого количества городских спекулянтов на хлебном рынке или около хлебного рынка, обдирающих у государевых крестьян хлеб и — главное — создающих атмосферу сдержанности среди держателей хлеба; 2) конкуренция между заготовительными организациями, дающая возможность держателям хлеба лавировать, не сдавать хлеба (ждать высоких цен), придержать хлеб, не торопиться со сдачей хлеба; 3) желание целого ряда колхозов (придержать хлебные излишки, придать хлеб на сторону. Наличие этих факторов, — которое будет усиливаться, если не примем теперь же срочных мер, — не даёт нашим заготовкам (и не дадут) развернуться вовсю. Следовало бы принять меры теперь же против этого зла, если мы в самом деле думаем кончить заготовки в марте — феврале и выйти из кампании победителями. Об этом прежде всего следовало бы сказать в поста...

First page of letter from Stalin to Molotov, 10 August 1929 (RTsKhIDNI f. 558, op. 1, d. 5388, l. 72).

1. Above the text of the letter is a notation: "Read it. A. Mikoian, J. Rudzutak, Yaroslavskii, Kaganovich."

2. A general agreement between the USSR and Great Britain on 8 August 1924 (*Dokumenty vneshnei politiki SSSR* [Documents of USSR foreign policy], vol. 7 [Moscow, 1963], 609–24).

3. In a resolution entitled "On Com. Bukharin," the X plenum of the Comintern Executive Committee (3–19 July 1929) approved the Central Committee's April decision to remove Bukharin from the work of the Communist International.

4. Rakovskii was expelled from the party in 1927. While in exile, he wrote a number of articles for *Biulleten' oppozitsii* (Bulletin of the opposition), which was published abroad by Trotsky. After Stalin's letter, Rakovskii was transferred from the lower Volga region to Barnaul [Barnaul is in western Siberia, south of Novosibirsk—U.S. Ed.].

5. The Kadets, or Constitutional Democrats, were the leading liberal party in the decade before the revolution—U.S. Ed.

Letter 41   [10 August 1929]

Hello, Com. Molotov,

I read the Central Committee's decree on grain procurements.[1] Despite all its merits, I think it is *completely inadequate*. The main problem with grain procurements at present is 1) the presence of a large number of *urban speculators* at or near the grain market who take the peasants' grain away from the government and—the main thing—create a wait-and-see attitude among the grain holders; 2) *competition between procurement organizations,* which creates the opportunity for grain holders to be obstinate and not give up the grain (while waiting for higher prices), to hide the grain, to take their time turning over the grain; 3) *the desire of a whole number of collective farms* to hide grain surpluses and sell grain on the side. The presence of these factors—which will grow worse if we don't take emergency measures **now**—prevents our procurements from increasing (and will continue to do this). Measures ought to be taken **now** against this evil if we really are thinking of finishing up the procurements in January or February and coming out of the campaign as victors. The Central Committee decree should have said this first of all. But the decree *skirts* this issue or, if it does address it, *mentions it in passing,* and what is said in this regard is *lost* in the endless number of other (secondary) points, liberally sprinkled through the whole six-foot-long decree. I'm afraid that, because of the way this is being handled, we will not collect enough grain.

My advice:

1) give a directive **immediately** to the [local] GPUs to **immediately** start punitive measures regarding urban (and urban-related) speculators in grain products (that is, arrest them and deport them from grain regions) in order to make the grain holders feel **right now** (at the beginning of the grain procure-

ment campaign) that little can be gained from speculation, that the grain can be given without trouble (and without loss) only to state and cooperative organizations;

2) give a directive **immediately** to the directors of the *cooperatives*, *Soiuzkhleb* [state grain purchasing agency], *OGPU*, and the *judicial agencies* to expose and **immediately** hand over to the courts (with **immediate** dismissal from their posts) all those procurement officials caught [trying to obtain grain by competing with other state agencies], as indisputably alien and Nepman elements (I don't exclude "Communists") who have burrowed into our organizations like thieves and have maliciously helped to wreck the cause of the workers' state;

3) establish surveillance of collective farms (through the Collective Farm Center, the party organizations, the OGPU) so that those **directors** of collective farms caught holding back grain surpluses or selling them on the side will be **immediately** dismissed from their posts and *tried* for defrauding the state and for wrecking.

I think that without these and similar measures, we will fail in our job.

Otherwise we will get only **speeches** and no **concrete** measures to help grain procurement.

Please show this letter to Mikoian.

I hope there won't be any disagreements among us on this.

I forgot to reply in the first letter to the question of the "uninterrupted week." It goes without saying that this idea should be promoted, brushing aside the objections of Uglanov and other whiners.[2] This will be one of the greatest achievements of our production policy and practice.

That's it for now.

Regards,

J. Stalin

10 August 1929

I agree wholly.

Voroshilov

1. Stalin was referring to the draft of the decree "On grain procurement," which was approved in final form by the Politburo on 15 August 1929 and which incorporated all of Stalin's comments. The decree ran as follows (RTsKhIDNI f. 17, op. 3, d. 753, l. 3):

> In order to fulfill completely the annual plan of grain procurements for January–February and to maintain a firm price policy, the Politburo decrees:
>
> a) To direct the OGPU to implement decisive punitive measures regarding urban and urban-related profiteers of grain products.
>
> b) To oblige Tsentrosoiuz, Khlebotsentr, and Soiuzkhleb [state grain purchasing agencies] to resolutely direct all their offices to immediately remove all purchasing officials caught engaging in price competition, not excepting Communists, for maliciously harming the cause of the workers' state. To instruct the OGPU and judicial bodies to issue through their channels a directive on combating competition of this kind.
>
> To propose that the Commissariat of Transport and the leadership of the unions of rail and water transport workers, along with the Commissariat of Trade, take additional measures to curb grain profiteering.

c) To propose that the Collective Farm Center maintain surveillance over collective farms: those directors who have been caught holding back surplus grain or selling it on the side should be immediately removed from office and tried for defrauding the government and for sabotage. Have the Commissariat of Trade, the OGPU, and party organizations ensure the implementation of this decree.

d) To send this decree to all party organizations in the regions with grain surpluses.

2. The uninterrupted workweek (with a system of revolving days off) was intended to increase the use of equipment. But the *nepreryvka* [the idiomatic noun formed from the adjective *nepreryvnaia*, "uninterrupted"] had many negative aspects that were discussed in a speech made on 22 July 1929 at a meeting of the Commissariat of Labor chaired by Commissar N. A. Uglanov. On the following day, Uglanov sent a report to the Council of Commissars stating that "to pass a resolution at the present time concerning an overall or even partial transition to the uninterrupted week would be impossible." On 22 August 1929, the Politburo approved the draft of a Council of Commissars resolution on the transition to the uninterrupted workweek (ibid., d. 754, l. 2).

Letter 42   [21 August 1929]

Hello, Com. Molotov,[1]

1) **On England.** Litvinov is wrong. Litvinov doesn't want to understand that Henderson has *replaced* the question of *procedure* with the question of a *settlement* (and not simply *negotiations*) of disputed (all!) questions. To accept this would mean losing our diplomatic gains, arming our enemies, and driving ourselves into a dead end. Whatever conversations Dovgalevskii might have *after* Henderson's declaration and the reply from Foreign Affairs,[2] they (the conversations) would be portrayed as negotiations *on the substance* of the matter, and we would end up in the most ridiculous position. I think that the transfer of the issue from the presidium to the full Central Executive Committee is not necessary, because if Henderson backs away from his position, the issue can be covered in the presidium, and if he doesn't, we can resolve the issue in the Central Executive Committee session itself (bypassing the presidium), tacitly proceeding from the premise that "plenum of the presidium" means a Central Executive Committee session. It would seem then that your question about "emphasizing the transfer of the issue from the presidium to the Central Executive Committee" no longer arises.

2) **On Azerbaidzhan.**[3] Gikalo must be supported in everything, because he is right *fundamentally* (he has retained anyone more or less capable of work from among the old cadre of the local officials). Artak and Shatunovskaia view Mirzoian's removal by the Central Committee as a victory for them, just as Shatskin views the party's victory over the rightists as his personal victory over the Slepkovites. This is all nonsense and stupidity. Both Shatunovskaia and Artak should be sent back to Moscow to the Communist Academy[4] (to which they had previously been assigned and from which they have now returned to Baku "by decision of the Baku party activists"). Nothing good can be expected from them in Baku. What can be expected from them is obvious

from *Krasnyi's* stupid article in *Komsomolskaia pravda* about Baku[5] (once again *Komsomolskaia pravda* is sticking its nose in other people's business!). Both Buniat-zade and the chairman of the Azerbaidzhan Council of Commissars must be kept.[6] (As officials, all the Shatunovskiis and Artaks put together aren't worth one Buniat-zade.)[7] **Bagirov** (despite his past sins)[8] will have to be confirmed as chairman of the Cheka in Azerbaidzhan: he is now the only person who can cope with the Musavatists[9] and Ittikhadists[10] who have reared their heads in the Azerbaidzhan countryside. This is serious business and there should be no fooling around. It is too bad (really too bad) about Kasumov. He was one of the best officials, capable of becoming a major official in the future. Please do not settle the matter of sending him somewhere without my involvement.[11]

3) **On the Transcaucasian Regional Committee.** The Transcaucasian Committee is not providing leadership to the national central committees [of the individual republics]. It is incapable of leading them. It must be fundamentally purged and renewed. This is a complex matter. It will have to be postponed until the fall.[12]

4) I. N. Smirnov's "statement" is trash. These gentlemen shouldn't be given any concessions—all they want to do is to escape from Art. 58[13] and then base themselves in Moscow for their wreckerist "work."[14]

5) You're right when you say that Bukharin is going downhill. It's sad, but a fact. What can you say?—it must be "fate." It's strange, though, that he hopes to *trick* the party with petty underhanded "maneuvers." He is a typical representative of the spineless, effete *intelligent* in politics, leaning in the direction of a Kadet lawyer.[15] The hell with him . . .

6) The Politburo has adopted my proposals concerning grain procurement. This is good, but in my opinion, it is inadequate. Now the problem is **fulfilling** the Politburo's decision. There is no need to insist that all procurement organizations (especially in Ukraine) will *evade* this decision. Furthermore, I'm afraid that the local GPU will not learn about the Politburo's decision, and it (the decision) will get bogged down in the "bowels" of the OGPU. Therefore, it is necessary to demand the following from procurement organizations, the OGPU, the Collective Farm Center, and so forth:

a) copies of their instructions to subordinate organs concerning the **fulfillment** of the Politburo's decision; b) regular reports every two weeks (even better, once a week) about the **results of the fulfillment** of the decisions. The Worker-Peasant Inspection and the Central Control Commission should be involved in this as well. I don't know how you regard this matter and the outlook for grain procurement (Mikoian probably thinks that since the decision has been reached, he now has 130 million poods of an untouchable reserve sitting in the grain elevators). But I think that our grain procurements are still poor. Judge for yourself: For the first ten days of August we fulfilled only 15 percent of the plan. Let us say that for the remaining two ten-day periods we will fulfill not 15 percent but 20 percent of the plan; this is still not what we need now. I'm afraid that this poor pace will become the standard for future procurements. And grain procurement this year will provide the basis for everything we're doing—if we foul up here, everything will be wiped out. And the danger of a foul-up will grow if we don't insist that the Central Committee's decision be **fulfilled** with unrelenting **firmness** and **ruthlessness**.[16]

7) Pay **serious** attention to the oil business in the Urals. It turns out they decided to place only ten derricks per year. The derrick equipment is largely percussive rather than rotary, so the drilling will be murderously slow. That means that the Supreme Economic Council and the "chiefs" of oil extraction agencies (Uralneft, Azneft and Grozneft)—are treating the extraction of oil in the Urals approximately as Nobel treated Ukhta.[17] This is a monstrosity and a crime. I think we must a) organize now a special trust, "Uralneft," freeing the Urals from its "chiefs" who are prepared to delay the extraction of oil there; b) put at the head of Uralneft an experienced Communist/oilman, after kicking out the **wrecker** Dobrynskii from the Urals (I think his name is Dobrynskii), who is the current "chief" of Grozneft ("what's god for you is no good for us"); c) oblige the Supreme Economic Council to erect between forty and eighty rotary derricks **this** very year. Without these and similar measures, the business will run into obstacles (or even perish), and we won't have any real new prospecting in the Urals.[18]

Well, that's it for now.

Regards,

J. Stalin

P.S. *On the Cotton Committee.* I have received information that members of the Cotton Committee as well as Gosplan workers (especially the Cotton Committee) *don't believe* in the correctness of the Politburo *decisions* regarding the increase in the cotton production five-year plan[19] and want to *defeat* it in practice in order to show **they** are right. If that's true (I think there's a good likelihood that it is), it must be acknowledged that such an "idea" from the Cotton Committee members is the most vile form of wrecking and deserves the **harshest** punishment. In general, I don't think that Mamaev has long to live as head of the Cotton Committee.[20] It's possible that he will be able to free himself from the old traditional routines of the Cotton Committee, but I think it's unlikely. Therefore it is entirely correct that the Central Committee has begun to think *now* about providing the Main Cotton Committee with new, outstanding workers. I suppose Fushman will be good for this. Kharitonov would perhaps do, if he is capable of honest work. Shadunts would be very good, but Sergo adamantly objects. Therefore it would be better to give Reingold to the Cotton Committee instead of Shadunts. In place of Fushman and Kharitonov, other officials of equal value should be given to the Worker-Peasant Inspection.[21]

J. Stalin

21 August 1929

1. In the upper left-hand corner is Mikoian's notation: "I've read it. A. M."

2. The Commissariat of Foreign Affairs' statement on the course of the negotiations to restore diplomatic relations between the USSR and Great Britain was published in the Soviet press on 2 August 1929 (*Dokumenty vneshnei politiki SSSR* [Documents of USSR foreign policy], vol. 12 [Moscow, 1967], 429–30).

3. The reference is to the struggle within the leadership of the Azerbaidzhan Communist Party. On 1 July 1929, the issue "On the Baku Affair" was reviewed at the Politburo and the following was decided (RTsKhIDNI f. 17, op. 3, d. 747, l. 4):

> b) Relieve Com. Mirzoian from his duties as secretary of the Azerbaidzhan party, recall him immediately to the Central Committee. Acknowledge the necessity of replacing the top officials of the GPU and Central Control Commission of Azerbaidzhan, after proposing that the Central Committee and the Central Control Commission of Azerbaidzhan nominate new candidates for the posts of chairmen of the Central Control Commission and the GPU of Azerbaidzhan and submit them for confirmation to the All-Union Central Committee. Recommend Com. Gikalo for the post of first secretary of the Azerbaidzhan party.

On 14 August 1929, Gikalo sent a telegram to the Central Committee that was discussed at the Politburo on the following day. The resolution acknowledged "that Com. Gikalo's line, especially with regard to keeping the best Turkic cadres, is correct" (ibid., l. 4).

On 26 September 1929, the Politburo approved the draft of directives to implement the Central Committee's decree regarding the Azerbaidzhan Central Committee report. The directives were based on Stalin's instructions as presented in the current letter (ibid., d. 759, l. 9):

> At the same time that new cadres are being promoted, it is necessary to preserve in every way possible the old cadres who have passed through the Bolshevist school—the Turkic officials, among others. . . . Special attention must be paid to stepping up the struggle with the counter-revolutionary parties of Musavatists and Ittikhadists who are reviving their activities.

4. Beginning in October 1929, Artak attended government courses on Marxism-Leninism and Shatunovskaia was a student in similar courses run by the party.

5. B. Krasnyi's article "Partiinye 'vospitateli' bakinskogo komsomola" (The party "educators" of the Baku Komsomol) was published in *Komsomolskaia pravda* on 21 August 1929. He discussed the participation of the Azerbaidzhan Komsomol leadership in the conflicts with the Transcaucasian Party Organization.

6. On 16 September 1929, the Politburo resolved: "Not to carry out the changes in the Azerbaidzhan Council of Commissars (chairman, Com. Musabekov; deputy chairman, Com. Buniat-zade)" (ibid., d. 758, l. 6).

7. On 30 January 1930, the Politburo approved the Transcaucasian Regional Committee's motion to nominate Buniat-zade to the post of chairman of the Azerbaidzhan Council of Commissars and Musabekov to the post of chairman of the Azerbaidzhan Central Executive Committee (ibid., d. 775, l. 11).

8. On 24 September 1929, at a meeting of the Central Control Commission, the question of the leaders of the Azerbaidzhan Party Organization was considered. The resolution on Bagirov ran as follows: "Inform Com. Bagirov that in 1924, as chairman of the GPU, he did not take measures against the intolerable methods of the GPU, and warn him that as chairman of the Azerbaidzhan GPU he will bear full responsibility if such incidents reoccur in the GPU apparat" (ibid., f. 613, op. 1, d. 90, l. 47).

9. Musavat [Equality], a bourgeois-national party in Azerbaidzhan from 1911 to 1920. With the support of Turkey and later of Great Britain, this party remained in power in Azerbaidzhan from September 1918 until April 1920. After Soviet rule was established, it ceased to exist.

10. Ittikhadists, members of the Turkish nationalist party Ittikhad ve terakki [Unification and progress] that was founded in 1899 and operated until 1926.

11. On 4 July 1929, the Central Control Commission's committee on the purging and checking of the Agdam City District of Karabakh Region removed Kasumov Mir Bashir from executive work

for two years and reprimanded him for committing "a number of crude political mistakes." The Central Control Commission amended the text of this committee's decision on 18 July and decreed that Kasumov should be "reprimanded for committing a number of mistakes that led to the distortion of the class line at the lower rungs of the soviet apparat" (ibid., f. 124, op. 1, d. 839, l. 38).

12. On 30 October 1929, the Politburo confirmed the Central Committee's directive on the future work of the Transcaucasian Regional Committee, which emphasized the need to improve the leadership exercised over the central committees of the republican Communist parties (ibid., f. 17, op. 3, d. 765, ll. 6, 16, 17). Personnel transfers were also made. On 5 January 1930, the Politburo confirmed the new composition of the presidium and secretariat of the Transcaucasian Regional Committee (ibid., d. 771, l. 11).

13. Article 58 was the all-purpose section of the criminal code under which political arrests were made. See Aleksandr I. Solzhenitsyn, *The Gulag Archipelago*, 3 vols. (New York, 1973–78), 1:60–67—U.S. Ed.

14. In 1929, after Trotsky was exiled abroad and Stalinist policy moved clearly to the left, many supporters of Trotsky in exile recanted and asked to be reinstated into the party. Among them were I. N. Smirnov and V. A. Ter-Vaganian. From July to the end of October 1929, the Smirnov group prepared several versions of its statement. In the first version, while recognizing their mistakes, they also criticized Stalin's policy and demanded that Trotsky be returned to the country. Gradually, they backed down and wrote a statement acceptable to Stalin. On 30 October 1929, the Politburo ruled: "Consider the statement of I. N. Smirnov acceptable" (RTsKhIDNI f. 17, op. 3, d. 765, l. 5). The statement was published in *Pravda* on 3 November 1929. Previously, on 25 October, the Politburo had passed the following resolution (ibid., d. 764, l. 6):

> Regarding those former Trotskyists against whom administrative measures were taken: the OGPU must terminate the administrative measures against those who openly declare their break with the opposition and [their desire for] the cessation of factional fighting and who acknowledge the general line of the party and the decisions of the party as correct (although their statements are not sufficient for acceptance into the party); as for the former Trotskyists, who remain active, the GPU must ameliorate the administrative measures applied to them, restricting them to semi-exile and designating places where residence is prohibited them.

15. The Kadets, or Constitutional Democrats, were the leading liberal party in the decade before the revolution—U.S. Ed.

16. All of Stalin's directives were incorporated in the Politburo's decree "On the course of grain procurements and implementation of Politburo directives," 29 August 1929. The resolution ran as follows (ibid., d. 755, ll. 3–4):

> a) The Politburo notes the slowness of fulfillment, and in some cases the virtual nonfulfillment, of Central Committee directives on the need to increase grain procurements and combat grain profiteering, to increase competition among grain purchasers, and to combat cases of state farms and collective farms withholding their grain and selling it on the side. b) The Politburo notes the weak course of procurement throughout the middle and lower Volga, throughout the North Caucasus, and also throughout Siberia and Kazakhstan. c) Coms. Molotov and Mikoian are assigned to draft Politburo directives to local party organizations on implementing Central Committee directives, on systematically checking up on fulfillment, and on informing the Central Committee concerning the measures taken. The draft directives should be put to a voice vote and sent out in the name of the Politburo. d) In the near future, information from the Commissariat of Trade on the course of the grain procurements and the implementation of the Central Committee's directives should be on the agenda of each Politburo meeting, with a summoning of leaders of the main procurement organizations and the OGPU. e) In order to check up on the fulfillment of the Central Committee's directives and to help local organizations improve grain procurement, send Com. Mikoian to the Volga and North Caucasus for a period of two weeks and send Com. Eismont to Kazakhstan. For the same purpose, mobilize Coms. Badaev, Kiselev, Antselovich, and Leonov. . . . f) Propose that OGPU guarantee the implementation of the Politburo's directives concerning resolute punitive measures against urban and urban-related grain speculators and report to the Politburo on the measures taken within a week.

17. Uralneft, Azneft, and Grozneft were agencies in charge of oil extraction in the Urals, Azerbaidzhan, and Groznyi (a town in the North Caucasus), respectively. Ukhta is a town in northern Russia—U.S. Ed.

18. On 5 September 1929, the Politburo passed a resolution "On Uralneft" (ibid., d. 756, l. 5):

a) to assign the Labor Defense Council and Gosplan: 1) to ensure that the target figures for 1929–1930 guarantee a pace of development for Uralneft that will provide an opportunity to erect fifty derricks, as well as to establish the most modern methods of oil extraction suitable for the soil, and to increase the size of construction projects correspondingly—approximately 15 million rubles; 2) to guarantee the necessary imports for Uralneft in the import plan for 1929–1930; 3) to incorporate in the target figures of the Commissariat of Transport all measures necessary to increase Uralneft's shipments by the main rail lines and to build underground pipelines in the area of the oil wells; b) to appoint Com. K. Rumiantsev chairman of the Uralneft trust.

19. The Central Committee's decree of 18 July 1929, "On the Work of Chief Administration of the Cotton Industry," stipulated a sharp increase in the recently approved five-year plan to develop cotton production. The original five-year plan called for a yield of 590,400 tons of cotton by 1932, but the new Central Committee decree demanded an increased yield of 787,200 tons (*Spravochnik partiinogo rabotnika* [Party worker reference manual], issue 7, chap. 11 [Moscow, 1930], 226–32).

20. Mamaev was dismissed from his position at the Chief Administration of the Cotton Industry on 30 November 1929 and was appointed deputy director of the board of Amtorg (American Trading Corporation) (RTsKhIDNI f. 17, op. 3, d. 767, l. 8).

21. On 23 August 1929, the Central Committee Secretariat reviewed the request of the Central Asian party bureau and the Main Cotton Committee for the assignment of certain officials, including Kharitonov, Shadunts, and Reingold, to work in the cotton-producing regions. The Secretariat approved only Reingold and released him from his duties at Gosplan (ibid., op. 113, d. 768, l. 18).

Letter 43   [23 August 1929]

23 August 1929

Hello, Com. Molotov,

1) Pay *particular* attention to the construction of *new* iron and steel works. I mean Telbes, Magnitogorsk, and so on. According to the figures, the situation is *poor* in this area. Lokatskov (I think that's his name) is the head of Main Ferrous Metals. His experience is in the Ural Mountains area, that is, with the old routines, because the methods of iron and steel production in the Urals (ferrous metals, blast furnaces, etc.) are really ancient. American and German specialists are either absent or brought in merely for show in the smallest numbers possible. Meanwhile, there is no greater need for foreign technical assistance than in this complex business. You should shake up Kuibyshev and Lokatskov and demand from them (at the beginning, and then we'll see) *written* reports on the status of this area, the type and amount of technical assistance,[1] and so on. Why, for example, couldn't we bring in Austin and Co. or some other firm on a *contract* basis to build the new plans? Etc., etc.

2) I read the Comintern's resolution on Bukharin. It didn't turn out too badly. I think the publication was a little late.

3) I just read Bystrianskii's report on his talk with Bukharin.[2] Just as I thought, Bukharin has slid into the swamp of opportunism and must now resort to gossip, forgery, and blackmail: he doesn't have any other arguments left. Talk of "documents" and "land nationalization" etc. is the fraud of a petty lawyer who has gone bankrupt in his "practice." If his disagreements with the present Central Committee are explainable in terms of Stalin's "personality," then how does one explain his disagreements with the Central Committee when Lenin lived? Lenin's "personality"? But why does he praise Lenin so much now, after his death? Isn't it for the same reason that all renegades like Trotsky praise Lenin (after his death!)? Our lawyer has completely tied himself in knots.

4) I read Shatskin's letter. It's a cowardly and dishonest letter. Shatskin will continue his "business."[3]

5) What if Krinitskii were to be made second secretary of the Transcaucasian Regional Committee (after first purging the Transcaucasian Committee of its old ballast), while leaving Orakhelashvili as first secretary (Krinitskii will find it difficult without him because he doesn't know a single local language)? Then we'll see.[4]

Well, bye for now.

Regards,
J. Stalin

P.S. When does Rykov arrive?[5]

1. The question of consulting foreign experts on iron production was reviewed more than once at the Politburo after Stalin's letter. On 10 January 1930, the Politburo approved a decree drafted by Rykov, "On the use of foreign technical assistance in iron and steel works" (RTsKhIDNI f. 17, op. 3, d. 772, ll. 11, 15–17).

2. The reference is probably to a routine denunciation of Bukharin. No documents related to this matter have been discovered.

3. The reference is to L. Shatskin's letter to the Central Committee dated 17 August 1929, where he protested charges made against him in a Komsomol decree and a *Pravda* editorial regarding his article "Down with Party Philistinism" (ibid., d. 754, ll. 10–14). On 22 August 1929, the Politburo approved the Komsomol's resolution condemning Shatskin's "opportunistic" views (ibid. 3, 15).

4. On 30 October 1929, the Politburo fulfilled Orakhelashvili's request to relieve him of his duties as secretary of the Transcaucasian Regional Committee and created a five-person secretariat that included A. I. Krinitskii (ibid., d. 765, l. 17). On 5 January 1930, the Politburo confirmed Krinitskii as secretary of the Transcaucasian Regional Committee (ibid., d. 771, l. 11).

5. By a Politburo resolution of 16 May 1929, Rykov was granted a three-month leave (ibid., d. 740, l. 9).

Letter 44

[29 August 1929]

Hello, Com. Molotov,

Received your letter of 27 August.

1) Regarding **England**. Our position is entirely correct. The Politburo's decision on Litvinov's proposal was correct.[1] The point is not only to achieve recognition without getting lost along the way. The point is that our position, based on the *exposure* of the "Labour government," is an appeal to the best elements of the working class of the whole world; our position unleashes *the proletariat's* revolutionary criticism of the "Labour government" and helps the cause of the revolutionary education of *workers* of all nations (England above all). It helps the Communists of the world educate the workers *in the spirit of antireformism*. It's a crime not to use a "God-given" occasion for this purpose; Litvinov does not see and is not interested in [the revolutionary aspect of policy]. But the Politburo should take all this into account.

2) *On China*. The same has to be said about China. The point is not only or not even mainly how to resolve this or that "conflict." The point is really to use our tough position to unmask completely and to undermine the authority of Chiang Kai-shek's government, a government of lackeys of imperialism, for attempting to become the model of "national government" for the colonial and dependent countries. There can be no doubt that each clash between Chiang Kai-shek's government and the Soviet government, just as each concession Chiang Kai-shek makes to us (and he is already starting to make concessions), is a blow against Chiang Kai-shek and exposes Chiang Kai-shek's government as a government of lackeys of imperialism and makes it easier to carry out the revolutionary education of the workers in colonial countries (and the Chinese workers above all). Litvinov and Karakhan (and they are not the only ones) don't see that. So much the worse for them.

3) Generally I would have to say that in taking a tough position with regard to the "Labour government" and Chiang Kai-shek's government, we are exposing (and have already exposed) a number of extremely interesting behind-the-scenes connections that make obvious (even to the blind) the **direct dependence** of these supposedly "popular" governments on the most reactionary forces of "their own" ("national") and international imperialism. *This is a very important and necessary revolutionary task, which will, at the same time, raise the prestige of the Soviet government in the eyes of the workers of all countries* (and above all in the eyes of the working class of the USSR). It is a crime against the USSR not to take this factor into account.

4) The campaign against petit bourgeois radicalism (Shatskin and Co.) went well.

5) Also the campaign went well against Bukharin, as the ideologue of the rightists, etc. The article in *Pravda* about Bukharin is superior.[2]

6) Regarding Mirzoian, I agree with you.[3]

7) It would be good to appoint Rumiantsev from Baku to head Uralneft [oil extraction agency in the Urals]. He knows the business well and would push things forward.[4]

8) I already sent [via] Mikoian (in reply to his letter) a letter congratulating the Politburo on its success in **smashing** the nest of Gromans, Vinogradskiis, and other such bourgeois politicians ensconced in Gosplan, the Central Statistical Administration, and so on. Hound them out of Moscow and put in their place young fellows, our people, Communists.[5]

9) The grain procurements have gone well. Stick to a firm policy regarding Siberia, Kazakhstan, Bashkiria. No concessions to Eikhe and other comrades wishing to shirk difficult responsibilities. We must and can accumulate 100 million poods of *emergency reserves*, if we are really Bolsheviks and not just full of hot air. If absolutely necessary, we could knock off 5–7 million, but no more, and only under the condition that it be made up in other regions. If we can beat this grain thing, then we'll prevail in everything, both in domestic and foreign policies.

10) I am beginning to recuperate in Sochi after my illness in Nalchik. Well, that's it for now. Regards.

J. Stalin
8/29/1929

P.S. Just received the text of the reply (ours) to the Chinese note.[6] Obviously you have lost your nerve somewhat and let the Chinese put one over on you. And this is at a time when victory was assured. What the Chinese want, that is, *the removal of Yemshanov and Eismont,* ended up in the declaration, implying that we and not the Chinese are to blame. And what we want, that is, the *removal of the* TAIPAN—an indication that we (and not the Chinese) are right—*did not get into the declaration* (you restricted yourself only to an "*oral report*" of this to Dirkesen)! Thus we are supposed to sign a paper (a declaration) saying we're wrong and the Chinese are right in spite of the obvious facts of the case! That means giving the defeated enemy the fruits of our victory. I see here the "wisdom" of Litvinov and Bukharin. And what if the Chinese don't agree to removing the taipan after such a declaration (signed by us)? After all, they have the right not to agree to it, since in the declaration we signed there is nothing said about appointing a new taipan. What do you intend to do then? Only one thing to do: swallow the bitter pill. It's too bad, really too bad.

J. Stalin

1. On 22 and 26 August 1929, Litvinov's proposal concerning England was discussed at the Politburo and the decision was sent to the Special File.

2. In the article, "Ob obshibkakh i uklone T. Bukharina" (On the mistakes and deviation of Com. Bukharin; *Pravda,* 24 August 1929), Bukharin was accused of being the "chief leader and inspirer of the deviationists."

3. On 30 September 1929, the Politburo decided to assign Mirzoian to party work in the Urals (ibid., d. 761, l. 51).

4. The Politburo accepted Stalin's proposal on 5 September 1929: Rumiantsev was appointed chairman of the Uralneft trust (ibid., d. 756, l. 5).

5. At a Politburo session on 22 August 1929, the question of the Central Statistical Administration and its Advisory Council was reviewed. The personnel of the Advisory Council had to be changed radically and the top positions of the Central Statistical Administration had to be reinforced with party members (ibid., d. 754, l. 3). In December 1929, the Central Statistical Administration was transferred to Gosplan (ibid., d. 769, l. 2). The new personnel of the Gosplan presidium and its statistical sector were confirmed at a Politburo session on 25 December 1929 (ibid., d. 770, l. 4).

6. The report of the Commissariat of Foreign Affairs concerning the draft Soviet-Chinese declaration about settling the Chinese Eastern Railway conflict was published in the Soviet press on 31 August 1929 (*Dokumenty vneshnei politiki SSSR* [Documents of USSR foreign policy], vol. 12 [Moscow, 1967], 481–83). On 6 January 1930, the Politburo reappointed Yemshanov vice-chairman of the board of the Chinese Eastern Railway (RTsKhIDNI f. 17, op. 3, d. 771, l. 8).

Letter 45
[1 September 1929]

9/1/1929

Hello, Com. Molotov,

1) From NKID reports published in the press,[1] it's obvious that my reproach on the Chinese question (see my previous letter—the *postscript) was unfair.* It turns out I didn't read the fine print in the coded report. Well, what of it, I am glad I was mistaken and ready to apologize for the undeserved reproach. That, of course, doesn't mean that Litvinov, Bukharin, and Karakhan have ceased to be opportunists. Not a whit!

2) Read the decision on contracting.[2, 3] It's a good thing. But I think it's a transitional thing. I think we'll soon have to go further and transfer all the grain procurements in the countryside to *agricultural cooperatives (Khlebo-tsentr [sic] and others),* taking *consumer cooperatives* and Khlebotsentr out of this business and turning *Khlebotsentr* into a collection agency for procured grain. This is particularly necessary after the successes attained with contracting. Without such a reform, competition [among ourselves] and its consequences are inevitable. We'll talk in more detail when I get to Moscow.

3) The procurements are now going well. That's very good. If we link this to the fact that we have already managed to take in more than 400 million rubles on the third industrialization loan, we can say with certainty that things are going fairly well for the time being. The main thing now is not to rest on our laurels and to move things forward.

4) What's going on in the Moscow [party] organization; why is Bauman thrashing Polonskii so mercilessly; what is this ugly *personal* squabble all about?

Well, bye for now. Regards,

J. Stalin

1. For the report of the Commissariat of Foreign Affairs (NKID), see note 6 to letter 44.

2. Contracting (*kontraktatsiia*) was a method briefly used in grain procurement. Under this method the peasants agreed, before the harvest, to deliver a set amount to the government in return for government promises to provide industrial goods.—U.S. Ed.

3. The Politburo decree "On the results and current tasks in the area of contracting grain sowing" was passed on 26 August 1929 (RTsKhIDNI f. 17, op. 3, d. 755, ll. 21–23).

Letter 46 {#letter-46}

Letter 46   [6 September 1929]

Hello, Com. Molotov,

1) I'm sending you a letter I just got from Mirzoian. You know that I'm not a supporter of the policy of "tolerance" regarding comrades who have committed grievous errors from the perspective of the party's interests. I must say, however, that it is not in the party's interests to *finish off* Mirzoian; however, I think you yourself wrote to me the other day about Mirzoian *in just this same* vein. His letter should be noted and his request fulfilled.

I think it wouldn't be a bad thing to appoint Mirzoian secretary to the Perm (Ural) Regional Committee and give him an urgent combat assignment: *to move the oil business forward* in the Urals.[1] He knows the oil business well, and *together with Rumiantsev* (I'm proposing to appoint Rumiantsev head of Uralneft [Urals oil extraction agency]), he could really develop the Ural oil fields. And oil in the Urals is *the most important* matter now, which our Supreme Economic Councilers[2] don't want to understand.

2) I supported Kabakov and Oshvintsev on the Zubarev matter[3] for two reasons: a) despite its increasingly enormous importance for the USSR, executives are terribly scarce in the Urals, and it can't be "plundered endlessly"; b) Zubarev is a specialist in agriculture, and in Arkhangelsk, strictly speaking, there isn't any agriculture.

Well, so long for now.

J. Stalin

9/6/1929

1. On 30 September 1929, the Politburo decided to assign Mirzoian to party work in the Urals (RTsKhIDNI f. 17, op. 3, d. 761, l. 51).
2. That is, the staff of the Supreme Economic Council.
3. On 12 September 1929, at Molotov's suggestion, the Politburo left Zubarev in the Urals instead of reassigning him to party work in the north (ibid., d. 753, l. 9, and d. 757, l. 6).

Letter 47 {#letter-47}

Letter 47   [9 September 1929]

Com. Molotov,

Received your letter of 9/6.

1) No haste should be displayed on the British question. Now Henderson needs a restoration of relations more than we do. It's not Henderson who is dangerous, since we have pushed him to the wall, but Litvinov, who believes

Wise and other bastards more than the logic of things. Especially dangerous are "our" Paris "advisors," who recommended that we send Henderson a "sympathetic" answer. These people are Henderson's agents, who inform the British government and disinform us. In short: no backing down from our position. Remember we are waging a struggle (negotiation with enemies is also struggle), not with England alone, but with the whole capitalist world, since the MacDonald government is the vanguard of the capitalist governments in the work of "humiliating" and "bridling" the Soviet government with "new," more "diplomatic," more disguised, and thus more "effective" methods. The MacDonald government wants to show the whole capitalist world that it can take more from us (with the help of "gentle" methods) than Mussolini, Poincaré, and Baldwin, that it can be a greater Shylock than the capitalist Shylock himself. And it wants this because only in this way can it win the trust of its own bourgeoisie (and not only its bourgeoisie). We really would be worthless if we couldn't manage to reply to these arrogant bastards briefly and to the point: "You won't get a friggin' thing from us."

2) Bauman must be disciplined sternly for trying to drag the organization into a struggle, not over political views, but "over individuals." That is precisely why Polonskii should not be budged (for the time being at least). Regarding Zhdanov, Postyshev and Rumiantsev, it would be better to wait until fall.

3) It's not good if Yaroslavskii begins to take over (apparently he's already begun) as, in effect, the editor in chief of Pravda. That is dangerous and harmful to the cause, because despite all his other outstanding qualities, he is weak in the political leadership department (he loves to swim along "with the tide" of the sentiment of the "masses"). No matter how it looks, in reality, Pravda is not directed by Yaroslavskii but by someone else, someone like Zinoviev or one of Zinoviev's pupils who knows how to flatter Yaroslavskii cleverly and who has it in for the Leningrad organization. Keep in mind that such a danger is quite real. At any rate, the shrill uproar about the Leningrad organization is suspicious.[1]

4) The decision on Rykov is correct.

Regards,
J. Stalin
9/9/1929

P.S. I almost forgot. The new (new!) statement from Smirnov, Vaganian, Mrachkovskii, and others must be rejected not only as unacceptable (and how!) but as a document from impudent counterrevolutionaries who are exploiting Yaroslavskii's easygoing nature and the trust he has shown them. Yaroslavskii must be forbidden to have anything to do with those upstarts who have exploited his easygoing nature to organize their counterrevolutionary faction on "new," "within-the-regulations" principles. We don't need them in the party. How can you not grasp this simple thing?[2]

Besides, I resolutely protest against the fact that, despite the Politburo reso-

lution,[3] Zinoviev has become one of the permanent staff members (and directors?) of *Pravda*. Can't an end be put to this outrage? Who's to blame for this? Is
it Yaroslavskii? Why are you tolerating this political depravity?

J. Stalin

1. On 1 September 1929, *Pravda* carried a large selection of materials on the "suppression of
self-criticism" and the "corruption" in the Leningrad Party Organization. A campaign to "unleash
self-criticism" was then launched in Leningrad and covered in detail in *Pravda*.
2. For information on Smirnov and others, see note 14 for letter 42.
3. On 9 May 1929, the Politburo took up the question of "the article by Com. Zinoviev in
Pravda and *Komsomolskaia pravda* of 8 May of this year" and decided "to reprimand the editorial
staff of *Pravda* and *Komsomolskaia pravda* for printing Com. Zinoviev's article on the Berlin events
and to remind them that articles by Coms. Zinoviev and Kamenev cannot be printed without
permission from the Central Committee Secretariat." [In other words, Stalin's description of
Zinoviev as a member of *Pravda*'s editorial staff was highly exaggerated—U.S. Ed.]

Letter 48

[9 September 1929]

9/9

Viacheslav,[1]

1) Poliudov absolutely must be removed from the Commissariat of Transport. This is the same nutcase that kept confusing the Central Committee and
Transport with new railroad constructions and has nothing Communist about
him (nothing left). Now he's sitting at Transport as head of (new) construction.
Come on, what kind of builder is he? He's the reason construction of the new
tracks between Siberia and European Russia haven't moved an inch forward.
Get that anti-party man out of Transport. He's been systematically violating
the Central Committee's resolutions and also systematically mocking the Politburo.[2]

2) Next, what is Chernyi doing at the Transport collegium? Why hasn't he
been transferred to another job?[3]

J. Stalin

1. In the upper right-hand corner is Molotov's notation: "1929=?"
2. On 30 December 1929, the Orgburo relieved Poliudov of his work in the Commissariat of
Transport and confirmed him as a member of the Soviet trade delegation in Berlin (RTsKhIDNI
f. 17, op. 113, d. 809, l. 5). On 5 January 1930, the Politburo reversed this decision and kept
Poliudov at Transport. On 5 March 1930, he was given editorial work in connection with the
training of executives (ibid., op. 3, d. 778, l. 8), and in September, he was appointed director of the
Belorussian-Baltic Railway (ibid., op. 114, d. 190, l. 1).
3. On 18 September 1929, the Central Committee Secretariat confirmed Chernyi as deputy
chairman of transport in charge of training specialists.

Letter 49

Coms. Molotov and Ordzhonikidze,

Received your coded telegram about self-criticism.[1] Your proposal is incorrect since a special decree from the Central Committee plus a speech by Molotov may be understood (**will** be understood!) by the party organizations *as a new course backward*, as an appeal: *"Rein in self-criticism,"* which is of course not desirable and which will undoubtedly undermine the authority of the Central Committee (and Molotov) in the eyes of the best elements of the party *in favor of all and sundry bureaucrats.*

The article in *Pravda* attacking the Leningrad leadership (which means **Kirov**-*Komarov*) was a grave error (especially the *way* it was done).[2] Someone (that is, an enemy of the party) wanted to portray the top officials in Leningrad as *opposing* the correction of the shortcomings (that's **not true**!) But those bunglers from *Pravda* swallowed the bait, and now "everything's in a commotion" to the delight of the party's enemies. They forgot that the Leningrad organization isn't just your *Sochi* or *Astrakhan* or *Baku* organization. They forgot that a blow to the chiefs of the Leningrad organization, which represents the most reliable bulwark of the Central Committee, is a blow to the very heart of the Central Committee. . . . The **Central Committee's fault** consists of *relinquishing the rudder* for a moment to *Pravda's* editorial collegium, having forgotten that someone who has turned self-criticism into a sport—Com. Yaroslavskii—is a member of the collegium and that he possesses the happy ability of not seeing anything further than his own nose.

The same must be said about *Komsomolskaia pravda* and local press organs.

Let the Central Committee Secretariat *take the rudder in hand again*, let it establish *monitoring* over *Pravda* and *Komsomolskaia pravda*, let it *change the tone and spirit* of self-criticism in these newspapers—and then everything will be all right.

Well, all the best.

Regards to you both,
J. Stalin
9/13/29

1. The coded telegram was not found.
2. For *Pravda*'s attack on the Leningrad leadership, see note 1 to letter 47.

Letter 50

To Molotov, Voroshilov, Ordzhonikidze:[1]

1) Did you read Rykov's speech? In my opinion, it's the speech of a *nonparty soviet bureaucrat* pretending to take the tone of a "loyal" person, "sympathizing" with the soviets. But not a single word about the party! Not a single word about the right deviation! Not a single word to say that the party's achievements, which Rykov underhandedly ascribes now to himself, were attained in struggle with the rightists, including Rykov himself! All our officials who give speeches usually consider it their duty to speak about the rightists and to call for struggle against the rightists. But Rykov, it seems, is free from such an obligation! Why?—I might ask—on what basis? How can you tolerate (meaning *covering up* as well) this political hypocrisy? Don't you understand that in tolerating such hypocrisy, you create the *illusion* that Rykov has separated from the rightists and you thus *mislead* the party, because everyone can see that Rykov has never had a thought of leaving the rightists? Shouldn't you give Rykov an alternative: either disassociate openly and honestly from the rightists and conciliators, or lose the right to speak in the name of the Central Committee and Council of Commissars. I think this should be done because it's the least the Central Committee can demand—less than that and the Central Committee ceases to be itself.

2) I learned that Rykov is still *chairing* your meetings on Mondays and Thursdays.[2] Is that true? If it's true, why are you allowing this comedy to go on? Who is it for and for what reason? Can't you put an end to this comedy? Isn't it time?

3) I think I'll stay in Sochi another week. What's your opinion? If you say so, I can return immediately.

Greetings,
Stalin
9/30/29

---

1. In the upper left-hand corner is Molotov's note:

Totally agree with everything said. Didn't read Rykov's speech, but only skimmed the headings. Will read.
   I do see now, however, that Stalin is right. Just don't agree that we're "covering" for Rykov. We have to fix things in the way Stalin proposes, however. V. Molotov. 10/3.

2. The reference is to Rykov's chairing of Politburo sessions.

Letter 51

[7 October 1929]

Greetings, Molotov,

Received your letter of 10/4.

1) Things really didn't turn out so badly with England. Henderson was shown up. Rykov, along with Bukharin and Litvinov, was also shown up. These people don't see the growth of the power and might of the USSR, nor those changes in international relations that have occurred recently (and will go on taking place).

2) There will be a lot of trouble with China. By the way, I think that it's time to think about *organizing* an uprising by a *revolutionary* movement in Manchuria. The isolated detachments being sent to Manchuria to perform isolated tasks of an episodic nature are a good thing, of course, but they are *not enough*. We have to go for *bigger things* now. We need to organize two double regiment brigades, chiefly made up of Chinese, outfit them with everything necessary (artillery, machine guns, and so on), put Chinese at the head of the brigade, and send them into Manchuria with the following assignment: to stir up a rebellion among the Manchurian troops, to have reliable soldiers from these forces join them (the others should be sent home after removing the officer corps), to form into a division, to occupy Harbin, and, after gathering force, to declare Chang Hsueh-liang overthrown, establish a revolutionary government (massacre the landowners, bring in the peasants, create soviets in the cities and towns, and so on). This is necessary. This we can and, I think, should do. No "international law" contradicts this task. It will be clear to everyone that we are against war with China, that our Red Army soldiers are only defending our borders and have no intention of crossing into Chinese territory, and if there is a rebellion inside Manchuria, that's something quite understandable, given the atmosphere of the regime imposed by Chang Hsueh-liang. Think about it. It's important.

3) I read the transcript of the Industrial Academy's party cell. The matter will have to be put on the agenda of the Central Committee plenum. I should think that Bukharin is going to be kicked out of the Politburo.

4) I read the Politburo resolution about Rykov. A correct resolution! This resolution is binding on us, of course. But we'll talk about that when I come.

5) Things are going well with the procurements. But you can't rest yet; you have to keep up the pressure. Otherwise people will fall asleep.

6) Generally, I'd have to admit that things are going pretty well for you [in Moscow] (that is, for us), at least for the time being. That's good.

I'll be in Moscow in a few days.

Regards,
J. Stalin
10/7/29

Letter 52   [earlier than 17 November 1929]

Molotov,[1]
The basic resolution (about the target figures) will be published, and we have to include a thesis concerning the *incompatibility* of party membership with the *propagandizing or defense of right-deviationist* views.[2]

> 1. In the upper left-hand corner of the note is Molotov's notation: "1930?"
> 2. At the Central Committee plenum of 17 November 1929, Rudzutak proposed adding to the resolution on economic target figures for 1929–1930 the phrase "to recognize that defending the views of rightist opportunists or appeasement with them is incompatible with membership in the party." The proposal was passed by the plenum (RTsKhIDNI f. 17, op. 2, d. 441, vyp. 2, l. 144).

Letter 53   [5 December 1929]

Hello Molotshtein,[1, 2]
Why the devil have you burrowed into your lair, like a bear, and why are you not talking? How are things there, good or bad? Write something.

Things are not bad here for now.

1) The grain procurements are progressing. Today we decided to expand the emergency stocks of food to 120 million poods. We are raising the supply quota for industrial cities like Ivanovo-Voznesensk, Kharkov, and so on.

2) The collective farm movement is growing by leaps and bounds. Of course there are not enough machines and tractors—how could it be otherwise?—but simply pooling the peasant tools results in a colossal increase in sown acreage (in some regions by as much as 50 percent!). In the lower Volga, 60 percent of peasant farms have been transferred (already transferred!) to collective farms. The eyes of our rightists are popping out of their heads in amazement. . . .[3]

3) You no doubt already know about our foreign affairs. Things with China should pick up. Obviously our fellows from the Far East Army gave them a good scare. I just received from Chang Hsueh-liang a telegram confirming his "complete agreement with the results of the meeting" between Ts'ai [Yunshan] and Simanovskii.[4] We rebuffed America and England and France rather harshly for their attempt to intervene.[5] We couldn't have done otherwise. Let them know what the Bolsheviks are like! I think the Chinese landowners won't forget the object lesson taught them by the Far East Army. We decided not to withdraw our troops from China until our conditions are guaranteed. You should read Litvinov's speech at the Central Executive Committee session—it's pretty good.[6]

4) You probably already know about the new appointments from the newspapers. What's new about these appointments is a) Tomskii's appointment as

deputy to Kuibyshev (Kuibyshev thinks—perhaps not without reason—that there will be some advantage in this); b) the appointment of Shvarts as chairman of the coal "association" (we don't have a better candidate).[7]

5) The rightists (the three) are working away, but so far they haven't made a move. Rykov took it into his head to bring Yakovlev as his assistant administrator (a "tea-drinkers society"!), but we nipped this in the bud.[8]

Well, that's it for now.

Regards,

J. Stalin

12/5/29

1. A jocular version of Molotov's name that gives it a Jewish flavor—Trans.

2. The letter was written in Moscow and sent to Molotov while he was on vacation.

3. For more information on the collectivization decision, see the Grain Tribute and Collectivization section in the Introduction—U.S. Ed.

4. Chang Hsueh-liang's telegram indicating agreement with the Nikolsk-Ussuriysk protocol on restoring the status quo on the Chinese Eastern Railway was received on 5 December 1929 (*Dokumenty vneshnei politiki SSSR* [Documents of USSR foreign policy], vol. 12 [Moscow, 1967], 639, 601, 602).

5. On 3 December 1929, the Soviet Union was handed a note from the governments of the United States, France, and England, which stated in part (*Dokumenty vneshnei politiki SSSR*, 605):

[There is] serious hope that China and Russia will refrain from or renounce any hostile measures and will find it possible to come to a peaceful settlement in the near future of all issues that are the subject of conflict between them at the present time.

A reply published in the Soviet press on 4 December 1929 noted (*Dokumenty vneshnei politiki SSSR*, 605):

The Soviet government cannot help but express its surprise that the government of the United States of America, which by its own wish does not have any official relations with the government of the Soviet Union, finds it possible to give it advice and instructions.

The text of the reply was first reviewed at a Politburo session on 3 December 1929 (RTsKhIDNI f. 17, op. 3, d. 767, ll. 12, 26, 27).

6. Litvinov's report was heard at the second session of the V Convention of the Central Executive Committee on 4 December 1929 (*Dokumenty vneshnei politiki SSSR*, 606–34).

7. On 30 November 1929, the Politburo appointed Tomskii deputy chairman of the Supreme Economic Council and Shvarts chairman of the coal industry (RTsKhIDNI f. 17, op. 3, d. 767, l. 12).

8. On 20 December 1929, the Politburo confirmed Yakovlev as RSFSR commissar of finance (ibid., d. 769, l. 4).

Letter 54   [25 December 1929]

Hello, Viacheslav,

Of course I got your first letter. I know you are cursing me in your heart for my silence. I can't deny that you are fully within your rights to do that. But try to see things my way: I'm terribly overloaded and there's no time to sleep (literally!). Soon I will write a proper letter.

1) Things aren't good with *Pravda*'s editorial staff. Kovalev and Naumov (both former Trotskyists) are apparently bossing everyone around there, including several other party officials. Kovalev has already taken Popov in hand. Krumin continues to "float." Perhaps this could be tolerated for a certain time, but the problem is that Kovalev is a "shadowy figure" and "incomprehensible" and apparently not completely one of us (I'm told he has sympathy for the Zinovievites). They let Shliapnikov through; even earlier they slipped up on Frumkin; and now there's Naumov's article.[1] They wanted to let Piatakov's recent article through, but Kaganovich and I caught on to it in time and managed to correct (late at night) some "unclear" "passages" in Piatakov's article. *We will straighten out the Shliapnikov affair today.* As for Frumkin, this is an old story and I think perhaps it could wait until a more opportune moment. I'm afraid Kovalev and his group will have to be dismissed. . . .

2) One of these days, the Politburo should decide on military affairs (there's a report from the Worker-Peasant Inspection on the artillery administration) in connection with measures *already passed* by the Commissariat for War that are designed to eliminate disruptions. We consider it inexpedient to make any noise about this. The resolution should go into the Special File.

3) Kaganovich has promised to move things forward on a school for people like Mikhailov (the Leningrader).

4) The nasty business (Desov-Komarov) against Kirov[2] *helped to accelerate* the purge of bureaucratized elements from the Leningrad organization. There's no cloud without a silver lining! The Leningrad Provincial Party Committee passed the Central Committee resolution—and, according to witnesses, not without a certain enthusiasm. It's a fact! Komarov's bureaucratism played a role here, and the Central Committee's authority, and the fact that Kirov has apparently earned the great respect of the Leningrad organization in recent times. Kodatskii, Alekseev, Lobov, Serganin (not as determinedly as the others) disassociated themselves instantly from Desov-Komarov. The Leningraders are thinking of nominating Kodatskii for the post of chairman. This Central Committee resolution should also go into the Special File.

5) You should already know about the Chinese matter. America has disgraced itself somewhat with its interference.

6) In a few days we'll make the decision on the pace of the collective farm movement. Yakovlev's commission has submitted a draft. In my opinion, it isn't suitable. You've probably already got it. Let me know your opinion via telegraph.[3]

Once again: I promise to write a proper letter.

Warm regards,
J. Stalin
12/25/29

1. Shliapnikov's article "Za industrializatsiiu—za sotsializm" (For industrialism and for socialism) was published in *Pravda* on 16 December 1929. No article with Naumov's byline was published in *Pravda* in December 1929. Either Stalin was referring to an unsigned piece, or an article submitted by Naumov was not published in the newspaper.

2. After hearing the report by Desov, a member of the Leningrad Control Commission, regarding press coverage of the abnormal phenomena in the Leningrad Party Organization, the Central Control Commission set up a committee to verify his information (RTsKhIDNI f. 613, op. 1, d. 81, l. 20).

3. For more on the collectivization decision, see the Grain Tribute and Collectivization section in the Introduction—U.S. Ed.

CHAPTER FIVE

1930

IN 1930, THE SOVIET UNION was approaching a state of civil war. In January and February the government unleashed a massive, violent collectivization campaign. By 10 March, 58 percent of all peasant households had been forced into the collective farms, and many peasants had been arrested and exiled. The countryside responded with massive unrest, the true dimensions of which are still not known. As a result of the forced collectivization and dekulakization of hundreds of thousands of peasants, agricultural production declined. The country survived on semistarvation rations that were constantly being reduced.

From the outset, the policy of forced industrialization was destructive and ineffective. As a result of this ill-conceived policy, many hundreds of millions of rubles were invested in unfinished construction. Factories producing consumer goods often had to reduce their output because of shortages of equipment and raw materials. The cost of industrial production escalated, and the output of defective products increased dramatically.

All of this was disastrous for the state budget. The huge deficit was patched up by raising prices, introducing obligatory promissory notes for loans, and, most important, printing money. In twenty-one months, from the end of 1928 to July 1930, 1,556 million rubles were put into circulation, although the five-year plan had called for the creation of only 1,250 million rubles.[1] The massive inflation led to inventories becoming exhausted, and bartering

1. RTsKhIDNI f. 85, op. 27, d. 397, l. 20b.

became the norm. At farmers' markets, peasants would sell agricultural products to urban dwellers, not for money, but for soap, thread, sugar, textiles, footwear, and so on.

One of the most graphic displays of the complete collapse of the budget was the so-called small-change crisis. Since paper money kept depreciating, people hoarded coins containing a tiny amount of silver. The monetary system split into two, with prices dependent on whether payment was in coins or paper bank notes. In a number of places, sellers refused to accept paper money. Large amounts of silver accumulated in people's homes. Although new coins were minted, the scarcity of imported silver meant that not enough was produced to cover the shortage.

On 19 July 1930, G. L. Piatakov, chairman of Gosbank (the state bank), sent Stalin a memo on the status of the coin supply and the country's finances. He candidly described the fiscal crisis and the coin shortage—the excessive printing of money, the rise in prices, the small-change crisis, and so on—and proposed the following remedies:

> To establish a clear and definite party position regarding money at this new stage of economic development. . . . To root out the apathetic and tailist[2] attitude some economic managers have to the question of money circulation. . . . A directive must be given to Gosplan to ensure that industries producing mass consumer goods . . . be given far greater scope than was originally intended. In particular, Group B industry [light industry] must at all costs attain a growth rate, not of 32 percent (as was originally projected by Gosplan), but of at least 35 percent or 36 percent . . .
>
> Imports must be made more efficient in every way possible, discarding from import [orders] everything that is not absolutely necessary . . . and maximizing the import of raw materials for consumer industries: an attempt should be made to import not just three but four million poods of cotton, and to increase somewhat the import of wool, rubber, boot leather, industrial fats . . .
>
> Exports should be reviewed and made more efficient. The export of animal products intended for human consumption (butter, eggs, meat, and so on) should be reduced or eliminated. Exports should also be

2. From *khvostizm*, "tailism," an expression condemning following the crowd or the momentary mass mood instead of providing leadership—U.S. Ed.

thoroughly analyzed, item by item, to eliminate any items exported at an excessive or outrageous loss . . .

The entire fiscal plan for the coming year must be implemented without creating a deficit, and the credit plan for Gosbank should be implemented without printing money. The budget should contain an unexpended reserve of 2 or 2.5 percent (that is, about 300–400 million rubles).

In addition, Piatakov proposed raising prices on a number of luxury items and expanding the system of loans from consumers to be repaid by the future production of consumer goods—sewing machines, pocket watches, carriages, bicycles, sugar, and so on. He proposed tightening control over construction projects to combat waste in this area; increasing the number of loans; regulating prices strictly without allowing procurement costs to rise; and changing the system that allowed any divergence from the budget to be covered by printing money or by permitting some payments to be postponed, and so on.[3]

In regard to the coin shortage, Gosbank directors supported the repeated suggestions of N. P. Briukhanov, commissar of finance, that silver money be replaced with nickel coins.[4] Until this could be done, Briukhanov and Piatakov advocated continued silver imports so that more coins could be minted.

In spite of Piatakov's attempt to show full support for the "general line" and his rejection of "any opportunistic conclusions aimed at exploiting the temporary disorder in coin circulation in order to discredit our economic policy and accuse us of overly ambitious and impossible tempos," Stalin must have realized that Piatakov was in effect advocating a real shift in course. To call for a fundamental change in attitude that would make the use of money acceptable, for an increase in the production of consumer goods, for the transfer of goods earmarked for export to the domestic market, and for stricter financing of large-scale construction projects—all these largely coincided with the "rightist, opportunist" sentiments from which Piatakov was so eager to disassociate himself.

As can be seen from the letters, Stalin sharply condemned these proposals and advocated his own solutions to the problem: "Defi-

3. RTsKhIDNI f. 85, op. 27, d. 397, ll. 5, 6.
4. GARF f. 5446, op. 6, d. 656, ll. 1–3.

nitely shoot two or three dozen wreckers" from the Finance Commissariat and Gosbank and conduct more vigorous OGPU operations against black-market coin dealers (letter 57). Stalin supervised these operations personally. On 2 August 1930, two weeks after receiving a report from Piatakov, Stalin sent OGPU Chairman V. R. Menzhinskii the following inquiry:

> Can you send a memo on the results of the struggle (through GPU channels) against the small-change speculators (how much silver was confiscated and for which period; what institutions are most involved in this; the role of foreign countries and their agents; how many people have been arrested, what sort of people, and so on). Report also on your thoughts about what measures to take for further struggle.[5]

The report requested was on Stalin's desk within a few days. After studying it, Stalin delivered a reprimand in writing to Menzhinskii on 9 August:

> I received your memo. Your point of view is correct. There is no doubt of that. But the problem is that the results of the operation to confiscate small silver change are almost pathetic. It wasn't even worth writing a report about 280,000 rubles—that's an insignificant sum. Apparently you took a bite out of the cashiers and let it go at that, as often happens in our country. That's not good enough.[6]

Although the Politburo had already passed a resolution about minting nickel coins, it is clear from the letters to Molotov that Stalin rejected this idea, and it was immediately withdrawn.[7]

After these instructions from Stalin, authorities stepped up the persecution of people who purchased coins. Piatakov and Briukhanov were soon removed from their posts. Just as Stalin had suggested (letter 63), the work of "inspecting and checking up by punching people in the face"[8] was conducted in their ministries.

The axe fell most heavily on the old specialists. Stalin's letters reflect a clear desire to deflect the responsibility for numerous problems and failures on to "wreckers" and "class enemies." In the 1920s, numerous engineers, experts, and scientists from the pre-

5. *Kommunist*, no. 11 (1990): 96 (RTsKhIDNI f. 558, op. 1, d. 5275, l. 1).
6. *Kommunist*, no. 11 (1990): 96–97 (RTsKhIDNI f. 558, op. 1, d. 5274, l. 1).
7. RTsKhIDNI f. 17, op. 3, d. 793, l. 12.
8. A more apt translation of *proverochno-mordoboinaia rabota* into American English would be "to take names and kick ass"—Trans.

revolutionary era worked in plants, factories, commissariats, and other institutions. Many of them had been members of various parties, ranging from Mensheviks to Kadets.[9] They had a great wealth of practical experience and excellent educations. In spite of their fundamental political disagreements with the Bolsheviks, these people had optimistically embraced NEP. They had done a great deal for the economic renewal of the country, and their political sympathies were with the moderate wing of the party leadership who advocated prudence and caution in both political and economic spheres. It can even be said that NEP's successes largely depended on the cooperation between the experienced specialists from the old intelligentsia and the moderate group of Bolshevik leaders.

The persecution of the "rightists" put an end to the old specialists' hopes for an evolutionary improvement of the Soviet government. Moreover, the *spetsy* (as they were called at the time) were some of the first victims of the leftist turn in the "general line" in the late 1920s. The famous Shakhty trial in early 1928 unleashed a powerful "anti-*spets*" campaign in the country.[10] Many representatives of the old intelligentsia fell victim to dismissals, arrests, and executions during this period. The Stalin government not only foisted all the blame on the "bourgeois specialists" for the growing difficulties brought about by its radical policies but rid itself of confirmed supporters of NEP and destroyed the intellectual allies of the rightists who were accused of fraternizing with and providing patronage to "wreckers." This was precisely the blueprint for the wide-scale campaign conducted in 1930, whose instigator, as the letters indicate, was Stalin himself.

In order to substantiate the claim that a widespread network of counterrevolutionary wreckers' organizations existed, the OGPU began to arrest major specialists from the central economic ministries in the summer of 1930. These were generally well known scientists and experts who had played a prominent role during the NEP years. For example, N. D. Kondratiev, a former Socialist Revolutionary and assistant minister of food supply in the Provisional

9. The Kadets, or Constitutional Democrats, were the leading liberal party in the decade before the revolution—U.S. Ed.

10. In 1928, more than fifty engineers were tried for sabotage at the Shakhty mines. It was one of the first show trials of wreckers—U.S. Ed.

Government, had worked in Soviet agricultural agencies and headed the Market Institute of the Commissariat of Finance; N. P. Makarov and A. V. Chaianov held posts in the RSFSR Commissariat of Agriculture; L. N. Yurovskii was a member of the collegium of the Finance Commissariat; and P. A. Sadyrin, an agronomist of peasant background who was elected to the Central Committee of the Kadet party in 1917, was a member of Gosbank. The experienced statistician V. G. Groman remained a Menshevik until 1921, then worked at Gosplan and the Central Statistical Administration. Another prominent Menshevik, V. A. Bazarov, had had a similar career and had worked as a Gosbank official since 1921. N. N. Sukhanov was a journalist who had debated Lenin; he worked in government economic agencies and in the Soviet trade delegations in Berlin and Paris during the 1920s. In 1930, Stalin demanded that Sukhanov's wife be interrogated under the pretext that "outrages [were] going on at their house." (Ironically, Sukhanov's wife had allowed her apartment to be used—without her husband's knowledge—in October 1917, prior to the Bolshevik revolution, for a crucial secret meeting of the party's Central Committee.)

Soon, through the efforts of the OGPU and under Stalin's careful supervision, materials were prepared describing the existence of a powerful network of interrelated anti-Soviet organizations in many government offices. Stalin's letters provide evidence of how the testimony of the arrested was used. Upon Stalin's order, testimonies were collected and published in the form of a printed brochure, *Materialy po delu kontrrevoliutsionnoy* 'Trudovoy krestianskoy partii' *i gruppirovki Sukhanova-Gromana (Iz materialov sledstvennogo proizvodstva OGPU)* (Materials on the case of the Counterrevolutionary "Toiling Peasants' Party" and the Sukhanov-Groman group [from OGPU investigation files]). The brochure contained the transcripts of the interrogations of Kondratiev, Yurovskii, Makarov, Chaianov, Sadyrin, Groman, and other arrested persons made from 27 July to 2 September 1930. The publication was widely distributed among party and state directors.

As can be seen from *Materialy,* the "testimonies" of "wreckers" followed a certain script: the OGPU supposedly discovered that a counterrevolutionary Toiling Peasants' Party (TPP), with Kondratiev as its chairman, had an organization in Moscow and "strong representation in the provinces." According to the OGPU's allegations, the Central Committee of this party met regularly and had even drawn up a list of officials for a future government under Kondratiev. It was supposed to come to power through armed insurrection. The TPP Central Committee had close contacts (or so the published "testimonies" claimed) with the White emigré Republican Democratic Association, to which such famous emigrés as P. Miliukov, S. Maslov, A. Kerensky, B. Brutskus, S. Prokopovich, and Ye. Kuskova belonged. OGPU investigators linked the TPP Central Committee with the "counterrevolutionary organization of Sukhanov-Groman-Bazarov" (soon to be dubbed the "Union Bureau of Mensheviks"). The TPP allegedly discussed the composition of the future government with this fellow "counterrevolutionary organization," as well as its participation in the organization of peasant uprisings and so on.

In fabricating the case, the OGPU also claimed that the TPP was in "informational contact" with a "center" made up of industrial engineers like L. K. Ramzin, director of the Institute of Thermal Technology; V. A. Larichev, member of the Gosplan presidium; A. A. Fedotov, chairman of the collegium of the Textile Research Institute; and S. V. Kupriianov, technical director of the Supreme Economic Council's textile division. This "center" was later called the Industrial Party (Promparty). Chaianov was slated to be the TPP representative to this "center." Supposedly he had regularly informed the TPP about measures to disrupt the entire economic life of the country in the event of foreign intervention.

Meanwhile, a case was being prepared concerning a counterrevolutionary organization of "wreckers in workers' food supply." The arrests were made in the chief government offices in charge of supplying food to the populace. The OGPU placed Riazantsev and Ye. S. Karatygin at the head of this "organization of wreckers." Karatygin had been a top official in the Ministry of Finance and the former editor in chief of *Torgovo-promyshlennaia gazeta* (Trade and industry newspaper). The Riazantsev-Karatygin group was declared a branch of the "wreckers' organization" run by Kondratiev-Groman. As we learn from the letters, Stalin made the decision to execute those who were arrested. At his order, a report from the OGPU was printed on 22 September 1930, concerning the discovery of a "wreckers' and spies' organization involved in the supply of the most basic food products"; the aim of this organization was to "cause hunger in the country and provoke unrest among the broad masses of workers and thus facilitate the overthrow of the dictatorship of the proletariat." Several days later, on 25 September, the newspapers reported the execution of forty-eight "supply wreckers." A loud propaganda campaign was organized around this event. The public, worn out by the food crisis, was told that the real people to blame for the conditions of poverty had been exposed and would now be punished.

A similar campaign was launched in December 1930 during the trial of the engineers who had supposedly formed the Promparty. The court's statement in the Promparty affair asserted that this organization was tied to the so-called Torgprom [Trade and Industry], a foreign counterrevolutionary group composed of former owners of Russian factories headed by Denisov, Nobel, and Montashev. The court claimed that the "Promparty was chiefly counting on a military intervention against the USSR and, in order to prepare for this, had entered into organizational contact with interventionist organizations both in the USSR (the Socialist Revolutionary, Kadet, and kulak group of Kondratiev and Chaianov, and the Menshevik group of Sukhanov and Groman) as well as abroad (Torgprom, Miliukov's group, and Parisian interventionist circles)."[11]

Evidence was given to show that a foreign expeditionary corps, combined with remnants of Wrangel's army and Krasnov Cossack units, was preparing for military intervention in 1930.[12] These formations were allegedly supposed to strike a combined blow against Moscow and Leningrad. According to the court's final statement, "The plan contained the notion of using some border incident as an excuse for an interventionists' attack against the USSR, so that as the conflict progressed, the armed forces of the countries allied with France—Poland and Romania—could be used as well as the armies of the border states (that is, the group of states on the periphery of the former Russian empire—Latvia, Lithuania, Estonia, and Finland)." The court further claimed that

11. Protsess "prompartii" (25 Noiabr–7 Dekabria 1930 g.) (Promparty trial, 25 November–7 December 1930) (Moscow, 1931).
12. Wrangel and Krasnov were tsarist generals who fought against the Bolsheviks during the civil war—U.S. Ed.

the time period for the intervention had been moved forward largely because of the absence "inside the USSR of conditions favorable to carrying out an intervention."

A letter from Stalin to Menzhinskii, head of the secret police, illustrates how all of these notions and "plans" came about, who their real instigator was, who in reality drafted the script for the trials of "spies and wreckers," and who thought up the "testimonies" that had to be obtained from the persons arrested:[13]

Com. Menzhinskii,

Received your letter of 10/2 and the materials. Ramzin's testimonies are very interesting. I think the most interesting thing in his testimonies is the question of intervention in general and the question about the timing of the intervention in particular. It seems they were plotting an intervention in 1930 but postponed it until 1931 or even 1932. This is quite likely and important. It's all the more important because it comes from a primary source, that is, from the group of Riabushinskii, Gukasov, Denisov, and Nobel, who represent the strongest socio-economic group of all those existing in the USSR and among the emigrés, the strongest both in financial backing as well as in ties with the French and British governments. It might seem as if the "TPP" or the "Promparty" or Miliukov's "party" represents the main force. But that's not true. The main force is the Riabushinskii-Denisov-Nobel group and the like—that is, Torgprom. The TPP, the Promparty, and Miliukov's "party" are errand boys for Torgprom. All the more interesting is the information about the timing of the intervention that has come from Torgprom. The question of intervention in general and the timing of the intervention in particular is obviously of primary interest for us.

Hence my proposals:

a) In any new (future) testimonies from the chiefs of TPP, Promparty, and Ramzin, pay particular attention to the question of intervention and its timing: 1) Why was the intervention in 1930 postponed? 2) Was it because Poland was still not ready? 3) Perhaps because Romania was not ready? 4) Perhaps because the border states had still not joined with Poland? 5) Why did they postpone the intervention until 1931? 6) Why were they "able to" postpone it until 1932? 7) and so forth and so on;

13. The inscription on the envelope reads: "To the OGPU, Com. Menzhinskii. In person only. From Stalin."

b) Bring charges against Larichev and other members of the "Promparty Central Committee" and interrogate them as strictly as possible about the same thing, after giving them Ramzin's testimony to read;

c) Interrogate Groman as strictly as possible; according to Ramzin's testimony, he once stated in the "United Center" that "the intervention is postponed until 1932";

d) Run Messrs. Kondratiev, Yurovskii, Chaianov etc. through the mill; they have cleverly tried to evade [the charge of having a] "tendency toward intervention" but are (indisputably!) interventionist; interrogate them as strictly as possible on the timing (Kondratiev, Yurovskii, and Chaianov should also know about that as well, just as Miliukov, whom they visited for a "chat," knows about it).

If Ramzin's testimonies are confirmed and corroborated in the depositions of other persons accused (Groman, Larichev, Kondratiev and company, etc.) that will be a serious victory for the OGPU, since we'll make the material available in some form to the Comintern sections and the workers of the world, and we'll launch the broadest campaign possible against the interventionists and will succeed in paralyzing them and in heading off interventionist attempts for the next one or two years, which is of great significance for us.

Everything understood?

Greetings,

J. Stalin[14]

This political persecution was accompanied by a further tightening of the domestic regime and a crackdown on dissent in the ranks of the ruling party. In spite of the harassment of "right deviationists," Stalin's policy provoked dissatisfaction even, in some cases, among the party figures who had until recently supported Stalin in his struggle with Bukharin. The most significant action against the apostates within the party's ranks in 1930 was the case of the "leftist right-wing bloc" of Syrtsov-Lominadze. Syrtsov was originally Stalin's protégé. For a time, he worked at the Central Committee, and he became prominent in 1928 as an active promoter of the policy of forcible grain procurement in Siberia. Subsequently Stalin brought Syrtsov to Moscow and set him up as the chairman of the RSFSR Council of Commissars and a candidate member of the Politburo, clearly opposing the young, energetic Syrtsov to Rykov.

14. *Kommunist*, no. 11 (1990): 99–100 (RTsKhIDNI f. 558, op. 1, d. 5276).

Syrtsov did not live up to the leader's hopes, however. Confronted with the fruits of Stalin's extremist policy, he began to criticize it and propose remedies that were increasingly reminiscent of the points made by the Bukharin group. Dissatisfaction with the "general line" united Syrtsov and another young protégé, V. V. Lominadze, who had been appointed to the executive position of first secretary of the Transcaucasian Regional Party Committee. A group of supporters gathered around Syrtsov and Lominadze; several meetings took place with frank conversations about and sharp criticism of Stalin.

To this day it is not known what practical actions this group had in mind. But on 21 and 22 October 1930, Reznikov, one of the members of the group, addressed two denunciations to Stalin at the Central Committee meeting. He informed the government in detail about the group's meetings and the issues discussed there. On the basis of Reznikov's statements, Syrtsov and Lominadze were grilled at the presidium of the Central Control Commission. A number of the group's members were arrested by the OGPU. Through the joint efforts of the Central Control Commission and the OGPU, the necessary testimonies were extracted. On 2 December 1930, a Central Committee and Central Control Commission resolution was published: "On the factional work of Syrtsov, Lominadze, and others." It stated that Syrtsov and Lominadze had organized a "leftist right-wing bloc" on the basis of a general political platform that coincided on all the basic points with the platform of the "right opportunists." Syrtsov and Lominadze were expelled from the party and removed from their posts. Other Communists suspected of disloyalty also fell victim to persecution.

One of Stalin's chief concerns in 1930 was the removal of Rykov from the post of chairman of the Council of Commissars. Throughout 1929–1930, as the letters illustrate, Stalin prepared various pretexts for attacking him. From Stalin's letters, it appears that one purpose behind the fabrication of the cases of the "counterrevolutionary parties" was to discredit Rykov (and also Kalinin, who had vacillated and not been sufficiently "staunch"). The majority of specialists arrested by OGPU worked in the government apparat and were in close contact with Rykov and Kalinin through their jobs. Interrogators made a special point of taking testimony from the arrested "wreckers" about these contacts. Political responsibility for the "activization" of the "counterrevolution" was constantly laid at the door of the "rightists," including Rykov.

Stalin first confidentially informed Molotov of his intention to remove Rykov in September 1930, apparently having decided that the conditions were ripe for it. True to his methods, Stalin conceived of an entire program to reorganize government bodies, in the context of which Rykov's removal was supposed to look like a mere detail. At the December Central Committee plenum, Rykov and the "rightists" as a whole were once again accused of ideologically abetting hostile forces. As Kuibyshev said in his speech, "The wreckers from the Promparty, the Chaianov-Kondratiev wing, and the Groman wing are all hoping for the victory of the right opportunists."[15] A decision was made at the plenum to remove Rykov and appoint Molotov to the post of chairman of the Council of Commissars.

As the new chairman, Molotov informed the plenum of the decision to reform the main government bodies and outlined in full Stalin's notions as conveyed to him in the letter of 22 September (letter 68). The plenum approved the proposal to bring Stalin into the Labor Defense Council and turn the Labor Defense Council into a "militant and viable economic management body." The plenum also decided to create a "Commission on Fulfillment" under the Council of Commissars, to be composed of the chairman of the Council of Commissars, the head of Worker-Peasant Inspection, the secretary of the Trade Union Council, and one of the secretaries of the Central Committee. The commission was charged with verifying the fulfillment of the party's directives and the Council of Commissars' decisions.

Virtually the entire reorganization was stillborn. The new bodies turned out to be a powerless appendage to the traditional mechanism of power. As before, all fundamental questions and the oversight of policy implementation were under the control of party bodies. Nevertheless, Rykov was removed, yet another purge had been conducted in the state economic apparat, and Stalin's real goals had been achieved.

15. RTsKhIDNI f. 17, op. 2, d. 460, l. 83.

Letter 55

We must reckon with Com. Bauman's categorical statement that he is not an advocate for any special line in our party, although he is the one who tolerated appeasement of the "leftist" deviationists.

Is that passage from my concluding speech suitable for the Moscow Party Committee?

Perhaps it should be said more forcefully that Bauman doesn't have a special *line?*

[V. Molotov]

Of course, it has to be said more bluntly that he doesn't have any special line, that he himself is *not* a "leftist" deviationist, but there are (or have been) only some examples of appeasement of "leftist" deviationists.²

[J. Stalin]

1. A note from Molotov (most likely written at one of the Politburo meetings) and Stalin's reply on the back of the note.

2. On 18 April 1930, the Politburo polled its members regarding the statement by the Moscow Regional Party Committee secretary, K. Bauman, in which he admitted the mistakes made by the Moscow Committee during collectivization and asked to be relieved from the post of secretary of the Moscow Committee. The Politburo noted that Bauman had "in practice displayed appeasement toward 'leftist' deviationists" and resolved (RTsKhIDNI f. 17, op. 3, d. 783, ll. 12, 13):

1) To satisfy the request of Com. Bauman regarding his release from the duties of secretary of the Moscow Regional organization. 2) To transfer Com. Bauman to work at the Central Committee in the capacity of a secretary. 3) To recommend that Com. Kaganovich take the post of first secretary of the Moscow Regional organization while maintaining his position as Central Committee secretary.

On 20 April 1930, the Politburo assigned Molotov to report to the plenum of the Moscow and Moscow Regional party committees on this resolution (ibid., l. 14).

On 22 April 1930, the joint plenum of the Moscow and Moscow Regional party committees "satisfied [Bauman's] request."

Letter 56

8/2

Viacheslav,

You have probably already received the new testimonies of Groman, Kondratiev, and Makarov. Yagoda brought them to show me. I think that all these testimonies plus Groman's first testimony should be sent to **all** members of the Central Committee and Central Control Commission and also the most active of our economic managers.[1] These are documents of primary importance.

Regards,

Stalin

1. On 10 August 1930, the Politburo resolved to distribute the testimonies of the persons arrested in the Toiling Peasants' Party case to members and candidate members of the Central Committee and Central Control Commission and to high-level economic managers (RTsKhIDNI f. 17, op. 3, d. 792, l. 11).

Letter 57

[No earlier than 6 August 1930]

Viacheslav,[1]

Received your letter of 8/6.

1) I'm against transferring Mirzoian to the Profintern [Trade Union International] because I have always been against and will continue to be against looting provinces, especially a province like the Urals, which is growing by leaps and bounds and is in need of officials.[2]

2) The results of the battle against the coin shortage are almost nonexistent. 280,000 rubles is nonsense. They probably clamped down on a few cashiers and let it go at that. But it's not only a question of cashiers. It's a question of Piatakov, Briukhanov, and their entourage. Both Piatakov and Briukhanov were for importing silver. Both Piatakov and Briukhanov preached the need to import silver and pushed a resolution to that effect through the conference of the deputies (or the Labor Defense Council)—a resolution we **rejected** *at Monday's meeting*, after branding them "blind followers" [*khvostiki*] of the financial wreckers. Now it's obvious even to the blind that Yurovskii directed Finance's measures (and not Briukhanov) and that wrecker elements from the Gosbank bureaucracy (and not Piatakov) directed the Gosbank "policy," as inspired by the "government" of Kondratiev-Groman. It is thus important to a) fundamentally purge the Finance and Gosbank bureaucracy, despite the wails of dubious Communists like Briukhanov-Piatakov; b) definitely shoot two or three dozen wreckers from these apparaty, including several dozen common cashiers; c) continue OGPU operations throughout the USSR that are aimed at seizing small change (silver).

3) I think that the investigation into the Kondratiev-Groman-Sadyrin affair must be continued—very thoroughly and without haste. This is a very important matter. All documents concerning this case should be sent to members of the Central Committee and the Central Control Commission. I don't doubt that a *direct* connection will be discovered (through Sokolnikov and Teodorovich) between these gentlemen and the rightists (Bukharin, Rykov, Tomskii). Kondratiev, Groman, and a few other scoundrels must definitely be shot.

4) A whole group of wreckers in the meat industry must definitely be shot and their names published in the press.

5) Is it true that you have decided to issue nickel coins **right now**? If that's true, it's a mistake. You should wait with that.[3]

6) Is it true that we imported shoes from England (for several million rubles)? If that's true, it's a mistake.

7) It's good that the United States has permitted the importation of our timber.[4] Our patience bore fruit. Wait on Bogdanov for the time being.[5]

8) The treaty with Italy[6] is a plus. Germany will follow suit. By the way, how are things with the German credits?[7]

9) Force the export of grain to the maximum. If we can export grain, the credits will come.

10) *Pay attention to the Stalingrad and Leningrad tractor factories.* Things are bad there.[8]

Well, regards,
Stalin

1. In the upper left-hand corner, Molotov has noted: "1930=?"

2. On 21 August 1930, the Politburo confirmed Mirzoian as third secretary of the Ural Regional Committee (RTsKhIDNI f. 17, op. 3, d. 793, l. 17).

3. On 20 August 1930, the Politburo rejected the proposal from the Politburo commission headed by Rudzutak on minting nickel coins (ibid., l. 12).

4. In 1930, the United States imposed barriers against Soviet exports of matches, timber, anthracite, manganese ore, and asbestos. On 25 July 1930, the U.S. Department of Commerce declared an embargo on the import of timber from the USSR. On 28 July, two ships carrying timber from the USSR were refused permission to unload. Following protests from the Soviet government and from a number of American companies, the Department of Commerce withdrew the embargo. But Soviet goods continued to be boycotted in the United States and other countries. The reasons for the embargoes and boycotts were allegations that the Soviets employed slave labor (in labor camps for the timber and mining industries) and dumped these products on the world market at below cost.

5. P. A. Bogdanov was director of Amtorg (American Trading Corporation) from 1930 to 1934. On 30 July 1930, the Politburo reviewed Bogdanov's statements. The decision was sent to the Special File (ibid., d. 791, l. 10). On 20 August 1930, the Politburo passed a resolution, "On Amtorg," noting that the Worker-Peasant Inspection had discovered substantial overpayments for oil and other products from America, and prescribed measures for "eliminating the shortcomings indicated" (ibid., d. 793, ll. 11, 32, 33).

6. The agreement between the governments of the USSR and Italy on the discount purchase of Italian products on a "most favored" basis was signed on 2 August 1930 (*Dokumenty vneshnei politiki SSSR* [Documents of USSR foreign policy], vol. 13 [Moscow, 1967], 439–41).

7. Talks on Germany's granting of credits to the USSR culminated in the signing, on 14 April 1931, of an agreement between the Supreme Economic Council and German industrial representatives that granted the Soviet Union substantial credits for the purpose of making large purchases from Germany (*Dokumenty vneshnei politiki SSSR*, vol. 14 [Moscow, 1968], 246–48).

8. On 25 August 1930, the Politburo discussed the question of tractor manufacture at the Stalingrad and Putilov factories. The resolution emphasized the need to fulfill the 1930–1931 manufacturing goals set for the factories. A commission that included Rykov, Kuibyshev, Osinskii, and others was formed to discuss the practical measures needed to fulfill this resolution (RTsKhIDNI f. 17, op. 3, d. 793, l. 3).

Letter 58

Viacheslav,

1) Doesn't it seem more than odd to you that the Siberians kept mum and didn't demand Eikhe's removal when the Siberian Regional Committee embraced both halves of Siberia, but now that Siberia has been divided into two sections and the Siberian Committee's sphere of activity has been halved (that is, *the Siberian Committee's job has been made easier*),[1] Eikhe **suddenly** turns out to be "unable to cope" with his assignments? I have no doubt that this is a crudely masked attempt to deceive the Central Committee and create "their own" artel-like regional committee based on mutual protection. I advise you to kick out all the intriguers and, above all, Klimenko (the Ukrainian "methods" of plotting!), along with all the Bazovskiis, Liaksutkins, Kuznetsovs, and so on and put full trust in Eikhe, in order to teach those intriguers never again to slander honest officials and deceive the Central Committee.[2]

2) The Central Committee's resolution on Azerbaidzhan should be published in full (in *Pravda*). Those clever ones from the Caucasus so twisted things in their own resolution (it has already been published) that Gikalo *comes out looking like the main* culprit (since he's at the head of the list of those recalled), and the [real] main culprits (Amas et al.) *come out looking like* secondary culprits, practically disciples of Gikalo. In order to smash this cleverness (this swindle), the Central Committee resolution must be published.[3]

3) The Politburo did absolutely the right thing in separating Maykop from Groznyi.[4]

That's all for now.

Regards,
J. Stalin

P.S. I'm getting better bit by bit.

8/13/30

1. In July 1930, changes were made in the administrative and territorial partitioning of Siberia. The Eastern Siberian Region was separated from the Siberian and Far Eastern regions.

2. In late July 1930, Kuznetsov, Bazovskii, Yeger, Klimenko, members of the Western Siberian Regional Party Committee; Liaksutkin, chairman of the Regional Control Commission; and others sent Stalin a letter criticizing the work of Eikhe, first secretary of the Siberian Regional Committee, and calling for his immediate replacement (RTsKhIDNI f. 17, op. 3, d. 793, ll. 21–23). On 19 August 1930, this statement was discussed at the Politburo. For "unprincipled cliquishness and un-party-like behavior" Klimenko, Kuznetsov, Bazovskii, and Yeger were reprimanded and dismissed from office (ibid., l. 7).

3. The internal party situation in Azerbaidzhan was reviewed at Politburo sessions on 20 July and 3 August 1930. The decree passed stated in part (ibid., d. 790, l. 8, and d. 791, ll. 23, 24):

Gossip, unprincipled cliquishness, intrigue, and counterintrigue have spread among the chief party activists, demoralizing the rank and file of the organization and disrupting the positive work of the party-Soviet and economic-cooperative bodies. . . . Although Com. Gikalo launched a large and energetic campaign to correct . . . those shortcomings, he was not able to sufficiently rally the basic mass of the party activists for further successful development of the work of the Azerbaidzhan Communist Party (largely because he was prevented from doing so by the above-mentioned cliques).

Gikalo, Bagirov, Amas, and others were recalled from work in Azerbaidzhan.

4. On 10 August 1930, the Politburo received a report on the fire in Maykop. The resolution passed noted that in view of the absence of elementary vigilance in the matter of protecting industries in Maykop it was necessary to "punish the guilty most severely." Since in the Politburo's view, Grozneft did not devote sufficient attention to Maykop's industries, they were removed and grouped in an independent organization (ibid., d. 792, l. 7 [Grozneft is the Russian acronym for the state organization that ran the Groznyi oil industry. Groznyi is the capital of what is now the Chechnia Republic of the Russian Federation, formerly the Chechen-Ingushetian Autonomous Republic of the RSFSR—Trans.]). On 10 September 1930, the Politburo accepted proposals from the Worker-Peasant Inspection and the Central Control Commission to institute legal and party proceedings against Grozneft manager Ganshin and other officials (ibid., d. 796, ll. 10, 38, 39).

Letter 59   [No earlier than 23 August 1930]

Viacheslav,[1]

The total for ten months is only 26 percent growth in *state industry* (instead of 32 percent). This is a worrisome total. You speak of the counterplan for industry and finance and the Central Committee manifesto.[2] I think we should be prepared to do anything to get that 30–32 percent growth. I'm afraid it's late to be speaking about this now—no major changes can be introduced before October (the end of the year) in any event. But perhaps we could try? Let's give it a shot—we really ought to try.

2) We have one and a half months left to export grain: starting in late October (perhaps even earlier), American grain will come on to the market in massive quantities, and we won't be able to withstand that. If we don't export 130–150 million poods of grain in these six weeks, our hard currency situation could become really desperate. Once again: *We must force through grain exports with all our might.*

3) Sukhanov, Bazarov, and Ramzin must definitely be arrested. Sukhanov's wife should be probed (she's a Communist!): she couldn't help but know about the outrages going on at their house. All testimonies without exception (both the basic and the supplementary) must be distributed to Central Committee members.[3] There can be no doubt that Kalinin has sinned. Everything reported about Kalinin in the testimonies is the absolute truth. The Central Committee must definitely be informed about this in order to teach Kalinin never to get mixed up with such rascals again.[4]

4) Received Osinskii's letter about the Automobile and Automotive Scientific Research Institute. Osinskii's wrong. I stand by my opinion. Klim [Voroshilov] will tell you about my reasons. Just like Osinskii's impudence.[5]

5) Am sending a clipping on the Mariupol Iron and Steel Factory.[6] This is the fourth of those provocateurs' escapades at that damned Metallurgical Institute. Can't the guilty parties be punished as an object lesson?
(It's *Pravda*, 23 August 1930)
Well, that's all for now.

Regards,

J. Stalin

1. In the upper right-hand corner is Molotov's notation: "8/1930."
2. The passing of the counterplan was organized in the fall of 1930. The Central Committee's appeal "On the Third Year of the Five-Year Plan" was published on 3 September 1930. This appeal called for using "storm" methods in an effort to complete the largely unfulfilled plan.
3. On 6 September 1930, the Central Committee passed a resolution to distribute the additional testimonies of Kondratiev, Groman, Sukhanov, and others (RTsKhIDNI f. 17, op. 3, d. 795, l. 6). See also the earlier decision to distribute testimonies mentioned in note 1 to letter 56.
4. While under arrest, Kondratiev testified that Kalinin was one of his sources of information about the political situation and internal party affairs.
5. The dispute between Osinskii, Supreme Economic Council deputy chairman, on the one hand, and Stalin and Voroshilov, on the other hand, arose in connection with the transfer of the aviation industry from the Supreme Economic Council to the Commissariat of War. On 20 August 1930 the Politburo charged Kuibyshev, chairman of the Supreme Economic Council, with "ensuring that the Automobile and Automotive Institute fully satisfies the needs of the military regarding the manufacture of airplane motors" (ibid., d. 793, l. 8.)
6. On 23 August 1930, *Pravda* carried a brief notice that the board of the State Institute for the Design of Metallurgical Factories had reviewed a proposal for a new factory in Mariupol. It was to be the largest metallurgical factory in the USSR and was expected to produce 816,000 tons of iron and 1,100,000 tons of steel.

Letter 60

[24 August 1930]

8/24/30

Viacheslav,

1) It's very good that you have taken Gosbank and its "director"[1] under *special* supervision. This very important matter should have been taken care of long ago. Kaktyn and Karklin have apparently not brought anything new to Gosbank. As for Piatakov, all indications are that he has remained the same as always, that is, a poor commissar alongside a specialist (or specialists) who are no better. He is a hostage to his bureaucracy. You really get to know people in practice, in daily work, in "trivial" matters. And here, in the practical matters of financial (and credit!) management, Piatakov has shown his true colors as a poor commissar alongside poor specialists. And I have to tell you that this type of Communist economic manager is the most harmful for us *at this time.*

Conclusion: he must be removed. Someone else (from the Worker-Peasant Inspection or OGPU) must be put in his place. We'll talk about it in October.[2]

2) Mikoian reports that grain procurements are growing, and each day we are shipping 1 to 1.5 million poods of grain. I think that's not enough. The quota for daily shipments (now) should be raised to 3–4 million poods at a minimum. Otherwise we risk being left without our new iron and steel and machine-building factories (Avtozavod, Cheliabzavod, etc.). Some clever people will come along and propose holding off on the shipments until the price of grain on the world market rises "to its ceiling." There are quite a few of these clever people in Trade. They ought to be horsewhipped, because they're dragging us into a trap. In order to hold off, we must have hard currency reserves. But we don't have them. In order to hold off, we would have to have a secure position on the international grain exchange. And we haven't had any position at all for a long time there—we'll only obtain it now if we can exploit conditions that have arisen at the present moment and are particularly favorable to us.

In short, we must push grain exports furiously.

3) Mikoian requests that Riabovol be appointed head of Neftexport [Central Oil Export Agency].[3] Lomov won't let him because he's already appointed Riabovol head of the production department of the oil syndicate. I think that in this case Lomov is more concerned about ensuring his own convenience inside the syndicate (the oil association) than about pushing exports. It would be better to put Riabovol in charge of the Oil Export Agency. The Oil Export Agency is sick, it has to be cured; the current directors of the Oil Export Agency have failed.[4]

4) We should replace Tumanov, who has completely rotted away. Does the Central Committee really hope to reform him in a French setting?[5]

5) How are things with the Chinese?

6) How is "Lena Goldfields"?[6]

I'm a little under the weather (strep throat!), but it'll pass soon.

Regards,
Stalin

Oh, I almost forgot. We keep forgetting about a certain "trivial matter," that is, that Trade is now one of the most important commissariats (and one of the most complicated, if not the most complicated of all). And what do we find? At the head of this commissariat is a person who is not coping with a job that, in general, is difficult, if not impossible, for one person to handle. Either we must remove Mikoian, which shouldn't be assumed, or we should prop him up with outstanding deputies which, I think, won't meet with any objection. That would all seem to be correct. The only question is: Why don't we immediately go from word to deed? Why? What are we waiting for? Why shouldn't we give Rozengolts to Mikoian (where else are we going to get outstanding people if not from the Worker-Peasant Inspection?) instead of Khinchuk, who has been an utter failure at running foreign trade? What more evidence is needed of Khinchuk's failure? Do people pity Khinchuk? But the cause should be pitied even more. Do they not want to offend Sergo? But what about the cause—can such an important and serious matter be offended?

I propose (formally):

1) to appoint Com. Rozengolts deputy of trade (for foreign trade) and to release him from his position at the Worker-Peasant Inspection.

2) to relieve Khinchuk from his position as deputy of trade and appoint him either as Ukhanov's assistant for the Moscow Soviet or as chairman of Grain Export.

If Sergo yells, give him Klimenko from Siberia in exchange. Rozengolts should be transferred to Trade *no matter what.* Trade has to be cured. It would be a crime to wait any longer.[7]

J. Stalin

1. At the 16 August 1930 session of the Council of Commissars, a decree was passed on reports from the Worker-Peasant Inspection and Gosbank on the credit reform. On 30 August 1930, the Politburo approved this decree and noted that Gosbank's implementation of the credit reform had been unsatisfactory (RTsKhIDNI f. 17, op. 3, d. 794, l. 5).

2. On the reorganization of Gosbank, see note 2 for document 63.

3. Soiuzneftexport, the Russian acronym for All-Union Association for the Export of Oil and Oil Products, also called Exportneft by Stalin—Trans.

4. On 18 January 1931, the Orgburo appointed Riabovol deputy chairman of the board of Soiuzneft. On 20 January 1931, the Politburo reviewed the issue of the management of oil export and resolved "to remove the export of oil from the jurisdiction of Soiuzneft and to transfer oil exports to the jurisdiction of the Commissariat of Foreign Trade" (ibid., d. 811, l. 8). On 25 January 1931, Riabovol was appointed director of oil export (ibid., l. 3).

5. On 25 November 1930, the Politburo discussed Tumanov's request to be relieved of his duties as Soviet trade representative in France. Tumanov was removed from this position but remained at the disposal of the Commissariat of Foreign Trade (ibid., d. 805, l. 3).

6. Lena Goldfields was a British stock company that signed a concession agreement in 1925 with the Soviet government to mine and refine gold, copper, iron, and mixed metals in a number of regions in Siberia, the Urals, and the Altai Mountains. In early 1930, Lena Goldfields filed a suit against the Soviet government in arbitration court. After negotiations to settle the accounts, an agreement was signed in 1934 resolving mutual claims. The Lena Goldfields matter was decided by a polling of Politburo members on 6 September 1930. The resolution was sent to the Special File (ibid., d. 795, l. 6).

7. On 10 September 1930, Rozengolts was appointed deputy commissar of trade. In the same resolution, Khinchuk was made chairman of Exportkhleb while retaining his post at Trade (ibid., d. 796, l. 9). On 15 September 1930, however, the Politburo changed its mind and appointed Khinchuk ambassador to Berlin (ibid., l. 4). On 15 November 1930, the Politburo discussed the reorganization of the Commissariat of Trade. It was divided into two independent commissariats: Commissariat of Provisionment and Commissariat of Foreign Trade. Rozengolts was appointed commissar of foreign trade and Mikoian was appointed commissar of provisionment (ibid., d. 804, l. 6).

Letter 61

Viacheslav,[1]

Received your latest letter.

1) I am **completely** in favor of moving up the collective agreements from January to October. There should be no delay! And for this we certainly don't need a Central Committee plenum.[2]

2) I'm against moving the Central Committee plenum to early October. In order to move the plenum to early October, we should have the target figures ready (no later than) mid-**September**. Obviously the target figures won't be ready in time. In addition, the plenum and its new decrees aren't the point—we've made a hellish number of decrees already. The new "appeals" and "proclamations" are even less the point: each issue of *Pravda* is an "appeal" or "proclamation." What's important now is to have a thorough and continuous *monitoring, checking up on fulfillment.* Until checking up on fulfillment is in order, our economic and trade union bodies, and consequently the fulfillment of plans, will be unsatisfactory. I think the most that can be done in terms of accelerating the plenum is to move it to late October, and only if *government agencies* will have the target figures fully in hand in early October.

3) You seem very unconcerned about the statute for settlement associations and the accompanying agitation in the press.[3] Keep in mind that this ill-omened statute was offered to us as the *new* word, which claims to *be setting itself up against* the "old" word, i.e., the statute for the agricultural *artel* [basic form of a collective farm]. And the whole point of the settlement (*new*) statute is the desire to give the individual the possibility of "*improving his (individual) farm.*" What kind of nonsense is this? Here we have the *collective farm* movement advancing in a growing wave, and then the clever ones from the Commissariat of Agriculture and from the agricultural cooperative societies want to *evade* the question of collective farms and busy themselves with "**improving**" the individual peasant farm! It seems to me that the rightists have achieved some sort of revenge here, sneaking in this statute on settlement associations, because people in the Central Committee, since they're overburdened with work, haven't noticed the little trick.

4) Regarding the plenum's agenda, I already stated my opinion by coded telegram. I think it could be beneficial only if the Central Committee plenums were to move away from *general* decrees on *general* issues and hear reports—*real* reports—from the economic commissariats that are doing badly. At present, provisions for workers are one of the most urgent questions. Consequently, the plenum cannot disregard this question. The consumer cooperatives must be turned upside down and bureaucratism shaken out of them. The meat supply must be checked and the relevant economic organizations must be improved. Hence my agenda proposal.[4]

5) It is best to appoint Khinchuk to Berlin. He is an economic administrator and will be more suited there than Surits, who isn't well versed in economic problems. Turkey is an important area for us. They like him there very much. I think it would be a mistake to remove him from that position. People from Grain Export will be found (Fridrikhson, Zalmanov, current deputies at Grain Export).[5] Khlebexport will do all right if only there is grain.

6) I propose [M. M.] Kaganovich from the Worker-Peasant Inspection[6] as the candidate for head of civil aviation.

7) What about Rozengolts's appointment?

That's it for now.

Regards,
J. Stalin

P.S. I am getting back on my feet bit by bit.

1. In the upper right-hand corner is Molotov's notation: "9/1930=?"

2. On 10 September 1930, the Politburo decreed that the new collective agreements to take effect on 1 October should be closely coordinated with the fulfillment of economic plans (RTsKhIDNI f. 17, op. 3, d. 796, l. 9).

3. The regulations on the settlement associations were published in the press on 30 August 1930.

4. Four issues were placed on the Central Committee plenum for 17–21 December 1930: the national economic plan for 1931; the summary report of the Commissariat of Provisionment, along with a report from the Worker-Peasant Inspection on meat and vegetable supplies; the summary report from the Central Union of Consumer Organizations on the work of the consumers' cooperative associations, accompanied by a supplementary report by the Worker-Peasant Inspection; and new elections to the soviets.

5. The appointment of Surits as ambassador to Germany was confirmed on 10 September 1930 (ibid., l. 9). On this appointment controversy, see also note 7 to letter 60.

6. On 15 October 1930, A. Z. Goltsman was confirmed by the Politburo as head of the Civil Aviation Association (ibid., d. 800, l. 7).

Letter 62

[1 September 1930]

9/1/30

Viacheslav,

Pay attention (for the time being) to two things:

1) The Poles are certain to be putting together (if they have not already done so) a bloc of Baltic states (Estonia, Latvia, Finland) in anticipation of a war against the USSR. I think they won't go to war with the USSR until they have created this bloc. This means that they will go to war *as soon as they have secured the bloc* (they'll find an excuse). To repulse both the Polish-Romanians and the Balts we should prepare to deploy (in the event of war) no fewer than 150 to 160 infantry divisions, that is, (at least) 40 to 50 divisions

more than are provided for under *our current guidelines*. This means that we'll have to bring our current army reserves up from 640,000 to 700,000 men. Without this "reform," it won't be possible to guarantee the defense of Leningrad and right-bank Ukraine[1] (in the event of a Polish-Baltic bloc). In my opinion, this is beyond doubt. And conversely, by this "reform" we would ensure the *victorious* defense of the USSR. But this "reform" will require considerable amounts of funds (a great quantity of ammunition, a great deal of hardware, and a surplus of officers, additional expenditures on uniforms and rations). Where can we find the money? I think vodka production should be expanded (*to the extent possible*). We need to get rid of a false sense of shame and directly and openly promote the greatest expansion of vodka production possible for the sake of a real and serious defense of our country. Consequently, this matter has to be taken into account *immediately*. The relevant raw material for vodka production should be formally included in the national budget for 1930–1931. Keep in mind that a serious upgrade of civil aviation will also require a lot of money, and for that purpose we'll have to resort again to vodka.[2]

2) We have a tremendous need for *road-building machinery*, equipment for *bread factories*, and *laundries*. The manufacture of these machines is a simple and quite manageable job for our plants. No one ever gives it serious attention (thinking it "trivial"), and therefore we are forced to spend hard currency. Ukhanov takes this matter seriously, but the Supreme Economic Council gives him no opportunity to do anything—it's like a dog in the manger, not doing anything itself but not letting others do anything either. We must put an end to this muddle. We must address this issue at the Central Committee and make it incumbent upon Ukhanov (Moscow Soviet) to become involved *immediately* in the manufacture of equipment for large-scale mechanized bakeries and laundries (and road-building machines as well). Some financial backing will have to be provided. But we must make up our minds to do it if we want to get this matter moving.[3]

Regards,

J. Stalin

P.S. I just received the Central Committee's "*Appeal*" concerning the industrial-financial plan and the Central Committee's "decree" on the practical means of implementing the "Appeal." It turned out better than I would have expected. Very good.[4]

J. Stalin

---

1. "Right-bank Ukraine" refers to that part of Ukraine that lies west of the Dnepr River—U.S. Ed.

2. On 2 July 1930, the Commissariat of Finance proposed a price increase for vodka. The Politburo rejected it (RTsKhIDNI f. 17, op. 3, d. 788, l. 5). On 15 September 1930, the Politburo reviewed the matter of increasing vodka production. The decision was sent to the Special File (ibid., d. 796, l. 7).

3. On 25 September 1930, the Central Committee established a committee consisting of

Kuibyshev, Ukhanov, and others to address all of these issues (ibid., d. 798, l. 5). Stalin's proposals were taken into consideration in the Politburo resolution "On the construction of road machinery" of 15 October 1930 (ibid., d. 800, ll. 3, 20–22).

4. On the Central Committee's appeal, see note 2 to letter 59.

Letter 63

[2 September 1930]

9/2/1930

Viacheslav,

1) I agree to Tomskii's "resignation": he is doing nothing for us in the chemical industry.[1]

2) An explanation of Kondratiev's "case" in the press would be appropriate *only in the event* that we intend to put this "case" on trial. Are we ready for this? Do we consider it necessary to take this "case" to trial? Perhaps it will be difficult to dispense with a trial.

By the way, how about Messrs. Defendants admitting their *mistakes* and disgracing themselves politically, while simultaneously acknowledging the strength of the Soviet government and the correctness of the method of collectivization? It wouldn't be a bad thing if they did.

3) Regarding the prosecution of Communists who rendered assistance to the Gromans and Kondratievs, I agree, but what is to be done with Rykov (who *unquestionably helped them*) and Kalinin (who evidently has been implicated in this "affair" by the *scoundrel Teodorovich*)? We need to think about this.

4) It is very good that you have finally taken in hand the "loose cannons" from Gosbank and Finance (which is rotten to the core). What are Karklin, Kaktyn, and others doing in Gosbank? Do they really echo Piatakov's every word? In my opinion, the leadership of Gosbank and Finance has to be replaced with people from the OGPU and the Worker-Peasant Inspection once these latter bodies have conducted some inspecting and checking up by punching people in the face.[2]

5) I don't think it's correct to triumphantly publish the new charter of the settlement associations and advertise it in the press.[3] There will be an impression that the slogan "Everyone into the settlement associations!" runs *counter* to the slogan "Everyone into the collective farms!" An illusion has arisen of a *retreat* from the slogan "For the collective farms!" to the slogan "For the settlement associations"! It doesn't matter what they want in Moscow—in practice there's been a *switch* from the vital and triumphant slogan "For or against the collective farms" to the mongrel, artificial slogan "For or against the settlement associations." And all of this at a time when we have a growing surge of peasants into the collective farms! I think this attempt to make us

retreat from a collective farm movement that is increasingly on the rise will confuse people and will weaken the influx into the collective farms. I already sent you a telegram on this. Maybe I shouldn't have sent it, but please do not berate me for this: it seemed to me that the earlier I informed you about my opinion the better.

I don't know whether you agree with me, but if you do, we can immediately start putting the brakes on this entire "settlement" ballyhoo. In my opinion, we should, *first*, give an *internal* directive to local party committees not to get carried away with settlement associations and not to substitute the slogan "Into the settlement associations" for the slogan "Into the collective farms" and to *focus all their attention* on organizing the movement into the collective farms.[4] In the second place, it would be well to overhaul *Pravda* and all of our press in the spirit of the slogan "Into the collective farms" and to oblige them to *systematically* devote at least *one page every day* to **facts** about the surge into the collective farms, **facts** about advantages of collective farms over individual peasant farms. In doing so, these *facts, reports, letters,* and the like should *not be printed in small print* somewhere in the back pages but should have prominent coverage. In a word, [we should] launch a systematic and persistent campaign in the press for the collective farm movement, which is the major and decisive factor in our current agricultural policy.

Well, that's all for now.

Regards,

J. Stalin

1. In 1929, Tomskii was appointed chairman of the All-Union Chemical Industry Association. On 6 September 1930, the Politburo fulfilled Tomskii's request to relieve him of this post because of illness (RTsKhIDNI f. 17, op. 3, d. 795, l. 5). On 25 September, Goltsman was appointed chairman of the chemical industry (ibid., d. 798, l. 3). On 15 October 1930, this post was given to Piatakov (ibid., d. 800, l. 7).

2. On 26 September 1930, the Orgburo reviewed the issue of "the radical improvement of Gosbank personnel in the center and provinces" and noted that "some improvement in the work of the Gosbank staff was achieved by thoroughly purging its personnel as well as by routinely eliminating those elements selected over a period of years by the former right-opportunist administration of Gosbank." The Orgburo's decree stipulated further shuffling of personnel at Gosbank. On 15 October 1930, by order of the Central Committee, Piatakov was relieved of his position as head of Gosbank and Briukhanov was relieved of his duties at Finance. Kalmanovich was appointed chairman of Gosbank, and Grinko was appointed commissar of finance (ibid., ll. 7, 8).

3. The regulations on the settlement associations were published in the press on 30 August 1930.

4. On 24 September 1930, the Politburo approved a letter on collectivization drafted by the Central Committee and addressed to all regional and provincial committees. An excerpt follows (*KPSS v rezoliutsiiakh* [Resolutions of the CPSU], vol. 5 [Moscow, 1984], 215):

> The Central Committee warns against an erroneous tendency observable in some organizations, namely, to substitute agricultural cooperative associations for artels. While restoring the agricultural cooperative associations in areas with a weak collective farm movement, we must firmly and persistently organize agricultural artels as the basic form of the collective farm movement at this stage.

Letter 64

9/7/30

Viacheslav,

There are two issues:

1) I'm told that Rykov and Kviring want to squelch the matter of the northern canal, contrary to the Politburo's decisions. They should be taken down a peg and given a slap on the wrists. Yes, the financial plan has to be cut as much as possible, but it's still a crime to squelch this matter.[1]

2) I'm told they want to take criminals (with sentences of more than three years) away from OGPU and give them to the [republican] NKVDs. This is an intrigue orchestrated by Tolmachev, who is rotten through and through. Syrtsov, to whom Rykov has been playing up, also has a hand in it. I think the Politburo's decisions should be implemented and the NKVDs should be closed down.[2]

Regards,
J. Stalin

1. On 5 May 1930, the Politburo approved the idea of constructing the entire Baltic–White Sea Canal. The resolution ran as follows (RTsKhIDNI f. 17, op. 3, d. 784, l. 2):

Calculations for the construction plan for the southern section of the canal should be based on the following requirements:

1) Construction work on this canal section (from Leningrad to Lake Onega) should start at the beginning of the next economic year and be completed within two years; 2) the canal should be dug to a depth that will allow the passage of ships drawing 18 feet.

The total cost of all construction work on the southern canal section should not exceed 60 million rubles.

The Commissariat of Transport with the participation of the armed forces and the OGPU should be charged with conducting a geological survey for the digging of the northern canal section (from Lake Onega to the White Sea).

The possibility of using prisoners in this work was used in determining the cost of the construction work on the northern section of the canal.

A note of Stalin's has been preserved, most likely written during this Politburo meeting (ibid., f. 558, op. 1, d. 5388, l. 150):

I think that it's possible to build it to Onega. As for the northern section of the canal, we should limit ourselves to surveying for now; I have in mind relying mainly on GPU [i.e., prisoners—Trans.]. At the same time, we must assign someone to calculate yet again the expenses in building this first section. 20 million plus 70 million. Too much.

On the back of the note is Molotov's reply:

I have my doubts about the expediency of building the canal. I read your note. The economic side is not thought through (it's not clear). Shouldn't this project be thought through first?

Molotov

On 5 October 1930, the Politburo told the OGPU that it should be guided by the decision of 5 May 1930, and the question of appropriations for the Baltic–White Sea Canal should be put off until consideration of the target figures for 1931 was completed (ibid., f. 17, op. 3, d. 799, l. 5).

Molotov and Stalin

Letter from Stalin to Molotov, 7 September 1930 (RTsKhIDNI f. 558, op. 1, d. 5388, l. 149).

2. On 27 June 1929, the Politburo approved the decree "On the use of the labor of criminal prisoners." It stipulated that persons sentenced to imprisonment for a term of three or more years should be transferred to prison camps run by the OGPU. To handle these prisoners, the existing concentration camps were to be expanded and new ones were to be established (around Ukhta [a town in northern Russia] and in other remote regions) "for the purpose of colonizing these regions and tapping their natural resources through the exploitation of prisoner manpower." Persons sentenced to terms of imprisonment of one to three years would remain in the custody of the NKVD of the Soviet republics and would be used by them for agricultural and industrial work (ibid., d. 746, ll. 2, 11).

These NKVDs, however, resisted the transfer of the prisoners with terms longer than three years, attempting to use them for their own economic projects. Early in August 1930, Shirvindt, deputy chairman of internal affairs of the Russian republic, sent a memo to the government asking for reconsideration of the decision to transfer prisoners to OGPU camps. This request was supported by Syrtsov, chairman of the RSFSR Council of Commissars. On 31 August 1930, the following decision was made by the Conference of Deputies chaired by Rykov: "Persons sentenced to imprisonment for a term of more than three years shall remain under the jurisdiction of [the police of the republics] if they can be used for work in colonies and factories" (GARF f. 5446, op. 6, d. 725, ll. 1–3, 13).

After receiving Stalin's letter, on 5 October 1930 the Politburo changed its mind and decided to go back to letting OGPU use these prisoners (RTsKhIDNI f. 17, op. 3, d. 799, l. 5).

Letter 65

Viacheslav,[1]

1) We must immediately **publish all** the testimonies of all the wreckers of the supplies of *meat, fish, tinned goods,* and *vegetables.* For what purpose are we preserving them, why the "secrets"? We should publish them along with an announcement that the Central Executive Committee or the Council of Commissars has turned over the matter to the OGPU collegium (it's a kind of judicial body in our system) and after a week have the OGPU announce that *all* these scoundrels will be executed by firing squad. They should all be shot.[2]

2) It would also be good to **publish** the testimonies of the "Intelligence Service" agents Neander, Gordon, Bondarenko, Akkerman, Bobrovshchikov, and others about the subversive activity of the Vickers employees, who have bombed, set fire to, and damaged our factories and buildings (Jackson, Lomans, Leap, and others).[3] Why is this rich material being kept secret? Now that negotiations with the British on debts and concessions are being opened, it would be most advantageous for us to publish Akkerman's and others' testimonies, precisely as testimony (as indisputable documents). These documents could be published (after careful preparation) five days after the publication of the testimonies of the wreckers in meat, fish, etc. For the time being, it is best to concentrate on their publication and not mention anything about the trial and execution.

3) It is quite clear that both the first and the second group of testimonies should not be published "just like that" but should be accompanied by an

introduction from the OGPU (or from Justice) and with a specific *interpretation* by our press. (The leitmotif of this *interpretation* should be: we have revealed everything, we know everything about the intrigues of the bourgeoisie and its robber-arsonists and wreckers, and we plan to rake them over the coals.) Early testimonies given by Pokrovskii, Strizhov, and others may be *added* to Akkerman's and other people's testimonies about the Anglo-scoundrels from the Intelligence Service.

4) I already sent you a coded telegram about Riutin.[4]

5) Our top Soviet hierarchy (Labor Defense Council, Council of Commissars, Conference of Deputies) suffers from a fatal disease. The Labor Defense Council has been transformed from an active, businesslike body into an idle parliament. The Council of Commissars is paralyzed by Rykov's insipid and basically anti-party speeches. The Conference of Deputies, which was previously the headquarters of Rykov-Sokolnikov-Sheinman, has now tended to become the headquarters of Rykov-Piatakov-Kviring or Bogolepov (I don't see a big difference between the last two) and is now *opposing* itself to the Central Committee. Clearly this can't go on. Radical measures are needed. As to what kind—I'll tell you when I get to Moscow. For the present, Piatakov should be watched closely. He is a genuine rightist Trotskyist (another Sokolnikov), and he now represents the most harmful element in the Rykov-Piatakov bloc plus the Kondratiev-defeatist sentiments of the bureaucrats from the soviet apparat. It would be good to accelerate Sergo's and Mikoian's return from vacation; together with Rudzutak and Kuibyshev (and also Voroshilov), they will be able to isolate Rykov and Piatakov in the Labor Defense Council and the Conference of Deputies.

6) I am now **completely** recovered.

Regards,

J. Stalin

1. In the upper right-hand corner is Molotov's notation: "9/13/30"

2. On 20 September 1930, the Politburo passed the resolution "On wreckers in meat et al." (RTsKhIDNI f. 17, op. 3, d. 798, l. 12):

> a) Publish immediately the testimonies of the wreckers concerned with the sabotage of meat, fish, canned food, and vegetables.
>
> Accompany this material with a brief introduction from the OGPU indicating that the case has been submitted by the Central Executive Committee and Council of Commissars to the OGPU for review.
>
> b) Publish articles clarifying the implications of this case, demonstrating that the work of this counterrevolutionary gang is totally unmasked and that all measures have been taken to undo the damage of wrecking. Set aside a page and a half for this material in the major newspapers on 22 September 1930.
>
> c) Charge a commission staffed by Coms. Menzhinskii, Yaroslavskii, Rykov, and Postyshev to review the material and introductory text from the OGPU prior to publication.

The testimonies of members of the so-called organization of wreckers of workers' food supply were published in newspapers on 22 September 1930, with an introductory statement that the "Central Executive Committee and the Council of Commissars submitted this case for review by the OGPU collegium," as Stalin had proposed.

On 25 September, newspapers carried a notice that the OGPU collegium had sentenced forty-eight "wreckers of workers' supply" to be shot and that the sentence had been executed.

3. Material on this issue has not been found.

4. Stalin's coded telegram was not found. On 23 September 1930, Riutin's file was reviewed by the Central Executive Committee (ibid., f. 613, op. 1, d. 142, l. 90). Riutin was condemned for sharply criticizing Stalin. A. S. Nemov's statement to the Central Committee formed the basis for the accusation against Riutin. The Central Control Commission ruled to expel Riutin from the party. On 5 October 1930, the Politburo passed a similar resolution (ibid., f. 17, op. 3, d. 799, l. 7). Shortly thereafter, Riutin was arrested for "counterrevolutionary agitation and propaganda."

Letter 66 [13 September 1930]

Viacheslav,

This is in addition to my other letter today.

1) With regard to Riutin, it seems to me that it's impossible to limit ourselves to expelling him from the party. When some time has passed after his expulsion, he will have to be exiled somewhere as far as possible from Moscow. This counterrevolutionary scum [*nechist'*] should be completely disarmed.

2) I talked to Ganshin. I think that the oil issue is certain to be raised in the Politburo in September in terms of *an increase in the number of refineries* for gasoline production. Without this, we'll get into big trouble. If we wait until October, it will be too late.[1]

3) For God's sake, stop the press's squawking about "breakdowns right and left," "endless failures," "disruptions," and other such nonsense. This hysterical Trotskyist–right-deviationist tone *is not justified* by the facts and is unbecoming to Bolsheviks. *Ekonomicheskaia zhizn'* [Economic life], *Pravda*, *Za industrializatsiiu* [For industrialization], and, to a certain extent, *Izvestiia* are all being particularly shrill. They screech about the "falling" in [production] rates or the *migration of workers* but they don't explain what's behind it. Indeed, where did this "sudden" flow of workers to the countryside come from, this "disastrous" turnover? What can account for it? Perhaps a poor food supply? But were people supplied any better last year compared to this year? Why wasn't such a turnover, such a flight, observed last year? Isn't it clear that the workers went to the countryside for the harvest? They want to ensure that the collective farms won't short them when they distribute the harvest; they want to work for a few months in the collective farm in full view of everyone and thus guarantee their right to a **full** collective farm share. Why don't the newspapers write about that, instead of just squeaking in panic? By the way, the Central Committee's "Appeal" left out this point.

Well, bye for now.

J. Stalin
9/13/30

1. The Supreme Economic Council's proposals on developing oil refineries in the USSR were submitted to the Politburo on 25 September 1930 (RTsKhIDNI f. 17, op. 3, d. 798, l. 16). The Politburo approved most of these proposals at its 5 October 1930 session (ibid., d. 799, ll. 2, 3).

Letter 67   [No later than 15 September 1930]

Viacheslav,[1]

Just received your letter.

1) It is very good that the Politburo has opened fire on Rykov and Co. Although Bukharin, so it seems, is invisible in this matter, he is undoubtedly the key instigator and rabble-rouser against the party. It is quite clear that he would feel better in a Sukhanov-Kondratiev party, where he (Bukharin) would be on the *"extreme left,"* than in the Communist Party, where he can only be a *rotten defeatist and a pathetic opportunist.* Bogolepov should be driven right out, of course.[2] But the matter can't stop there. In addition, the disciples of Bogolepov-Groman-Sokolnikov-Kondratiev should be turned out. This means that Rykov and his lot must go as well. This is now inevitable. It is impossible to go on tolerating this rottenness in government economic management. **But for the time being, this is just between you and me.**

2) The Central Committee's directives on procurements are very good. Procurement will take off.[3]

3) I think Amosov's replacement by Semenov would fix things.[4]

4) You ought to hold off on your vacation. Without you there (at the Politburo), it will be very difficult. I will be in Moscow in mid-October. If you cannot postpone your vacation until then, wait at least until Sergo comes back.[5] Otherwise, there may be a predicament.

5) How is Voroshilov? Did he get back already? Say hello to him.

Regards,

J. Stalin

P.S. If Rykov and Co. try to stick their noses in again, beat them over the head. We have spared them enough. It would be a crime to spare them now.

P.P.S. I propose that we distribute the statement by Kuznetsov (from Gosplan) to members of the Central Committee and Central Control Commission.[6]

1. In the upper right-hand corner is Molotov's notation: "1930=?"

2. On 30 November 1930, the Politburo passed Gosplan's proposal "On Prof. M. I. Bogolepov's dismissal from his post in the Gosplan presidium" (RTsKhIDNI f. 17, op. 3, d. 806, l. 13).

3. The grain procurement directives were approved on 15 September 1930 by the Politburo, which noted that the 1930 harvest exceeded those of past years and that the market potential of the grain crops had increased considerably. The Central Committee resolved to increase procurement by 117 million poods by increasing the annual grain procurement plan of republics, regions, and provinces (ibid., d. 796, ll. 5, 22–27).

4. On 16 August 1930, the Orgburo reviewed the preparation of the transportation system for fall and winter freight. The resolution urged all party, trade union, and economic transportation organizations to note the highly unsatisfactory implementation of the Central Committee's 8 May decision on this issue. Molotov demanded that all executives on leave be recalled. On 17 August, Postyshev sent an express telegram to Amosov urging him to return immediately (ibid., op. 114, d. 181, ll. 1, 2, 38, 58, 59). On 10 September 1930, the Politburo reviewed reports on the fall–winter deliveries and railroad accidents. Because of poor performance in transportation, the trade unions in particular were criticized (ibid., op. 3, d. 796, ll. 8, 30–37). Perhaps this was the reason that Stalin wrote about replacing Amosov, the chairman of the Central Committee of the Rail Workers' Union.

5. By a decision of the Politburo on 11 October 1930, Molotov was granted a leave. Originally scheduled to begin on 15 September, it was postponed until 16 October 1930 (ibid., d. 791, l. 16, and d. 800, l. 14). On 20 July 1930, Ordzhonikidze was given a two-month leave to begin 21 July, and Voroshilov was granted leave from 1 August to 15 September 1930 (ibid., d. 790, l. 14).

6. The statement was not found. Subsequently, on 5 December 1930, in deciding the issue of the deputy chairman of Gosplan, the Politburo decreed: "To relieve Com. Kuznetsov of his duties as deputy chairman of USSR Gosplan, in view of his transfer to other work. The decision should be made official after Com. Kuznetsov is appointed to the board of the Chinese Eastern Railway" (ibid., d. 806, l. 15).

Letter 68   [22 September 1930]

22 September 1930

Viacheslav,

1) It seems to me that the issue of the top government hierarchy should be finally resolved by the fall. This will also provide the solution to the matter of leadership in general, because the party and soviet authorities are closely interwoven and inseparable from each other. My opinion on that score is as follows:

a) Rykov and Shmidt need to be relieved of their posts, and all their bureaucratic advisory and secretarial staff should be sent packing.

b) You'll have to take over Rykov's place as chairman of the Council of Commissars and Labor Defense Council. This is necessary. Otherwise, there will be a split between the soviet and the party leadership. With such a setup, we'll have complete unity between soviet and party leaders, and this will unquestionably double our strength.

c) The Labor Defense Council should be converted from a body of chatterers into a militant and viable economic management body, and the number of Labor Defense Council members should be reduced to about ten or eleven (a chairman, two deputies, the chairman of Gosplan, the Commissariats of Finance and Labor, the Supreme Economic Council, the Commissariats of Transport, War, Trade, and Agriculture).

d) Under the Council of Commissars, a standing commission ("Commission on Fulfillment") should be established for the sole purpose of systematically *checking up on the fulfillment* of the center's decisions. It should have the right to call both party members as well as nonparty people *to answer*, rapidly and directly, for bureaucratism, nonfulfillment, mismanagement, or evasion of the center's resolutions, and so on. This commission should have the right to make direct use of the services of the Worker-Peasant Inspection (in the first place) and the GPU, Procuracy, and press. Without such an authoritative and rapidly acting commission, we will not be able to break through the wall of bureaucratism and [improve] the slipshod performance in our bureaucracies. Without such reforms, the center's directives will remain completely on paper. Sergo ought to be put at the head of the commission (as the deputy chairman of the Council of Commissars and the head of Worker-Peasant Inspection).

Thus the Council of Commissars will have three important commissions: Gosplan, Labor Defense Council, and the Commission on Fulfillment.

e) The existing *Conference of Deputies* should be dismantled, and the chairman of the Council of Commissars should be allowed to consult with his deputies (bringing in various officials) at his own discretion.

All of this is *just between you and me* for the time being. We'll speak in more detail in the fall. Meanwhile, consult with our closest friends and report on any objections.

2) Things are going badly in the Urals. Millions of pounds of ore are lying in the pits, but there's nothing to haul the ore out with. The whole problem is that there isn't any track that can be used to run spur lines and branch lines through factories. Why couldn't we *suspend new rail construction for a year, somewhere in Ukraine or elsewhere* and take about 200–300 versts of track and give it immediately to the Urals? I think we could do this. That would save the Ural iron works from dependency (a cursed dependency!) on horses, oats, and other idiocy. Can you push this?

Why isn't Kosior going to Sverdlovsk?[1]

3) Rozengolts was here to see me. He asked me to help him transfer to the Supreme Economic Council (instead of Trade). I answered that I would fight for him to stay at Trade. Then he asked me to help him to take three or four officials along with him from the Worker-Peasant Inspection (Sudin, Belenkii—an engineer, Izrailovich, and another person whose name I can't recall). I promised my support and said that I'd tell you about it.[2]

4) Hold off on the question of turning over the Kondratiev affair to the courts. This matter is not completely without risk. Wait until the fall to resolve this issue. We'll decide this question together in mid-October. There are certain reasons I have for *not* turning it over. Well, so long.

Best regards,
Stalin

1. On 25 July 1930, the Politburo confirmed I. V. Kosior as chairman of Eastern Steel in Sverdlovsk (RTsKhIDNI f. 17, op. 3, d. 790, l. 4). On 20 December 1930, the Politburo reversed its decision and left Kosior in his position as assistant chairman of the Supreme Economic Council (ibid., d. 808, l. 13).

2. On 28 November 1930, the Politburo confirmed the membership of the collegium of the Commissariat of Trade; Sudin was included (ibid., f. 17, op. 3, d. 806, l. 6).

Letter 69

Viacheslav,

1) Have you received my letter of 9/22? I sent it through Yagoda. In it I wrote, among other things, about the creation of a "Commission on Fulfillment." I think that if Sergo for some reason refuses the post of chairman of this commission, you would have to assume the post and Sergo could then be your assistant for checking up on fulfillment. I consider such a commission to be absolutely essential as a means of invigorating our apparat and our struggle against the bureaucratism that is consuming us.

2) However, [creating] the "Commission on Fulfillment" addresses just one side of the matter, turning its edge against the bureaucratism of our apparat. But in order to get our construction of socialism fully on track, we must incorporate yet **another** aspect of the matter. I mean the "turnover" at enterprises, "transients," labor discipline, the shrinking cadre of permanent employees, socialist competition, and shock work, organizing supplies for workers. As the situation now stands, some of the workers labor honestly in accordance with socialist competition; others (the majority) are irresponsible and transient, yet the latter are as well provisioned as the first (*if not better*), enjoy the *same* privileges of vacations, sanatoria, insurance, etc., as the first. Is this not an outrage? This can undermine any real foundation for socialist competition and shock work! In addition to this outrage, we are essentially tearing away from production ("upward mobility"!) all the workers who show some initiative and handing them over to some office or other where they die of boredom in unfamiliar surroundings, decimating in this way the basic core of workers involved in production. That is, once again we are undermining the foundations of socialist competition and weakening its army.

To accept this sort of thing is to go against the interests of the construction of socialism.

What should we do?

We need to:

a) **Reserve** supplies for workers in the **basic** and decisive districts (the special list) and, accordingly, **reorganize** the cooperative and trade organizations in these districts (and, if need be, break them up and establish new ones) in order to supply workers rapidly and fully—keeping these districts **under special observation** by members of the Central Committee (special list).

b) Separate out the **shock workers** at each **enterprise** and supply them **fully** and in **first order** [of priority] with food and clothing as well as housing; **fully** guarantee them **all** rights of insurance.

c) Divide the non–shock workers into two categories, those who have worked at **a specific enterprise** for at least a year and those who have worked for less than a year, in order to supply the former with goods and housing in **second** order [of priority] but in **full** measure and the latter in **third** order [of priority] and **in reduced amounts.** Regarding insurance for sickness, etc., tell them approximately the following: If you have worked at an enterprise for less than a year, you are pleased to "be a transient," so please do not expect full wages in the event of illness, but, let's say, two-thirds, and those who have worked at least a year, let them receive full wages. And so on.[1]

d) **Prohibit** the promotion [*vydvizhenie*] of workers **from the shop floor** to any and all bureaucracies, and encourage their promotion *only* within *production* (or perhaps within the trade unions). Let workers from the shop floor (who know their trade) be promoted to assistant craftsmen, craftsmen, shop stewards, and so on. **This** is the kind of promotion we need now like air and water. Without it, we will squander our entire basic core of industrial workers and hand over our factories to parasitical spongers.[2]

e) Break with Tomskii's petit bourgeois traditions regarding **absenteeism** and **labor discipline;** eliminate every single "legal" *loophole* for absentees (putting them in a **privileged** position relative to honest and hardworking workers) and make extensive use of workers' courts and expulsion from trade unions for absenteeism.

f) Break with Tomskii's petit bourgeois traditions regarding the unemployed, by organizing a functioning register of *genuinely* unemployed people and systematically purging the lists of people unemployed for specious reasons or elements unquestionably **not** unemployed. Establish a regime where an unemployed person who has already twice refused offers of work will automatically be denied the right to receive unemployment compensation.[3]

g) And so forth and so on.

I do not doubt that these and similar measures will find great support among the workers.

This is, of course, a serious and complicated matter. We should think about it from all angles. Whether or not these measures can be applied **immediately** in **all** branches of industry is also disputable. Still, this entire matter is extremely necessary and **unavoidable.**

Think this matter over (and also the question of the "Commission on Fulfillment") in a small circle of our closest friends and afterward inform me of their opinion.

Keep in mind, however, that Syrtsov's commission on workers' provisionment will not be able to provide any help along these lines. A new commission is needed, created on different principles. I could be on such a commission if necessary.[4]

Regards,
J. Stalin
9/28/30

P.S. Just received your letter from the Donbass. It looks like Shvarts wasn't suitable for such a big job.[5]

1. A decree, "On provisions for workers," that incorporated Stalin's basic proposals was approved by the Politburo on 15 December 1930 (RTsKhIDNI f. 17, op. 3, d. 807, l. 5).

2. On 25 March 1931, the Council of Commissars and the Central Committee passed the resolution "On the full termination of the mobilization of workers from the shop floor for ongoing campaigns by local party, soviet, and other organizations" (*Spravochnik partiynogo rabotnika* [Party worker reference manual], 8th ed. [Moscow, 1934], 385–86).

3. On 20 October 1930, the Central Committee passed the decree "On measures for planned provision of manpower and for the struggle against worker turnover" (ibid., op. 3, d. 801, l. 9). The decree noted in particular that the Commissariat of Labor "exhibited a clearly bureaucratic attitude toward economic issues and instead of efficiently organizing, assigning, and using the requisite manpower or combating transients or malingerers, it paid tens of millions of rubles in stipends to hundreds of thousands of 'unemployed.'" The decree stipulated that "in the event that registered persons refuse available work, they should be immediately removed from the lists of labor agencies . . . deserters and transients should be denied the right to be sent to work at industrial plants for a six-month period" (*Spravochnik partiinogo rabotnika*, 396–98).

4. On 6 September 1930, the issue of supplying meat to Moscow was discussed at a Politburo meeting. It was decided to examine how goods in short supply were distributed and to institute unconditional punitive measures against "counterrevolutionary and speculator elements" who disorganized the work of the supply apparat.

A commission made up of Syrtsov (chairman), Postyshev, Shvernik, Yanson, Khlopliankin, Eismont, and others was assigned to draft measures for improving methods for workers' provisionment (eliminating queues, monitoring workers in the cooperative system, and so forth). The commission was told to report on the results of its work twice a month (RTsKhIDNI f. 17, op. 3, d. 795, l. 5).

On 15 October 1930, the Politburo's commission on workers' provision was joined by Stalin and L. Kaganovich (ibid., d. 800, l. 3).

5. On 25 July 1930, Shvarts was confirmed as chairman of the board of Soiuzugol [Union coal] for the south (ibid., d. 790, l. 4). The status of the coal industry was often discussed by the Politburo during August and September. On 19 August 1930, the Politburo passed the decree "On the Donbass coal industry": "The coal-mining situation and the fulfillment of basic production goals in the Donbass is most ominous and requires the passing of a number of immediate, urgent measures" (ibid., d. 793, ll. 8, 27–29).

In September 1930, the Central Committee received information about a speech Shvarts made at a meeting of Rutchenkovka workers and specialists; on 20 September, the Politburo decreed: "To consider the nature of this speech . . . unacceptable . . . for a Communist economic manager" (ibid., d. 798, ll. 2, 3). On 5 October 1930, the Politburo relieved Shvarts from his duties as chairman of the board of Soiuzugol (ibid., d. 799, l. 6).

Letter 70   [10 October 1930]

Viacheslav,

Received your letter of 10/6.

1) Your work on the Donbass turned out well.[1] You've achieved a sample of Leninist checking up on fulfillment. If it is required, let me congratulate you on your success.

2) The proposal to reinforce the planning agencies is good. I'm sending it back with a few of my corrections. The only thing needed is to "outfit" the planning agencies with students, not wholesale, or indiscriminately, but through a comprehensive individual screening and without speeding everything up, as [they do] in the movies.[2]

3) I'm sending you Ganshin's letter with some other materials. If it's true that the Politburo is bringing legal charges against him, then I think Ganshin will have to be removed from executive work, and we will lose him for a time. Can't the Politburo decision be mitigated and the phrase "brought up on legal charges" be removed from his record? I'm personally for that. It would be much better to remove Lomov from the oil agency (he doesn't know the oil business and never will) and put Ganshin in his place.[3] That would be much better. We'll talk about this in more detail when I get to Moscow.

Well, bye for now.

Regards,

J. Stalin

Sergo,[4]

I'm sending you Koba's letter from yesterday. We'll put Ganshin on the Politburo agenda for 10/15 and soften the previous decision.

Return Koba's letter and the "draft" with his corrections.

Molotov

10/11

1. In September 1930, Molotov took a trip to the Donbass. On 25 September 1930, the Politburo discussed Molotov's telegram from the Donbass (RTsKhIDNI f. 17, op. 3, d. 798, ll. 3, 19):

> Given the significant increases in the coal-mining effort since October, especially considering the need to compensate for this year's shortfall, and given the certain possibility of significantly increasing the mechanical extraction of coal, the matter of mechanizing the Donbass has become an extremely urgent task. . . . It is necessary for the economic, party, and trade union organizations to focus immediately on mechanizing the Donbass. . . . In fulfilling the October, quarterly, and annual industrial plans for the Donbass, we must broaden the struggle for a new, mechanized, and genuinely socialist Donbass. . . . In the event [my proposal] is approved, we will move directly to working out a series of practical measures for economic, party, and trade union agencies, since the work of all Donbass organizations will have to be restructured.

Molotov's proposal was approved by the Politburo.

2. On 15 October 1930, the Politburo passed the resolution "On the improvement of state planning" (ibid., d. 800, l. 15):

> a) Immediately strengthen the qualified party and nonparty staff of Gosplan and of the planning agencies of the commissariats—Supreme Economic Council, Transport, Agriculture, Trade—and cooperative organizations, etc., by transferring a significant group of senior students from the economic faculties for this work (offering the students assigned to the commissariats the additional opportunity of continuing their theoretical work in the relevant institutions of higher education).
>
> b) Establish a planning academy in Moscow. Along with the permanent cadre of students— qualified party members who are economic managers—comrades working in the economic commissariats should also take a number of basic courses (accounting, improvement of production methods, economic geography, the theory of planning, the five-year plan and its fulfillment).

3. For an earlier decision about Ganshin, see note 4 for letter 58. On 15 October 1930 the Politburo retracted its decision of 10 September 1930 to turn Ganshin over to the courts and decided to limit his punishment to a party reprimand (ibid., d. 800, l. 7). On 15 November 1930, Ganshin was appointed chairman of Soiuzneft (ibid., d. 804, l. 8).

4. Molotov's note to Ordzhonikidze was attached to Stalin's letter.

Letter 71   [23 October 1930]

10/23

Viacheslav,

1) I'm sending you two reports from Reznikov on Syrtsov's and Lominadze's anti-party (essentially right-deviationist) factional group. It's unimaginable vileness. Everything goes to show that Reznikov's reports correspond with reality. They played at staging a coup; they played at being the Politburo and went to the lowest depths.

2) As for the T-chevskii affair,[1] he turns out to be 100 percent *clean*. That's very good.

3) Things are going more or less all right for us. Lezhava and Kviring were removed (from Agriculture). We will formalize it one of these days.[2, 3]

How are things going for you?

Regards,
Stalin

1. The facts remain unclear. The reference is probably to Tukhachevskii.

2. On 20 October 1930, the Politburo passed a resolution recalling Kviring and relieving Lezhava from his duties as deputy chairman of the RSFSR Council of Commissars (RTsKhIDNI f. 17, op. 3, d. 801, l. 11). Soon afterward, Lezhava was appointed chairman of Union Fisheries and given a high position in the Commissariat of Trade. On 30 June 1931, Kviring was confirmed as chairman of the Credit Guarantee Bank in Berlin (ibid., op. 114, d. 243, l. 226).

3. Er. Kviring should not be confused with the Emmanuil Kviring who excited Stalin's anger in earlier letters. Er. Kviring was a minor official who Stalin may have mentioned only because he had worked as Molotov's assistant in the mid-1920s—U.S. Ed.

CHAPTER SIX

1931–1936

THE FEW LETTERS from the years 1931–1936 that Molotov handed over to the Central Party Archive are only a fragment of the correspondence for this period. The contents of these letters suggest that only the most "harmless" documents, those that in no way touched upon Stalin's and Molotov's darkest and most criminal activities, were selected for the archive. Surely if we suppose that Stalin was as honest with his closest comrade-in-arms in the 1930s as he had been in the preceding period (and we have no reason to doubt this), Molotov would have had a great deal to conceal from future generations.

The first half of the 1930s is one of the most tragic periods in Soviet history. Stalin's policies plunged the country into a state of virtual civil war, creating millions of victims. Mass arrests, executions by firing squad, and deportations attended the campaign of forced collectivization. Hundreds of thousands of peasant families were subjected to the so-called special resettlements, transported to remote districts of the country, and often left to starve. Those who survived were confined in special settlements under the custody of the OGPU, and their labor was exploited for the most difficult jobs in the timber, construction, and mining industries.

The rigors of forced industrialization fell not only on the peasants; life became progressively difficult for the urban population as well. In the industrial centers, it was common for workers to be housed in barracks or earthen bunkers, to receive scanty food rations, and to engage in back-breaking labor for many hours of the day.

The race toward collectivization and industrialization finally culminated in severe crisis. In the years from 1931 to 1933, the country was gripped by a harsh famine that claimed the lives of several million people. In spite of huge investments, industrial production grew only slightly. With such an extreme decline in living standards, social tensions grew more acute. In the countryside, people voiced their apprehensions, silently engaged in sabotage, or frequently fled from the collective farms altogether. In the cities, there were open demonstrations against the government. The authorities were constantly confronted by anti-Soviet sentiments, even within the largest and therefore most privileged industrial enterprises. Criticism of Stalin himself was in fact quite common. Within the party, the opinion was widespread that he was incapable of leading the country out of the crisis or placating the peasantry and that, for these reasons, he had to go.

Stalin himself and his immediate circle thought otherwise, however. Rallying all their resources, they proceeded to pacify society by force. As usual when confronted with a crisis, Stalin advanced the theory of the intensification of the class struggle. At the January 1933 Central Committee plenum, he declared that the difficulties that had emerged during industrialization were the fault of enemy opposition. And so the flow of mass arrests, executions, and deportations reached even greater proportions. The tally made at the time ran into many hundreds of thousands. As N. V. Krylenko, Russian commissar of justice, reported to Stalin and Molotov, 738,000 people were sentenced in the first half of 1933 alone, and 687,000 in the second half.[1] Yet these extraordinary figures did not include the many categories of people persecuted in other ways: those deported when an internal passport system was imposed on urban residents; those purged as "transient elements" from the famine regions; and so on. The mass arrests led to overflowing prison and jail cells: by May 1933, at least 800,000 had been detained. On 8 May 1933, Stalin and Molotov were obliged to authorize special instructions on reducing the jail population to 400,000 and prohibiting further unsanctioned deportations and arrests.[2]

Beginning in late 1932, the crackdown on society at large was

---

1. RTsKhIDNI f. 17, op. 120, d. 171, l. 50.
2. Ibid., op. 3, d. 922, ll. 58, 580b.

paralleled by a purge within the party itself that continued in various forms for several years. Many Communists were expelled from the party and then arrested. A series of dramatic events created the rationale for persecuting "heretical" party members. A large group of party activists, including former opposition leaders Kamenev and Zinoviev, were faced with criminal charges in connection with the so-called Union of Marxist-Leninists. The intellectual driving force behind this union was M. N. Riutin, who in mid-1932 had written two anti-Stalinist documents, "Stalin and the Crisis of Proletarian Dictatorship" and the open letter "To All Members of the Party." Riutin was arrested and spent several years in prison before his execution by firing squad in 1937.[3]

In late 1932 and early 1933, thirty-eight people were arrested on trumped-up charges of belonging to the so-called Anti-Party Counterrevolutionary Group that consisted of Slepkov and other members of the right deviation ("the Bukharin school"). The group included prominent scholars, students, and those who sided with Bukharin during the period of his struggle with Stalin, as well as N. A. Uglanov, one of the leading activists of the right deviation, who had held the post of Moscow Party Committee secretary until 1929. At the January 1933 Central Committee plenum, the so-called anti-party faction of Eismont, Tolmachev, and Smirnov was ruthlessly condemned. Informers revealed that these longtime party members were having conversations that were critical of Stalin's policies, and this information was then used as evidence of an "underground opposition faction." In connection with this case, new charges were brought against Tomskii and Rykov. These dramatic events in Moscow sent smaller shock waves throughout the country. Provincial GPU officers who received the relevant decrees on these cases concocted their own local "counterrevolutionary groups."

The assassination of Sergei Kirov in December 1934 sparked a new round of Stalin's repressions. To this day, historians cannot agree on this tragic incident. Unclear and mysterious circumstances point to the possibility that Stalin may have had a hand in Kirov's murder. Regrettably, Stalin's letters for the year 1934 are missing entirely from the selection that Molotov delivered to the archive.

3. Riutin's long denunciation of Stalin has only recently been published in *Izvestiia TsK*, nos. 8–12 (1990)—U.S. Ed.

The years 1935 and 1936 were marked by steadily increasing preparations for the mass persecution that would come to be known as "the Year 1937," "Yezhovschina,"[4] and "the Great Terror." One campaign followed another—the review and reissuance of party cards; the Stakhanovite "shock-workers'" movement, for example—accompanied by arrests, expulsions from the party, and terminations of employment. In the summer of 1936, the Moscow show trials opened against the former opposition. Kamenev and Zinoviev were put on trial, and Bukharin, Rykov, Tomskii, and Piatakov were criticized along with many other leaders from the Lenin era. Local campaigns to discover "enemies" were set in motion.

These campaigns of persecution led to strife among the chief government leaders and prefigured the conflict between Stalin and Ordzhonikidze that culminated in Ordzhonikidze's death. By the end of 1936, a rumor was circulating that even the trusted Molotov had fallen into Stalin's disfavor. To this day, almost nothing is known about the political history of this period, and the letters published here are of very little help in this respect.

All this does not mean that Stalin's letters to Molotov for the years 1931–1936 are of no interest. Although they do not reveal sensational incidents or hitherto unknown secrets of the Soviet past, they nevertheless contain important information about the day-to-day activities of top government officials. Stalin's thoughts on the economic target figures for the year 1936 illustrate how very important economic decisions were made (letters 80, 81). The letter on the new Constitution provides ample evidence of Stalin's role in its drafting (letter 83).

Of particular note are the letters from the fall of 1933 (letters 78, 79), which contain Stalin's reaction to the conflict between Ordzhonikidze and A. Ya. Vyshinskii, Soviet deputy procurator, who enjoyed Stalin's full support. After Ordzhonikidze insisted that the Politburo consider the question, other top party leaders entered the fray. This episode offers a rare opportunity to assess the situation within Stalin's Politburo after the destruction of the opposition, particularly Stalin's relationship with his closest comrades in the early 1930s, before the onset of the Great Purge.

4. After Nikolai Yezhov, Stalin's secret police chief from 1936 to 1938—Trans.

Letter 72

[before March 1931]

Molotov,

I read only the part about "dumping" and "forced" labor.[1] The section on "dumping" is good. The section on "forced" labor is incomplete and unsatisfactory. See the comments and corrections in the text.

J. Stalin

P.S. Regarding the kulaks' labor, since they are not convicts, either they should not be mentioned at all, or we should explain in a special section and with thorough documentation that the only ones who work among the deported kulaks are those **who want to work** and [that they do so] with all the rights of voluntary labor.

1. The reference is to Molotov's speech at the VI Congress of Soviets (*Pravda*, 11 March 1931).

Letter 73

[24 September 1931]

Hello, Viacheslav,

I received the letter.

You are right that in light of the new circumstances (the financial crisis in England, etc.) we will have to **reduce** our imports.[1] I am certain we will not be able to get by without a reduction in the import quotas approved at the beginning of the year. The conditions at the start of the year were one thing, but now they have changed (worsened). We absolutely must take this into consideration.

Regarding the stores the Supreme Economic Council wants to establish, you are right, of course.[2]

Regards,
J. Stalin
9/24/31

1. The question of imports was often taken up by the Politburo in September and October 1931. On 29 October 1931, the resolution "On the export-import and currency exchange plan for the fourth quarter of the year 1931" was adopted. The resolution was sent to the Special File (RTsKhIDNI f. 17, op. 3, d. 857, l. 5).

2. The question of stores was considered by the Council of Commissars and the Labor Defense Council in September and October 1931 at the initiative of the Supreme Economic Council, which requested permission to open seventy-seven stores to serve workers at the largest enterprises exclusively. At the suggestion of the Supreme Economic Council, the plant directors were granted the right to establish regulations for distributing goods. By January 1932, eighty-three stores attached to specific factories had been opened, selling goods in short supply solely to employees from those factories (GARF f. 5446, op. 13, d. 1058, ll. 6, 29).

Voroshilov, Khrushchev, and Stalin

The Congress of Victors, 1934. Back row: Einukludze, Voroshilov, Kaganovich, Kuibyshev. Front row: Ordzhonikidze, Stalin, Molotov, Kirov

Letter 74   [19 June 1932]

Hello, Viacheslav,

I received your letter dated 13 June.

1) United States—this is a complicated matter. Insofar as they want to use flattery to drag us into a war with Japan, we can tell them to go to hell. Insofar as the oil industrialists of the United States have agreed to give us a loan of 100 million rubles without requiring from us any political compensation, we would be foolish not to take their money. We must rein in Rozengolts and correct the error in the agreement with the oil industrialists![1] We need the hard currency!

2) The proposal from Nanking about a nonaggression pact is utter chicanery. Really, the Nanking government consists entirely of petty crooks. This does not mean, of course, that we should not deal with these crooks or with their proposal for a nonaggression pact, but it certainly pays to keep in mind that they are petty crooks.[2]

3) Regarding the Ukrainians (Chubar and others), I already wrote Kaganovich and you must already know my opinion.[3] The rest is a matter for the Politburo.

4) You and Kaganovich should by now have received my letter about the meeting of the council of secretaries and chairmen of regional committees on the organization of grain procurements. I think that we ought to hurry ahead with this important matter, so we'll be able to **prevent** the recurrence of the Ukrainian mistakes in the area of grain procurement. This is a most important matter.[4]

5) Tebandaev asks that we give him several million rubles (4–5 million rubles) for the construction of an **earthen** dam on the Manich River (east of the Don).[5] This is a straightforward matter and is apparently necessary.

Bye for now.

Regards,
J. Stalin
6/19/32

1. The facts remain unclear.
2. After Japanese forces invaded northeastern China in September 1931, the proponents of normalization of Sino-Soviet relations within the Chiang Kai-shek government grew more powerful. On 6 June 1932, the Kuomintang central policy council passed a resolution on secret negotiations with the USSR, the contents of which were leaked to the press. On 26 June 1932, the Chinese representative at the Geneva disarmament convention delivered a letter to the Soviet commissar for foreign affairs proposing the consideration of a nonaggression pact between the USSR and China. On 6 July, Litvinov proposed beginning negotiations on a nonaggression pact and on establishing diplomatic relations. In December 1932, diplomatic relations between the USSR and China were established, but the two countries failed to agree on a nonaggression pact.

3. Forced collectivization resulted in widespread famine. On 17 June 1932, the Ukrainian Politburo sent Kaganovich and Molotov the following telegram:

> On the instructions of our Central Committee, Chubar has initiated a request to grant food assistance to Ukraine for districts experiencing a state of emergency. We urgently request additional means for processing sugar beets and also supplemental aid: in addition to the 220,000, another 600,000 pounds of bread.

In Stalin's view, Ukrainian crop failures were caused by enemy resistance and by the poor leadership of Ukrainian officials. On 21 June 1932, the Central Committee sent a telegram, signed by Stalin and Molotov, to the Ukrainian Central Committee and Council of Commissars, proposing to ensure the collection of grain "at all costs." The telegram stated:

> No manner of deviation—regarding either amounts or deadlines set for grain deliveries—can be permitted from the plan established for your region for collecting grain from collective and private farms or for delivering grain to state farms.

On 23 June 1932, in response to S. V. Kosior's telegram requesting aid, the Politburo passed the following resolution: "To restrict ourselves to the decisions already adopted by the Central Committee and not to approve the shipment of additional grain into Ukraine." (All quotations are from *The 1932–1933 Ukrainian Famine in the Eyes of Historians and in the Language of Documents* [in Ukranian Kiev, 1990], 183, 186, 187, 190).

4. On 21 June 1932, the Politburo resolved to call a meeting on 28 June 1932 of the secretaries and chairmen of the executive committees of Ukraine, North Caucasus, Central Black Sea region, the lower and middle Volga, etc. on the problems of organizing grain reserves and of fulfilling the established plan for grain reserves (RTsKhIDNI f. 17, op. 3, d. 889, l. 16). On 28 June, the Politburo decided not to present a general report to the conference but to authorize Molotov to deliver a keynote address on the problems and to emphasize that Stalin's proposals had been approved by the Politburo and must form the basis for any decisions regarding grain procurement (ibid., d. 890, l. 8). [For the "Ukranian mistakes," see note 3—U.S. Ed.]

5. On 10 July 1932, the Politburo confirmed the decision of the Council of Commissars to release 4 million rubles from its reserve fund to enable the North Caucasus Regional Executive Committee to construct a dam on the Manich (ibid., d. 891, l. 13). [No information is available concerning Tebandaev—U.S. Ed.]

Letter 75   [1932, before June 1932]

Hello, Viacheslav,[1]

1) Received the letter on revolutionary legality. It came out well. See my minor corrections to the text. I think that the Central Committee directive, namely, *the first two points including several corrections,* ought to be publicized, but the third point of the directive should have only restricted distribution.[2]

2) Did you receive my telegram about Lancaster with the proposal of the new terms (100 million dollars, 10 years, 3 percent interest, 15–20 percent of orders from 100 million dollars)? It's advantageous to us. It is also beneficial to Lancaster, since the total of his claims is thus raised to 60 million rubles (40 million rubles under the original terms), and the total orders to 40 million rubles (7 million rubles under the original terms).

3) What is the situation regarding the conference of secretaries and procurements?[3]

Regards,

P.S. The number of Politburo inquiries has no effect on my health. You can send as many inquiries as you like—I'll be happy to answer them.

J. Stalin

1. In the upper right-hand corner is Molotov's notation: "1928=?" In fact the letter was written in spring 1932.

2. The government decree "On revolutionary legality" was approved by the Politburo on 25 June 1932. The Politburo sent the following directive to all the local party organizations (RTsKhIDNI f. 17, op. 3, d. 890, l. 11):

The Central Committee wishes to bring to the attention of all party organizations the decree published on 27 June by the Central Executive Committee and the Council of Commissars on the measures to be undertaken to enforce revolutionary legality and to require all party organizations to enact the most stringent measures.

Emphasizing the special role that the court and the procurator must play in the matter of enforcing revolutionary legality, the Central Committee proposes that all party organizations:

1. Provide the committee all manner of aid and support in the matter of enforcing revolutionary legality.

2. Implement thoroughly the party decrees on the strict responsibility of Communists for the most minor infringements of the law. . . .

Categorically forbid the involvement of party organizations in specific separate judicial matters, as well as the removal or transfer of any court employees in connection with their activities, without the consent and approval of the senior party, judicial, and procuratorial bodies.

The government decree was published on 27 June 1932 in *Pravda*.

The Central Executive Committee and the Council of Commissars propose that the governments of Soviet and autonomous republics, procuratorial bodies, and the regional executive committees:

1. Investigate any allegations about violations of revolutionary legality by officials and guarantee the speediest consideration of these matters; impose punishment, up to and including arrest, on officials responsible for these offenses and on those guilty of a bureaucratic attitude toward workers' allegations. . . .

3. Eliminate the practice of imposing burdensome [grain] obligations, dekulakization, etc., in violation of the laws of the Soviet government in regard to individual collective farms as well as farms of middle peasants, while implementing thoroughly the obligations and measures established by Soviet law for kulak elements.

4. Require the courts and procurators to prosecute officials in all instances involving the violation of toilers' rights, especially in the cases of unlawful arrest, searches, confiscation, or expropriation of property, and impose strict punishment on those found guilty.

5. The Central Executive Committee and the Council of Commissars of the USSR wish to bring to the attention of all local organs of Soviet power and all procurators' offices that strict compliance with revolutionary legality regarding collective farms and the masses of collective farm workers is especially important given that the majority of peasant laborers are concentrated on collective farms.

6. In the interest of further enforcing revolutionary justice and of improving and raising the status of the judicial-procuratorial bodies, it is categorically forbidden to remove or transfer people's judges other than by the decree of regional executive committees or to remove and transfer district procurators other than by the decision of the regional procurator or the supreme procuratorial bodies of the procuracy or Commissariat of Justice.

3. On the secretaries and grain procurement, see note 4 to letter 74.

Letter 76

Viacheslav![1]

Today I read the section on international affairs.[2] It came out well. The confident, contemptuous tone with respect to the "great" powers, the belief in our own strength, the delicate but plain spitting in the pot of the swaggering "great powers"—very good. Let them eat it.

J. Stalin

1. In the upper right-hand corner is Molotov's notation: "1/1933." In the lower right-hand corner is another notation by him: "January 1933."

2. The reference is to Molotov's speech on 23 January 1933 to the Central Executive Committee (*Pravda*, 24 January 1933).

Letter 77

Viacheslav,[1]

I think we should satisfy Sholokhov's[2] request **in full,** *that is, grant an additional 80,000 poods* to Veshensk residents and 40,000 poods to Verkhnedonsk residents. This matter has apparently received wide public attention, and after all the shameful behavior that has been tolerated, we can only gain politically. The extra 40,000–50,000 means little *to us,* but it is decisive right now for the population of these two districts.

And so, let's vote on this immediately (tell Chernov).

Besides this, we must send someone—anyone—there (perhaps Com. Shkiriatov) to clear up the matter and call on Ovchinnikov and all the others who created this mess to account for themselves. We can do this tomorrow.[3]

J. Stalin

1. In the upper right-hand corner is Molotov's notation: "1929=?" In fact this letter was written in April 1933.

2. On 20 April 1933, M. A. Sholokhov wrote to Stalin about the forcible expropriation of cattle from the peasants. On 23 April 1933, with Stalin and Molotov present, the Politburo reviewed the situation in the Veshensk District. Shkiriatov was assigned to travel to the Veshensk District to conduct an inquiry into the causes of the intolerable violations during grain procurement committed by local officials and by representatives of regional agencies.

3. On 4 July 1933, the Politburo heard Shkiriatov's report on the violations in the Veshensk District in connection with grain procurement. Among those questioned were Zimin, the second secretary of the Azov–Black Sea Regional Committee; Ovchinnikov, representative of the committee in the Veshensk District; a series of workers in the Veshensk District; and Sholokhov, as a witness. The Politburo noted (RTsKhIDNI f. 17, op. 3, d. 926, ll. 5, 6):

The Regional Committee is chiefly responsible for such violations as the mass eviction of collective farm workers from their homes and forbidding other collective farm workers from offering temporary shelter to those evicted. [The committee] did not take timely measures to rectify these violations or even issue warnings regarding them.

The Central Committee considers that the entirely correct and absolutely necessary policy of applying pressure to the collective farm workers who sabotaged the grain production effort was distorted and compromised in the Veshensk District because the committee did not exercise effective oversight.

The Politburo criticized the committee for inadequately overseeing the activities of their representatives and agents. Zimin and Ovchinnikov were removed from their posts. The leaders of the Veshensk district were given strict warnings and reprimands.

Letter 78   [1 September 1933]

To Comrade Molotov,[1]

1) To be honest, neither I (nor Voroshilov) like the fact that you are leaving for vacation for six weeks instead of two weeks as was agreed upon when we made the **vacation schedule.** If I had known beforehand that you wished to leave for six weeks, I would have proposed a different vacation schedule. Why did you change the schedule—I don't understand it. Are you running away from Sergo? Is it so hard to understand that you simply can't leave the Politburo and Council of Commissars to Kuibyshev (he may start drinking) or to Kaganovich **for long?** True, I did [originally] agree (in a telegram) to the extended leave, but you will understand that I cannot act otherwise [now].

2) I consider Sergo's actions with respect to Vyshinskii the behavior of a hooligan. How can you let him have his way? By his act of protest, Sergo clearly wished to disrupt the campaign of the Council of Commissars and Central Committee to provide proper equipment.[2] What's the matter? Did Kaganovich pull a fast one? So it seems. And he's not the only one.

J. Stalin

9/1

1. In the upper right-hand corner is Molotov's notation: "9/31 =?" In reality, the letter dates from 1933.

2. On 16–20 August 1933, the chief judicial collegium of the USSR Supreme Court heard the case against officials responsible for the production of agricultural machinery; they were accused of delivering combines without the full complement of parts. At the hearings on 22 August, the state prosecutor and deputy Soviet procurator, Vyshinskii, delivered a speech excerpted as follows (RTsKhIDNI f. 17, op. 3, d. 929, l. 21):

> This allows us to ask some questions about the work of Soviet economic organizations in general. We have no reason to paint all the economic organizations completely black, but we must, regardless of the institution or the person who heads it, expose the genuinely "black" marks that indicate the immense failure of the work methods of some of the most important government institutions. I mean the Commissariat of Agriculture in the first place as represented by its agricultural supply agency, . . . I mean the Commissariat of Heavy Industry as represented by its agricultural machinery association.

Vyshinskii's statement outraged Ordzhonikidze and Yakovlev, who were the heads of Heavy Industry and Agriculture, respectively. In Stalin's absence, they managed to persuade the Politburo to issue a resolution criticizing Vyshinskii for his allegations: "To point out to Com. Vyshinskii that he should not have formulated his views in a way . . . that allows incorrect accusations to be made against Heavy Industry and Agriculture."

On 1 September 1933, the Politburo revoked this decision (ibid., d. 930, l. 13).

Letter 79

[12 September 1933]

Hello, Viacheslav,

1) I agree that we should not budget more than 21 billion rubles for capital investments for 1934 and that the growth in manufacturing should not be more that 15 percent. This will be for the best.[1]

2) I also agree that we should set the gross yield for the 1932 [sic] grain harvest at 698 million centners.[2] No less.

3) The behavior of Sergo (and Yakovlev) in the affair concerning "production with full equipment" can only be characterized as "anti-party," since their objective is to defend reactionary party elements [who are acting] **against** the Central Committee.[3] In fact, the whole country is crying out against the lack of full equipment. The party began a campaign on this subject in the press with clearly publicized punitive measures. The sentencing of enemies of the party—that is, of all those who maliciously infringe on the decisions of the party and the government—has already been declared, and Sergo (with Yakovlev), who bears the responsibility for these violations, is attempting to attack the procuracy instead of confessing his sins! For what reason [is he doing this]? Of course, not in order to rein in the reactionary violators of party decisions[4]—rather to support them morally, to justify them in the eyes of party opinion, and, in this way, to discredit the party's unfolding campaign— which in practice means to discredit the policy of the Central Committee.

I wrote Kaganovich to express my surprise that he turned out to be in the camp of the reactionary elements in the party.

4) I am a little uncomfortable with being the reason for your early return from your vacation. But this awkwardness aside, it's obvious that it would be rash to leave the center's work to Kaganovich alone (Kuibyshev may start drinking) for any length of time, because Kaganovich must divide his time between his central and local responsibilities. I will be in Moscow in one month, and you will be able to go on vacation then.

5) I have resolutely decided that it would be useless for you to travel to Turkey.[5] Let Voroshilov and Litvinov go.

Regards,
J. Stalin
9/12/33

1. The references are to the target figures for the Soviet economy in 1934.
2. One centner equals 100 kilograms—Trans.

3. Concerning the controversy over *komplektnost* (providing equipment with a full complement of parts), see note 2 to letter 78.

4. By "reactionary violators of party decisions" Stalin means bureaucrats within the Soviet government and party. For more about these violators, see the Introduction—U.S. Ed.

5. In May 1932, Ismet-Pasha, chairman of the Council of Ministers of the Turkish Republic, and Tenfik Rushtubeibi, minister of foreign affairs, visited the Soviet Union.

On 20 September 1933, the Politburo approved a reciprocal visit to Turkey (RTsKhIDNI f. 17, op. 3, d. 931, l. 17). At the end of October 1933, a Soviet government delegation headed by Voroshilov departed for Ankara to take part in celebrations on the occasion of the tenth anniversary of the Turkish Republic.

Letter 80   [21 July 1935]

Hello, Viacheslav,

Today we discussed the target figures for 1936.[1] Based on a figure of **19** billion for construction projects, Mezhlauk [head of Gosplan] proposed this distribution among the ministries: Heavy Industry would receive 6 billion; Transport—3 billion plus; Agriculture, Light Industry, Food Industry, Timber—reduced numbers. Health, Education, Municipal Services, Local Industry, and so on—also reduced numbers. Even allowing for the most economical approach, it doesn't work out, especially if we consider that Defense must be fully provided for under any circumstances. I proposed a figure of 22 billion rubles. With this number, Heavy Industry would receive 6 billion 500–700 *million* (along with 8 billion plus in the year '35); Transport an additional 400–500 million; Light Industry—200 million; Food Industry—400–500 million; Education, Health Care—around 300 million; Agriculture, State Farms, Local Industry, Municipal Services, Communications, etc.—all that remains. Heavy Industry (they want to get 9 billion) and Transport (they want to get 4 1/2 billion), Food Industries, and all the others are howling.

Mezhlauk and Chubar were told to make a distribution (roughly) based on a total of 22 billion. We shall see.

Some things can't be cut. *Defense;* repair of roads and moving stock, plus payments for new trains and steam engines for *Transport;* the construction of schools for *Education;* re-equipping (technical) for *Light Industry;* paper and cellulose factories for *Timber;* some essential industries (coal, oil, blast furnaces, rolling-mills, viscous materials, electric plants, chemicals) for *Heavy Industry.* This complicates things. We'll see.

How's life? Are you getting any rest?

My health is good; my friends are well also.

Regards to Com. Zhemchuzhina.

J. Stalin
21 July 1935

P.S. The final resolution on the target figures, like the conversion of prices, was put off until the fall.[2]

1. The reference is to a meeting on target production figures for 1936 that took place on 26 July 1935 [sic]. The government and party directive establishing target figures was confirmed by the Politburo on 28 July 1935 (RTsKhIDNI f. 17, op. 3, d. 969, ll. 31–38).
2. This probably refers to substantial changes in factory wholesale prices that occurred in 1936 to eliminate the need for huge subsidies. For price movements during this period, see Alec Nove, *An Economic History of the U.S.S.R.*, 1st ed. (Harmondsworth, Eng., 1969), 246–51—U.S. Ed.

Letter 81
[Later than 28 July 1935]

Hello, Viacheslav,[1]

1) I received your letter. We are considering organizing military schools for the artillery, aviation, and navy.

2) I am sending the directive on the target figures for 1936 to the Council of Commissars and Central Committee.[2] As you can see, the total amount budgeted for construction has been set at 27 billion rubles, with financing at 25 billion rubles. If the cost of those construction projects is reduced by 8 percent—and this is an obligatory directive—the amount budgeted for construction will be reduced to 27 billion, with a government subsidy of 25 billion rubles. This will create a material interest in reducing the cost of construction projects.

Twenty-two billion was insufficient and, as is evident, would never have been enough. The increase for school construction (up 760 million), for Light Industry, Timber, Food Industry, Local Industry (up 900 plus million rubles in all), for Defense (up 1.1 billion), for Health Care, Moscow Canal construction, and other items (more than 400 million rubles) determined the nature and size of the target figures for 1936.

I do not regret this, since everything that increases the production of products for mass consumption must be strengthened each year. Otherwise there is no possibility of moving ahead.

Well, greetings,
Greetings to Com. Zhemchuzhina
J. Stalin

1. In the upper left-hand corner is Molotov's notation: "1935=?"
2. On the meeting on target figures for 1936, see note 1 to letter 80.

Letter 82

[5 August 1935]

5 August 1935

Hello, Viacheslav,

I received your letter. With respect to the complete abolition of ration books for food and consumer goods this year, of course you're right. We must see this matter to its conclusion.[1]

The Comintern Congress wasn't so bad.[2] It will be even more interesting after the reports from Dimitrov and Ercoli [P. Togliatti]. The delegates made a good impression. The draft resolutions came out pretty well. I think now is the time to create within the Comintern the office of first secretary [gensek]. I imagine Dimitrov could be appointed first secretary. Piatnitskii, Manuilskii, and others (from among the foreigners) can be put in as secretaries in the Secretariat of the Comintern Executive Committee.

I am indeed a little tired. I had to spent a lot of time with the Comintern members, with the 1936 target figures, with all sorts of ongoing questions—inevitably you get tired. But it's not a disaster—tiredness passes quickly, with a day's rest, or even a few hours'.

Greetings,

J. Stalin

1. The rationing system for meat and fish products, sugar, oils, and potatoes was abolished on 1 October 1935, and for manufactured goods on 1 January 1936.

2. The XII Congress of the Comintern took place in Moscow from 25 July to 20 August, with 513 delegates representing sixty-five Communist parties and a number of international organizations that had joined the Comintern. The Congress discussed the following issues: Comintern activities (W. Pieck reporting), the work of the International Control Commission (Z. Angaretis reporting), the fascist offensive and the Comintern's tasks in fighting for the unity of the working class against fascism and war (G. Dimitrov reporting), imperialist preparation for war and the tasks of the Comintern (M. Ercoli [Togliatti] reporting), results of the construction of socialism in the USSR (D. Manuilskii reporting), elections to the highest bodies of the Comintern.

The Congress elected ruling bodies for the Comintern: the Executive Committee of the Comintern, which was composed of forty-six members and thirty-three candidate members, and the International Control Commission, which consisted of twenty people. The following were full members of the Comintern Secretariat: G. Dimitrov (general secretary), P. Togliatti, D. Manuilskii, W. Pieck, O. Kuusinen, A. Marty, K. Gottwald; candidate members of the Secretariat were M. Moskvin (Trilisser), F. Florin, Van Min.

Letter 83

[September 1935]

Hello, Viacheslav,[1]

Regarding the Constitution, I think that under no circumstances should it be confused with the party program. It must contain [only] what has *already* been achieved. The program, however, must contain what we are *still striving for.*

I have the following preliminary plan. The Constitution must consist of (approximately) **seven** sections: 1) *Social system* (the soviets, socialist property, socialist agriculture, etc.); 2) *Government system* (union and autonomous republics, the union of these republics, equality of nations, races, etc.); 3) *Supreme government bodies* (the Central Executive Committee or the body that replaces it; the two chambers and their powers; the presidium and its powers, the Council of Commissars, etc.); 4) *Administrative bodies* (commissariats, etc.); 5) *Judicial bodies*; 6) *Rights and responsibilities of citizens* (civil liberties, freedom of unions and associations, the church, etc.); 7) *Electoral system*.

In the Constitution, the *principles* should not be separated from the other articles but must instead be incorporated as the first articles of the Constitution.

In my opinion, a preamble is not needed.

I think we need to hold a *referendum.*

As far as grain purchases are concerned, the plan will have to be somewhat curtailed. Everyone is complaining that the plan is too big. If the allotment for Ukraine is to be cut by 10 million poods, for the North Caucasus [by] 7 million poods, for the Azov–Black Sea region by 5 or 6 million poods, and if the plans for the other regions are to be cut by another 25–30 [million poods], then we could still have a plan for 250–240 million poods.

Regards,
Yours, J Stalin
9/26/35

1. In the upper right-hand corner is Molotov's notation: "2/1936."

Letter 84

[February 1936]

Reviewed. Not bad. See comments in the text.

J. Stalin[1,2]
2/1936

1. This letter is Stalin's notation on the following note from Molotov:

To Comrade Stalin
   Sending you text of my report on the Soviet Constitution.
   Waiting for your comments during the day on 2/6.
   Molotov

2. When Molotov sent a copy of his report on the Constitution to Stalin for his approval in February 1936, he evidently attached Stalin's letter from the previous September (letter 83). Stalin wrote the same marginal note on both his own letter and Molotov's cover letter—U.S. Ed.

Letters with Undetermined Dates

Letter 85

Viacheslav![1]
   I am sending you Zinoviev's letter to Sergo.[2] Read it and weep. It turns out that all these "notes" (from Kamenev and then from Zinoviev) came about not so that copies could be sent to Trotsky (to whom, even after the "break," our "Leninists" found it necessary to give an account), but rather *because* Kamenev and Zinoviev have the habit of talking among themselves via special "notes." And these geniuses want the Central Committee to trust them "in advance"!

Regards,
J. Stalin

1. In the upper right-hand corner is Molotov's notation: "1926=?"
2. Zinoviev's letter to Ordzhonikidze has not been found.

Letter 86

Hi, Molotov,
   The waters here are truly remarkable. Terrific. I'll tell you in detail when we meet.
   I will be in Sochi (most likely!) by 1 September, if not earlier.
   Greetings from Nadia [N. S. Allilueva, Stalin's wife] to Zhemchuzhina.

J. Stalin.

The Eastman Affair

Excerpt from Lenin's Testament
(translated by the U.S. editor from *Polnoe sobranie sochinenii,*
5th ed., 344–46)

24 December 1922. I have in mind stability as a guarantee against a schism in the immediate future, and I intend to deal here with a few ideas concerning purely personal qualities.

I think that from this standpoint the prime factors in the question of stability are such members of the Central Committee as Stalin and Trotsky. I think the relationship between them constitutes the greater part of the danger of a schism, which could be avoided, and this purpose, in my opinion, would be served, among other things, by increasing the number of Central Committee members to 50 or 100.

Comrade Stalin, having become general secretary, has boundless power concentrated in his hands, and I am not sure whether he will always be capable of using that power with sufficient caution. Comrade Trotsky, on the other hand, as his struggle against the Central Committee on the question of the Commissariat for Transport has already proved, is distinguished not only by outstanding ability. He is personally perhaps the most capable man in the present Central Committee, but he has displayed excessive self-assurance and shown excessive preoccupation with the purely administrative side of the work.

These two qualities of the two outstanding leaders of the present Central Committee can inadvertently lead to a schism, and if our party does not take steps to avert this, the schism may come unexpectedly.

I shall not give any further appraisals of the personal qualities of other members of the Central Committee; I shall just recall that the October episode with Zinoviev and Kamenev was, of course, no accident, but neither can the blame for it be laid upon them personally, any more than unbolshevism can upon Trotsky.

Speaking of the young Central Committee members, I wish to say a few words about Bukharin and Piatakov. They are, in my opinion, the most outstanding figures (among the youngest ones), and the following must be borne in mind about them: Bukharin is not only the most valuable and important theorist of the party; he is also rightly considered the favorite of the whole party, but his theoretical views can be classified as fully Marxist only with great reserve, for there is something scholastic about him (he has never made a study of dialectics, and, I think, never fully understood it).

25 December 1922. As for Piatakov, he is unquestionably a man of outstanding will and outstanding ability, but he shows too much zeal for administration and the administrative side of the work to be relied upon in a serious political matter.

Both of these remarks, of course, are made only for the present, on the assumption that both these outstanding and devoted party workers will fail to find an occasion to enhance their knowledge and amend their one-sidedness.

4 January 1923. Stalin is too crude, and this defect, although quite tolerable in our own midst and in dealings with us Communists, becomes intolerable in a general secretary. That is why I suggest that the comrades think about a way of removing Stalin from that post and appointing another man in his stead who in all other respects differs from Comrade Stalin in having only one advantage, namely, that of being more tolerant, more loyal, more polite, and more considerate to the comrades, less capricious, etc. This circumstance may appear to be an insignificant trifle. But I think that from the standpoint of safeguards against a split and from the standpoint of what I wrote above about the relationship between Stalin and Trotsky, it is not a trifle, or it is a trifle that can assume decisive significance.

Inaccuracies in Eastman's Account of Lenin's Testament
(prepared by the U.S. editor)

1. According to Eastman's account in *Since Lenin Died*, Lenin reserves the word *outstanding* for Trotsky alone, thus showing that Lenin thought Trotsky

was "the ablest and the greatest." In actuality, Lenin calls Trotsky *and* Stalin "the two outstanding leaders" of the Central Committee; he also describes Bukharin and Piatakov as outstanding figures among the younger generation.

2. Eastman quotes Lenin as describing Trotsky as a "devoted revolutionist." No such words appear in Lenin's Testament.

3. In the Testament, Lenin also mentions Trotsky's "struggle against the Central Committee" at the time of the trade union dispute in 1920—a black mark on Trotsky's record in the eyes of most party members. Eastman does not mention this remark.

4. In Eastman's version, Lenin is indulgent, not only of Trotsky, but of his followers, for he "did not qualify his praise of Pitiakov [*sic*]—who has stood with Trotsky throughout this crisis" (30). In reality, Lenin states that Piatakov became too absorbed in the administrative side of things and was therefore unreliable in political matters. Eastman seems unaware that Lenin also portrays Trotsky as too absorbed in the administrative side of things.

5. According to Eastman, Lenin uses the emotive term *apostasy* in his discussion of Zinoviev's and Kamenev's actions in 1917. Lenin actually restricts himself to the euphemistic phrase "October episode." More important, Eastman fails to mention that Lenin put this "October episode" on a par with Trotsky's "unbolshevism."

6. Eastman cites Lenin's remark that Bukharin did not fully understand the dialectic and implies that Lenin thought Bukharin was worthless as a theoretician. In reality, Lenin calls Bukharin "the most valuable and important theorist of the party."

7. According to Eastman, Lenin attacks Stalin as "too brutal." This is a tendentious translation of *grubyi*, which is usually rendered as "crude."

Both Stalin and Trotsky alluded to the Eastman affair in later years. In 1927, at the height of the struggle with the left opposition, Stalin provided a lengthy refutation of the charge that Lenin's Testament had been suppressed. In the course of his remarks, he mentions Trotsky's letter of 1925 and asks in effect: "Trotsky told the truth in 1925; why does he deny it now?"

Trotsky seems to have commented on this affair only once: in a letter he wrote in 1928 with the intention of rehabilitating Eastman's personal reputation. There, he does not comment on any of the substantive issues involved, nor does he suggest that his public statement of 1925 contains anything untrue. Trotsky does not even retract his criticism of Eastman's action in publishing *Since Lenin Died*. All Trotsky says in this letter is that, if the Politburo had not pressured him, he would not have publicly criticized Eastman on this issue.

Trotsky's Letter
(translated by the U.S. editor from *Bolshevik*,
1925, no. 16:67–70)

I learned of the publication of Eastman's book *Since Lenin Died* from a query telegraphed to me by Comrade Jackson, editor of the London *Sunday Worker*, soon after my return from Sukhumi to Moscow. This book was being used by the bourgeois press to attack our party and Soviet power. Although my [telegraphed] answer to Comrade Jackson was published in due course in the press, I consider it useful to reproduce the opening section here: "I know nothing of the Eastman book you asked me about. The bourgeois papers that have cited the book have not reached me. It goes without saying that I reject a priori and categorically any comments directed against the Russian Communist Party." In the rest of the telegram, I challenged absurd insinuations about my alleged turn toward bourgeois democracy and free trade.

I later received a copy of Eastman's *Since Lenin Died* from the secretary of the British Communist Party, Comrade Inkpin, with a letter similar to Comrade Jackson's telegram. I did not intend to read, much less to react, to Eastman's book, because I felt that my telegram to Comrade Jackson—which by that time had been published in the British and foreign press in general—was sufficient. After my closest party comrades became familiar with the book, however, they expressed their opinion that, in view of the book's references to conversations with me, my silence might provide indirect support to a book directed in its entirety against our party. This prompted me to take the book more seriously and, first of all, to read it more attentively. Basing himself on certain episodes of our party life—from the discussion on the methods of party democracy and state regulation of the economy—Eastman proceeds to conclusions that are completely and utterly directed against our party and capable, if taken on faith, of discrediting the party and Soviet power.

Let us dwell first of all on a theme that not only has historical significance but is still a very urgent one at present: the Red Army. Eastman implies that the change in individual leadership has led to a disintegration of the army and to its loss of fighting capacity and so on. Where Eastman got his ridiculous information is completely unknown, but its absurdity strikes one immediately. We certainly don't advise the imperialist governments to build their calculations on Eastman's discoveries. By the way, Eastman seems not to realize that his description of the Red Army also nourishes the completely rotten menshevik legend about Bonapartism, praetorianism, and so on, for it is clear that an army capable of "falling to pieces" because of a change in individual leadership would not be a Communist or a proletarian army, but rather a Bonapartist and praetorian one.

The author cites in the course of his book a large number of documents and brings in many episodes, often from second-, third-, and fourth-hand accounts. Clearly erroneous and false assertions can be found in this book in no small number. We will discuss only the most important.

In several places in his book, Eastman says that the Central Committee "hid" from the party a number of highly important documents that Lenin wrote in the last period of his life (letters on the national question, the so-called testament, and so forth); this cannot be termed anything other than a slander of the Central Committee of our party. These letters give advice on matters of internal party organization, yet from Eastman's words, the conclusion could be drawn that Vladimir Ilich [Lenin] meant them to be printed. In fact, this is completely untrue. After the onset of his illness, Vladimir Ilich turned more than once to the leading institutions of the party as well as to the Party Congress with proposals, letters, and so on. It goes without saying that all these letters and proposals came to the attention of the addressees and to the knowledge of the delegates of the XIII Party Congress; these [letters], of course, always had their due influence on party decisions. If they were not published, that is because their author did not intend for them to be published. Vladimir Ilich did not leave any "testament," and the character of his relation to the party, not to mention the character of the party itself, excludes the possibility of such a "testament." When the emigré, foreign bourgeois, and menshevist press uses the term *testament*, it usually has in mind a letter—in a form distorted beyond recognition—in which Vladimir Ilich gave advice of an internal party character. The XIII Congress gave this letter, like all the others, its close attention and drew the conclusions appropriate to the circumstances of the moment. Any talk of a hidden or violated "testament" is a spiteful invention aimed against the real will of Vladimir Ilich and the interests of the party he created.

Just as false is Eastman's assertion that the Central Committee wanted to keep under wraps (that is, not publish) Lenin's article about the Worker-Peasant Inspection. The dispute in the Central Committee about this article (if *dispute* is the proper word) involved a question of secondary importance, namely, whether the publication of Lenin's article should be accompanied by an announcement from the Central Committee to the effect that there was no danger of a schism. This question was settled unanimously in the same session, and a letter was written by the members of the Politburo and Orgburo who were present. This letter was sent to party organizations and contained the following:

"In this strictly informational letter we will not consider the possible long-range dangers that Comrade Lenin appropriately raised in his article. The members of the Politburo and Orgburo, however, wish to state with complete unanimity, in order to avoid any possible misunderstandings, that in the work of the Central Committee *there are absolutely no circumstances that would provide any basis whatsoever for fears of a 'schism.'*" Not only does this document have my signature, along with those of ten or so others, but I myself drafted the text (27 January 1923).

Since Comrade Kuibyshev also signed this letter—which expresses the Central Committee's unanimous opinion of Lenin's proposal about the Worker-Peasant Inspection—another of Eastman's false assertions is also refuted: the allegation that Comrade Kuibyshev was appointed to head the Worker-Peasant Inspection as an "opponent" of Lenin's organizational plan.

Eastman's assertions that the Central Committee confiscated or in some way held up my pamphlets in 1923 or 1924 or at any other time are false and based on fantastical rumors.

Also completely incorrect is Eastman's assertion that Lenin offered me the post of chairman of the Council of Commissars or of the Labor Defense Council. I learn of this for the first time from Eastman's pamphlet.

No doubt a more attentive reading of the book would uncover a number of other inaccuracies and errors, but there is hardly any need to do this. Using Eastman's information and citing his conclusions, the bourgeois and especially the menshevik press have tried in every way to emphasize his "closeness" to me as the author of my biography and his "friendship" with me, clearly trying by this *indirect* means to give his conclusions a weight they do not and could not have on their own. It is therefore necessary to dwell on this matter. Perhaps the best way of showing the real nature of my relationship with Eastman is to quote a business letter I wrote before there was any talk of his book *Since Lenin Died*.

During my stay in Sukhumi, I received from a party comrade who is involved in publishing my works in Moscow a manuscript by Eastman entitled *Lev Trotsky: Portrait of a Youth*. From my associate's accompanying letter, I learned that the author had submitted this manuscript to the State Publishing House so they could consider publishing a Russian edition and that its sentimental tone produced a strange and, for us, unaccustomed impression. I replied to this letter on 3 April 1925:

"Even before becoming acquainted with Eastman's manuscript, I am in complete agreement with you that it would be absolutely inappropriate to publish it. Thank you for sending the manuscript, but I have no stomach for reading it. I am quite willing to believe that it is unappetizing, especially to our Russian Communist taste. Eastman was very insistent in trying to convince me that it was very difficult for Americans to interest themselves in *communism*, but that they could be interested in *Communists*. His argument was not entirely unconvincing. That is what moved me to give him help, although of a very limited kind: its limits are indicated in my letter to him. (On 22 May 1923, I responded to Eastman's repeated requests for help with the following words: 'I am willing to help by providing you with accurate information, but I cannot agree to read your manuscript. That would make me responsible, not only for its facts, but also for its personal evaluations and judgments. It should be evident how impossible that would be. I am willing to take some limited responsibility for the factual statements I made to you at your request. For everything else, the responsibility must be yours alone.' The manuscript does not go further than 1902.) I didn't know that he intended to publish the book in Russia; otherwise I would probably have already advised the State Publishing House not to publish it. In no way am I able to interfere with Eastman's publication of his book abroad. He is a 'free' writer who lived in Russia, where he collected material, and now lives in France or America. Ask him not to publish the book as a personal favor? *I am not close enough to him to make that request.* And in general it would hardly be appropriate."

The topic here, I repeat, is a completely innocent book about my youth (up to 1902), but the tone of my letter leaves no room for doubt that my relationship to Eastman differs in no way from my relationship to very many Communists or "sympathetic foreigners" who turn to me for help in trying to learn about the October revolution, our party, and the Soviet state—certainly no closer.

With vulgar self-assurance, Eastman waxes ironic about my "quixotic" attitude to my closest comrades on the Central Committee, since according to him I referred to them in friendly fashion [even] during the "fierce discussion." Eastman, evidently, feels called upon to correct my "mistake" and gives a description of the leaders of our party that is impossible to describe as anything other than slander.

We saw earlier how rotten is the foundation on which Eastman has constructed his edifice. With a scandalous disregard for facts and for proportion, he uses individual aspects of the intra-party discussion in order to blacken our party's name and destroy confidence in it. It seems to me, however, that any really serious and thoughtful reader does not even need to verify Eastman's citations and his "documents"—something, in any event, that not everyone can do. It is sufficient to ask oneself this simple question: if the malicious evaluation of the leaders of our party given by Eastman is true even in part, then how could such a party have gone through long years of underground struggle, carried out a great revolution, led masses many millions strong, and aided in the formation of revolutionary parties in other countries? *Not one honorable worker will believe the picture given by Eastman.* It contains its own internal contradiction. It makes no difference what Eastman's own intentions are. His book can be of service only to the most malicious enemies of communism and the revolution, and it is therefore, objectively speaking, a tool of counterrevolution.

Excerpt from Krupskaia's Letter
(translated by the U.S. editor from *Bolshevik*,
1925, no. 16:71–73)   1 July 1925

Comrade Trotsky now knows exactly how Lenin felt about him at their meeting in 1902 (from the letter to Plekhanov published in the third *Leninskii sbornik*) and also how Lenin felt about him at the end of his life, because of Lenin's letters to the Party Congress. Mr. Eastman writes all sorts of unbelievable nonsense about these letters (calling them a "testament"). Mr. Eastman has no understanding of the spirit of our party. For Mr. Eastman a Party Congress is a congress of party bureaucrats. For us Bolsheviks, the Congress is the highest party body, where each member of the party is supposed to speak with complete sincerity, without fear or favor. This is how Lenin viewed a Party Congress. For him, its decisions had exceptional significance: he was always agitated before a Party Congress and always prepared for it with great care. His Congress speeches were always particularly distinguished by careful thought and weightiness of content.

Lenin's letters on intra-party relations (the "testament") were also written for a Party Congress. He knew that the party would understand the motives that dictated this letter. Such a letter could only be addressed to people who would undoubtedly put the interests of the cause first. The letter contained, among other things, personal descriptions of the highest party comrades. There is no lack of faith [nedoverie] expressed in the letters toward these comrades, with whom V. I. worked for many years. On the contrary, there is much that is flattering—Eastman forgets to mention this. The letters had the aim of helping the other comrades get work moving in the proper direction, and, for that reason, they mention not only virtues but also defects (including Trotsky's), since it is necessary to take into account these defects when organizing the work of the party collective in the best possible way.

As Lenin wished, all members of the Congress familiarized themselves with the letters. It is incorrect to call them a "testament," since Lenin's Testament in the real sense of the word is incomparably wider: it consists of V. I.'s last articles and discusses the basic questions of party and Soviet work. These are the articles "On Cooperation," "On Rabkrin," "Page from a Diary" (on education), and "Our Revolution." Taken together with what Lenin said previously, these articles will illuminate the path we must take for a long time to come. They have all been published. But Mr. Eastman is not interested in them.

The enemies of the Russian Communist Party are trying to use the "testament" in order to discredit the present leaders of the party and to discredit the party itself. Mr. Eastman is energetically working to achieve the same purpose: he slanders the Central Committee by shouting that the "testament" has been suppressed. In this way he tries to inflame an unhealthy curiosity, thus distorting the real meaning of the letter.

Glossary of Names

The term *repressed,* which appears repeatedly in this glossary, indicates that the person concerned was expelled from the Communist Party, arrested, and then probably either was executed or died in the camps. When only a single date is provided, it indicates that the position was assumed at that time.

Akhundov, Rukhulla Ali ogly (1897–1938). Party member from 1919. Secretary of Azerbaidzhan Central Committee, 1924. Azerbaidzhan commissar of public education. Member of USSR Central Executive Committee, 1922–27. Repressed.

Alekseev, P. A. (1893–1939). Party member from 1914. Central Committee candidate member, 1927. Central Committee member, 1930. Chairman of Leningrad Regional Trade Union Council.

Aleksinskii, G. A. (1879–1967). Activist in Russian Social Democratic movement. Sided with Bolsheviks, 1905. Member of second Duma. "Recallist," 1908. Menshevik, 1917. Emigré, 1918.

Allilueva, Nataliia S. (1901–1932). Party member from 1918. Wife of Joseph Stalin. Attended Moscow Industrial Academy, 1929–32.

Amas (real name: Amirbekov), A. S. (1904–1937?). Party member from 1917. Secretary of Abkhazian Regional Party Committee, February 1928 to May 1929. Chairman of Batumi Party Purge Commission, June to September 1929. Head of organization department of Azerbaidzhan Central Committee, October 1929 to July 1930. Deputy head of organization department of Moscow Party Committee. Repressed.

Amosov, A. M. (1896–1937). Party member from 1914. Chairman of Central Committee of Rail Workers' Union from 1929. Central Committee candidate member, 1930–34. Chief of Northern Railway from 1933.

Andreev, A. A. (1895–1971). Party member from 1914. Central Committee secretary, 1924–25. Chairman of Central Committee of Rail Workers' Union, 1922–27. Secretary of North Caucasian Regional Committee, 1927–30.

Antselovich, N. M. (1888–1952). Party member from 1905. Chairman of Central Committee of Agriculture and Forestry Workers' Union, 1923–30. Member of Trade Union Central Council presidium.

Aralov, S. I. (1880–1969). Party member from 1918. Ambassador to Lithuania, Turkey, Latvia, 1921–25. Member of collegium of USSR Commissariat of Foreign Affairs. Appointed Soviet ambassador to China's national government on 30 December 1926.

Artak (Astamboltsian), A. A. (1895– ?). Party member from 1916. Secretary of Bailov-Bibi-Eybat District Committee of Azerbaidzhan Communist Party, 1926–29. Student in courses on Marxism-Leninism under the auspices of USSR Central Committee from October 1929.

Asribekov, Ye. M. (1898– ?). Party member from 1917. Secretary of Tiflis Committee of Georgian Communist Party, 1925.

Astrov, V. N. (1898– ?). Party member from 1917.

Avdeev, I. A. (1877–1937?). Party member from 1901. Chairman of Stalingrad Provincial Economic Council, 1927. Central Committee candidate member.

Averbakh, L. L. (1903–1939). Party member from 1919. Editor of *Na literaturnom postu* (On literary guard) and *Vestnik inostrannoi literatury* (Foreign literature review), 1929. Repressed.

Badaev, A. Ye. (1883–1951). Party member from 1904. Chairman of Consumers' Union (Leningrad), 1921–29. Chairman of Central Union of Consumers' Organizations (Moscow), 1930–33.

Bagirov, Mir Jafar Abbasovich (1896–1956). Party member from 1917. Chairman of Azerbaidzhan Cheka (security police); chairman of Azerbaidzhan GPU (security police), commissar of internal affairs and deputy chairman of Azerbaidzhan Council of Commissars, 1921–27. Chairman of Azerbaidzhan GPU (Baku), 1929–30. Student in courses on Marxism-Leninism at USSR Central Committee, 1930–32. Executive instructor sent out by the Central Committee, 1932. Chairman of Azerbaidzhan Central Committee, 1932–33. First secretary of Azerbaidzhan Central Committee, 1933. Sentenced to death and executed by firing squad, 1956.

Bakaev, I. P. (1897–1936). Party member from 1906. Chairman of Leningrad Provincial Control Commission, 1925. Member of Central Control Commission, 1925–27. At XV Party Congress, expelled from party for joining Trotskyist opposition group. Repressed.

Baldwin, Stanley (1867–1947). British statesman, Conservative prime minister, 1923–29.

Bauman, K. Ya. (1892–1937). Party member from 1907. Politburo candidate member, 1929–30. Second and then first secretary of Moscow Party Committee, 1928–30. Central Committee secretary, April 1929 to February 1934. Repressed.

Bazarov, V. (real name: V. A. Rudnev) (1874–1939). Philosopher and economist. Involved in revolutionary movement, 1896. After February revolution, coeditor of newspaper *Novaia zhizn'* (New life). Worked for USSR Gosplan, 1921.

Bazovskii, N. A. (1895–1938?). Party member from 1919. Deputy chairman of Siberian Regional Executive Committee, 1929. Member of Siberian Regional Party Committee, 1930. Repressed.

Bednyi, Demian (real name: Ye. A. Pridvorov) (1883–1945). Writer. Party member from 1912.

Belenkii, A. Ya. (1883–1941). Party member from 1902. Official of All-Russian Cheka (security police) and USSR OGPU (security police) of Council of Commissars. Chief of Lenin's bodyguard, 1919–24.

Belenkii, Z. M. (1888– ?). Party member from 1905. Chairman of North Caucasian Regional Trade Union Council, 1925. Member of collegium of Worker-Peasant Inspection, 1928–31. Deputy commissar of Worker-Peasant Inspection, 1931–34.

Bogdanov, P. A. (1882–1939). Party member from 1905. Chairman of RSFSR Economic Council, 1921–25. Chairman of North Caucasian Regional Executive Committee, 1926. Head of American Trading Corporation, 1930–34. Repressed.

Bogolepov, M. I. (1879–1945). Economist, corresponding member of USSR Academy of Sciences. Head of budget and finance department of Gosplan, 1930.

Bordiga, Amadeo (1889–1970). Activist of Italian working-class movement. Cofounder and early leader of Italian Communist Party, 1921. Held leftist views; opposed Italian Communist Party leaders, 1926. Expelled from party for factional activity.

Borodin, M. M. (1884–1951). Party member from 1903. Comintern representative in China, 1923–27; political advisor to Kuomintang leadership, 1923–27.

Briukhanov, N. P. (1878–1942). Party member from 1902; commissar of finance, 1926–30. Repressed.

Brutskus, B. D. (1878–1938). Economist and agronomist. Author of a number of works on agriculture and economics. Expelled from Russia, 1922.

Budenny, S. M. (1883–1973). Party member from 1919. Inspector of Red Army Cavalry, 1924–37.

Bukharin, N. I. (1888–1938). Party member from 1906. Politburo member, 1924–29. Repressed.

Buniat-zade, D. Kh. (1888–1938). Party member from 1908. Deputy chairman of Azerbaidzhan Council of Commissars, 1908. Chairman, 30 January 1930.

Bystrianskii, V. A. (1886–1940). Party member from 1907. Historian, journalist. Worked for *Izvestiia VTsIK* (All-Union Central Executive Committee news) and *Petrogradskaia pravda* (Petrograd truth), 1917. Lecturer at Communist University (Leningrad), 1922.

Chaianov, A. V. (1888–1937). Agrarian economist. Director of Research Institute of Agricultural Economics and Politics, 1930. Repressed.

Chamberlain, Austin (1863–1937). British politician. Foreign secretary, 1924–29.

Chang Hsueh-liang. (1901– ?). Chang Tso-lin's son, commander of Northeastern Army. De facto ruler of Manchuria.

Ch'en Tu-hsiu (1872–1942). General secretary of Chinese Communist Party, 1921–27.

Chernov, M. A. (1891–1938). Menshevik, 1909–18. Social-Democrat-Internationalist, 1918–20. Party member from 1920. Ukrainian commissar of domestic trade, 1925–28. Chairman of Committee on Procurement of Agricultural Products and member of USSR Commissariat of Trade, 1930. USSR commissar of agriculture, 1934–37. Repressed.

Chernyi, V. N. (1891– ?). Party member from 1918. Head of Research Administration, March 1929. Head of United Administration of River Transport from January 1930.

Chiang Kai-shek (1887–1975). Head of Kuomintang regime from 1927.

Chicherin, G. V. (1872–1936). Party member from 1905. Commissar of foreign affairs, 1918–30.

Chubar, V. Ya. (1891–1939). Party member from 1907. Central Committee member, 1921. Chairman of Ukrainian Council of Commissars, 1923–34. Repressed.

Desov, G. A. (1884– ?). Party member from 1902. Chairman of Leningrad Provincial Control Commission, 1926–29. Director of Gelts Precision Machine-Building Works, October 1930.

Deterding, Sir Henri. Head of Royal Dutch Shell, a British-Dutch oil trust.

Dimitrov, Georgi (1882–1949). Activist in Bulgarian and international labor movement. Secretary general of Comintern Executive Committee, 1935.

Domski, G. G. (1883–1937). Member of Polish Social Democratic Party, 1904. Member of editorial board of *Svit* (World, Polish newspaper in Moscow). Member of Central Committee of Polish Communist Party, March 1926.

Dovgalevskii, V. S. (1885–1934). Party member from 1908. Soviet ambassador to France, 1928–34.

Dzerzhinsky, F. Ye. (1877–1926). Party member from 1895. Central Committee member. Head of Cheka (security police) from late 1917; head of OGPU (security police), 1922–26. Also chairman of Supreme Economic Council, 1924.

Eastman, Max. (1883–1969). American journalist and writer.

Eikhe, R. I. (1890–1940). Party member from 1905. Central Committee candidate member, 1925–30. Chairman of Siberian Regional Executive Committee, 1925–29. First secretary of Siberian and West Siberian Regional Party Committees.

Eismont, N. B. (1891–1935). Party member from 1917. Commissar of trade of RSFSR and deputy commissar of foreign and domestic trade of USSR, 1926. Arrested, 1933. Released, 1935. Killed in a car accident. (This is not the Eismont who was an employee of the Chinese Eastern Railway.)

Eliava, Sh. Z. (1888–1937). Party member from 1904. Chairman of Georgian Council of Commissars, 1923. Chairman of Transcaucasian Council of Commissars, 1927. Repressed.

Fedorov, G. F. (1891–1936). Party member from 1907. After the civil war, involved in major trade union, party, and Soviet work. At the XV Party Congress, expelled from party for membership in Trotskyist opposition group, 1927. Restored to party by decision of Central Control Commission, 1928. Worked in metallurgical industry. Expelled again, 1934.

Feng Yü-hsiang (1882–1948). Chinese general, member of the Kuomintang.

Fischer, Ruth (1895–1961). Headed a leftist group of the German Communist Party in the 1920s. Member of Central Committee of German Communist Party, 1923–26. Candidate member of Comintern Executive Committee, 1924. Removed from official positions in Comintern by Executive Committee official at proposal of Soviet party (approved by Politburo, 19 June 1926). Expelled from German party by decision of Central Committee of German Communist Party, 19 August 1926.

Fotieva, L. A. (1881–1975). Party member from 1904. Secretary of Labor Defense Council, 1918–30. V. I. Lenin's secretary, 1918–24.

Fridrikhson, L. Kh. (1889–1937?). Party member from 1908. Head of State Grain Trade, 1926. Appointed chairman of the board of the joint-stock company Grain Export, 21 August 1930. Repressed.

Frumkin, M. I. (1878–1938). Party member from 1898. Deputy commissar of finance of USSR, 1929. Repressed.

Frunze, M. V. (1885–1925). Party member from 1904. Central Committee member, 1921. Politburo candidate member, 1924. Army Commander of Ukraine and Crimea, 1920–24. Deputy chairman of Revolutionary Military Council and deputy commissar of military and naval affairs, 1924. Also Red Army chief of staff. Chairman of Revolutionary Military Council, commissar of military and naval affairs, January 1925.

Fushman, A. M. (1889–1936). Party member from 1921. Chairman of textile import agency.

Gallacher, William (1881–1965). Activist in British and international labor movement. Member of British Communist Party, 1921.

Ganshin, S. M. (1895–1937). Party member from 1914. Head of Groznyi oil industry, 1928–30. Deputy chairman of Soviet oil industry, 1931. Repressed.

Gegechkori, A. A. (1887–1928). Party member from 1908. Deputy chairman of Georgian Council of Commissars, 1922. Simultaneously commissar of internal affairs, commissar of agriculture.

Gei, K. V. (1896–1939). Party member from 1916. Secretary of Perm District Party Committee, 1924. Head of organization and distribution department of Central Committee, Central Committee candidate member, 1925–26. Confirmed as secretary of Ural Regional Committee by Politburo, 28 August 1926.

Gikalo, N. F. (1897–1938). Party member from 1917. Secretary of North Caucasian Regional Committee from 1925. First secretary of Uzbekistan Central Committee and Azerbaidzhan Central Committee. Repressed.

Goltsman, A. Z. (1894–1933). Party member from 1917. High official at Supreme Economic Council, Central Control Commission, main directorate of air force from 1922.

Grinko, G. F. (1890–1938). Party member from 1919. Deputy chairman of Gosplan from 1926. Deputy commissar of agriculture, 1929. Commissar of finance, 1930–37. Member of Central Executive Committee. Repressed.

Grisha. See Zinoviev, G. Ye.

Groman, V. G. (1874–1932?). Economist, statistician. After October revolution, member of Gosplan and of Central Statistical Administration presidium, consulting editor at All-Union Association of Sugar Industry.

Guralski, A. (real name: A. Ya. Kheifets) (1890–1960). Party member from 1918. Comintern representative in France in 1924.

Guseinov, Mirza Davud Bagir ogly (1894–1938). Party member from 1918. Azerbaidzhan and Transcaucasian commissar of finance; deputy chairman of Transcaucasian Council of Commissars, 1920.

Henderson, Arthur (1863–1935). Leading figure in British Labour Party, 1911–34; British Foreign Secretary, 1929.

Ilin, N. I. (1884– ?). Party member from 1910. Member of presidium of combined Central Control Commission and Worker-Peasant Inspection, 1923–34.

Inkpin, Albert (1884–1944). Secretary general of British Communist Party.

Ishchenko, A. G. (1895–1937). Party member from April 1917. Chairman of Water-Transport Workers' Union Central Committee; member of collegium of Commissariat of Transport; member of committee for construction of Volga-Don rail link, 1927. Repressed.

Ivanov, P. Deputy head of main board of Fuel Industry.

Izrailovich, A. I. (1883–1937?). Party member from 1918. Manager of mining and fuel group at Worker-Peasant Inspection, 1929. Deputy chief of main directorate of Coal Industry; member of collegium of Commissariat of Heavy Industry, 1933. Repressed.

Kabakov, I. D. (1891–1937). Party member from 1914. First secretary of Ural Regional Party Committee, 1929. Central Committee member. Repressed.

Kaganovich, L. M. (1893–1991). Party member from 1911. Central Committee secretary, 1924–25 and 1928–39. General secretary of Ukrainian Central Committee, 1925–28. First secretary of Moscow Party Committee, 1930–35. Simultaneously first secretary of Moscow City Party Committee, 1931–34. Central Committee department head, 1933.

Kaganovich, M. M. (1888–1941). Party member from 1905. Member of Worker-Peasant Inspection collegium, 1928–30. Presidium member of Supreme Economic Council, department head and deputy chairman of Machine-Building Industry Administration of Supreme Economic Council, 1930–31. Head of main directorate of Machine-Building Industry, 1931–32. Deputy commissar of heavy industry, 1933. Head of technology and production department of Commissariat of Heavy Industry, 1933–34. Head of main directorate of Aircraft Industry of Commissariat of Heavy Industry, 1935–36. Committed suicide.

Kaktyn, A. M. (1893–1937). Party member from 1916. Deputy business manager of Council of Commissars and Labor Defense Council, 1926–29. High official at Gosbank, 1930. Member of Worker-Peasant Inspection collegium, 1931–34.

Kalinin, M. I. (1875–1946). Party member from 1898. Central Committee member, 1919. Politburo member, 1926. Chairman of Central Executive Committee, 1922.

Kalmanovich, M. I. (1888–1937). Party member from 1917. Deputy commissar of agriculture, 1929. Member of Central Control Commission. Repressed.

Kamenev, L. B. (1883–1936). Party member from 1901. Deputy chairman of Council of Commissars; chairman of Labor Defense Council, 1922. Commissar of domestic and foreign trade, January to August 1926. Soviet ambassador to Italy; chairman of Technical and Scientific Administration of Supreme Economic Council and of Main Concession Committee, 1926. Repressed.

Kamenev, S. S. (1881–1936). Military commander. Party member from 1930. Deputy commissar of military and naval affairs and deputy chairman of Revolutionary Military Council, 1927–34.

Karaev, A. G. (1896–1938). Party member from 1917. Member of Transcaucasian Regional Committee of Worker-Peasant Inspection.

Karakhan, L. M. (1889–1937). Party member from 1917. Soviet ambassador to China, 1923–26. Deputy commissar of foreign affairs, 1927. Repressed.

Karklin, R. Ya. (1894– ?). Party member from 1914. Head of industrial department of Gosbank, 1930–32.

Kartvelishvili, L. I. (real name: Lavrentiev) (1890–1938). Party member from 1910. Georgian Central Committee secretary and Transcaucasian Regional Committee secretary; chairman of Georgian Council of Commissars, 1923.

Kasumov Mir Bashir Fattakh ogly (1876–1949). Party member from 1910. Deputy chairman of Azerbaidzhan Central Executive Committee; member of Transcaucasian Regional Party Committee, 1921–25. Member of Baku Revolutionary Committee, April 1929. Chairman of Karabakh District Executive Committee of Azerbaidzhan, September 1929.

Kerensky, A. F. (1881–1970). Politician, lawyer. Minister of justice; minister of military and naval affairs; prime minister and supreme commander in chief in Provisional Government, 1917.

Kerzhentsev, P. M. (1881–1940). Party member from 1904. Soviet ambassador to Italy, 1925–26.

Khinchuk, L. M. (1868–1944). Party member from 1920. Deputy commissar of trade, 1927. Ambassador to Germany, 1930–34. Repressed.

Kirov, S. M. (1886–1934). Party member from 1904. Central Committee member, 1923. Politburo member, 1930. First secretary of Leningrad Provincial (Regional) Party Committee. Assassinated.

Kiselev, A. S. (1879–1937). Party member from 1898. Chairman of Small Council of Commissars, 1921–23. Member of Central Control Commission presidium, 1923–25. Secretary of All-Russian Central Executive Committee, 1924. Central Committee candidate member, 1925–34.

Klim. See Voroshilov, K. Ye.

Klimenko, I. Ye. (1891– ?). Party member from 1912. Appointed deputy commissar of agriculture, 1927. Chairman of main directorate of tractor center; chairman of USSR Agricultural Cooperation; and deputy commissar of agriculture, 1929. Chairman of Siberian Regional Executive Committee, Central Committee candidate member, 1930.

Koba. Nickname for Stalin.

Kodatskii, I. F. (1893–1937). Party member from 1914. Deputy chairman and chairman of Leningrad Regional Economic Council, 1928–29. Central Committee candidate member, 1925. Repressed.

Komarov, N. P. (real name: F. Ye. Sobinov) (1886–1937). Party member from 1909. Chairman of Leningrad Soviet Executive Committee, 1926–29. Worked for Supreme

Economic Council, 1930–31. RSFSR commissar of municipal services, 1931. Central Committee member. Repressed.

Kondratiev, N. D. (1892–1938). Economist. Director of Market Institute of Commissariat of Finance. Arrested and sentenced in connection with case of so-called Toiling Peasants Party, 1930. In 1987, this "case" was acknowledged to have been falsified, and the accused were fully exonerated.

Kopp, V. L. (1880–1930). Party member from 1917. Member of collegium of Commissariat of Foreign Affairs, 1923–25. Soviet ambassador to Japan, April 1925. Soviet ambassador to Sweden, 1927–30.

Kosior, I. V. (1893–1937). Party member from 1908. Deputy chairman of Supreme Economic Council; deputy commissar of heavy industry, 1927. Representative of Council of Commissars in Far Eastern Region, 1933.

Kosior, S. V. (1889–1939). Party member from 1907. Secretary of Siberian Bureau of Russian Communist Party, 1922. Central Committee secretary, 1926. Secretary general (first secretary) of Ukrainian Central Committee, 1928–38. Repressed.

Kotov, V. A. (1895–1937). Party member from 1915. Moscow Party Committee secretary, 1925–28. Member of collegium of RSFSR Commissariat of Labor, 1929. Repressed.

Kotovskii, G. I. (1881–1925). Party member from 1920. Civil war hero.

Kovalev. Head of *Pravda* Party Department. Member of *Pravda*'s editorial board from 10 June 1929. Elected party cell secretary of *Pravda*.

Krasin, L. B. (1870–1926). Party member from 1890. Commissar of foreign trade, 1920–23, 1925–26.

Krinitskii, A. I. (1894–1937). Party member from 1915. Secretary, first secretary of Belorussian Central Committee, 1924. Central Committee department head, 1927–29. Secretary of Transcaucasian Regional Party Committee, 1929–30. Deputy commissar of Worker-Peasant Inspection, 1930. Repressed.

Krumin, G. I. (real name: Kruminsh) (1894–1943). Party member from 1909. Editor of newspaper *Ekonomicheskaia zhizn'*(Economic life), 1919–28. Editorial staff member of *Pravda*, 1928. Editor of *Izvestiia VTsIK i TsIK sovetov* (News of All-Union Central Executive Committee and Central Executive Committee of Soviets), 1930.

Krupskaia, N. K. (1869–1939). Party member from 1898. Wife of Lenin. Elected member of Central Control Commission at XIII and XIV Party Congresses and member of Central Committee at XV through XVII Party Congresses. Head of Main Political Education Committee of Commissariat of Public Education, 1920. Deputy RSFSR commissar of public education, 1929.

Krylenko, N. V. (1885–1938). Party member from 1904. Chairman of Supreme Tribunal; RSFSR chief public procurator, 1918. RSFSR commissar of justice, 1931. Repressed.

Kuibyshev, V. V. (1888–1935). Party member from 1904. Central Committee member, 1922. Politburo member, 1927. Chairman of the Central Control Commission; commissar of Worker-Peasant Inspection; deputy chairman of Council of Commissars and Labor Defense Council, January to November 1926. Chairman of Supreme Economic Council, 1926–30. Deputy chairman and chairman of Gosplan; deputy chairman of Council of Commissars and Labor Defense Council, 1930–34.

Kulikov, Ye. F. (1891–1937 ?). Party member from 1910. Repressed.

Kuskova, Ye. D. (1869–1958). Journalist; advocate of "economism" at the turn of the century. Involved in foundation and work of Committee for Famine Relief. Expelled from USSR in 1922.

Kuznetsov, S. M. (1891– ?). Collegium member of Commissariat of Finance, 1923–29. Deputy chairman of Gosplan, 1929–31. Approved as vice-chairman of the board of Chinese Eastern Railway, 10 April 1931.

Kviring, Er. I. (1892– ?). Party member from 1912. Assistant to Central Committee secretary Molotov, 1926–28. Member of collegium of Commissariat of Agriculture, 1928–29. Chairman of Agricultural Cooperation Council, 1929–30. RSFSR deputy commissar of agriculture, early 1930 to September 1930.

Kviring, Ye. I. (1888–1937). Party member from 1912. Central Committee member, 1923–24. Deputy chairman of Supreme Economic Council, 1927. Deputy chairman of Gosplan, 1927. Deputy commissar of transport, 1931. Deputy chairman of Goods Committee of Labor Defense Council, 1932–34. Repressed.

Larichev, V. A. Member of Gosplan presidium, 1929–30.

Lashevich, M. M. (1884–1928). Party member from 1901. Deputy commissar of military and naval affairs and deputy chairman of the Revolutionary Military Council, 1925. Central Committee candidate member, 1925–26.

Leonov, F. G. (1892– ?). Party member from 1893. Central Committee member.

Lezhava, A. M. (1870–1937). Party member from 1904. Deputy chairman of RSFSR Council of Commissars and chairman of RSFSR Gosplan, 1924–30. Repressed.

Liaksutkin, F. F. (1896– ?). Party member from 1913. Chairman of Siberian Regional Control Commission, 1929–30. Head of complaints office and leader of procurement group for Worker-Peasant Inspection, 1931–33.

Litvinov, M. M. (1876–1951). Party member from 1898. Deputy commissar of foreign affairs of USSR, 1921. Commissar of foreign affairs of USSR, 1930–39.

Liubimov, I. Ye. (1882–1937). Party member from 1902. Board member of central cooperative agency, 1926–30.

Lizdin, G. Ya. (1864– ?). Party member from 1892. Member of factory trade union committee of Baltic Factory; member of Central Control Commission, 1925.

Lobov, S. S. (1888–1937). Party member from 1913. Central Committee member, 1924–37. Chairman of RSFSR Council of Commissars, 1926–30. Deputy commissar of provisionment, 1930. Commissar of timber industry, 1932–36. Repressed.

Lokatskov, F. I. (1881–1937). Party member from 1904. Central Committee candidate member, 1927–30.

Lominadze, V. V. (1897–1935). Party member from 1917. Presidium member of Comintern Executive Committee, 1925–29. Secretary of Executive Committee of Youth Communist International, 1925–26. Secretary of Transcaucasian Regional Party Committee, 1930–31. Committed suicide.

Lomov, G. I. (real name: Oppokov) (1888–1938). Party member from 1903. Member of presidium of Supreme Economic Council, 1929. Repressed.

Lozovskii, A. (real name: S. A. Dridzo) (1878–1952). Party member from 1901. General secretary of Profintern (Red International of Trade Unions). Repressed.

Lukashin (real name: Srapionian), **S. L.** First secretary of Central Committee of Armenian Communist Party, 1921. Elected to Transcaucasian Regional Party Committee, 1922. Member of Central Executive Committee of USSR.

MacDonald, James Ramsey (1866–1937). Cofounder and leader of British Labour Party. Prime minister, 1924 and 1929–31.

Makarov, N. P. (1887–1980). Agrarian economist. Professor at Timiriazev Academy of Agriculture and Voronezh Institute of Agriculture; presidium member of Land Planning Commission of RSFSR Commissariat of Agriculture.

Makharadze, F. I. (1868–1941). Party member from 1903. Chairman of Central Executive Committee of Georgian SSR from 1922; chairman of Georgian Council of Commissars; chairman of Central Executive Committee of Transcaucasian Soviet Federative Socialist Republic.

Mamaev, A. S. (1892–1938?). Party member from 1917. Chairman of main administration of the cotton industry, 1924–29. Deputy chairman of American Trading Corporation, January 1930.

Manuilskii, D. Z. (1883–1959). Party member from 1903. Central Committee member, 1923. Presidium member of Comintern Executive Committee, 1924. Secretary of Comintern Executive Committee, 1928–43.

Maretskii, D. P. (1901–1938). Party member from 1891. Until 1925, contributed to *Pravda*. Academic secretary of planning commission and head of Economic Cabinet of USSR Academy of Sciences, Leningrad, 1929–32.

Mariia Ilinichna. See Ulianova, M. I.

Maslov, S. L. (1873–1938). Right Socialist Revolutionary. Minister of agriculture in Provisional Government. Subsequently worked for economic organizations and scientific institutions.

Medvedev, S. P. (1885–1937). Party member from 1900. Trade union work in Central Committee of Metalworkers' Union, 1920. Subsequently worked for Commissariat of Labor. Chairman of Syndicate of Nonferrous Metallurgical Enterprises, 1928–29.

Menzhinskii, V. R. (1874–1934). Party member from 1902. Chairman of OGPU (security police), 1926. Central Committee member from 1927.

Mezhlauk, V. I. (1893–1938). Party member from 1917. First deputy chairman of Gosplan, 1931. Chairman of Gosplan, 1934–37; Deputy chairman of Council of Commissars and Labor Defense Council. Repressed.

Mikoian, A. I. (1895–1978). Joined Bolshevik party, 1915. Secretary of North Caucasian Regional Committee of All-Union Communist Party (Bolshevik), 1924–26. Commissar of foreign and domestic trade of USSR, August 1926. Commissar of food provisionment, 1930. Commissar of food industry, 1934–38.

Miliukov, P. N. (1859–1943). Politician, historian, and journalist.

Mirzoian, L. N. (1897–1939). Party member from 1917. Secretary of Central Committee of Azerbaidzhan Communist Party, 1925–29. Central Committee candidate member, 1927. Repressed.

Monatte, Pierre (1881–1960). French trade union figure and journalist. Editorial staff member of publication of French Communist Party, 1921–24. Published Trotskyist organ *La Révolution prolétarienne*, 1925.

Mrachkovskii, S. V. (1888–1936). Party member from 1905. Commander in chief of, first, Ural and, then, West Siberian Military District, 1920–25. Chairman of board of State Committee of Textile Machinery, 1927. Expelled from party for factional activity, September 1927. Restored and appointed construction chief of Baikal-Amur Main Railway Line, 1928. Repressed.

Mravian, A. A. (1886–1929). Party member from 1905. Deputy chairman of Council of Commissars and commissar of public education of Armenian SSR, 1923. Member of Transcaucasian Regional Party Committee, 1924.

Muralov, N. I. (1877–1937). Party member from 1903. Rector of Timiriazev Academy of Agriculture; member of RSFSR Gosplan presidium, 1925. Member of the Central Control Commission. Repressed.

Musabekov, G. M. (1888–1938). Party member from 1918. Chairman of Council of Commissars, 1922. Chairman of Central Executive Committee of Azerbaidzhan SSR, 1929. Repressed.

Mussolini, Benito (1883–1945). Fascist leader of Italy, 1922–43.

Nazaretian, A. M. (1889–1937). Party member from 1905. Secretary of Transcaucasian Regional Party Committee; chairman of Central Control Commission and of Worker-Peasant Inspection of Transcaucasian Soviet Federative Socialist Republic, 1924.

Nechaev, N. V. (1887– ?). Party member from 1915. Instructor working for Kursk Provincial Party Committee, 1925. Head of organization department and then secretary of Belgorod Party Committee, 1926.

Nikolai. See Bukharin, N. I.

Nobel, Emmanuel (1859–1932). Headed enterprises of Nobel family in Russia prior to 1917.

Orakhelashvili, M. D. (1881–1937). Party member from 1903. Secretary of Transcaucasian Regional Party Committee of All-Union Communist Party (Bolshevik); chairman of Council of Commissars of Transcaucasian Soviet Federative Socialist Republic, 1926. Central Committee member, 1926–34. Repressed.

Ordzhonikidze, G. K. (Party pseudonym: Sergo) (1886–1937). Party member from 1903. First secretary of the Transcaucasian and North Caucasian Regional Party Committees, 1922–26. Chairman of Central Control Commission and commissar of Worker-Peasant Inspection, 1926–30. Deputy chairman of Council of Commissars and Labor Defense Council. Chairman of Supreme Economic Council, 1930. Commissar of heavy industry, 1932. Committed suicide.

Oshvintsev, M. K. (1889– ?). Party member from 1917. Chairman of Ural Regional Executive Committee; Central Committee candidate member, 1930.

Osinskii (real name: Obolenskii), V. V. (1887–1938). Party member from 1907. Deputy chairman of Supreme Economic Council; Central Committee candidate member, 1930. Repressed.

Oudegeest, Jan. Social Democrat, leader of Dutch Rail Workers' and Tram Workers' Union in the 1920s.

Ovchinnikov, G. F. (1893–1937). Party member from 1918. Secretary of Party Committee of Rostov Agricultural Machine-Building Plant, 1932–33. First secretary of Rostov City Committee of All-Union Communist Party, 1933. Chief of North Caucasian Regional Communication Board, November 1933. Repressed.

Peterson, A. A. (1895– ?). Party member from 1917. Investigator for Central Control Commission.

Petrovskii, G. I. (1878–1958). Party member from 1897. Chairman of All-Ukrainian Central Executive Committee and of Central Executive Committee of Ukrainian SSR, 1919–38. Also co-chairman of USSR Central Executive Committee, 1922.

Piatakov, G. L. (1890–1937). Party member from 1910. Deputy chairman of Supreme Economic Council, 1923. Trade representative to France, 1928. Chairman of board of Gosbank, 1929. Deputy commissar of heavy industry, July 1931. Central Committee member, 1923–36. Head of Gosbank, 1929–30. Repressed.

Piatnitskii, I. A. (1882–1938). Party member from 1898. Secretary of Comintern Executive Committee, 1923. Central Committee member, 1927–37. Repressed.

Pilsudski, Jozef (1867–1935). Marshal, activist in the right-wing of the Polish Socialist Party. Polish prime minister, 1926–28, 1930.

Poincaré, Raymond (1860–1934). French president, 1926–29.

Poliudov, Ye. V. (1887– ?). Party member from 1907. Collegium member of Commissariat of Transport, 1929.

Pollitt, Harry (1890–1960). Activist of British and international labor movement, cofounder and member of British Communist Party, 1924–43. Member of Comintern Executive Committee, 1924–43.

Polonskii, B. I. (1893–1937). Party member from 1912. Central Committee candidate member, 1927. Secretary of Moscow Party Committee, 1928. First secretary of Central Committee of Azerbaidzhan Communist Party; secretary of Transcaucasian Regional Party Committee, 1930. Repressed.

Popov, N. N. (1890/91–1938). Party member from 1919. (Member of Russian Social Democratic Workers' Party, 1906.) Editorial staff member of *Pravda*, 1920. Secretary of Central Committee of Ukrainian Communist Party, 1933–37. Central Committee candidate member, 1930. Repressed.

Postyshev, P. P. (1887–1939). Party member from 1904. Secretary of Central Committee of Ukrainian Communist Party (Bolshevik), 1926. Central Committee member, 1927. Repressed.

Preobrazhenskii, Ye. A. (1886–1937). Party member from 1903. Statesman, economist; member of Commissariat of Finance and member of Communist Academy presidium prior to 1927. Repressed.

Prokopovich, S. N. (1871–1955). Journalist, economist. Member of Committee for Famine Relief. Deported, 1922.

Radek, K. B. (1885–1939). Member of Russian Social Democratic Workers' Party from 1903. Member of Polish Social Democratic Party, 1902. Member of Social Democratic Party of Poland and Lithuania, 1904. Active figure in left wing of German Social Democratic movement, 1908. Member of Central Committee of Russian Communist Party (Bolshevik), 1919–24. At XV Congress of Communist Party (1927), expelled as active member of Trotskyist opposition group; reinstated in 1929. Repressed.

Rakovskii, Ch. G. (1873–1941). Party member from 1917. Soviet ambassador to Great Britain, 1923–25; ambassador to France, October 1925. Expelled from Communist Party, 1927; reinstated, 1935. Repressed.

Ramzin, L. K. (1887–1948). Thermal engineer. Director of All-Union Institute of Thermal Engineering, 1930.

Reingold, I. I. (1887–1936). Party member from 1917. Worked for Gosplan, 1929. Appointed chairman of main administration of cotton industry, 30 November 1929. Worked as deputy commissar of agriculture prior to December 1934. Repressed.

Reznikov, B. G. (1898– ?). Party member from 1917. Secretary of party cell at department of literature of Institute of Red Professors. In October 1930, wrote two denunciations to Central Committee concerning Syrtsov's factional activity.

Riabovol, K. S. (1894–1937?). Party member from 1919. Worked as a high official in the oil industry from 1927. Chairman of Central Oil Export Agency, 1931–33.

Riabushinskii, P. P. (1871–1924). Industrialist and political activist; emigrated after October revolution.

Riutin, M. N. (1890–1937). Party member from 1914. Secretary of Krasnopresnenskii District Party Committee, Moscow, 1925–28. Central Committee commissioner on collectivization, 1929. Appointed chairman of Photography and Cinematography Industry Administration and presidium member of Supreme Economic Council, March 1930. Repressed.

Romanov, M. A. (1878–1918). Grand duke, brother of last Russian emperor, Nicholas II.

Roy, Manabendra Nat (1892–1948). Activist in Indian national liberation movement. Worked in 1920s for Comintern. Comintern representative in China, 1927. Expelled from Comintern, 1929.

Rozengolts, A. P. (1889–1938). Party member from 1905. Deputy commissar of Worker-Peasant Inspection, 1928. Deputy commissar and subsequently commissar of foreign and domestic trade, 1930. Member of Central Control Commission. Repressed.

Rudzutak, Jan E. (1887–1938). Party member from 1905. Central Committee member, 1920–37. Politburo member, 1926–32. Central Committee candidate member, 1923–26. Commissar of transport, 1924–30. Deputy chairman of Council of Commissars and Labor Defense Council, 1926–37. Also chairman of Central Control Commission and Worker-Peasant Inspection, 1931–34. Repressed.

Rumiantsev, K. A. (1891–1932). Party member from 1916. In the 1920s, deputy chairman of Azerbaidzhan oil trust, member of Transcaucasian Regional Committee, member of Azerbaidzhan Central Committee. From 1925 candidate member of Communist Party.

Rykov, A. I. (1881–1938). Party member from 1898. Central Committee member, 1920–34. Politburo member, 1922–30. Chairman of Council of Commissars, 1924–30. Also chairman of Labor Defense Council, 1926–30. Commissar of communications, 1931–36. Repressed.

Sadyrin, P. A. (1877– ?). Board member of Gosbank, 1930.

Sassenbach, I. Leader of German Saddlers' Union. Activist in International Secretariat of Trade Unions in 1920s.

Savelev, M. A. (1884–1939). Party member from 1903. Director of V. I. Lenin Institute, 1928–30. By Politburo resolution, made editorial staff member of *Pravda,* 30 July 1928.

Serebriakov, L. P. (1888–1937). Party member from 1905. Deputy commissar of transport, 1922–24. Subsequently performed economic work within commissariat. Member of collegium, 1929. Head of main directorate of Paved Roads of Commissariat of Internal Affairs, 1931. Repressed.

Sergo. See Ordzhonikidze, G. K.

Shadunts, S. K. (1898–1937?). Party member from 1917. Worker-Peasant Inspection staff member.

Shatskin, L. A. (1902–1937). Party member from 1917. Member of Central Control Commission of All-Union Communist Party (Bolshevik), 1927–30.

Shatunovskaia, O. G. (1901–1990). Party member from 1916. Head of a department of Bailov-Bibi-Eibat District Party Committee, 1927–29. Student in courses on Marxism-Leninism under the auspices of USSR Central Committee, October 1929.

Sheinman, A. L. (1886– ?). Party member from 1903. Deputy commissar of finance, 1926–29.

Shkiriatov, M. F. (1883–1954). Party member from 1906. Member of Central Control Commission, 1922–34. Member of collegium of Commissariat of Worker-Peasant Inspection, 1927.

Shliapnikov, A. G. (1885–1937). Party member from 1901. Leader of Workers' Opposition group, 1920–22. Chairman of board of joint-stock company Metallimport, 1926.

Shmidt, V. V. (1886–1938). Party member from 1905. Central Committee member, 1925–30. RSFSR and USSR commissar of labor, 1918–28. Deputy chairman of Council of Commissars and Labor Defense Council, 1928–30. Deputy commissar of agriculture, 1930. Chief arbitrator of Council of Commissars, 1931. Repressed.

Sholokhov, M. A. (1905–1984). Writer, public figure. Academician at USSR Academy of Sciences. Won Nobel Prize for Literature in 1965.

Shvarts, I. I. (1879–1951). Party member from 1899. Board member (southern area) of All-Union Association of Coal Industry, 1930.

Shvernik, N. M. (1888–1970). Party member from 1905. Central Committee member, 1925. Member of Central Control Commission presidium and Worker-Peasant Inspection, 1924. Secretary of Leningrad Provincial Party Committee and Northwestern Bureau of Central Committee, 1925–26.

Simanovskii, A. A. (1874– ?). Party member from 1917. Official of Commissariat of Foreign Affairs, 1926–30.

Skvortsov-Stepanov, I. I. (1870–1928). Party member from 1896. Editor of *Izvestiia*, deputy editor of *Pravda*; editor of *Leningradskaia pravda*, 1925. Central Committee member, 1925.

Slepkov, A. N. (1899–1937). Party member from 1919. Contributed to *Pravda, Bolshevik*, 1924–28. Also executive instructor and head of agitation and propaganda department of Comintern Executive Committee. Bureau member and head of agitation and propaganda department of Mid-Volga Regional Party Committee, 1928–32.

Smilga, I. T. (1892–1938). Party member from 1907. Deputy chairman of Gosplan, autumn 1923. Member of Labor Defense Council, 1924–26. Central Committee member, 1925–27. Repressed.

Smirnov, I. N. (1881–1936). Party member from 1899. Commissar of postal and telegraph service, 1923–27. At XV Party Congress (1927) expelled for factional activity. Repressed.

Smirnov, V. M. (1887–1937). Party member from 1907. Member of Gosplan presidium. Repressed.

Sokolnikov, G. Ya. (1888–1939). Party member from 1905. Central Committee member, 1922–30. RSFSR commissar of finance, 1922–26. USSR commissar of finance, July 1923. Deputy chairman of Gosplan, 1926. Head of oil syndicate, 1928. Soviet ambassador to Great Britain, 1929–32. Repressed.

Sorin, V. G. (1893–1944). Party member from 1917. Member of Moscow Party Committee; member of bureau of Moscow Party Committee, 1920–25. Worked at V. I. Lenin Institute, 1924.

Sten, Ya. Ye. (1899–1937). Party member from 1914. Deputy director of Institute of Marx and Engels, 1928–30. Professor at Institute of Red Professors and staff member at USSR Academy of Sciences, 1932.

Stetskii, A. I. (1896–1938). Party member from 1915. Member of Northwestern bureau of Central Committee and department head of Leningrad Provincial Party Committee, 1926–29. Head of departments of Central Committee, 1930–38. Editor in chief of *Bolshevik*, 1934.

Strumilin, S. G. (1877–1974). Party member from 1923. Well-known Soviet economist and statistician. Worked for RSFSR and USSR Gosplan, 1921–37.

Sturua, I. F. (1870–1931). Party member from 1896. Member of Transcaucasian Regional Party Committee.

Sudin, S. K. Party member from 1918. Worked in field of transportation, 1920–27. Member of Central Control Commission, 1928.

Sukhanov, N. N. (1882–1940). Economist, journalist. Member of Land Planning Commission presidium of Commissariat of Agriculture; member of council of First Labor Army, 1920; member of USSR trade delegations to Berlin and Paris; full member of Institute of Foreign Trade Monopoly. Repressed.

Sukhanova, G. K. (1888–1958). Party member from 1905. Wife of N. N. Sukhanov.

Surits, Ya. Z. (1882–1952). Party member from 1903. Soviet ambassador to Turkey, 1930.

Sverdlov, Ya. M. (1885–1919). Party member from 1901. Chairman of Russian Central Executive Committee of RSFSR.

Syrtsov, S. I. (1893–1937). Party member from 1913. Central Committee member, 1927–30. Politburo candidate member, 1929–30. Secretary of Siberian Regional Party Committee, 1926. Chairman of RSFSR Council of Commissars (head of government), 1929–30. Subsequently performed economic work.

T'an Ping-shan (1886–1956). Member of Central Committee and Politburo of Chinese Communist Party, 1926–27. Minister of agriculture in Wuhan government of Kuomintang.

T'ang Shen-chih (1889–1970). Chinese military leader; member of Wuhan government; chairman of Hunan Province.

Teodorovich, I. A. (1875–1940). Party member from 1895. General secretary of Peasants' International, 1928–30. Repressed.

Ter-Vaganian, V. A. (1893–1936). Party member from 1912. At the XV Party Congress (1927), expelled for "aggressive Trotskyist activity." Expelled initially to Biisk and then to Kazan, January 1928. Repressed.

Thomas, James Henry (1884–1949). General secretary of British National Union of Rail Workers.

Togliatti (pseudonym: Ercoli), Palmiro (1893–1964). General secretary of Italian Communist Party, 1926. Member of Comintern Executive Committee Secretariat, 1935.

Tolmachev, V. N. (1886–1937). Party member from 1904. RSFSR commissar of internal affairs.

Tomskii, M. P. (1880–1936). Party member from 1904. Central Committee member, 1919–34. Politburo member, 1922–30. Chairman of Trade Union Council, 1922–29. Head of association of state publishing houses, 1932–36. Committed suicide.

Tovstukha, I. P. (1889–1935). Party member from 1913. Central Committee staff member, 1921–24. Assistant director of V. I. Lenin Institute, 1924–26.

Trotsky, L. D. (1879–1940). Participated in revolutionary movement from 1897. Party member from 1917. Politburo member of Central Committee, 1919–26. Commissar of military and naval affairs and chairman of Revolutionary Military Council, 1919–25. Presidium member of Supreme Economic Council; chairman of Main Concession Committee, 1925.

Tsiurupa, A. D. (1870–1928). From the beginning of 1918, commissar of food supply. From the end of 1921, assistant chairman of Council of Commissars and Labor Defense Council. Head of Worker-Peasant Inspection, 1922. Head of Gosplan, 1923. Commissar of trade, 1925. Central Committee member from 1923.

Tukhachevskii, M. N. (1893–1937). Party member from 1918. Marshal of Soviet Union. Chief of staff of the Workers' and Peasants' Red Army, 1925–28. Repressed.

Tumanov, N. G. (1887–1936). Party member from 1917. Soviet trade representative in France, 1930.

Uglanov, N. A. (1886–1937). Party member from 1907. Central Committee member, 1923–30. Candidate member of politburo, 1926–29. Central Committee secretary, 1924–29. Simultaneously, first secretary of Moscow Regional Party Committee and Moscow City Party Committee, 1924–28. Commissar of labor, 1930. Repressed.

Ukhanov, K. V. (1891–1937). Party member from 1907. Central Committee member, 1923–37. Chairman of Moscow Soviet, May 1926 to March 1927. Chairman of Moscow Region Executive Committee, 1929. Deputy commissar of provisionment, February 1932. Repressed.

Ulianova, M. I. (1878–1937). Party member from 1898. Editorial staff member and executive secretary of *Pravda*, 1917–29. Subsequently member of Central Control Commission.

Unshlikht, I. S. (1879–1938). Party member from 1900. Deputy chairman of Revolutionary Military Council and deputy commissar of military and naval affairs, 1925–30. Central Committee candidate member, 1925. Repressed.

Vaganian. See Ter-Vaganian, V. A.

Valentinov, G. B. (1896– ?). Party member from 1915. Deputy editor of *Trud* (Labor), 1924–29. Repressed.

Voikov, P. L. (1888–1927). Party member from 1917. Soviet ambassador to Poland, 1924. Assassinated.

Voroshilov, K. Ye. (1881–1969). Party member from 1903. Member of Central Committee, 1921–61. Commissar of military and naval affairs; chairman of Revolutionary Military Council, 1925–34.

Vujovich, Vujo Dmitrievich (1897–1936). Member of Serbian Social Democratic Party, 1912. Party member from 1918. Member of Comintern Executive Committee.

Vyshinskii, A. Ya. (1883–1954). Party member from 1920. Menshevik from 1903. RSFSR procurator and deputy commissar of justice from 1931; Soviet deputy procurator, 1933.

Wang Ching-wei (1883–1944). A leader of the Kuomintang. Chairman of National Government of Chinese Republic in Canton, 1925–26. Elected chairman of Kuomintang Central Executive Committee, January 1926. Chairman of Central Military Council, January to April 1926. Chairman of National Government in Wuhan, April to September 1927.

Warski, A. (**real name: A. Warszawski**) (1868–1937). Participated in Polish Communist movement. Cofounder and leader of Social Democratic Party of Kingdom of Poland and Lithuania and of Polish Communist Party. Member of Polish Central Committee, 1919–29. Member of Polish Politburo, 1923–29. Forced to emigrate to USSR, where he took up research work, 1929.

Wise, Edward Frank (1885–1933). British political figure. Economic advisor on foreign trade at London branch of central cooperative agency of USSR. Took part in informal talks on resuming British-Soviet diplomatic relations.

Yagoda, G. G. (1891–1938). Party member from 1907. Deputy chairman of OGPU (security police), 1924.

Yakovlev, Ya. A. (1896–1938). Party member from 1913. Commissar of agriculture, 1929–34. Central Committee member, 1930. Repressed.

Yakovleva, V. N. (1884–1941). Party member from 1904. RSFSR commissar of finance, 1929–37. Repressed.

Yanson, N. M. (1882–1938). Party member from 1905. Deputy commissar of Worker-Peasant Inspection, 1925.

Yaroslavskii, Ye. M. (1878–1943). Party member from 1898. Member of Central Control Commission, 1923–34. Secretary of party collegium of Central Control Commission and member of collegium of Worker-Peasant Inspection, 1923.

Yeger, V. Yu. (1895– ?). Party member from 1917. Head of organization and instruction department of Novosibirsk Regional Party Committee, 1930.

Yemshanov, A. I. (1891–1937?). Party member from 1917. Chief of Chinese Eastern Railway, 1926 to June 1931. Head of Gosplan's railway transport department, 1931. Repressed.

Yevdokimov, G. Ye. (1884–1936). Party member from 1903. Central Committee secretary; member of Central Committee Orgburo, 1925–27. Repressed.

Yurovskii, L. N. (1884– ?). Chief of Currency Administration of Commissariat of Finance of USSR; member of collegium of Commissariat of Finance of USSR, 1929.

Zaitsev, A. D. (1899–1937?). Party member from 1919. Repressed.

Zalmanov, M. M. (1879– ?). Party member from 1919.

Zhdanov, A. A. (1896–1948). Party member from 1915. First secretary of Nizhegorod Provincial Party Committee, 1924. Central Committee candidate member, 1925.

Zhemchuzhina, P. S. (1897–1970). Party member from 1918. Wife of V. M. Molotov.

Zinoviev, G. Ye. (1883–1936). Party member from 1901. Central Committee member; Politburo member, 1921–26. Chairman of Comintern Executive Committee, 1919–26. Repressed.

Zubarev, P. T. (1886–1938). Party member from 1904. Deputy chairman of Sverdlovsk Regional Party Executive Committee, 1923–28. Second secretary of Sverdlovsk Regional Party Committee, 1929–31. Repressed.

Index

Absenteeism, 220
Advisers, to Chinese Communist Party, 142
Agrarian reform, in China, 31
Agriculture, 85, 233*n*2, 234, 235. *See also*
   Collectivization
Alekseev, P. A., 185
Allilueva, N. S., 239
American Federation of Labor (AFL), 109
American Trading Corporation (Amtorg),
   172*n*20, 201*n*5
Amosov, A. M., 216, 217*n*4
Amsterdam International of Trade Unions,
   108, 109, 110*n*2
Amtorg. *See* American Trading Corporation
Andreev, A. A., 95
Anglo-Russian Committee, 28, 107, 109,
   110*n*5, 134, 136, 138*n*2, 143
Anti-Party Counterrevolutionary Group, 226
Anti-Soviet organizations, in government of-
   fices, 192–93
Anti-*spets* campaign, 190–96
Aralov, S. I., 117, 118*n*5
Army. *See* Red Army
Artak, A. A., 167, 170*n*4
Astrov, V. N., 160
August bloc (*1912–14*), 127, 128*n*7, 129
Austin and Co., 172
Automobile and Automotive Institute, 203,
   204*n*6
Averbakh, L. L., 162

Aviation industry, 204*n*6
Azerbaidzhan Communist Party, 170*n*3, 202
Azerbaidzhan, 104*nn*2,3, 167–68

Bagirov, Mir Jafar Abbasovich, 168, 170*n*8
Baku, Azerbaijan, 104*nn*2,3, 129, 167–68
Baltic–White Sea Canal, 212*n*1
Bauman, K. Ya., 88, 176, 178, 199
Bazarov, V. A., 192, 203
Bazovskii, N. A., 202
Bednyi, Demian, 127, 129–30
Belenkii, Z. M., 103, 218
Bliucher, Vasilii, 30
Bogdanov, P. A., 201
Bogolepov, M. I., 216
Bolshevik: Kamenev's telegram to Great
   Prince Mikhail Romanov and, 102–3;
   Krupskaia's letter on Eastman affair, 22,
   83, 91, 93, 248–49; Trotsky's letter on
   Eastman affair, 21–22, 84, 244–48
Borodin, M. M., 30, 137*n*3, 140, 142
Boycottism, 66
Bread factories, 209
Brezhnev, Leonid, 59
Britain. *See* Great Britain
British Communist Party, 70–71, 107, 109
Briukhanov, N. P., 189, 190, 200, 211*n*2
Brutskus, B. D., 193
Budget, target figures for, 234, 235–36, 237
Bukharin, N. I., 7–8, 34, 114, 127, 138,

Bukharin, N. I. (continued)
168, 173; All-Union Congress of Atheists, speech at, 150–51, 155; Anti-Party Counterrevolutionary Group and, 226; leftist right-wing bloc and, 216; Lenin on, 242, 243; letters to Central Committee (13 August 1929), 154–55, 164; miners' strike in Great Britain and, 100, 106, 112–14; petit bourgeois attitude of, 54–55; Platonov's letters, communication on, 152–54, 155; Politburo, membership in, 66, 182; as right deviationist, 54–55, 174, 216; on Stalin, 61; Supreme Economic Council, appointment to, 149; "Theory of 'Organized Mismanagement,'" 150–51, 154–55; Vorobiev affair and, 160–61; Voroshilov and, 149–50; on world revolution, 27
Bukharin group, 148–50, 155–61, 184, 227
Buniat-zade, D. Kh., 168, 170n7
Buranov, Yuri, 19n16
Bystrianskii, V. A., 173

Capitalist world, relations with, 35–36
Central Committee, 65; Eastman affair and, 94n2, 245–46; grain procurement, decree on, 165–67, 168–69, 171n6, 175; July 1926 plenum of, 101; October 1925 plenum of, 95–96; October 1926 plenum of, 101; Organizational and Assignment Department of, 88–89, 92; schism in, 75–77; semerka and, 68
Central Control Commission, 66, 101, 135, 168
Central Executive Committee, 65
Central Statistical Administration, 175, 176n5
Chaianov, A. V., 192, 193, 196
Chamberlain, Austin, 133, 136
Chang Hsueh-liang, 7, 182, 183
Chang Tso-lin, 7, 125, 126, 137
Checking up on fulfillment, 14–15, 16–17, 42, 52, 171, 190, 207, 210, 218–19, 221
Ch'en Tu-hsiu, 141
Chernyi, V. N., 179
Chiang Kai-shek, 6, 31, 33, 136, 137, 144, 149, 174, 229
China: agrarian reform in, 31; nonaggression pact with, 229; Northern Expedition, 6, 31; Wuhan government, 31, 136, 139, 140. See also Kuomintang; Manchuria
Chinese Communist Party, 6–7, 31–33, 111, 134–35, 140–42
Chinese Eastern Railway, 7, 118n5, 126, 217n6; armed intervention over, 34–35, 147–48, 175, 176n6, 184n4

Chinese revolution, 30–33, 110, 112n4, 130, 138, 143
Chistka, 50
Chubar, V. Ya., 69, 229, 230n3, 235
Class enemies, 13–14
Class struggle, 13–14, 225
Cleansing, 50
Coal industry, 221n5
Coal shipments to Great Britain, embargo on, 119, 120n3, 125, 126n2
Cognitive insecurity, in Stalin, 46–47, 62
Cohen, Stephen, 163n2
Coin shortage. See Small-change crisis
Collective farms, 166. See also Settlement associations
Collectivization, 8, 36–42, 183, 187, 224–25
Comintern, 20, 27, 29, 115, 121, 140, 237. See also Guralski and Vujovich affair
Commissariat of Agriculture, 233n2
Commissariat of Finance, 210, 211n2
Commissariat of Heavy Industry, 233n2
Commissariat of Trade, 117, 118n2, 127–28, 205–6
Commissariat of Transport, 179
Commission for Fulfillment, 15, 198, 217–18, 219
Communist International. See Comintern
Conference of Deputies, 214, 218
Confession, forced, 44, 46–47
Confrontation (ochnaia stavka), 46
Constitution of 1936, 9, 238
Consumer cooperatives, 207
Contracting, in grain procurement, 176
Cotton Committee, 169
Cotton Industry, Chief Administration of, 169, 172n19
Council of People's Commissars, 65, 214

Daniels, Robert V., 63
Davies, R. W., 57
Death penalty, 138n3
Defense industry, 235, 236
Desov, G. A., 185
Deutscher, Isaac, 19, 24–25
Dimitrov, Georgi, 237
Diplomatic recognition of USSR by United States, 35
Dneprostroi project, 4, 68–69, 86–88, 91, 92
Donbass, 221
Dovgalevskii, V. S., 46, 146
Dzerzhinskii, F. Ye.: industrial construction, role in, 95; Labor Defense Council, role in, 89, 90n2; Politburo, membership in,

116; Supreme Economic Council, role in, 88, 89*n3*

Eastman, Max, 5, 19, 20, 69–70
Eastman affair, 5, 18–24, 69–84, 90–94; *Bolshevik,* Trotsky's letter in, 21–22, 84, 244–48; Central Committee and, 94*n2*; Inkpin's letter, Trotsky's reply to, 71; Krupskaia and, 18, 19, 22, 78, 83, 91, 93, 248–49; *L'Humanité,* Trotsky's statement in, 83, 90; Stalin's memorandum, 21, 22, 70–82; Trotsky's letter to Stalin, 71–73; Zinoviev's letter to Manuilskii, 93*n2*
Economy, 3–4
Education, 235
Eikhe, R. I., 175, 202
Eismont, N. B., 147, 148, 175, 221*n4*, 226
Ekonomicheskaia zhizn', 86, 89, 215
Embargo on coal shipments to Great Britain, 119, 120*n3*, 125, 126*n2*
Emotional range, of Stalin's letters, 63
Engineers, trial of. *See* Industrial Party (Promparty)
England. *See* Great Britain
Estonia, 194, 208–9
Execution of White Guards (*9 June 1927*), 136, 137*n2*, 138*n3*

Factionalism: Guralski and Vujovich affair, 97–99; Kamenev, conflict with, 101–3; Lashevich affair, 100–101
Fedorov, G. F., 102
Fedotov, A. A., 193
Feng Yü-hsiang, 126, 128*n4*, 136, 137*n3*
Finance, Commissariat of, 210, 211*n2*
Finland, 194, 208–9
Fischer, Ruth, 113, 114*n1*
Florin, F., 237*n2*
Food industry, 235, 236
Food stamps, 237
Food supply services, wreckers in, 193–94
Forced confession, 44, 46–47
Forced labor, 35, 212*n1*, 213*n2*, 228
Foreign expeditionary corps, 194–96
Foreign policy, 5–6
Foreign technical assistance, 172, 173*n1*
Fotieva, L. A., 79
French Communist Party, 73*n8*, 113, 114
Fridrikhson, L. Kh., 208
Frumkin, M. I., 185
Frunze, M. V., 93
Fulfillment Commission. *See* Commission for Fulfillment
Fushman, A. M., 169

Ganshin, S. M., 203*n4*, 215, 222, 223*n3*
Gei, K. V., 88, 92, 93*n1*
German credits, 201
Gessler, Gertrud, 97–98
Gikalo, N. F., 167, 170*n3*, 202
Gipromez, 204
Goltsman, A. Z., 211*n1*
Gosbank, 188–90, 200, 204, 210
Gosplan, 52, 65, 89, 175, 235–36
Gottwald, K., 237*n2*
Government: anti-Soviet organizations in, 192–93; selection of officials, Stalin's views on, 13, 14; Stalin's views on, 10–11
GPU. *See* Security police
Grain exports, 201, 203, 205
Grain harvest, 85, 234
Grain procurement, 14–15, 36–39, 182, 183, 216*n3*, 229, 238; Central Committee's decree on, 165–67, 168–69, 171*n6*, 175; contracting and, 176; quotas for daily shipments, 205; security police, role of, 51–52; violations in connection with, 232–33
Great Britain, 5–6, 7, 24; coal shipments, embargo on, 119, 120*n3*, 125, 126*n3*; imports from, 201; miners' strike in, 99–100, 104, 106–14, 118*n5*, 119–20; restoration of diplomatic relations with, 46–47, 145–46, 163–64, 167, 174, 177–78, 182; trade unions in, 28–30. *See also* Anglo-Russian Committee; British Communist Party
Great powers, 232
Great Terror, 227
Grinko, G. F., 211*n2*
Groman, V. G., 52–53, 89, 192, 196, 199, 200
Grozneft, 203*n4*
Groznyi, 172*n17*, 202, 203*n4*
Guralski, A., 97–99
Guralski and Vujovich affair, 97–99, 101, 116

Hankow, China, 31, 130
Harbin, China, 182
Harvest. *See* Grain harvest
Health care, 235, 236
Health insurance, 220
Heavy industry, 235; Commissariat of, 233*n2*
Henderson, Arthur, 46–47, 119, 120*n5*, 146, 163–64, 167, 177–78, 182
"How We Should Reorganize Rabkrin" (Lenin), 75–77, 245–46
Hydroelectric power stations. *See* Dneprostroi project

Imports, 201, 228
Industrial construction, 95
Industrialization, 85, 187, 224–25. *See also* Wreckerism
Industrial Party (Promparty), 193, 194–96, 198
Infection, imagery of, 50
Inflation, 57
Inkpin, Albert, 70–71, 73, 244
Institutional background, to Stalin's letters, 65–66
International Association of Socialist Parties, 108, 110n3
Internationalism. *See* Comintern; World revolution
Iron and steel works, 172
Ishchenko, A. G., 138
Italy, treaty with, 201
Ittihad ve terakki party (Turkey), 168, 170n10
Izrailovich, A. I., 218
Izvestiia, 215

Jail population, 225
Japan, 118n5, 121, 125, 126

Kaganovich, L. M., 185, 208, 229, 230n3, 233; Moscow Regional Party Committee, secretary of, 199; Politburo, membership in, 66, 221n4, 234
Kaktyn, A. M., 204, 210
Kalinin, M. I., 47, 197, 203, 204n4; leftist right-wing bloc and, 210; Politburo, membership in, 66
Kalmanovich, M. I., 211n2
Kamenev, L. B.: in Commissariat of Trade, 117, 118nn2,4; Eastman affair and, 94; Japan, ambassador to, 121, 126n3; Lenin on, 243; telegram of greetings to Great Prince Mikhail Romanov, 101–3, 131–32; trial of, 227; Union of Marxist-Leninists and, 226. *See also* Guralski and Vujovich affair
Karakhan, L. M., 31, 117, 118n5, 126, 130, 174, 176
Karatygin, Ye. S., 193
Karklin, R. Ya., 204, 210
Kasumov Mir Bashir Fattakh ogly, 168, 170n11
Kerenskii, A. F., 193
Kerzhentsev, P. M., 117
Kharitonov, M. M., 169, 172n21
Khinchuk, L. M., 206, 208
Khlebexport, 208
Khlevniuk, O. V., 48
Khlopliankin, I. I., 221n3

Khoper county, collectivization in, 39–40
Khrushchev, Nikita, 61–62
Kirov, S. M., 66, 180, 185, 226
Klim. *See* Voroshilov, K. Ye.
Klimenko, I. Ye., 202, 206
Koba. *See* Stalin, Josef
Kodatskii, I. F., 185
Kolkhozy. See Collectivization
Komarov, N. P., 180, 185
Kommunisticheskiy internatsional, 119, 120n6
Komsomolskaia pravda, 162, 164, 168, 170n5, 179n3, 180
Kondratiev, N. D., 191–93, 196, 199, 200, 204n4, 210, 218
Kopp, B. L., 117, 118n5, 125, 126, 128n2
Kosior, I. V., 218
Kosior, S. V., 66, 88, 230n3
Kotov, V. A., 157
Kotovskii, G. I., 93
Krasnyi, B., 168, 170n5
Krinitskii, A. I., 88, 173
Krumin, G. I., 151, 155, 159
Krupskaia, N. K.: Eastman affair and, 18, 19, 22, 78, 84, 91, 93, 248–49; *Pravda*, on reorganization of, 155, 158; Zinoviev, defense of, 117n4
Krylenko, N. V., 69, 225
Krylenko, Ye. V., 69
Kuibyshev, V. V.: drinking problem of, 233, 234; on Guralski and Vujovich affair, 97–99; in Labor Defense Council, 214; Politburo, membership in, 66; on Promparty, 198; Supreme Economic Council, appointment to, 117, 118n7, 172, 184, 204n6; Worker-Peasant Inspection, role in, 79–80, 246
Kulaks, liquidation of, 40
Kulikov, Ye. F., 157
Kuomintang, 6–7, 30–31, 111, 134, 137, 139, 140–41, 143, 229n2
Kupriianov, S. V., 193
Kuskova, Ye. D., 193
Kuusinen, O., 237n2
Kuznetsov, S. M., 202, 216, 217n6
Kviring, Emmanuil, 212
Kviring, Ye. I., 223

Labor Defense Council, 65, 89, 90n2, 198, 214, 217
Labor discipline, 220
Larichev, V. A., 193, 196
Lashevich, M. M., 100–101, 113, 115, 116, 118
Latvia, 194, 208–9

Laundries, 209
Leadership struggle within Politburo, 4–5
Leadership theory of Stalin: checking up on fulfillment, 14–15; government, views on, 10–11; selection of officials, 13, 14; state *apparat*, 12–13
Leftist right-wing bloc, 196–97, 199
Left opposition, right deviation and, 49
Legality, revolutionary, 230, 231*n2*
Lena Goldfields, 205, 206*n6*
Lenin, Vladimir: on Bukharin, 242, 243; on Kamenev, 243; on nationalities question, 78–79; on Piatakov, 242, 243; on selection of officials, 16–17; on Stalin, 241, 242–43; on state *apparat*, 12–13; testament of, 73, 77–78, 79, 241–43, 245, 248–49; on Trotsky, 241, 242–43; Worker-Peasant Inspection (Rabkrin), views on, 12, 75–77, 245–46; on Zinoviev, 243
Leningrad, 24, 25
Leningrad party organization, 178, 179*n1*, 180, 185
Lev Trotsky: Portrait of a Youth (Eastman), 246–48
L'Humanité, 83, 90
Liaksutkin, F. F., 202
Light industry, 235, 236
Liquidationism, 66
Liquidation of kulaks, 40
Lithuania, 194
Litvinov, M. M., 34, 126, 146, 174, 175, 175*n1*, 177–78, 183, 234
Liubimov, I. Ye., 149
Lobov, S. S., 185
Lokatskov, F. I., 172
Lominadze, V. V., 45, 162, 196, 197, 223
Lomov, G. I., 205, 222
Lozovskii, A., 109

MacDonald, James Ramsey, 164, 178
Maikop, 202, 203*n4*
Makarov, N. P., 192, 199
Mamaev, A. S., 169, 172*n20*
Manchuria, 7, 147–48, 182
Manich river dam, 229, 230*n5*
Manuilskii, D. Z., 83–84, 90–91, 92–93, 94, 237
Maretskii, D. P., 157, 159, 160
Mariupol Iron and Steel Factory, 204
Marty, A., 237*n2*
Maslov, S. L., 193
Meat industry, wreckers in, 43, 200, 213–14
Medvedev, S. P., 104*nn2,3*, 130*n5*
Menzhinskii, V. R., 44, 190, 195–96, 214*n2*

Merl, Stephan, 37
Mezhlauk, V. I., 235
Mikoian, A. I., 117, 118*nn2,4*, 122, 168, 205–6, 214
Military intervention against Soviet Union, 194–96, 208–9
Military schools, 236
Miliukov, P. N., 193, 196
Miners' strike, in Great Britain, 99–100, 104, 106–14, 112–14, 118*n5*, 119–20
Mirzoian, L. N., 167, 174, 177, 200
Molodaia gvardiia, 162
Molotov, V. M., 2–3, 53–54, 66, 198
Monatte, Pierre, 73
Moscow Regional Party Committee, 199*n2*
Moskvin, M., 237*n2*
Mrachkovskii, S. V., 178
Musabekov, G. M., 170*n3*
Musavat party (Azerbaidzhan), 168, 170*n9*

Nadtocheev, Valerii, 23
Nanking government. See Chiang Kai-shek
Nationalities question, 78–79
Nazaretian, A. M., 127
Nechaev, N. V., 127, 129*n9*
Nemov, A. S., 215*n4*
NEP. See New Economic Policy (NEP)
Neustadt, Richard, 16
New Economic Policy (NEP), 3, 50–51, 67, 191
Nickel coins, minting of, 201
Nobel, Emmanuel, 169, 194
Nonaggression pact with China, 229
Northern Expedition (Kuomintang), 6, 31

Ochnaia stavka. See Confrontation
OGPU. See Security police
Oil extraction agencies, 169, 172*n18*, 222
Oil industry, 14, 215
Opportunism, 66
Orakhelashvili, M. D., 173
Ordzhonikidze, Sergo, 8, 55, 58, 135, 169, 206, 214, 216, 218, 227; Commission for Fulfillment, chairman of, 219, 234; Transcaucasian Regional Party Committee and, 122–25, 127; Voroshilov's letter to, 148–50; Worker-Peasant Inspection, head of, 14, 59, 123, 125*n7*
Organization and Assignment Department of Central Committee (Orgraspred), 88–89, 92
Osinskii, V. V., 203
Ovchinnikov, G. F., 232*n3*

Party unity, 4–5
Petrograd. See Leningrad

Piatakov, G. L., 8, 53, 55, 56–58, 185, 214, 227; All-Union Chemical Industry Association, chairman of, 211nn1,2; Gosbank, chairman of, 188–90, 200, 204–5, 210; Lenin on, 242, 243; Zinoviev and, 116
Piatnitskii, I. A., 237
Pieck, Wilhelm, 237n2
Pilsudski, Jozef, 110, 111, 112n3
Platonov, G., 152–54, 155
Poland, 194, 195, 208–9
Polish Communist Party, 111
Politburo, 65, 89; leadership struggle within, 4–5; members of, 66; semerka, 5; shadow Politburo, 5
Poliudov, Ye. V., 179
Polonskii, B. I., 176, 178
Popov, N. N., 151, 155, 159, 185
Postyshev, P. P., 178, 214n2, 217n4, 221n4
Pravda, 155–60, 178–79, 179n3, 180, 185, 207, 211, 215
Preliminary checking of speeches, 131
Preobrazhenskii, Ye. A., 48, 103
Prison population, 225. See also Forced labor
Profintern. See Trade Union International (Profintern)
Prokopovich, S. N., 193
Promotion off the shop floor. See Upward mobility
Promparty. See Industrial Party (Promparty)
Purge. See Cleansing

Rabkrin. See Worker-Peasant Inspection (Rabkrin)
Rakovskii, Kh. G., 20, 164, 165n4
Ramzin, L. K., 193, 196, 203
Ration books, 237
Recallism, 66, 106–7
Red Army, 81, 244–45
Reingold, I. I., 169, 172n21
Republican Democratic Association, 193
Revolutionary interests, state interests and, 33–35, 36
Revolutionary legality, 230, 231n2
Reznikov, B., 197, 223
Riabovol, K. S., 205, 206n4
Riazantsev-Karatygin group, 193
Right deviation, 49–60, 196–97
Riutin, M. N., 50, 214, 215, 215n4, 226
Road-building machinery, 209
Romania, 194, 195, 208–9
Romanov, Great Prince Mikhail, 101–3, 131–32
Rosmer, Alfred, 73
Roy Manabendra Nat, 140, 141, 142

Rozengolts, A. P., 206, 208, 218, 229
Rudzutak, Ya. E., 66, 117, 150, 183n2, 214
Rumiantsev, I. P., 172n18, 175, 177, 178
Rykov, A. I., 3–4, 7–8, 34, 58, 114, 178, 182, 217, 227; Anti-Party Counterrevolutionary Group and, 226; Baltic–White Sea Canal and, 212; in Council of Commissars, 197–98, 214; execution of White Guards and, 138; leftist right-wing bloc and, 210; Politburo, membership in, 66, 181; Pravda, on reorganization of, 155–57, 158–60; on prisoners' jurisdiction, 213n2; specialists, defense of, 55–56, 59; speech at Moscow region Congress of Soviets, 160, 161; on Trotsky, 25. See also Bukharin group
Ryskulov, T. R., 39–40

Sabotage, 16–17, 43
Sadyrin, P. A., 200
Savelev, M. A., 159
Scapegoating, 48
Schapiro, Leonard, 19
Schism, in Central Committee, 75–77
School construction, 236
Security police, 44, 45, 51–52, 56, 65–66, 200, 212, 213n2. See also Anti-spets campaign
Selection of officials, 13, 14, 16–17
Self-criticism, 180
Semerechensk Railroad, 69
Semerka, 5, 68, 85, 87, 90–93, 95, 105n3
Serebriakov, L. P., 125, 126
Serganin, M. M., 185
Settlement associations, 40–41, 207, 210–11
Shadow Politburo, 5, 68
Shadunts, S. K., 169, 172n21
Shatskin, L. A., 145, 162, 167, 173, 174
Shatunovskaia, O. G., 167, 170n4
Sheinman, A. L., 214
Shirvindt, Ye. G., 213n2
Shkiriatov, M. F., 232n3
Shliapnikov, A. G., 104nn2,3, 114, 130n5, 185, 186n1
Shmidt, V. V., 217
Shock work, 219, 227
Sholokhov, M. A., 232–33
Shvarts, I. I., 221
Shvernik, N. M., 88, 92, 221n4
Simanovskii, A., 148, 183
Since Lenin Died (Eastman). See Eastman affair
Slave labor. See Forced labor
Slepkov, A. N., 159, 160, 162, 163n6, 167, 226

Small-change crisis, 187–88, 189, 200, 201
Smilga, I. T., 52, 89, 95, 102
Smirnov, I. N., 168, 171n14, 178, 226
Smirnov, V. M., 129, 130n4
Socialist competition, 219
Soiuzneftexport, 205
Sokolnikov, G. Ya., 113, 114, 200, 214
Souvarin, Boris, 19, 23
Soviets, 65
Soviet Union, diplomatic recognition of by
    United States, 35
Specialists: anti-*spets* campaign, 190–96;
    Rykov's defense of, 55–56, 59
Stalin, Josef: as a Bolshevik, 16–17;
    Bukharin on, 61; cognitive insecurity in,
    46–47, 62; emotional range found in let-
    ters of, 63; as an individual, 17;
    Khrushchev on, 61–62; leadership theory
    of, 10–17; as an official, 16; on prelimi-
    nary checking of speeches, 131; on
    Zinoviev, 27. *See also* Leadership theory of
    Stalin
State *apparat*, 12–13
State interests, and revolutionary interests,
    33–35, 36
Steel works, 172
Sten, I. Ye., 145, 162
Stetskii, A. I., 121–22
St. Petersburg. *See* Leningrad
Strumilin, S. G., 52, 89
Sudin, S. K., 218
Sukhanov, N. N., 192, 203
Sunday Worker, 70
Sun Yat-sen, 6
Supreme Economic Council, 65, 89n3, 209,
    228
Surits, Ya. Z., 208
Syndicates, in textile industry, 88–89
Syrtsov, S. I., 44–45, 196–97, 212, 213n2,
    220, 221n4, 223
Syrtsov-Lominadze affair, 44–45, 196–97

Tailism, 66
T'ang Shen-chih, 139
T'an Ping-shan, 141
Teodorovich, I. A., 200, 210
Ter-Vaganian, V. A., 171n14, 178
Testament of Lenin, 73, 77–78, 79, 241–43,
    245, 248–49
Textile industry, 88–89
"Theory of 'Organized Mismanagement'"
    (Bukharin), 150–51, 154–55
Thomas, James Henry, 109, 110n6, 111,
    119, 120n5
Timber, 235, 236

Timber export, 201
Togliatti, Palmiro, 237
Toiling Peasants' Party (TPP), 192–93, 195,
    199–200
Tolmachev, V. N., 212, 226
Tomskii, M. P., 29, 109, 138, 149, 227; All
    Union Chemical Industry Association,
    chairman of, 210, 211n1; Anti-Party
    Counterrevolutionary Group and, 226;
    miners' strike in Great Britain and, 112–
    14, 119, 120n8; petit bourgeois attitude
    of, 220; Politburo, membership in, 66; Su-
    preme Economic Council, appointment to,
    183–84. *See also* Bukharin group
Torgprom, 194, 195
Torture, use of, 48
Tovstukha, I. P., 91, 112
Trade, Commissariat of, 117, 118n2, 127–
    28, 205–6
Trade Union International (Profintern),
    104n3, 109, 110n4, 200
Trade unions: Amsterdam International of
    Trade Unions, 108, 109, 110n2; Anglo-
    Russian Committee, 28; in Great Britain,
    28–30
Transcaucasian Regional Party Committee,
    122–24, 127, 168
Transport, 217n4, 235; Commissariat of,
    179
Trotsky, L. D.: Central Committee, removal
    from, 135; Lenin on, 241, 242–43; Polit-
    buro, membership in, 66, 101, 129,
    130n3; Rykov on, 25; *semerka* and, 68;
    workers' opposition group and, 104n3;
    world revolution, views on, 27; Zinoviev
    and, 24–25. *See also* Dneprostroi project;
    Eastman affair; *Lev Trotsky: Portrait of a
    Youth* (Eastman)
Trud, 135
Ts'ai Yun-shan, 148, 183
Tseitlin, Ye., 159
Tucker, Robert, 48
Tumanov, N. G., 205, 206n5
Turkey, 208, 234, 235n5

Uglanov, N. A., 155, 158, 160, 166, 167n2,
    226
Ukhanov, K. V., 209
Ukhta, 169, 213n2
Ukraine, famine in, 230n3
Ukranian Central Committee, 95, 96n3,
    229, 230n3
Ukranian Poor Peasants' Committees, 95,
    96n3
Ulianov, Vladimir. *See* Lenin, Vladimir

Ulianova, M. I., 79, 156, 157, 159
Unemployment, 220
Uninterrupted workweek, 166, 167*n2*
Union Bureau of Mensheviks, 193
Union of Marxist-Leninists, 226
United States, 229; American Federation of Labor (AFL), 109; diplomatic recognition of USSR by, 35; import of timber from Soviet Union, 201
Upward mobility, 8, 219, 220
Ural Mountains: extraction of oil in, 169, 172*n18*, 175, 177; iron and steel works in, 172, 218
Uralneft, 175

Vacation schedules, 233
Valentinov, G. B., 138
Van Min, 237*n2*
Verney, Eric, 70
Vodka production, 209
Voikov, P. L., 133
Volkogonov, Dmitrii, 23
Vorobiev affair, 160–61
Voroshilov, K. Ye., 66, 140, 142, 148–50, 203, 214, 216, 234
Vujovich, V. D., 97–99
Vydvizhenie. See Upward mobility
Vyshinskii, A. Ya., 227, 233

Wages, 129, 130*nn1,2*
Wang Ching-wei, 137*n4*, 139*n2*
Wan-hsien, China, 130
Warski, A., 113
White Guards' execution (*9 June 1927*), 136, 137*n2*, 138*n3*
White Sea. *See* Baltic–White Sea Canal
Worker-Peasant Inspection (Rabkrin), 11–12, 42, 66; grain procurement and, 168; Kuibyshev's role in, 79–80; Ordzhoni-

kidze's role in, 123, 125*n7. See also* "How We Should Reorganize Rabkrin" (Lenin)
Workers' opposition group, 104*nn2,3*, 129, 130*n5*
Worker turnover, 221*n3*
World revolution, 27–36
Wreckerism, 42–49, 193–94, 200
Wuhan government, China, 31, 136, 137, 139, 140

Yagoda, G. G., 199, 219
Yakovlev, Ya. A., 185, 234
Yanson, N. M., 88, 221*n4*
Yaroslavskii, Ye. M., 151, 155, 159, 178–79, 180, 214*n2*
Yeger, V. Yu., 202*n2*
Yemshanov, A. Ye., 147, 148, 175
Yeniseiskii kray, 103
Yezhovshchina, 227
Yurovskii, L. N., 192, 196, 200

Za industrializatsiiu, 215
Zaitsev, A. D., 160
Zalmanov, M. M., 208
Zhdanov, A. A., 178
Zhemchuzhina, P. S., 235, 236, 239
Zinoviev, G. Ye.: campain against, 24–27, 113–15, 135, 143, 227, 239; on Chinese Communist Party, 111; Comintern, removal from, 101, 121, 122*n1;* Eastman affair and, 93*n2*, 94; Lenin on, 243; miners' strike in Great Britain and, 100, 106–14; Polish Communists, directives to, 111, 113; Politburo, membership in, 66, 116*n2; Pravda,* as director of, 179; Trotsky and, 24–25; Union of Marxist-Leninists and, 226; workers' opposition group and, 104*n3. See also* Guralski and Vujovich affair
Zubarev, P. T., 177